Predictive Astrology Textbook
Mastering Forecasting

Revised and Expanded Edition, Combining Material from
the Two Volumes of the "Mysteries of Medieval Astrology"
Series

Alexey Borealis

The Wessex Astrologer

Published in 2025 by
The Wessex Astrologer Ltd
PO Box 9307, Swanage, BH19 9BF, England

For a full list of our titles go to
www.wessexastrologer.com

Copyright 2025 ©Alexey Borealis

Alexey Borealis asserts the moral right to be recognized
as the author of this work

ISBN: 9781916625365

Second edition ISBN: 9798281442091 (Pbk.)   9798283795225 (Hdbk.)
First edition ISBN: 9798328424912 (Vol. 1)   9798328648097 (Vol. 2)

A catalogue record for this book is available at The British Library

No part of this book may be reproduced or used in any form or by any means without the written permission of the publisher. A reviewer may quote brief passages.

Disclaimer: The information provided in this book, including astrological forecasts and algorithms, is intended for educational purposes only. The author and publisher do not assume responsibility for any losses, damages, or adverse outcomes from using this material.

Readers should be aware that astrology does not guarantee specific results. Any actions taken based on this book's astrological content are solely the reader's responsibility.

Before making decisions influenced by this book's content, it is advisable to seek guidance from qualified professionals in relevant fields, including (but not limited to) medical, legal, and financial matters.

Using this book's information is voluntary and at the reader's discretion and risk.

Praise for the Book

"Alexey's Predictive Astrology Textbook is a breath of fresh air in a field that, as the author himself notes, has in recent years become diluted with pseudo-psychological jargon and trendy esotericism.

Unlike many "how-to" manuals that begin with setting out the symbols and signs and their potential meanings, Alexey starts with a compelling look at neuroscience—specifically, how a newborn's neural network experiences a brief, but critical postnatal spark, during which the planetary configuration at birth is imprinted on the brain.

The book then transitions into a methodical, well-structured guide to horary astrology. Each chapter is thoughtfully designed to build upon the last, progressively deepening the reader's understanding and practical skill. What helps sets this work apart from others is the inclusion of exercises and "homework" at the end of each chapter—complete with answers and chart analysis—which transforms passive reading into active learning. Even as someone who has studied horary astrology over three decades, I found Alexey's approach stimulating. This book is now on my students' list of must-have manuals.

The chapter on natal astrology is a worthy successor that boldly confronts a controversial topic in modern astrology: the very concept of prediction. In a time when the word "prediction" can send some contemporary astrologers into a panic, Alexey offers a clear and scientifically grounded method for forecasting using Primary Directions. For anyone serious about astrology—particularly horary and predictive techniques—Predictive Astrology Textbook is a groundbreaking work. Alexey doesn't just teach you about astrology; he teaches you how to do it well. And perhaps most importantly, he restores a level of clarity, precision, and respect to a discipline too often lost in abstraction."

— **Sharon Knight**
QHP, MA, the Chair of APAI

"This book by Alexey Borealis is an excellent endeavor in this postmodern era to explore Renaissance Astrology, grounded in the works of William Lilly and Jean-Baptiste Morin, encompassing horary and natal astrology. As for natal astrology, perhaps one of the clearest introductions written in English on the astrological practice based on Jean-Baptiste Morin, functioning as a textbook, simple and direct, aimed at both novice and experienced astrologers.

What I consider the heart of the book is the didactic explanation of primary directions. This task is accomplished by presenting, in a simple manner, what promissors and significators are and their characteristics; we have clear examples and practical experiences to substantiate what is stated. Of particular importance is the clear explanation of the specific geometry of primary directions, something that few current astrology books manage to offer, coupled with an excellence in the graphical representation of concepts, which permeates the entire book and is especially highlighted in this section.

Furthermore, it is here that, perhaps for the first time in modernity and with exactitude, the circle of planetary aspects with latitude, as conceived by Morin, is presented; this point alone would justify reading the book. All those who are in any way involved in astrological practice, following in Morin's footsteps, have at least a duty to thank the author for this exposition.

Approaching the end of the book, planetary revolutions and transits are presented with mastery, along with their principles, differences, and practical examples. It is evident that directions, revolutions, and transits are not predictive techniques without interconnection; quite the contrary, they form part of a chain, and this is explained with examples. In fact, not only is the interconnection of natal directions with revolutions briefly presented, but also the sublime refiners: directions derived from solar and lunar revolutions, something rarely studied and presented in astrological literature."

— **Rodolfo Melchior**
Translator of *Morin's Astrologia Gallica*

Contents

Praise for the Book iii

List of Figures   xiii

List of Tables   xvii
Preface xix
Foreword by Penelope Sitter xxi

Chapter 1   Introduction to Predictive Astrology   1
How Much Do The Stars Influence Our Fate? 1
    The Context Rules 2
    How The Stars Affect Us 3
    To What Extent Can a Person Influence Their Fate? 6
    Modern Use of Astrology 8
Three Types of Predictive Astrology 8
    Natal Astrology 8
    Mundane Astrology 9
    Horary Astrology 10

Chapter 2   Horary Astrology   15
Definitions 15
The List of Techniques 16
    Signification Techniques 16
    Descriptive Techniques 18
    Object Interaction Techniques 20
    Event Prediction and Timing Techniques 22
    The Table of Main Techniques in Horary Astrology 23
    Homework Assignment №1 24
    A Simple Algorithm to Make a Prediction 27
Signification Techniques: House Rulership 28
    Universal and Accidental Meaning of Planets 29

The House Systems	30
House Cusps	30
The Domiciles of the Planets	31
The Lord of the House	32
The Angles of the Chart	35
Homework Assignment №2	37
House Meanings	37
Identifying the Unknown Planet	41
Homework Assignment №3	42
House Meanings in Natal Astrology	42
Descriptive Techniques: Celestial State Assessment	44
Rulership	45
Exaltation	46
Triplicity	47
Debilitated Planet	48
Detriment	49
Fall	50
Peregrine	50
The Table of Essential Dignities	50
Example №1: Working with Planetary Dignities	51
Homework Assignment №4	52
Descriptive Techniques: Sign Properties	54
The Table of Sign's Properties	57
Homework Assignment №5	57
Object Interaction Techniques: Reception	59
Reception by Exaltation	60
Reception by Triplicity	60
Modification of the Celestial State Due to Reception	60
Negative Reception	61
Influence of the Celestial State on Reception	62
The Table of Receptions	63
Multiple Receptions Towards the Same Planet	63
Mutual Receptions	65
Reception As a Signification Technique	66
Homework Assignment №6	68
Your First Prediction	69
Solution	71
What Happened in Reality	72
Signification Techniques: Derived Houses	73

Homework Assignment №7	76
Signification Techniques: Alternative Rulers	77
Co-rulers of the House	77
Planet Inside the House	78
How To Choose the Right Co-ruler Among Several	78
If There Are No Alternative Rulers	81
Homework Assignment №8	82
Signification Techniques: Locking of Significators	83
The Special Role of the Moon in Horary Astrology	84
Signification Techniques: Universal Rulership	87
When Do We Use Natural Rulership?	90
How to Find a Universal Ruler of a Particular Object	91
Homework Assignment №9	91
Ptolemaic Aspects	94
Event Prediction Techniques: Exact Aspects	95
Object Interaction Techniques: Close Aspects	96
Difference Between Exact and Close Aspects	97
Influence in Close Aspects	97
Mutual and One-Sided Aspects	98
The Strength of Close Aspects	101
The Effect of Aspect in Connection With Its Form	103
The Effect of the Aspect in Connection with the Place It Falls	104
Homework Assignment №10	105
The Cumulative Effect of Close Aspect and Reception	107
The Orbs of the Seven Planets	108
Graphical Representation of Aspects and Beholding Signs	110
Aspects on the Borders of Non-Beholding Signs	111
Homework Assignment №11	112
Event Prediction Techniques: Exact Aspects Perfection	115
Exact Aspects and Events	115
Type of Aspect & Event	116
Applying and Separating Aspects	117
Aspects Within Signs and Context of the Question	118
Cutting Off the Light	119
Homework Assignment №12	120
Translation and Collection of Light	121
Homework Assignment №13	123
Planetary Movements	125
Homework Assignment №14	126

Homework Assignment №15	128
Descriptive Techniques: the Fixed Stars	132
Homework Assignment №16	135
Signification Techniques: Arabian Parts	136
Example №2: Part of Fortune	140
Timing Techniques: the Symbolic Timing in Exact Aspects	141
Real-Life Example	145
Radicality of the Chart	148
Reflection of the Current Situation in a Horary Chart	149
How a Horary Chart Highlights a Client's Deep Concern	153
Example №3: Radicality Assessment	154
Homework Assignment №17	156
The Horary Chart Analysis Algorithm	158
Example №4: Flight to Turkey	159
Homework Assignment №18	162
The Planet Interposing the Question	166
Signification Techniques: Antiscia	166
Antiscia and Chart Radicality	168
Example №5: Antiscion in Action	170
Special Case: The Question on Behalf of the Group	174
Homework Assignment №19	174
Three Ways How the Chart Shows the Future	177
1. The Snapshot of the Future	178
2. The Short Movie	178
3. A Full Movie	179
The default option	179
Short Examples	180
A Real-Life Example	181
Choosing the Right Timing Technique	184
Timing Technique: Long Term Aspects	186
Prohibition of Long-Term Aspect	188
Several Long-Term Aspects	189
Example №6: Part-Time Job	190
Example №7: Film Release Date	193
Example №8: Job Search	197
Timing Technique: Symbolic Timing in Ingress	199
Example №9: Investment Payback Date	200
Example №10: Dismissal	203
Supplementary Timing Techniques	207

Contents

- Transit Time ... 207
- Freezing the Significator ... 207
- Aspects to House Cusps ... 208
- Refining the Number of Time Units ... 209
- Example №11: Lockdown ... 209
- Example №12: Power Supply Restoration ... 212
- Homework Assignment №20 ... 215

Accidental Strengthening: Strong Testimonies ... 217
- Position in the House ... 217
- Example №13: Football Match ... 219
- Lunar Nodes ... 222
- Short Examples ... 223
- Combustion ... 227
- Example №14: Missing Person ... 229
- Station of the Planet ... 232

Accidental Strengthening: Moderate Testimonies ... 233
- Retrograde Motion ... 233
- Example №15: Permission From Authorities ... 234
- Close Aspects and Receptions ... 236
- Example №16: First Reaction ... 240
- Affliction/Strengthening of the House ... 242
- Example №17: Exhibition ... 244
- Example №18: Failed Prediction ... 247
- Example №19: Money Transfer ... 251
- The Position of a Planet Relative to Luminaries ... 253

Accidental Strengthening: Weak Testimonies ... 254
- A Planet Void of Course ... 254
- The Elevated Planet ... 255

Special Forecasting Techniques ... 256
- Death Questions ... 256
- Example №20: Death ... 258
- Example №21: Date of Departure ... 260
- Search Horaries ... 262
- Example №22: Search Question ... 266
- Relationship Questions ... 269
- Example №23: Relationship Models ... 272
- Example №24: Relationship Development ... 277
- Example №25: Betrayal ... 282

Summary of Chapter 2 ... 288

Before Judgment 288
During Judgment 289

Chapter 3   Natal Astrology   291
Roles of Planets in the Natal Chart 291
   The Diversity of Roles of the Same Planet 291
   Changing Roles Over Time 292
Celestial States of the Planets 294
   Precursor of the Event 294
   Close Aspects 295
   The Dispositor of the Planet 297
   Receptions 297
   Universal Benefics and Malefics 299
House Rulership 300
   House Meanings in Natal Astrology 300
   Derived Houses 302
   Position in the House 302
The List of Techniques 303
   Delineating a Natal Chart 303
   Primary Directions 304
   Revolutions of the Planets 306
   Final Transit 308
Delineation of the Natal Chart 309
   Four Types of Determination 309
Celestial Determination 312
   Mechanics of Celestial Determination 312
   Reading the Celestial State 313
   Example №26: Aspects of the Planet 316
   The Position of the Aspect and Its Dispositor in the Houses . . 321
   Example №27: Terrestrial Determination of Venus's Aspect . . 322
   Example №28: Planet-Trendsetter 323
   Summary 324
Terrestrial Determination 325
   Types of the House Rulership 326
   Coincidence of the Planet's and the House's Natures 331
   Example №29: Strength of Terrestrial Determination 332
Multiple Aspects of Planets 334
Examples of Delineation 335
   Example №30: Delineating the 10th House 335

Example №31: Non-Determining Chart	343
Example №32: Fatal Chart	351
The Myth of Destiny	356
Homework Assignment №21	358
Primary Directions	363
Promissors and Significators	363
Special Role of the 1st House	365
Celestial State of the Promissor	366
Initiating Directions	368
Example №33: Initiating Directions in Action	368
Example №34: False Prediction	373
Geometry of Primary Directions	377
Rectification of Birth Time	382
Example №35: Rectification	382
Revolutions	390
General Principle	390
Example №36: Venusian Return	391
Solar and Lunar Returns	394
Event Details in Solar/Lunar Return Charts	396
Example №37: Solar Return Chart	397
Example №38: Lunar Return	404
Narrowing Down Planetary Meanings	410
Revolutions Confirming Initiating Directions	411
Example №39: Solar Return Confirming Initiating Direction	412
Relocation	418
General Principle	418
Example №40: Relocated Solar Return	419
Planetary Transits	427
General Principle	427
How Not to Use Transits	428
Example №41: Predicting the Exact Day of the Event	430
Astrological Compatibility of Couples	449
Example №42: Shared Events	450
Forecasting as a Part of Life	454
Strategic Planning	454

Chapter 4 Conclusion 457

Refutation of Modern Astrologers' Arguments against Accurate
    Forecasting 457

Memo for Reading Ancient Texts 459
    How to Correctly Read Ancient Texts 459
    Avoid Cherry Picking 461

Appendix A   The Geometry of Celestial Sphere   463

The Zodiac Circle 463
    The Ecliptic, Solstice, and Equinox 463
    Zodiac Signs and Constellations 467
    Precession 468
    Tropical and Sidereal Zodiac Circles 469
    Great Cycles and Ages 470
Planetary Loops 470
    The Local Horizon 471
    Cardinal Signs and Mystical Cults 473
    Different Coordinate Systems 474

Appendix B   List of the Brightest Stars   477

Appendix C   Determination by Ecliptic   479

Bibliography   485

Index of Terms   487

List of Figures

The Twelve Spatial Places Called Houses _____ 29
House Cusps in Regiomontanus System _____ 31
The Twelve Houses Represented in an Old-Fashioned Style ___ 35
Example Chart With Venus in the 1st House _____ 52
Example Chart With Various Planets _____ 53
Example Chart For Various Questions _____ 59
Chart: Will My Single Enter the Chart and Become a Hit? _____ 70
Mutual Aspect _____ 99
One-Sided Aspect _____ 99
One-Sided Sinister Trine _____ 100
Interference Picture of the Zodiac Circle _____ 101
The Orb of the Sun _____ 108
The Orb of Venus _____ 109
Aspect's Ruler _____ 111
Chart: What Will Happen If I Buy That House? _____ 113
Buying the House: Chart with Planetary Speeds _____ 127
Chart: Moving Abroad _____ 129
Chart: When Will My Car Arrive? _____ 145
Transit Chart: The Car Arrival _____ 147
Chart: The Future of the Single With PoF _____ 157
Chart: Will the Flight to Turkey Be Safe? _____ 160
Chart: Will He Fire Me? _____ 162
Antiscia _____ 167
Chart: A Gigolo-Lover (With Antiscion) _____ 169
Chart: House Purchase (With Antiscion) _____ 171
Chart: The Exam _____ 175
Chart: Who is My Biological Father? _____ 182
Chart: When Will I Get a Private Job Again? _____ 191
Transit Chart: Getting the Job _____ 192

Chart: When Will the Film Be Released on TV? — 194
Transit Chart: Film Release — 196
Chart: When Will I Find a New Job? — 197
Chart: When Will the Bank Return My Dividends? — 201
Chart: Will I Lose My Job? If So, How Soon? — 204
Chart: The Dates of Lockdown — 210
Chart: When Will the Electricity Be Restored? — 213
Chart: The Exact Day of the Child's Arrival — 216
The Moon on 3D-Sphere — 218
Chart: Will We Win? — 220
Lunar Nodes — 222
Chart: House Purchase (with Nodes) — 224
Chart: Film Release (with Nodes) — 225
Chart: Dismissal (with Nodes) — 226
Chart: Is He Alive? And Where Is He Now? — 230
Chart: When Will We Obtain Permission? — 234
Chart: Future of This Book — 240
Chart: How Will This Exhibition Go? — 244
Chart: When Will I Get a Contract With the Publisher? — 248
Chart: When Will I Get $25,000? — 252
Chart: Where Is My Cat? — 259
Chart: How Much Time Does He Have? — 260
Chart: Where Is My Thermometer? — 267
Chart: How Will Our Relationship Develop? — 273
Chart: Relationships No. 2 — 278
Transit Chart: Relationship — 281
Chart: Betrayal — 282
Transit Chart: Betrayal — 286

Alexey Borealis. Rectified Figure — 317
A Non-Determining Chart — 344
A Highly Determining Chart — 352
A Blind Chart №1 — 358
A Blind Chart No. 2 — 369
Donald Trump — 374
Mundane Conjunction — 377
Zodiacal Directions With Latitude — 379
A Circle of Aspects — 380
Antiscia — 380

Alexey Borealis. The Birth Chart According to Records.	383
Mean Average and Standard Deviation	389
Alexey Borealis. Venusian Return Chart	392
The Following Venusian Return Chart	395
Alexey Borealis. A 43rd Solar Return Chart	398
Alexey Borealis. A 44th Solar Return Chart	403
Alexey Borealis. A 6th Lunar Return.	405
Alexey Borealis. A 5th Lunar Return	406
Albert Einstein	413
Albert Einstein's Solar Return	414
Radical Chart for Relocation	420
Solar Return for Place of Residence	422
Relocated Solar Return	424
A Woman's Chart	430
Venus in a 3D Sphere	431
A Woman's Solar Return Chart	436
Eighth Lunar Return for 2014	441
Transit Chart: 10 Oct 2014	446
Prince Philip	451
Rotation of the Earth	463
Rotation of the Sun	465
Zero Degree of Zodiac Circle	465
Zodiac Signs	466
Signs vs Constellations	468
Precession	468
Cosmic Epochs	469
Planetary Cycles	471
Local Horizon	472
Primary Motion	473
Ecliptical Coordinates	475
Equatorial Coordinates	476
Horizontal coordinates	476
The north and south poles of the ecliptic	480
The circle from the planet to the pole	480
Four poles	481
Three main circuits	481
Twelve aspects	482
Ptolemaic aspects	483

Ptolemaic aspects in space ___483

List of Tables

Main Techniques in Horary Astrology 23
Zodiac Signs: Their Degrees and Dispositors 32
Four angles of the chart 36
The domiciles of the planets 46
The places of exaltation of the planets 46
The triplicities of the planets 47
Essential Dignities of Planets 51
Sign's properties 58
Receptions 64
Example of Aspects Perfection 120
Example of Past Aspects 124
Example of Future Aspects 124
Major Fixed Stars 134
Determining Time 143
Average Speeds of Planets 144
House Meanings in Search Questions 262

Celestial States of Planets in Houses 315
Alexey Borealis: Aspects of Venus 320
Alexey Borealis: Direction of Venus' Aspects 321
Blind Chart: Directions for Career 348
Homework: Promissors and Their Action 360
Blind Chart: Expected Dates of Child's Birth 362
Blind Chart: Most Expected Dates of Child's Birth 362
Blind Chart: Less Expected Dates of Child's Birth 362
Events for Rectification 386
Rectification: Shifting the birth time 387
Borealis: Directions from Venus' return chart 393
Alexey Borealis: Directions From 43rd Solar Return Chart . . 402

Alexey Borealis: Directions From Lunar Return Chart 409
A Woman: Directions for Marriage 433
A Woman: Directions in 2009 434
A Woman: Directions for 2014 434
Directions for Marriage from the Solar Return 440
Intersection of Dates 440
Directions for Marriage from the Lunar Return 444
Intersection of Dates from All Charts 445
Key Dates in Queen Elizabeth II's Horoscope 450
Prince Phillip. Promissors of Children 452
Prince Phillip. Directions for Children 453
Prince Phillip & Queen Elizabeth II. Shared Dates 453

List of royal stars 478

Preface

Astrology has been developed and designed as a predictive discipline. Unfortunately, in recent years, it has taken on the role of a pseudo-psychological science. Surprisingly, many modern astrologers have become so fascinated with trendy esoteric beliefs that they have stopped accepting the idea of accurate astrological predictions (see the section "Refutation of Modern Astrologers' Arguments against Accurate Forecasting"). Nevertheless, astrology enables the precise prediction of dates and details of events. Soon, you will see for yourself.

This book is a textbook that guides you from beginner to expert in making predictions. It will teach you to make independent and accurate forecasts and explain how to use your knowledge of the future.

Astrology thrived as a scientific discipline in European universities in the 17th century. Thus, the works of renowned astrologers of that time—William Lilly and Jean-Baptiste Morin de Villefranche, whose precise predictions earned them lasting fame—lie at the foundation of this book.

I find great pleasure in writing this book while being in Warsaw, at the very heart of the country that became the cradle of European astrology in the 15th and 16th centuries. The sons of this land, such as Jan of Głogów, Marcin Biem of Olkusz, Nicolaus Copernicus, Marcin Bylica of Olkusz (a colleague of Regiomontanus), and many others, brought fame to the Chairs of Astrology and Mathematics at the University of Kraków across Europe.

Continue Your Journey

This book introduces a predictive framework designed for astrologers seeking clarity, precision, and accountability in their work.

As a reader, you gain access to The Case Study Pack — three complete predictive examples (natal, horary, and medical) that demonstrate the method in action.

https://morinus-astrology.com/bookbonus/

Let's take predictive astrology to the next level — with clarity, precision, and results.

Foreword by Penelope Sitter

In this PREDICTIVE ASTROLOGY TEXTBOOK, Alexey Borealis teaches astrologers how to use horary and natal astrology to make reliable predictions and to forecast the exact date of their occurrence. The textbook is a revised edition of Borealis' two-volume *Mysteries of Medieval Astrology* (2024). The first volume of the first edition teaches horary astrology, and the second teaches predictive natal astrology. Now this revised edition offers astrologers a well structured course in two major branches of horoscopic astrology in a single volume.

With a background in mathematics, physics and astrophysics, Borealis wished to use astrology to make accurate predictions of future events. After study in various schools of modern astrology, he became dissatisfied with the vague statements he encountered. Following his study of medieval astrology with Robert Zoller and of horary with John Frawley, he entered a period of some fifteen years during which he assiduously studied horary techniques to understand which ones work and which fall short. As a result, he became able to make horary predictions with near-perfect accuracy and to consistently time the occurrence of predicted events within days, and sometimes within hours.

During the years he worked to develop his horary skills, Borealis also studied many traditional natal techniques, including among others, for example, firdaria and profections. After finding that these techniques failed to reliably enable specific predictions and exactly timed forecasts, he began to doubt that one can use natal techniques to make the consistently realized specific predictions he sought.

Despite these doubts, Borealis was piqued by Zoller's report that his teacher, Zoltan Mason, had said, "If you want real astrology, study Morinus." He did exactly that. He took up the study of the work of the 17th century French astrologer, J.B. Morin de Villefranche (1583–1656), whose work is most fully presented in his 26-book treatise, *Astrologia Gallica*, published posthumously in 1661. Upon encountering that work, Borealis was amazed, he has said, to find in Morin the work of a true scientist who makes well reasoned arguments and substantiates them with sound demonstrations of the efficacy of the method and techniques he advocates.

Though he wished to test Morin's natal method as fully and critically as he had tested numerous traditional techniques, Borealis found that no existing software could calculate primary directions according to Morin's prescriptions. To fill that gap, he created a software program to make those calculations, and he tested Morin's method and predictive system as rigorously as he had tested other approaches to prediction. He found that Morin's approach enables consistently accurate predictions of major life events and exactly timed forecasts that fall within a few days of the date of an event's occurrence. He realized that he had found in Morin's work what he had been looking for since he began studying astrology years earlier. After years of fully developing the tenets of his practice and perfecting their use, Borealis now teaches horary and natal astrology as predictive disciplines.

Although Morin rejected horary astrology on incorrectly conceived theoretical grounds, Borealis puts Morin's method for delineation of horoscopic charts to good use in both horary and natal practice. He uses Morin's method to make proper use of the houses and their rulers to determine which particular things a planet will signify and act on. He shows also how to assess and use a planet's celestial state—its placement in the Sky—to determine the quality and efficacy of the planet's action. As Morin identifies the receiver of celestial influence as a crucial determinant of what a planet signifies and will effect, so Borealis stresses the determining importance of the receiver's identity and the context in which a chart operates. As Morin emphasizes the powerful role of analogy in astrological practice, so Borealis attends carefully to the repetition of similar patterns and conforming testimonies that accumulate to determine meaning and produce effects.

The portion of the book on horary practice guides the student through a carefully structured course on horary method that even a beginning student can use to develop into a proficient practitioner. Borealis fully covers the usual traditional horary rules and techniques, and teaches how and when to use each technique. In doing so, he in multiple ways refines or adds to the understanding and use of these techniques.

For example, Borealis has developed a highly effective approach to discern whether a querent's true question may hide beneath the question as stated. Using this approach, one also can reliably determine the radicality of a horary chart. Following William Lilly, Borealis focuses on whether the chart reflects the situation in which the question is posed,

Foreword by Penelope Sitter

and he introduces a novel way to make that assessment. The approach he explains enables the astrologer to avoid two most fundamental errors to which a horary practitioner may fall victim. That is, with this approach, one can avoid answering the wrong question in a chart that is radical for the querent's true but unstated concern, and can avoid treating as radical a chart that in fact is non-radical.

Borealis also has discovered a way to increase the accuracy of timing techniques. He distinguishes three ways a horary chart can show the future: as a snapshot, a short movie, or a full movie. He teaches use of these distinctions to aid in the selection of the appropriate timing technique to enable more precise forecasts of the time a promised event will occur.

In a striking innovation, Borealis introduces a technique that demonstrates the wonderful way planets act. He shows that, at the time a horary chart's promise is realized, confirming transits occur that fulfill the predicted promise of the chart cast for the question. Such concordant transits also signify the matter's future development. These transits raise interesting theoretical questions and, as Borealis shows, have great practical value. I am unaware that any other astrologer has recognized this quite amazing phenomenon and put it to use in horary practice.

Borealis also introduces a system, or algorithm, practitioners can use to efficiently organize their approach to horary questions and to assure they use the right techniques to answer any question. He classifies available horary techniques, states the purpose for which each is designed, and gives keywords that direct the practitioner to the techniques best suited to a given question. He outlines this system in a handy table, and in ensuing sections of the book he explains and demonstrates in example charts how and when to use each technique. I find this system to be of enormous practical use in organizing the approach to a horary question, and I believe it may well prove useful even to quite experienced practitioners.

As a natal astrologer who practices in accord with horoscopic method as Morin explains it, I particularly value the portion of this book that teaches how to make precise predictions from natal charts. A natal astrologer should be able to answer two fundamental questions: *What can the native expect during the life the chart represents?* and: *When* will the predicted events occur? Borealis demonstrates mastery of the ability to answer these two essential questions. Unfortunately, few astrologers can do the same. Fortunately, Borealis sets out in this book a well designed course that any natal astrologer can use to become proficient at making consistently correct predictions and exact forecasts.

Borealis uses Morin's method to delineate the natal chart. The method provides an especially efficient and effective means to gauge the goals, focus, strength and persistence of the native's motivations, and to assess the native's likely actions and their probable consequences. The book teaches how to begin with a planet's most general potential significations and progressively narrow to the planet's actual significations at a particular time and in the context of the native's life. Even astrologers who do not seek to forecast future events can find great value in what this textbook teaches about use of Morin's method to discern from the natal chart the native's motivations and likely actions.

As he teaches how to delineate the nativity for the purpose of the prediction of major events, Borealis makes a nice distinction between highly determining natal charts and those that are less determining of the course of the native's life. This distinction has significant implications for questions about fate and human self-determination. Moreover, the means he uses to make this distinction is instructive for the delineation of any natal chart.

Borealis adopts Morin's predictive system, which uses primary directions, solar and lunar revolutions, directions taken in the charts of the revolutions, and finally transits, which trigger a predicted event. He thoroughly explains and demonstrates in example charts how to perform each step of this procedure in accord with proper method.

The book teaches a unique, highly practical and efficient approach to identify and assess primary directions relevant to a matter under investigation. It shows how to identify potential significators and promissors, and how to use short, simple statements to evaluate the power each potential promissor has to realize, deny, promote or hinder the major event in question. This very practical teaching is for me one of the most valuable of the many valuable teachings in this fine textbook. Nothing else I have seen has even come close to giving me such a clear, thoroughly explained, wonderfully practical, and well organized approach to the use of primary directions.

Foreword by Penelope Sitter

This textbook is the work of a true teacher. Both portions of the book, that on horary and that on natal practice, begin with basics and build section-by-section on what has gone before. For example, the portion on horary practice offers a simple algorithm that a beginning student can use to soon begin to realize predictive success. Later in the book, Borealis expands that algorithm for more advanced use to determine the querent's true question and the radicality of the chart. The book demonstrates the method, principles and techniques it teaches in numerous example charts that deserve, and will reward, careful study. Homework assignments are well designed to help students develop skill in practice step-by-step. The well reasoned and fully explained answers to the homework problems themselves act almost as a teacher who is present to guide the student's development. One of the book's appendices explains the geometry of the celestial sphere; another sets out the mathematics for calculation of primary directions as Morin and Borealis calculate them.

A practicing astrologer or student of predictive method will find in this textbook an eminently practical approach designed to teach the hands-on art of predictive practice. The approach is also refreshingly parsimonious—in method and guiding principles, in the range of, and relationships among, the techniques deployed, and in the goals of practice. Borealis is a scientist by training. He approaches astrological theory and practice with logic, common sense, adherence to sound method and strict rules, attention to the context in which a chart operates, and an abiding commitment to logical synthesis. As a result, the book teaches an unusually sound and effective approach to predictive practice.

Alexey Borealis' excellent predictive astrological work should inspire every serious astrologer to study and practice what this textbook teaches. The work should at least move those who practice predictive astrology to put these teachings to sincere and careful test. It should challenge all of us to raise the level of our astrological practice, and to give the great predictive art its true deserts.

— Penelope Sitter
Translator of *Morin's Book 21*

Chapter 1

Introduction to Predictive Astrology

How Much Do The Stars Influence Our Fate?

Some say that a person is entirely free from a superior destiny, while others argue that they are subject to a fate determined from above. Practice shows that the truth lies somewhere in between.

Indeed, one can accurately predict future events down to the day using astrology. Thus, we cannot claim that the stars do not influence our lives. Some time ago, I led a research group where we conducted a statistical study to measure the accuracy of astrological predictions. The results were impressive.[1]

In astrology, the following rule applies: *the more specific the context, the more accurate the result.*

For example, consider answering a programmer's question: "When will I find a new job as a developer?" If you are familiar with the current context—companies are operating and hiring developers—you can pinpoint the exact day of employment. You might also predict whether it will be an average IT company or a large corporation like Google, whether the job will involve frequent business trips, and what the relationships

---

[1] A. Borealis. Pilot study of predicting the timing of events using horary astrology methods. *Correlations*, 36(1):63–68, 2024

with colleagues will be like. Of course, you cannot pinpoint the company's name or the exact salary figure from the horoscope, but you can accurately forecast many details.

The situation changes if the question is: "How will my life unfold next year?" Here, much depends on the unknown context. Even if you determine that a new job awaits by the end of the year, you may not know whether it will be in-office or remote. It could happen that shortly before employment, an epidemic outbreak forces companies to switch to remote work exclusively.

Thus, we observe a combination of random and "fateful" factors. Random factors typically shape the context of one's life (specific education, place of residence, etc.), while major "fateful" events manifest only within a particular context.

The Context Rules

Suppose you have a natural inclination for the humanities. During your school years, you met companions who were publishing a newspaper, and it captivated you. As a result, you enrolled in the journalism faculty. There were good job opportunities at the local journal's editorial office, and your education and experience were a perfect fit. So, for the past five years, you've been working as the deputy chief editor of the journal. And that's your life context.

You have a twin brother born at the same moment with an identical horoscope. But his destiny unfolded differently. He is also inclined toward the humanities. During his school years, he stumbled upon a literary club and became fascinated by poetry. He enrolled in the philology faculty and studied the history of poetry but couldn't find a job in that field. As a result, he earns a living as a street artist, and poetry remains his main hobby. And that's his life context.

If, as an astrologer, I predict a significant career breakthrough for you and your brother on the 24th of September, this forecast unfolds within the specific contexts of your lives. On that day, you will get the position of chief editor, and your brother will be offered the opportunity to organize a small art exhibition.

As you can see, the same horoscope produces different biography milestones—a position as a chief editor on the 24th of September for you and a small exhibition at the end of October for your brother. It combines predefined events and particular contexts formed by random events.

How The Stars Affect Us

Skeptics and science enthusiasts often criticize astrology for its inability, even roughly, to explain the planets' influence on a person. Scientists rightly point out that no known long-range fields can directly impact or shape a person's destiny.

And they are right. Indeed, stars and planets do not directly influence people—electromagnetic and gravitational waves from distant planets are negligibly small. Besides, the connection between electromagnetic fields and a person's destiny is unclear.

We must admit that we have no fundamental theory explaining astrological influence. However, this does not make predictive astrology a matter of belief.

Just as physicists use so-called wave function to predict the state of a quantum system, astrologers use their computational tools to predict the state of a macro-system—the external circumstances of a particular person's life.

And just as physicists do not understand the nature of quantum effects, astrologers do not understand the mechanism of stellar influence on the course of events. But both physicists and astrologers do one thing—they make accurate predictions without fully grasping some of the underlying mechanisms. This principle is known in science as "shut up and calculate."

Nevertheless, I'll share my perspective on how planets might influence our lives in this chapter.

Studies suggest that planetary movements cause "spikes" in the concentrations of specific particles in the Earth's atmosphere.[2] These particles, called ultra-low-energy neutrinos, can actively affect any biological substance, particularly the neurons in the brain.

---

[2] A. Parkhomov. Dark Matter as a Cosmic Interaction Agent. (Russian). *Institute for Time Nature Explorations*, 2007. URL http://chronos.msu.ru/old/RREPORTS/parhomov_temnaya.pdf

At the moment of birth, a person's neural network experiences an early postnatal neural burst that lasts about a day. Scientists believe this period is crucial for forming synapses and shaping the brain's future development.

It is logical to assume that the presence of chemically active substances in the Earth's atmosphere at birth and in the first hours after birth can significantly affect the formation of neural connections, i.e., subconscious motives. In other words, there is a correlation between the positions of planets at the time of birth and the movements of the celestial sphere in the first hours after birth and the future development of the brain.

The brilliant 17th-century astrologer J.B. Morinus[3] hinted at this effect, claiming that neither stars nor horoscopes directly influence human life. He asserted that stars only "shape the inner nature of a person," and then the person acts according to that nature. Further, the stars can only "trigger" the inner nature to express itself at a specific moment.

I'll give you an example of how the mechanism of astrological prediction works. Suppose at the moment of birth, the Scorpio sign was descending on the western horizon. Astrologers say Mars "rules" the horizon of the west, which is associated with wars and conflicts. Such a celestial configuration may contribute to stimulating the brain region responsible for aggression at the moment of birth. It may create a long-term pattern in the early structure of the brain as part of the *natal chart*.

Let's say, 20 minutes later, the celestial sphere turned by 34 degrees, and the "ruler" of the descendant, Mars, ascended on the eastern horizon. The atmospheric chemical pattern changed again at that moment, leaving an additional "imprint" of aggression on the forming neural connections. The motion that potentially creates such secondary patterns is known as *primary directions* in astrology.

Over the years, the brain develops a root desire for aggression, according to what was "imprinted" at birth. However, this doesn't mean the person will constantly engage in conflicts.

There's a fascinating connection—the number of degrees the celestial sphere turns at birth corresponds to the number of years when a similar celestial configuration is likely to repeat.

---

[3] J.-B. Morinus. *Astrologia Gallica.* Hagae (ex Typograhia Adriani Vlacq), 1661a

So, after 34 years, it's quite probable that the stars will form a similar pattern in the sky, triggering a similar chemical pattern in the atmosphere that "activates" the internal need for aggression. In the 35th year of life, the person will unconsciously seek ways to enter conflict. Such triggering moments are known as *solar returns* in astrology.

However, it doesn't mean this need will turn into action. It requires the stars to repeat a similar pattern in a specific month of that year. The monthly repetition of the root patterns is known as *lunar return charts*. If a suitable lunar return happens, the person's brain will unconsciously plan conditions for engaging in a fight. For example, they may start noticing dark alleys in the city and paying attention to crime-ridden areas.

When the planets repeat a similar pattern on a specific day, the cumulative potential of aggression leads to action. This triggering moment is known as *transit chart* in astrology. On that day, the person will take action and unconsciously choose a path through a dangerous alley. On that very day, the brain fulfills its deep-seated need to engage in a confrontation. As a result, the person gets injured.

In this cause-effect chain, the astrologer sees the ultimate result—an event like "injury" and the date it happens. It is worth noting that the brain is the actual active force that makes the person take micro-decisions every day, resulting in the foreseen events at the planned time.

The brain, not the planets, serves as the "vessel" of destiny. Planets act as "shapers" of the brain in the first hours of life, and later, they play the role of triggers that make the brain react and perform pre-known actions at pre-known times.

Morinus described the same effect using the words of a 17th-century scientist (Book 21 of his *Astrologia Gallica*). He said that the homogeneous rays or *virtue* of the *Primum Caelum* (the Primary Heaven) pass through the degrees where the planets were at the moment of birth. This *determines* the primary radiation to leave a specific imprint on the body according to the intrinsic nature of the planets it passes through.

According to Morinus, this primary imprint is embedded in a person's body and remains with them for life. Each person's body perceives the zodiacal circle in its own unique way—it is sensitive to the degrees that were *determined* by the planets at the moment of birth. This means that the body perceives the degree of the zodiac where the Sun was at birth as if this degree constantly emanates the energy of the Sun. This is the essence of the term *determination*.

Whenever the planets pass through these determined degrees in their real motion during a person's life, the human body responds sensitively to these moments with an irresistible urge to take action or be subject to external action, leading to a known result.

What fascinates me the most in this remarkable game of planets is the interaction of people within the framework of their destinies.

Suppose someone is predetermined to enter a conflict, get married, or be in a car accident on a particular day. In that case, there will always be a second part—a person (or even a group of people) with the same date of the same event in their horoscopes. Remarkably, these people find each other on a specific day during a seemingly random social encounter.

I once conducted a small study. I calculated the exact day and hour when my wife and I moved to Warsaw. Interestingly, this date was the same in both her and my horoscopes.

The way people, during seemingly random encounters, form pairs where two or more horoscopes share the same dates of similar events is astonishing. Morinus called this phenomenon nothing less than a "miracle of the Lord."

Of course, this miracle only happens in societies with many social connections. Suppose you live as a hermit on an island. No matter how many indications of childbirth, divorces, and conflicts you have in your horoscope, they simply won't manifest due to the lack of a suitable context. So, a woman who was supposed to meet you on the appointed day will meet someone else that day.

To What Extent Can a Person Influence Their Fate?

Morinus wrote that a person can principally influence any aspect of their life, except for choosing parents and siblings. However, it's challenging for a person to resist their inner nature.

I agree with this. Suppose my assumption is correct and the stars, to some extent, imprint a person's destiny in the brain's neural network.

Chapter 1. Introduction to Predictive Astrology

In that case, each of us can influence the outcome of our lives to the extent that we can change our behavior patterns. Psychotherapy has made significant progress in this regard.

Psychologists would agree that a person can change many aspects of their stereotypical behavior, but not everything. Some deep configurations of neurons are so stable that it is nearly impossible to alter them in adulthood.

In such cases, as Morinus wrote, "rational will" comes to the rescue.

Let me give an example of how it works. According to a man's horoscope, there are about a dozen moments when he could die. But only one of them will come to pass. He could die, for example, at the age of 5 from a fall, then at 16 from an enemy's attack, then at 27 from a car accident, and so on. All these episodes would have something in common—a violent death. The man is predisposed to realize this scenario.

If parents watch over a child and don't allow him to climb high walls, falling from a height at five years old is unlikely to threaten him. Suppose a child grows up in a cultured family, away from criminal areas. In that case, he is unlikely to fall victim to an enemy's attack by age 16. But he may well develop a passion for extreme driving closer to age 27. It would be challenging to resist this passion since the urge for risk is deeply rooted in a person's subconscious and cannot be easily suppressed.

But if a man knew that this urge for speed would be fatal, he could use his rational will in advance to restrain himself from this inclination (at least during the specific period when the mortal threat is predetermined to be realized). And this is precisely where predictive astrology shines in its power—it allows one to apply rational will in a specific direction and at a specific time.

Certainly, this doesn't mean that a person can escape death every time. Sooner or later, on one of the predetermined dates, death will still come, at least from the wear and tear of the body. But it's better for death to happen later rather than sooner.

Morinus claimed an obvious thing—knowing the negative consequences of internal inclinations (what astrology provides) plus applying rational willpower to resist these inclinations can rid our lives of many troubles. And that's true.

Predictive astrology is an excellent risk management tool.

Modern Use of Astrology

Since astrology ceased to be a university discipline and fell into the hands of the general public, it has undergone a total transformation. From what I see, astrology today is a tool to comfort or entertain the masses:

- It assures people that everything is fine with them, and all their problems are due to poorly positioned planets in the horoscope. It relieves a person of responsibility for their actions.
- Modern astrology gives hope for some miracle to come with no or minimal effort, which the average person desperately needs.
- It flatters the ego—astrologers are ready to talk about a person's talents and great mission for hours.
- Astrological forecasts have been replaced by trivial recommendations, such as "refrain from spending during a certain period" or "celebrate the New Year in a red dress for good luck."

Moreover, the code of modern astrology prohibits predicting any adverse events, let alone death. I have often heard at professional astrological conferences that an astrologer can tell clients anything as long as it makes them happy.

But such use of astrology contradicts the very essence of predictions. Knowing the future is vital information for making managerial decisions in critical moments. And knowing about possible negative scenarios is the most valuable data from a risk management perspective.

Three Types of Predictive Astrology

There are three types of predictive astrology, each serving different purposes and employing various techniques.

Natal Astrology

The most well-known type is called *natal astrology*. The name originates from the Latin *"natalis,"* i.e., birth date. It focuses on identifying key life events and predicting their dates based on your birth chart. Some mistakenly believe that a natal chart can reveal the most minor details of a day, but that's not the case in practice.

Indeed, significant events in your life are relatively few—maybe one or two per year—and sometimes no notable events occur throughout the year. The appearance of a new boss in your office, a casual romance, or a night out with friends are not critical life events; they are more like random social encounters.

On the other hand, events such as childbirth, moving to a new city, divorce, changing careers, legal disputes, meeting a future spouse, life-threatening situations, severe illnesses, and so on stand out from the ordinary. Natal astrology is capable of "seeing" such events.

As mentioned in the section "The Context Rules," you must know the person's life context to make a specific prediction. Making accurate predictions ten years ahead is unlikely because various random factors can alter the future life context.

Let's assume a newborn's horoscope consistently shows the connection of Mars and the Sun with the western horizon and zenith. This configuration equally indicates success in sports, in the criminal world, or warfare. It would be foolish to predict success in sports at 30 if the person grows up in a criminal environment and becomes a gang leader during their school years. These factors are random and unknown.

Therefore, natal astrology works well in the short term—you can make reasonably accurate predictions for a year or two ahead. And you can only name a few critical events in the coming years.

Over the years, I've learned to apply natal astrology in the most practical way possible.

- I check for any sudden upheavals in the upcoming year so I can take countermeasures in advance.
- I also look for exceptionally favorable events to prepare and maximize their positive impact.
- When facing a major decision, I analyze the potential consequences beforehand to make an informed choice.

Mundane Astrology

Personal horoscopes may predict a wedding for someone this year. Still, a sudden war, epidemic, or another disaster that may strike before that day will ruin these promises. They overwrite the context of peaceful life, leaving no space for the expected marriage.

As mentioned earlier in the section "How Much Do The Stars Influence Our Fate?," major social upheavals cannot simultaneously reflect in every horoscope of every citizen.

Individuals miraculously unite to realize personal events like weddings, moving with family, conflicts, or road accidents with the other party. These events are part of personal "fate" and are visible in each participant's natal chart.

However, simultaneous social disruptions affecting thousands of people at the same time and place are not tracked in the horoscopes of each resident. If it were so, nearly every horoscope of every person on Earth would contain an indication of the COVID outbreak in early 2020. But no astrologer noticed anything like that.

Group dynamics result from the behavior of an entire group (e.g., a region's economic prosperity) or the collision of distinct groups (e.g., war). They rise above individual behavior, developing traits absent in the isolated individuals who drive the collective process.

There is a branch of astrology that specifically examines the influence of stars on collective processes. This branch is called *mundane astrology*, derived from the Latin word *"mundanus,"* meaning civil or worldly.

Mundane charts are entirely insensitive to events in the lives of individual citizens. In contrast, individual natal charts usually do not indicate social processes.

In ancient times, before making personal yearly forecasts, astrologers carefully examined the situation in the current area to understand the social context in which the promises of the natal chart would unfold.

Horary Astrology

As you've understood, a natal chart only shows significant events in your life. However, there's an area of astrology focused on predicting the development of everyday situations.

You can predict where you'll find a lost key, how your favorite football team will play in the next match, or your boss's decision about the

Chapter 1. Introduction to Predictive Astrology

vacation you requested for next Friday. You can make forecasts in areas where natal astrology is powerless. For example, your natal chart won't show how your favorite football team will play the next game—the fate of a football team isn't part of your horoscope.

This type of astrology is called *horary*, originating from the Latin word "*hora*"—the current moment in time. The forecasting of specific events occurs not based on a person's birth chart but on the horoscope of the current moment, which determines the development of a particular situation, that is, a group process involving small collectives of people.

The natal chart shows the imprint stars made in your neural network at birth. The horary chart reflects the imprint stars made in the collective process.

Imagine several people involved in the same situation, already having clear unconscious tendencies toward its outcome. For instance, if two people are predetermined to break their relationship this Friday, each partner's brain unconsciously decides to separate in advance. An astrologer sees this collective decision in the chart before the actual separation.

Another example is a girl actively seeking love. Suppose the Sun has recently returned to the position it was in at her birth, and the stars formed a configuration called solar return. The solar return repeated the pattern of her horoscope related to family formation. It activated the girl's unconscious desire to find her future husband this year.

According to the solar return chart, she will meet her future husband this year, precisely in 12.5 weeks. Imagine several men in her city also have astrological indications of a significant encounter in 12.5 weeks. One of them will become her husband—he has a corresponding configuration in his solar return chart.

Both horoscopes will guide these two people toward meeting on a specific date. Without even realizing it, they are drawn into a shared dynamic with a predetermined outcome—family formation. In some way, incomprehensible to our current understanding, the girl's and her future husband's subconscious minds will begin steering them toward the same locations, increasing the chance of their encounter. How exactly people recognize their destined partners remains unknown, but it appears to be a poorly understood aspect of brain function. Almost certainly, on the destined day, they will meet each other.

We may not know the girl's or her future husband's horoscopes. Yet, based solely on the horary chart, which captures the evolution of specific group dynamics, we can predict with reasonable accuracy (within a margin of a few days) that the girl will meet her future husband in 12.5 weeks. We may even determine the circumstances of their meeting, which are not trackable in the natal charts.

As you can see, with horary astrology, you can predict not only ordinary situations that are outside the scope of natal astrology but also forecast vital events in a person's life just as effectively as with the use of the natal chart.

Sometimes, global social dynamics are directly connected to a particular situation you predict. In that case, you can observe the development of the significant social process with the horary chart as if you were a mundane astrologer.

Later in this book, we'll delve into a real-life case where a girl needed to know if the government would impose a lockdown in her city due to COVID. We will accurately pinpoint the date she will lose the ability to move around the city due to the lockdown. And we will see how, on that exact day, the authorities announced the restriction of movement across the whole country.

Notice that we will not use a mundane chart. Still, indirectly, we will see an event concerning the entire city. It will happen because the girl's circumstances are so closely intertwined with the context of a large-scale lockdown.

As you can see, horary astrology sometimes allows predicting mundane processes. Furthermore, unlike other types of astrology, horary astrology is straightforward and provides results within minutes.

A reasonable question arises: If horary astrology is so good, why not use it all the time? Despite its first-glance appeal, horary astrology has three severe limitations:

– The stars do not, in every moment, form a configuration that shows the future development of a specific situation. Several crucial factors must come together simultaneously—we'll discuss them later in the section "Radicality of the Chart."

Chapter 1. Introduction to Predictive Astrology

- To predict the outcome of a process, it must already be taking place and developing at the current moment. You can say where exactly a person will find lost keys only if they've already lost them. You can predict the date of a future wedding only if the girl is already seeking a husband. You can only predict a COVID epidemic if you are in a situation where the beginning of the epidemic is a significant part of the current circumstances. Simply put, you cannot predict anything unexpected—something the person isn't even aware of yet.
- Finally, horary astrology is a field where predictions can be relatively easy to "cancel." Simply changing the context and stepping outside the group dynamics is often enough. For instance, if you're searching for a lost key, you might stop looking and make a duplicate instead. In this case, the astrologer's prediction about where and when you'd find the key (assuming you continued searching) would no longer hold true. However, not everything can be changed. For example, if your friend is ill and an astrologer predicts the progression of their illness, your friend can't simply "decide to recover."

Chapter 2

Horary Astrology

Definitions

We'll start our journey into the world of accurate predictions with the simplest form of astrology—horary. By the end of this part, you can make your first forecast. Follow the instructions carefully, and you'll do great.

Horary astrology predicts the future of a particular life situation. The astrologer casts a chart when accepting the client's question. The horary horoscope includes seven planets, representing *external objects* (people, organizations, illnesses, money, etc.) in the context of the situation.

Let's get acquainted with the symbols of the seven planets in the horary chart. I have divided them into three groups to make it easier for you to remember them.

- The first group is the Moon and the Sun: ☽, ☉. These symbols are self-explanatory and easy to remember.
- The second group is the planets Mercury and Venus: ☿, ♀. See how the symbols of these planets are similar. The Venus symbol resembles a hand mirror.
- There are three planets left—Mars, Jupiter, and Saturn: ♂, ♃, and ♄. You may often encounter the symbol of Mars in books. I'm sure you are already familiar with it.

So, the only new symbols to remember are those of Jupiter and Saturn. With this knowledge, let's move on to our first definition.

Significator. It is a planet that signifies an object. We often phrase this as: "The significator of a dog is planet A" or "Planet B signifies a salary in that chart." There are two more essential definitions.

The querent. It is the person asking the question, usually the client. But sometimes the astrologer can be the querent and ask about their own future. In this case, the time to accept the question is when the astrologer is ready to hear the stars' honest answer.

The quesited. It is the subject or subjects in question. You may ask about your brother's health, a lost key, or your prospective career—they all are quesited.

With these simple definitions, we are ready to move on and learn the fundamental techniques for making an accurate forecast in horary astrology.

The List of Techniques

Before studying each technique separately, we will determine how they are applied and what tasks they solve.

Signification Techniques

As we have already said, each planet in the horary chart signifies some external object. It could be a thing, a person, or a circumstance. Therefore, we need to juxtapose external items to the planets to predict. There is a whole class of astrological techniques for this. Let's call them "signification techniques." They essentially answer two questions:

– "Which planet signifies that particular object, person, or circumstance?" and
– "Whom does this planet signify?"

We ask the second question when we know the planet has an essential role in the horoscope, but we do not know its meaning and need to find it. There are several techniques for determining the objects' significator.

1. Universal Rulership

You've probably heard that Mars represents war, while Venus signifies love. Each planet has a list of external objects and processes associated

Chapter 2. Horary Astrology

with it. This connection is constant and identical for all people on Earth. It doesn't depend on the horoscope and is called *universal rulership*. We'll only occasionally use this correspondence.

2. Accidental Rulership

In a specific horoscope, the universal nature of a planet undergoes significant changes. For instance, the planet of love, Venus, due to its position relative to the horizon, may indicate a mother, a car, or credit. In another horoscope, the same Venus may signify entirely different things. We call this modified correspondence between a planet and external objects *accidental rulership*. We'll almost always search for correspondence between a known object, person, or circumstance and some planet in the horoscope.

Here is a list of techniques for that:

- House rulership
- Derived house rulership
- Alternative lords
- Arabian Parts disposition

Sometimes, we must do the reverse—we must establish a connection between a known planet and an unknown object or person it signifies. There are several techniques called *identification of an unknown planet*.

N.B. on natal astrology

Natal astrology is more complex. In a horary chart, you have 2–3 external elements to match with planets within an ultra-specific situation. With seven planets available, it's a simple task. One planet shows only one specific object in context.

However, in natal astrology, seven planets describe all possible external events in your life.

For example, you might have three marriages, several relocations, encounter the bankruptcy of your younger brother, etc. Yet, you still have only seven planets to work with. This means that each planet in the natal chart can play not just one role but several.

For instance, in my horoscope, Venus represents my wife, my money, certain diseases, and people scheming against me.

It doesn't mean Venus plays all its roles simultaneously. Each role belongs to a specific period of life. A planet in the natal chart may signify something particular during a given period.

Descriptive Techniques

When we have chosen a planet that signifies an external object, we need to investigate that significator. By considering the planet's condition, we describe that object's current or future state. There is a class of techniques for this.

1. Sign Properties

This technique assigns specific properties to the planet through the properties of the sign where it resides. There is a limited number of these properties, such as coldness, warmth, multiplicity, loudness, and so on. We will study them in detail later in the section "Descriptive Techniques: Sign Properties." For example:

- The planet might signify your neighbor and reside in a loud sign.
- It may signify food and be in a cold sign.
- It may represent a job and reside in a double-bodied sign.

Thus, you know in advance that your roommate will be noisy, the breakfast at the hotel will be cold, and you will be working on two projects simultaneously.

2. Position of the Planet in a House

We will talk about the so-called *houses* in detail later. For now, it is enough to understand that a house is just a sector of the sky from the eastern to the western horizon. Each house is responsible for a particular sphere of life. You will find the planets in the horoscope distributed among these sectors.

A significator may have a relation to one or another house—that is, a connection to one or another sphere of your life. For instance, your boss might have a close relationship with your secret enemies and plan your dismissal. Your spouse may spend time with friends at a lake tomorrow. We use the planet's position in the house to extract this information from the chart.

The house (the sector of the sky) may be afflicted or strengthened by the presence of a benefic or malefic planet (we'll talk about the celestial states of the planets later). In that case, we say that a particular sphere of life is affected for better or worse by the presence of a specific object. For instance, you may have an excellent job, but it is impacted by a colleague who constantly annoys you.

3. Conjunction with a Fixed Star

A prospective meeting with an external object (a job, a person, etc.) may bring unexpected consequences, such as great joy, protection, success, or regret. The conjunction of the planet with a fixed star may reveal these particular details.

4. Celestial State

In most cases, we will be interested in a qualitative assessment of the object rather than its specific properties. A qualitative assessment always answers "how good" or "how bad" that object is. We may want to know whether a person is healthy or sick, or whether a high or low salary awaits us at a new job.

That is where the technique of the celestial state of the planet comes into play. The dignity or debility of the significator describes the state of the objects it signifies. It answers three simple questions.

- Is this object in a bad or good condition? (in the context of the question).
- Is this object harmful or helpful *per se*?
- And if we are talking about a person—does he feel bad or good?

For example, a client asks, "Is it worth reading this book?" It implies that the book can be dull or exciting. The condition of the significator of a book shows this—it may be dignified or debilitated.

Suppose a client asks the astrologer what position he will receive in a company—high or middle. In that case, we can assess the celestial state of his future work. If the significator is dignified, then the job will be highly managerial.

The logic of judgment is straightforward here. So, the celestial state of the planets shows the state of objects signified by those planets. We will almost always use the celestial state assessment.

Only sometimes will we apply the techniques for identifying the specific properties of the object when it is part of the context. For example, in the question, "How wet will the weather be next Friday" we are interested in humidity. Humidity is a specific property (see above).

5. Accidental Strengthening of the Planet

This technique answers "how actively a given object can act or resist external influences."

For example, a company can be aggressive and not play by the rules (that is, harmful to the market). Meanwhile, it can be a powerful player and consist of excellent professionals.

Another example: there is an excellent company manager with extensive experience. But at the moment, they are ill and cannot manage the business. In this case, the planet showing the boss is dignified but accidentally weakened.

Here are the typical questions we can answer exclusively by the accidental strengthening/weakening assessment.

– Will our team win?
– Will the company survive the crisis?
– Is this glass fragile or durable?

We are asking here exclusively about the strength or resistance of the objects against external pressure.

Object Interaction Techniques

Well, we know a list of techniques to describe objects. But what about the interconnections between objects? How do significators interact with each other?

Chapter 2. Horary Astrology

Here is the third class of techniques that comes into play. It shows the interaction between the planets.

- There are tools for determining people's motives—what they want and in what direction they will act.
- There are techniques for assessing the enduring influence of one planet on another.

1. Receptions

The first technique is *reception*. It answers three simple questions.

- Does a person love, appreciate, or want to save/support/defend something or otherwise?
- Will the object help (because it fits explicitly or intends to support) or harm another object?
- And finally, is an object in someone's power?

For example, in the question, "Will my boss agree to give me this position?" we are interested in the boss's motive. And this is what reception describes.

In the question, "Is it safe to eat this food?" we are interested in the possible harm the food can cause. It may happen because the food is destructive innately—say, it is not fresh. In this case, we will assess the celestial state (the quality) of the food's significator. But it could also be because this food doesn't fit the querent—say, he has an allergy to nuts, even if they are of excellent quality. In this case, we discuss a specific impact and apply the reception technique.

Finally, in the question, "Who has hidden control over my competitors?" we are interested in the presence of control by a third party. And this is also the subject of receptions.

2. Close Aspect and Antiscion

These techniques show the close connection between the two planets. They answer the questions:

- Is there any long-lasting influence from the other planet, and does it signify something?
- Is there a connection between the two planets, that is, between the objects they describe?

For example, in the question, "Does my friend's mother interfere with his relationship?", we are interested in the mother's constant influence. Astrologically speaking, we are interested in whether the mother's planet affects the friend's planet. Influence is the subject of close aspects and antiscia. It often applies with the *reception technique*—the mother at least should have a *motive* to support or disrupt the son's relationship.

In the question, "Is he involved in a dirty business?" or "Is he tied with Harry?", we are interested in the presence of a close connection between the two significators. And this is also what close aspects and antiscia describe.

As I mentioned above, the position of the significator in the house can also show the connection between two objects. So please keep it in mind.

Event Prediction and Timing Techniques

Finally, the most intriguing part is the techniques for identifying events and the time of their occurrence. It is what *exact aspects* and *timing tools* are responsible for. They answer two simple questions:

- Will a particular event occur?
- And if it will, then when will it happen?

1. Exact Aspects

This technique is most often used in conjunction with *reception* and *accidental strengthening* techniques. It determines whether a particular event occurred in the past or will happen in the future. Typical questions it answers:

- Will I get this job?
- Did he steal my wallet?
- Will he come before 15:00?

2. Timing Techniques

These techniques answer the question "when?"

- When will I meet him?
- When will my business double in size?

– When did it happen?

The Table of Main Techniques in Horary Astrology

So, let's recap what we've learned so far. In Table 2.1, I have listed astrological techniques and their purposes. I also highlighted the focus keywords that characterize each method. When you hear these keywords in a question, you immediately understand which techniques are appropriate to use in response.

You will remember this table with time, but for now, keep it handy—you will return to it frequently.

Table 2.1: *Main Techniques in Horary Astrology*

Task	The keywords in question	The technique
To choose a planet	—Which planet **signifies** a given object? —Whom does this planet **signify**?	Signification techniques
To describe an object	—Is it **good** or **bad**? —Is it **helpful** or **harmful** by nature? —Does he **feel good** or **bad**?	Celestial state assessment
To describe an object	Does it have a **specific property**?	—Conjunction with the fixed stars —Sign's properties —Position in a house
To describe an object	Is it **strong** or **weak**?	Accidental strength
		Continued on next page

Table 2.1 — Continued from previous page

Task	The keywords in question	The technique
To understand motives or subordination	—Does he **love** or **hate**? —Is that object in someone's **power**? —Is there **control** of one object over another?	Reception
To describe the effect of influence	Does it **support** or **harm** that particular object?	—Reception —Position in the house —Close aspect
To identify influence or connections	—Is there long-lasting **influence**? —Is there close **connection**?	—Position in the house —Close aspect and antiscia
To predict specific events	Will the event **happen**?	Exact aspects
To predict the date of event	**When** will the event happen?	cell1.3inTiming techniques

Homework Assignment №1

So now it's time for your first homework. I will give you five questions, and your task is to choose appropriate astrological techniques to answer.

Here is an example of how it might look. Suppose you got the question, "Why is my business not growing?" In such a formulation, it is entirely unclear where to start. Let's restate it to include familiar focus words from the previous table.

"Why is my business not growing?" is equivalent to "What influences my business, preventing it from growing?" The idea is the same, but now we have a clue for specific techniques. We have a focus keyword—

"**influence**." Influence is a subject of reception, antiscia, and close aspects.

So we need to choose these techniques. The second focus word is "**what**". We need to find the correspondence between the planet and some physical objects it signifies. And this is a subject of signification techniques.

The correct answer would look like this: We will examine the receptions and close aspects and apply signification techniques.

Now, please find appropriate techniques to answer each of the questions below.

– I am going to England for three days. Do I need to take warm clothes with me?
– If I buy this used car, will driving be safe?
– When will I sell my house?
– What feelings does he have for me?
– Who leaks information to competitors?

The accuracy of an astrological forecast is 90% dependent on the correctness of the chosen tools. Therefore, read these questions carefully and take some time to think. As soon as you finish this task, read the solution below.

Solution

Question 1. "I am going to England for three days. Do I need to take warm clothes with me?" In this formulation, it is entirely unclear where to start. Let's reformulate the question to include familiar focus words. What interests the querent? Clothing (its condition), weather, or England? Of course, they are interested in the weather.

What exactly do they want to know about the weather? They desire to see if it is warm or cold. Great, the property of *heat* or *cold* is something familiar. So we can formulate this question as "Will it be *cold* in England?" The keyword here is "cold"—it's a specific property of the sign. So, we will apply the sign properties technique to the weather's significator.

Question 2. The next question is, "If I buy this used car, is it safe to drive?" Again, we must clarify this formulation to understand how to approach the query. But what does the client want to know? They desire to know if driving the car will harm them or not. "Harm" is a familiar keyword. Let's reformat the question: "Will driving that car harm me?"

The significator of the car in the horary chart may harm in two ways:

- It may be harmful by itself. Let's say the car is in poor condition, or
- The planet of the car can be fine, but it may harm the querent specifically. The car is fine, but it doesn't suit the querent's driving habits. For example, this car has a unique gearbox that the querent is unfamiliar with.

In the first case, we will involve the technique of celestial state assessment; in the second, the tool of reception and the position of a planet in a house.

Astrologically speaking, we find the planet, which signifies the car. Then we assess that planet's essential dignity and see if it harms the querent by reception or position in their 1st house.

Question 3. The next question is, "When will I sell my house?" Everything is quite simple here. We hear the word "when," so we apply timing techniques.

Question 4. The same short approach is in the next question, "What feelings does he have for me?" Feelings and desires are the fields of human motives, and reception is responsible for them.

Question 5. The last question is challenging. "Who leaks information to competitors?"

If you have no idea how to restate the question, go through the list of keywords to find something that fits the context. And look, there are the words "close connection with someone" and "control over someone" in our list.

- Does one of the employees have a secret connection with competitors?
- Do competitors control one of the employees?

Isn't it what the querent wants to know? Yes, this is an entirely appropriate formulation. The keywords here indicate that we can involve reception techniques, close aspects, and position in a house.

Chapter 2. Horary Astrology

Suppose we cast a chart and found a particular planet connected with competitors' significators or controlled by them. And let's suppose this is Saturn. That is, we know that Saturn shows the informant. But look at the wording of the question. Querent wants to know *who exactly* leaks information. That is, we need to find whom Saturn signifies. We need to locate a connection between the planet and a real man. And for that purpose, we require the techniques of signification. They will help us extract tons of information about the informant, including where they live and how they look.

A Simple Algorithm to Make a Prediction

For the first time, this approach may seem very sophisticated. But this is only at first. I have prepared a simple algorithm for analyzing a horary chart to make it easier for you to assimilate this knowledge. Use it until it becomes a habit.

- First, look at the keywords in the question. You may need to restate it.
- Then, based on the keywords found, create the list of techniques you will use.
- Then cast a chart and find the main significators—the querent, the mother, a job, or a car—everything you need in the context.
- Then, apply techniques from your list to these planets.

To consolidate these steps, let's walk through them with another question. A man asks, "I have two job offers. Which one to choose?" He wants to know which job is better.

First, we'll reformulate the question to include familiar keywords. On the one hand, the job can be excellent *per se* (great company, fantastic social package, etc.). On the other hand, the job can be average by itself, but satisfy the querent's particular needs. For instance, it may be a middle position, but it gives an emotional return, a warm relationship with the team, etc.

So, we have two subquestions here.

- Which job is better *per se*, and
- Which one is more supportive?

In the first case, we will assess the celestial state of the significator of the job; in the second, we will evaluate the reception between the job and the querent. Then, we cast a chart and find the main significators. Suppose that in the particular chart,

- Saturn is the 1st job
- Jupiter is the 2nd job
- The Moon is the querent

Now, we will apply the celestial state assessment and reception techniques to our significators.

Let's start with the celestial state.

- We will assess the state of the first work (Saturn). Is it debilitated or dignified?
- Similarly, we will look at the second work (Jupiter). Is it in excellent or poor condition?

After that, we can confidently say which of the jobs is better by itself—where are the best conditions: position, salary, career prospects, etc.

Finally, we will apply the reception technique. Remember that reception involves the interaction between two planets, so we use it for a pair of significators. We look at:

- If Saturn supports the Moon, or
- If Jupiter supports the Moon by reception.

This quick assessment will inform us how well two jobs satisfy the querent's needs and expectations, such as emotional returns, special privileges, etc. Based on this judgment, we can give a detailed answer.

As you can see, horary astrology stands out for its straightforward approach.

Signification Techniques: House Rulership

There is a whole series of techniques for determining an object's significator. In this chapter, we will closely examine one of them, namely, *house rulership*. It is the most commonly used technique and is a good starting point.

The horary chart represents the distribution of planets in the sky when an astrologer accepts the question. In astrology, they divide the celestial sphere into 12 unequal parts called "spaces" or "houses,"[4] as shown in Fig. 2.1.

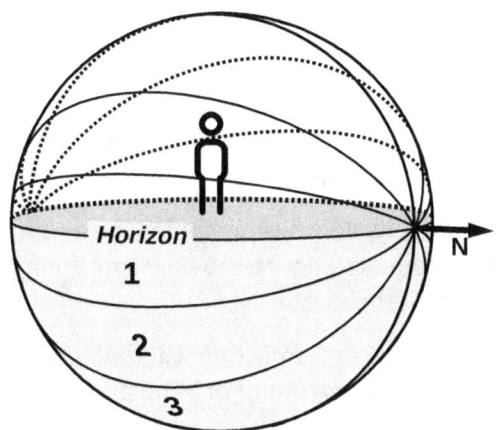

Figure 2.1: *The Twelve Spatial Places Called Houses*

Universal and Accidental Meaning of Planets

Each sector has a specific action: it forces the planet to manifest itself within a particular area of life. Some sectors are related to health, some to money, others to family. In astrology, we often say that if a planet falls into a specific sector, *it is determined* to manifest itself in that particular area.

You've probably heard that Mars is associated with aggression. It is the god of war. But this is its *universal* meaning, valid at all times and for all residents of Earth. However, in a particular city where an astrologer casts the chart, Mars may occupy a sector of the sky related to work. In that case, Mars will indicate someone at work. Suppose another astrologer, living 10,000 kilometers to the east, casts the chart at the exact same moment. He will find Mars descending on the local horizon—and then the same Mars will indicate, let's say, a wife's lover.

---

[4] Morinus divided houses into *primary* and *secondary*. Primary houses are the sections of the sky that you see in Fig. 2.1. Secondary houses are the sections of the zodiac circle or *Primum Caelum* that are enclosed in these areas.

You see how dramatically a planet changes its meaning due to its location in one or another sector of the sky relative to the horizon. It depends on the geographical area where the astrologer casts the chart. For this reason, these sectors are called *terrestrial places* or the *houses* of the planets.

Astrological houses modify the universal meaning of planets, narrowing them down to specific roles in certain life situations. Morinus wrote that houses *determine* the planets to influence specific areas of life. These modified significations of planets are called *accidental meanings*.

For example, *universally*, Venus represents love and romance. But *accidentally*, due to its connection with the house of siblings, it may indicate a brother in a particular chart.

The same Venus in another horoscope will indicate a distant trip—this will be another *accidental meaning* of Venus.

The House Systems

There are mathematical algorithms for splitting the celestial sphere into 12 parts, called *the house systems*. Each system is named after its founder—the astronomer of old who invented it. You may hear about Regiomontanus, Koch, Placidus, and other house systems. We will use the Regiomontanus house system in this book. Practice shows that it provides the most accurate predictions. So, when you work with astrological programs, remember to select this house system in the application settings.

Each house has its meaning and its serial number. House numbers start at the eastern horizon and go counterclockwise, as shown in the picture above.

House Cusps

The boundary between the previous and the current house is called the *house cusp*.

For example, the boundary between the twelfth and first houses is called the first house cusp. It coincides with the eastern horizon, where the 1st house begins, as shown in Fig. 2.2.

Chapter 2. Horary Astrology

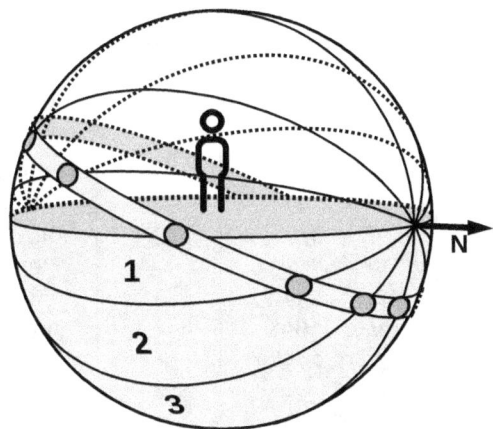

Figure 2.2: *House Cusps in Regiomontanus System*

Planets in the sky are arranged along a circle called the *zodiacal circle*. House cusps intersect that circle at 12 points.

Since the zodiacal circle consists of twelve 30-degree segments, known as *zodiac signs*, we often say that house cusps *fall into specific zodiac signs*. We also call those signs *the signs of the cusps*.

When examining a horoscope, we often use the term "cusp," referring to the zodiacal degree of the cusp.

The Domiciles of the Planets

Each zodiac sign corresponds to a particular planet; it "reflects" its ruler. Morinus said that the zodiac sign is *determined* by the planet to reflect its intrinsic nature. This correspondence is universal and constant. For instance, Aries ♈ corresponds to Mars ♂. We use the following notation for that correspondence:

– Mars rules Aries
– Mars disposes Aries
– Aries is the domicile of Mars

These are synonyms. Table 2.2 denotes this correspondence.

Table 2.2: *Zodiac Signs: Their Degrees and Dispositors*

Sign	Zodiac Degrees	Symbol	Ruler	
Aries	0°..29°	♈	Mars	♂
Taurus	30°..59°	♉	Venus	♀
Gemini	60°..89°	♊	Mercury	☿
Cancer	90°..119°	♋	The Moon	☽
Leo	120°..149°	♌	The Sun	☉
Virgo	150°..179°	♍	Mercury	☿
Libra	180°..209°	♎	Venus	♀
Scorpio	210°..239°	♏	Mars	♂
Sagittarius	240°..269°	♐	Jupiter	♃
Capricorn	270°..299°	♑	Saturn	♄
Aquarius	300°..329°	♒	Saturn	♄
Pisces	330°..359°	♓	Jupiter	♃

This correspondence works in one direction: if something affects a planet, it influences the zodiac sign it rules.

The Lord of the House

As we mentioned, each degree of the zodiac sign is a miniature copy of the sign's ruler. This means that each degree of the sign Leo emits rays of the Sun's nature. Leo will act destructively if the Sun is in Libra—the sign of its detriment. On the contrary, if the Sun is in Leo or Aries, then Leo will act constructively.

Thus, a zodiac sign is an active force. This becomes evident when a planet comes bodily to the cusp of the house, which is simply the point in space corresponding to an empty degree of the sign. Such a conjunction with the cusp often measures the time until the event, meaning that the zodiac degree is the active point of the chart (see example in the section "Affliction/Strengthening of the House").

As you remember, a house focuses any radiation of Primum Caelum that passes through it on specific objects. Moreover, the closer the radiation is to the cusp, the stronger this focus becomes, meaning the more effective the terrestrial determination is. This rule applies to radiation emitted via planets and the zodiac signs.

Suppose Leo occupies a specific house. The house focuses radiation emitted from the sign of Leo in a specific sphere of life. However, Leo

Chapter 2. Horary Astrology

will emit beneficial or hostile rays when the Sun is in Aries or Libra. The house doesn't modify Leo's beneficial or maleficent influence but only directs this influence to particular objects.

Therefore, if the cusp of the 2nd house falls in Leo, then the state of the Sun significantly affects the querent's wealth. We say that the Sun rules money, and the state of the Sun indicates the state of the querent's finances.

There's a rule—the closer a celestial object is to the house cusp, the stronger its influence is determined by that house on the specific things it describes. This also applies to zodiac signs. This means that the sign on the cusp exerts the most targeted influence on a specific object. For example, if the sign of Leo falls on the cusp of the 2nd house of possessions, then the sign's influence focuses on the specific type of possession in question, such as a bank account or certain shares owned by the querent.

For example, the cusp of the 10th house falls at 17 degrees of Sagittarius (17° ♐). This means that Jupiter, "reflected" in Sagittarius, influences a particular object in question—let's say, a specific job. Whatever the state of Jupiter is, it determines the state of the job you will get.

The 10th house may also include the sign of Capricorn ♑, which follows Sagittarius. This means that Saturn also signifies something related to the 10th house. It may be another job you have, the private business you run, or something else that is not directly connected to the particular job in question (i.e., in a given group dynamics).

So, Jupiter mainly impacts the state of a particular subject. We express this as:

- Jupiter is the ruler of the 10th house, or
- Jupiter governs the 10th house, or
- Jupiter is the Lord of the 10th house.

Since the degree of a zodiac sign is like a small copy of a planet, the reflection of Jupiter in the sign of Sagittarius is weaker than the presence of Jupiter in the 10th house. In other words, Jupiter in the 10th house has a more noticeable effect on the matters of the 10th house than its reflection in the sign of Sagittarius on the cusp.

However, Jupiter in the 10th house exerts a broader influence, as the 10th house signifies the querent's activities in general, including their job, profession, startups, and so on.

Although weaker, Jupiter's reflection on the cusp establishes a very focused connection between Jupiter and the specific job in question.

This means that in horary astrology, where we are interested in the fate of a particular position in a company, we prefer the house ruler as the significator of that position rather than the planet in the house. The planet in the house may signify something else within the same area of life, not directly related to the question—for example, social activity, the head of the department in your prospective job, etc.

Exceptions may occur when the planet is located right on the cusp of the house. In that case, we prefer the planet on the cusp, especially if it describes the object better than the house ruler.

For example, if Saturn is on the cusp of the 2nd house of possessions in a question about a missing umbrella, we would prefer Saturn over the ruler of the 2nd because:

- The rays emitted by Saturn are more concentrated (i.e., influential) than the rays emitted from the empty sign, which only reflects its ruler.
- Saturn's rays affect the particular umbrella in question, not the car, clothes, or other possessions, since Saturn is right on the cusp.
- In addition, Saturn naturally describes all things that serve as barriers—walls, fences, umbrellas, bulletproof vests, safes, and so on. We will discuss the natural rulership of planets in more detail in the following lessons.

Usually, a planet inside a house is the ruler of another house. Therefore, in horary astrology, planets in a house often indicate specific details related to the object. For example, the planet ruling the 11th house of friends inside the 2nd house of possession will indicate a friend connected with the querent's property (for example, a friend who borrows a querent's car), while the ruler of the 2nd will denote that car and its condition.

N.B. on natal astrology

In natal astrology, things are different. We lack a particular context and are more interested in the planet that has more influence on the specific area of life. That's why, in natal astrology, we prefer a planet in a house over the house ruler whenever possible.

The second significant difference in natal astrology is that planets often combine universal and accidental meanings since the birth chart lacks a specific context, unlike a horary chart. For example, Mars in the 8th house in a birth chart indicates death on the one hand and violence on the other (according to its universal nature). In summary, it signifies a violent death when debilitated.

The Angles of the Chart

In Fig. 2.3, you see the skeleton of a horary chart—12 astrological houses and the signs where their cusps fall. The houses are always displayed so that the cusp of the 10th house is at the top of the chart. We will draw the houses with equal length, in an old-fashioned style, though the houses have different lengths in reality.

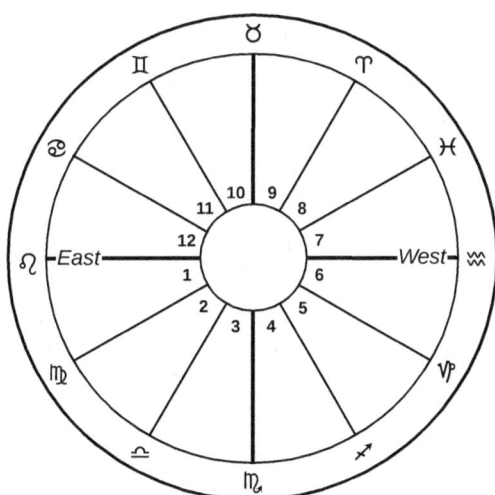

Figure 2.3: *The Twelve Houses Represented in an Old-Fashioned Style*

Geometrically, the peak of the 10th house—the line running from the South to the North through the Zenith—always rises above any other cusps. That's why the 10th house is always positioned at the top of the chart. The cusp of the 1st house coincides with the eastern horizon, and the cusp of the 7th house coincides with the western horizon.

The eastern horizon intersects the zodiac circle at a point called the *ascendant*, abbreviated as ASC. The name indicates the zodiac sign rising above the horizon at the moment the question is accepted.

Similarly, the zodiac sign where the cusp of the opposite 7th house falls is called the *descendant* and is denoted as DSC.

The zodiac sign where the 10th house cusp falls is called the *medium caeli* (midheaven) and is denoted as MC. The opposite sign is called the *imum caeli* (IC), which means "the bottom of the sky."

These four cusps form the so-called *angles of the chart*. We often use the expression "angular planet" or "planet in an angle" to indicate a planet that occupies the 1st, 4th, 7th, or 10th house.

Table 2.3 summarizes the names and descriptions of the four angles of the chart.

Table 2.3: *Four angles of the chart*

House	Position of the cusp	Name
1	Eastern horizon (a line of the horizon from south to north through the east	Ascendant, ASC
4	Main meridian below the feet (a line from South to North through Nadir	Imum Caeli, IC
7	Western horizon (a line of the horizon from South to North through the West)	Descendant, DSC
10	Main meridian above the head (a line from South to North through Zenith)	Medium Coeli, MC

Chapter 2. Horary Astrology

Homework Assignment №2

Look at the skeleton of a horary chart above and tell which planet rules the tenth, eighth, and fourth houses. For instance, the 2nd house falls in Virgo, which is ruled by Mercury. So, Mercury is the ruler of the 2nd house.

Solution

The cusp of the 4th house falls into the sign of Scorpio. Scorpio is ruled by Mars, which means that Mars is the ruler of the 4th house.

The cusp of the 8th house falls into the sign of Pisces, which is ruled by Jupiter. Finally, the 10th house cusp falls into Taurus, meaning Venus rules that house.

House Meanings

Now let's explore the meaning of the astrological houses. By "meaning," I refer to the areas of life that an astrological house focuses planetary influence on, when planets rule or reside in that house.

Opposite houses often have opposite meanings. Therefore, it is more convenient to consider houses in pairs. Let's start with the axis of the 1st and 7th houses.

1st–7th Houses

The 1st house represents the querent themself—their body, health, safety, talents, and abilities. In contrast, the 7th house represents all other people who interact with the querent as equals, not as superiors or inferiors, and not as blood relatives. Lovers, spouses, business partners, and competitors fall into this category. Consultants, attending physicians, the other party in a deal, or anyone with whom the querent interacts on equal terms are also appropriate examples. The 7th house also includes open enemies and allies.

The 1st house signifies the querent's current location, their "here." This could be their home, a hotel where they are staying, or any other immediate environment. In contrast, the 7th house signifies the opposite place. This can be taken literally—such as a room opposite theirs, a house across the street—or it may represent a new place to which the querent wishes to move.

2-8 Houses

The following two houses are 2nd and 8th. The second house shows the querent's resources. It can be their savings—cash, bank account, or stock. It can be their movable possessions—a car, furniture, or clothes. The 2nd house shows people who support the querent in challenging times—their closest advisers, seconds in a duel, lawyers in court. The 8th house, on the contrary, shows the resources and the circle of trust of your opponents, partners, or other people, signified by the 7th house.

The 2nd house shows the material entry points—food, throat, and eating places, like food courts and cafes. The opposite 8th house represents material exit points—toilets, bathrooms where we wipe off the dirt, and death, as a great liberation from material bonds.

3-9 Houses

Now, let's look at the axis of the 3rd and 9th houses. The 3rd house traditionally represents the territory close or familiar to the querent. In the physical sense, these are neighboring houses and neighbors. It is movement along familiar routes—a trip to work or the store.

In contrast, the 9th house points to distant, unexplored territories. These are foreign countries, foreigners, and special trips, such as a trip on a long-awaited vacation or a pilgrimage.

In a psychic sense, the close, familiar territory is the essential skill laid in childhood. It is literacy, primary education, and school. It is a primary skill that does not require substantial intellectual effort—the ability to clean, type on a computer, etc. The 3rd house is responsible for this.

The opposite 9th house shows unique, higher knowledge that one must earn. It also notes the places where one acquires this knowledge. These are higher education and universities, libraries, and scientists. Also, religion, the church, and the keepers of this sacred knowledge—priests—traditionally belong to the 9th house. Also, special knowledge includes wisdom acquired over the years.

The 3rd house shows everything related to daily communications—the Internet, email, communication hubs, and post offices. The 9th house, on the contrary, shows supreme communication—prophetic dreams, prophecies and prophets, monasteries, and places of deep prayers and meditation.

3rd house shows pupils, 9th—teachers. 3rd house shows close relatives—siblings and cousins, and 9th house—distant relatives—brothers-in-law and sisters-in-law.

Let's do a short exercise before we go further with the houses.

A Short Exercise

Suppose you received a question, "Is it worth reading this spiritual book?" The task is to determine which planet shows the book on the chart. First, ask yourself, what the querent is interested in, the book or its content.

Please refer to the chart (Fig. 2.3 on page 35), and answer which house is responsible for the book in this context. Then, find the ruler of this house. It will be the significator of the book.

Solution

The querent is not interested in the book as stuff. They are interested in what it teaches. The 9th house is what represents spiritual knowledge. The cusp of the 9th house falls into the sign of Aries, which corresponds to Mars. So Mars is the ruler of the 9th house, that is, the significator of the book. Mars is the correct answer here.

Let's continue our study of houses and their meanings. We come to the axis of the 4th and 10th houses.

4-10 Houses

It is the vertical axis, so it denotes the top-bottom symbolism. The 4th house shows your social start—your family roots. It shows your family home, your parents, and your grandparents. In contrast, the 10th house shows your social zenith—your profession, work, social success, and recognition.

The 4th house shows ground & lands. It shows underground places (wells, graves, buried treasures, metro). It also denotes the querent's land, property, and everything that grows on it—trees and plants. In contrast, the 10th house indicates heights—mountains, hills, roofs, and upper floors.

The 4th house represents the father (at least in patriarchal societies), and the 10th house denotes the mother (as it is the opposite house of spouses relative to the 4th house).

5-11 Houses

The 5th house indicates pleasure. It could be a pleasant process of creativity and the results of that creativity. For example, it could be books the querent wrote for fun, or pictures they created, or hobbies they have.

The most apparent pleasure is sex and its result—the conception of children. Therefore, pregnancy and children are the particular meanings of the 5th house.

The 5th house is a house of fun and pleasant places. It can show a barbecue party, the theater, nightclub, cinema, etc.

Partners who share the querent's hobbies and passions become their friends. Maybe that is the reason why the opposite, the 11th house, shows the querent's close friends.

6-12 Houses

Traditionally, the 6th house indicates humble and hard labor or service to one's master. It also shows servants. Nowadays, these are people who serve the querent and follow their instructions. It is a project team member if the querent is a team leader; it is a house-keeper who provides a long-term service to the querent.

The 6th house also denotes small animals—cats, dogs, chickens, goats, pigs, etc. In contrast, the 12th house shows large animals—horses, cows, buffaloes.

The 12th house represents diseases, including addictions of any type—alcoholic, narcotic, sexual.

Chapter 2. Horary Astrology

The 12th house shows envious people and hidden enemies—those who weave a web of lies against the querent or attack from behind. It also denotes everything hidden from the querent's eyes in the literal sense of the word, which is why this house is often called the house of secrets.

The 12th house also indicates imprisonment, captivity, and exile.

N.B.

Understanding the question context is crucial. Different houses will describe the same object depending on the context. For instance, if you were buying a car and trying to assess its quality, the vehicle is an item, the 2nd house. In a question about safe driving in that car, you are interested in the vehicle as a space where you are on the road. You are concerned about that place's safety and your body's safety—that's a 1st house question.

Identifying the Unknown Planet

Sometimes, you may notice that an unknown planet interferes with the flow of events in the horary chart. As you remember from the section "The Table of Main Techniques in Horary Astrology," the planet may influence the process by

- A close aspect
- Reception
- Position in a house

Suppose we need to find out what this planet signifies. Who or what is going to change the flow of events? For example, you may see that Venus stops you from going on a vacation. You do not know what Venus signifies, but you must find it out.

The technique of identifying the unknown planet through house rulership is quite simple. First, find the zodiac signs that correspond to the planet in question. In our case (see picture below), Venus corresponds to the signs of Libra ♎ and Taurus ♉. Then, find the numbers of the houses whose cusps are in those signs. In our case (Fig. 2.3 on page 35), these are the 3rd and 10th houses.

Then, you need to choose the one meaning of these houses that fits the context. You may use the principle of Occam's razor here. It says that of the many explanations, the simplest one will be correct. In our example, the 3rd house shows siblings and neighbors. But the querent has no siblings, and neighbors are unlikely to influence their vacation.

In turn, the 10th house shows the project they are working on, which does not go as smoothly as expected. The unforeseen problem with that project may be the reason for the vacation delay. This explanation is the simplest one and perfectly fits the context. It means that we will choose that option.

The project will stop the querent from taking the vacation.

Homework Assignment №3

Now, with this knowledge, let's do our next homework. Suppose you are a complainant in court. As a newbie astrologer, you found that a strong Jupiter supports your opponent. Someone helps them to win in court. Look at the chart (Fig. 2.3 on page 35) and answer the question, "What does Jupiter signify in this context? Which person?"

Solution

Someone signified by Jupiter protects your opponent in court. Jupiter corresponds to the signs of Sagittarius ♐ and Pisces ♓. These signs are at the 8th and 5th house cusps. It means that someone described by these houses is protecting the defendant.

The 5th house denotes children, and the 8th house denotes the resources of your opponent—money, close advisers, and lawyers in court. We follow the principle of Occam's razor. The simplest option is resources (it could be money, lawyers, or evidence for the court). So, we choose that option as it perfectly fits the context and is the easiest one to explain. Therefore, Jupiter is your opponent's resource.

House Meanings in Natal Astrology

In horary astrology, the context of the situation determines the main significators. We look for planets that correspond to pre-known objects. For example, if the question is about the mother, we look at the 10th house of the mother and its ruler. The 10th house has many other meanings, but we pick a particular one because we know the object whose significator we are searching for.

In natal astrology, it's the opposite. Our task is to understand, looking at a planet, what exactly it will signify in a given period.

For instance, we see that Venus is prominent this year. Multiple houses may determine Venus's influence over different areas of life. Venus may rule the 8th and 10th houses and occupy the 7th house. The 10th house has particular meanings—the mother, boss, or a business project. The 8th house has specific meanings, like a colleague's lawyer, a spouse's finances, etc. The more particular meanings for each house we involve, the lower the chance of finding Venus' true meaning.

Therefore, in natal astrology, we stick to general house meanings. For instance, the 10th house generally represents the native's actions and undertakings. The 4th house generally shows the native's family roots (including mother and father for both patriarchal and matriarchal societies) and lands. The shorter the list of areas of life to examine, the higher the chance to find the right path.

Once we know the general meaning of the planet, then we narrow it down to a specific object.

For example, Venus rules the 8th, 4th, and 7th houses. However, two special techniques of natal astrology—*primary directions* and the *lunar return chart*—emphasize the 4th house. So we know Venus indicates one of the parents (without specifying exactly who). Then, we seek a way to identify a particular relative within the native's family.

For instance, we may observe that Venus is a feminine planet and separates from the native. In the general context of the native's life, we know their mother left them when they were a kid. We also see that in other prognostic charts, like lunar return, Venus conjoins with the Moon—the natural ruler of mothers. And so, with many coinciding testimonies, we conclude that Venus represents the native's mother in a given period of their life.

Notice, we didn't use the special meaning of the 10th house (as a house of the mother) as we normally do in horary astrology. We focused on the 4th house—the house of ancestors—and then narrowed down the meaning of its ruler to a specific person.

Thus, houses are more generalized in natal astrology. Here's a list of house meanings in the most general sense.

1. Life in general, state of health, moral and mental qualities.
2. Wealth, goods of acquired estates.
3. Siblings.
4. Parents, successions.
5. Children, bodily pleasures.
6. Servants, subordinates, domestic animals.
7. Marriage, open enemies, lawsuits.
8. Death.
9. Religion, journeys.
10. Action, profession, dignity, fame.
11. Friends.
12. Sickness, imprisonment, exile, secret enemies, hardships.

Descriptive Techniques: Celestial State Assessment

Let's remember what we have already learned so far. There are several techniques to identify which planet represents external objects. We have studied one of them—*house rulership* and, partly, the *unknown planet identification*.

When we've found the significator, we need to describe its properties. And that's what descriptive techniques do. One of them is the *celestial state assessment*. As you remember, a planet's celestial state shows the state of the object it signifies. It answers one of three questions:

– Is this object **good** or **bad** in the context of the question?
– **How** does this or that person **feel**?
– Is this object **harmful** or **supportive** by itself?

Technically, a planet changes its celestial state when it occupies one or another sign of the zodiac. In some signs, the planet can be dignified. In others, it can be neutral or debilitated. This happens because of the dissonance or consonance between the inner nature of the planet and the nature of the zodiac sign it occupies. The condition of the planet in a sign will tell us about the state of the external object.

There are six states in which a significator can be:

- Dignity by rulership
- Dignity by exaltation
- Dignity by triplicity
- A state of peregrine (a neutral state)
- Debility by fall
- Debility by detriment

N.B.

A great British astrologer, William Lilly[a], utilized Ptolemy's table of dignities[b], which encompassed minor dignities such as term and face. However, these minor dignities are insignificantly small and can be safely disregarded in practical application. So, we will skip them in this book.

[a] W. Lilly. *Christian Astrology*. Printed by John Macock, 1669
[b] C. Ptolemy. *Tetrabiblos: Translated from the Greek paraphrase of Proclus by J. M. Ashmand*. Davis and Dickson, London, 1882

Let's explore how the planet acquires these states and what they mean.

Rulership

We learned in the section "The Domiciles of the Planets" that each planet rules one or two zodiac signs. This means there is a connection between the sign and its ruler. It happens due to a simple fact—the sign "reflects" the nature of one of the seven planets. Morinus wrote in his 21st book of *Astrologia Gallica* that when the world was created, the zodiac signs were *determined* to "reflect" the planetary natures so that Aries reflects Mars, Taurus—Venus, etc.

What happens if a planet occupies the sign it rules? It comes to its domain. "My home, my rule" principle works here. The significator feels good and produces good things.

Astrologers assign 5 out of 5 dignity points to a planet in its domicile.

For example, you have the question, "Is this movie good?" The significator of the film is the Sun in Leo. We interpret it as "the Sun is in its domicile." It is an excellent state of the Sun (the film). So, yes, the film is amazing.

More examples of the readings of a planet in its sign:

- The wage is **high**.
- The employee is **promising**.
- The person **feels good**.
- The diet is **very healthy**.

We interpret the goodness of the significator in the current context. Nothing complicated. Table 2.4 shows the *domicile of planets*—the signs where the planets gain maximum dignity.

Table 2.4: *The domiciles of the planets*

Planet	Domicile
☉	♌
☽	♋
☿	♍ ♊
♀	♉ ♎
♂	♈ ♏
♃	♐ ♓
♄	♑ ♒

Exaltation

Imagine a planet intensively but briefly expresses some of its best qualities when it enters a particular sign. This state is called the *exaltation*. It's like the planet entering its honor hall for a ceremonial award for specific merits. The ceremony enhances some virtues of the significator, and it doesn't last long. Table 2.5 shows the places of exaltation.

Table 2.5: *The places of exaltation of the planets*

Planet	Exaltation
☉	♈
☽	♉
☿	♍
♀	♓
♂	♑
♃	♋
♄	♎

So, a planet in exaltation will also show the excellent condition of the subject, but with a touch of exaggeration. For instance, the Sun rules the 2nd house and indicates a car in the chart. The Sun is in Aries, so it is in an exalted state. Overall, the car is beautiful, but it's not as perfect as it seems—there are minor defects you don't see.

Another example: The exalted planet shows dividends from your company. You'll get a great income, even more than usual, but it will only last for a while.

Astrologers assign 4 out of 5 dignity points to the exalted planet.

N.B.

Please do not add up dignity points. If a planet is simultaneously exalted and in its sign, as it happens with Mercury in Virgo, it doesn't mean it accumulates nine dignity points.

Mercury already shares a common nature with Virgo. For this reason, it has a maximum of five dignity points in this sign. Mercury in Virgo doesn't gain extra dignity from its exaltation. The same principle applies to other dignities.

Triplicity

The following essential dignity is *triplicity*. The twelve zodiac signs consist of four sets of three signs each. These sets share common elemental qualities, forming the signs of fire, earth, air, and water.

Table 2.6: *The triplicities of the planets*

Elements	Name	Triplicity	Ruler	
			Day	Night
Hot & Dry	Fire	♈ ♌ ♐	☉	♃
Cold & Dry	Earth	♉ ♍ ♑	♀	☽
Hot & Moist	Air	♊ ♎ ♒	♄	☿
Cold & Moist	Water	♋ ♏ ♓	♂	♂

Planets rule these sets, meaning they share a common nature with three signs of the same element (the triplicity). Notably, the triplicity rulers change depending on whether the question is asked during the day or at night. The Table 2.6 shows triplicity rulers in day and night charts.

When a planet enters a sign of its triplicity, it acquires a moderate celestial state. This indicates the healthy condition of the external object.

Astrologers assign 3 beneficence points out of 5 to a planet in its own triplicity. Again, do not add up dignity points. The Moon in Taurus in a night chart has dignity by exaltation and triplicity, but it is still less dignified than the Moon in Cancer.

Here are examples of how to interpret this dignity in context:

- The movie is **not bad**.
- The wage is **above average**.
- He feels **generally good**.
- This guy **is a reliable**.
- This diet is **generally healthy**.

Debilitated Planet

Since the sign reflects its ruler, you can think of it as each degree of the sign being a miniature copy of the planet that rules the sign. For example, each degree of Capricorn is like a miniature Saturn directing its rays toward the center of the Earth, and the entire sign of Capricorn consists of 30 such miniature copies of Saturn.

What happens to a planet if it enters the sign ruled by another planet? It mixes its nature with the nature of the miniature copy of that sign's ruler.

It's good if the nature of the sign's ruler aligns with the planet's nature. Then, the significator feels like a guest at a good friend's place. But what if their natures are incompatible?

For instance, universally, the Sun signifies life, while Saturn signifies death. They have diverse natures. If the Sun is in a sign that Saturn rules alone (♒), we say the Sun is in a sign of a diverse nature. The same is true for Saturn in Leo.

It's like walking into a shady club in a crime-ridden area. A planet in a sign of incompatible nature feels suppressed and starts manifesting its worst qualities.

Such a planet is called *debilitated* and signifies things in bad condition.

> **N.B.**
>
> Strictly speaking, planets do not influence each other but influence the Earth. If the Sun is at 10° Aquarius, it emits rays of the Sun's nature, while each degree of Aquarius emits rays of Saturn's nature. The 10th degree of Aquarius emits two types of rays—one of the Sun's nature and another (lesser) of Saturn's nature.
>
> These two rays do not affect each other, but their mixture produces a destructive effect. It is like two people in a boat rowing in different directions. Although they do not interact with each other, the overall impact on the ship is destructive. The boat does not move forward; it rocks and risks capsizing.
>
> However, since the state of the significator reflects the state of objects on Earth, for the sake of simplicity, we will use terms such as "Planet A worsens the state due to Planet B" or "Planet A feels weakened due to the influence of Planet B."

Detriment

If the planet enters the sign opposite to the sign it rules, we say it is *exiled* or *in detriment*. It is the worst condition for the significator. Astrologers assign 5 points of debility out of 5 to the planet in a detrimental state.

In the context of the question, we assign a negative characteristic to the object shown by the exiled planet; for example,

- The movie is **awful**.
- The wage is **low**.
- The employee is **useless**.
- Someone feels **bad**.
- This person is **dangerous**.

Fall

When the planet enters the sign opposite to the sign of its exaltation, it is *in fall*. It is also a bad state of the significator but not as bad as if it were in detriment. If the sign of exaltation is like a hall of fame, the sign of fall resembles a hall of shame. It also has a shade of exaggeration, which doesn't last long.

For instance, the planet in fall shows the return on investment. You'll get practically nothing from this trade, though you will not lose 100% of your money as you might fear.

Astrologers assign 4 points of debility out of 5 to the planet in fall.

Again, do not add up these points. Venus in Virgo is in triplicity in the daytime chart. At the same time, it is in fall. Venus has both—3 points of dignity and 4 points of debility. Venus may signify the condition of your father—he feels bad due to physical sickness, but simultaneously, he is satisfied with the progress in his business. These points refer to the different qualities of the object or person, which coexist in the context of the situation.

We will use these dual qualities when it comes to the *aspects*.

Peregrine

If a planet does not have any dignity and, at the same time, is not in detriment or fall, then such a planet can be called neutral or *peregrine*. We interpret the neutral state in the context of the question; for example,

- The movie is **neither bad nor good**;
- The salary is **average**;
- They feel **as usual**, and so on.

The Table of Essential Dignities

Let's summarize everything in one table (see Table 2.7).

Table 2.7: *Essential Dignities of Planets*

Sign	Domicile	Exaltation	Triplicity Day	Triplicity Night	Fall	Exile
♈	♂	☉	☉	♃	♄	♀
♉	♀	☽	♀	☽		♂
♊	☿		♄	☿		♃
♋	☽	♃	♂	♂	♂	♄
♌	☉		☉	♃		♄
♍	☿	☿	♀	☽	♀	♃
♎	♀	♄	♄	☿	☉	♂
♏	♂		♂	♂	☽	♀
♐	♃		☉	♃		☿
♑	♄	♂	♀	☽	♃	☽
♒	♄		♄	☿		☉
♓	♃	♀	♂	♂	☿	☿

N.B. on natal astrology

In natal astrology, the assessment of celestial conditions goes far beyond a planet's position in a sign (see the section "Celestial Determination" on page 312).

In horary astrology, if Mars enters Capricorn, where it is exalted, it indicates the object is in good condition. That's the end of the story.

In natal astrology, we must discover what Mars signifies and explore all its possible manifestations. In particular, we consider its dispositor—Saturn—to understand where the ruler of the sign directs Mars' force.

In natal astrology, we also assess the so-called *close aspects* (which we explore further), meaning Mars' connections with other planets—they can modify Mars' influence for better or worse.

Example №1: Working with Planetary Dignities

Let's take an example of how to work with dignities. Suppose the querent asks if they can avoid traffic jams on their way home. I cast a chart for this question (Fig. 2.4). You can see a familiar picture below—12 houses and signs on the cusps.

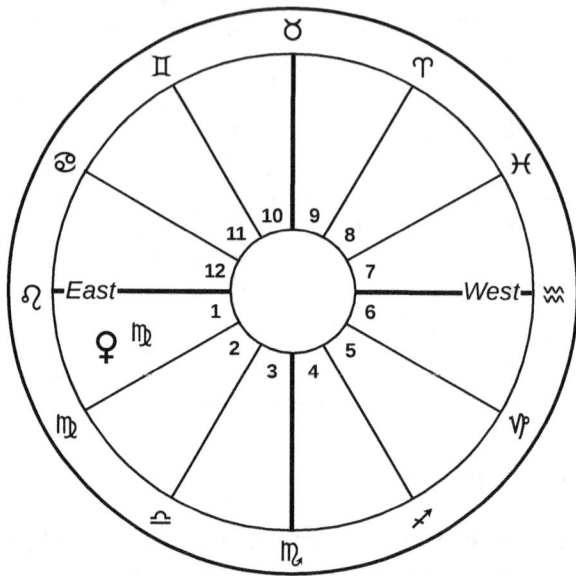

Figure 2.4: *Example Chart With Venus in the 1st House*

We begin our analysis. The question is about the way home. The 3rd house represents regular movements, so we choose it. The cusp of the 3rd house falls into the sign of Taurus. It corresponds to Venus, which means Venus signifies the way home.

Venus is in its fall—the way back is difficult, meaning there will be a traffic jam. But the fall always means an exaggeration. We expect traffic jams to be stronger than usual. Still, on the other hand, they will have a local or short-term manifestation.

Isn't it cool? We got the exact answer just from one planet.

Homework Assignment №4

Now it's your turn.

- On the chart (Fig. 2.5), find the planets in their own signs.
- Then find exalted planets.

Chapter 2. Horary Astrology

- Finally, answer the question, "Will the party be fun?" Give a simple yes/no answer.

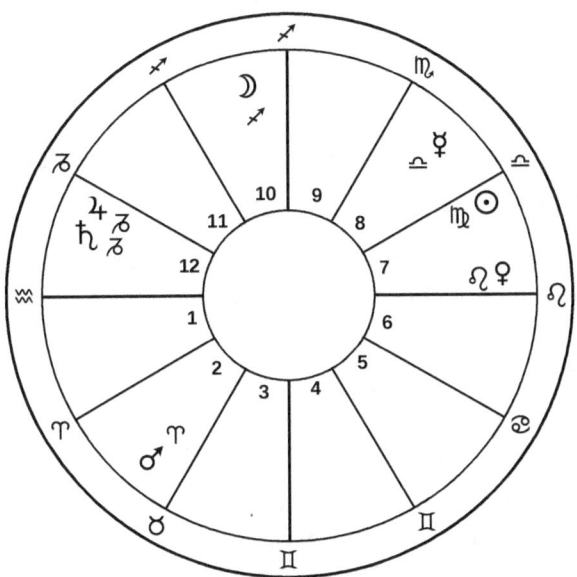

Figure 2.5: *Example Chart With Various Planets*

Solution

In this chart, only two planets are in their signs: Saturn and Mars. And no planet is exalted. Further, the 5th house always shows the party. The ruler of the 5th house is Mercury. Since Mercury has no dignities, the party will not be fun.

Another assignment

Now, it is your turn to work with the essences in practice. Look at the chart (Fig. 2.5). Your task is to answer the following questions.

- What is the condition of the house I am about to buy?
- How does my brother feel?
- How will I feel next month?
- What position will I be offered (high, medium, or low)?

Solution

I highlighted the quesited—the main subject in the context—with an italic font. Each quesited has its significator.

- My future *property* is the lord of the 4th house, Mercury.
- My *brother* is the ruler of the 3rd house, Venus.
- *I am* the lord of the 1st house, Saturn.
- Finally, my future *position* is the lord of the 10th house, Jupiter.

The essential dignities of these planets are:

- Mercury (a house) is in an airy sign, which it rules by night. But the ☉ is over the horizon—this is a day-time chart. So, Mercury is peregrine.
- Venus (my brother) is peregrine.
- Saturn (me) is in its domicile.
- And Jupiter (my position) is in the fall.

Now, let's translate this into human language.

- What is the condition of a house I want to buy? The condition is neutral; it is neither bad nor good.
- How does my brother feel? He feels calm—nothing special.
- How will I be feeling next month? Just great.
- What position will they offer me (high, medium, or low)? I will receive a low position in the company, although it will seem worse than it is.

Descriptive Techniques: Sign Properties

Let's remember what we have already explored. There are several techniques to signify external objects, people, and circumstances. We have studied one of them—*house rulership*. We have learned how to describe an object's state by assessing the significator's *celestial state*.

There are several methods for reading the particular features of external objects. We will explore one of them—*the properties of the zodiac signs*.

There are eight main properties of zodiac signs.

1. Sign's Gender

All odd signs are *masculine*, while all others are *feminine*, starting from Aries. This property of signs is used to determine the gender of the person in question. For example, it applies to the question, "Will I conceive a son or daughter?" or "Who will deliver the lecture—Mr. or Mrs. Brown?" The use of these signs is straightforward. If a female planet (the Moon or Venus) falls into a feminine sign, this indicates a woman, and if any other planet falls into a masculine sign, then this indicates a man.

Suppose a masculine planet is in a feminine sign or vice versa. In that case, we do not have enough evidence to determine the person's gender.

2. Modality

There are four signs—Aries, Cancer, Libra, and Capricorn—which are called *cardinal* or *fast*. The signs following them (Taurus, Leo, Scorpio, and Aquarius) are called *fixed* or *slow*. The signs preceding them (Pisces, Gemini, Virgo, and Sagittarius) are called *mutable* or of *medium speed*. When the significator of some process falls into one of these signs, it determines the speed of that process.

For example, in the question, "Will this disease be long-lasting?" the significator fell into a fast sign—the disease will pass quickly. "Will our marriage be long-lasting?" The significator of marriage falls into a fixed sign—yes, you will live with this person for a long time. "Will I receive the package in three days or three weeks?" The package is in a fast sign. Wait for delivery in three days.

3. Elements

We discussed this in the section "Triplicity"—signs vary by elemental qualities. There are hot and dry signs of *fiery nature* (Aries, Leo, and Sagittarius), cold and dry signs of *earth nature* (Taurus, Virgo, and Capricorn), hot and wet signs of *airy nature* (Gemini, Libra, and Aquarius), and cold and moist *water signs* (Pisces, Cancer, and Scorpio).

Astrologers commonly use these properties in search questions, questions about destination, and weather forecasts. For example: "Where is my husband?" The ruler of the 7th house is in a water sign—he is by the lake. The husband's planet is in a fire sign—he's at the barbecue. "Will I become a farmer?" The querent's planet is in an earth sign—yes, you will. "Will it be rainy today?" My city's planet is in a fire sign—no, today it will be hot and dry.

4. Multiplicity

There are *double-bodied* (Pisces, Gemini, Virgo, and Sagittarius) and *single-bodied* signs (all the rest). Suppose the significator falls into a double-bodied sign. In that case, it shows two or more objects.

For example, if it rules the 10th house, it shows several simultaneous jobs, two bosses, and so on. It is handy if you receive a question about the amount of something. For example, "Will I conceive one or more children," or "Will one or more people interview me?"

5. Fertility

There are three types of zodiac signs—*fertile* (Pisces, Cancer, and Scorpio), *barren* (Gemini, Virgo, and Leo), and signs of medium fertility (all the rest). This property is helpful in matters of conception.

For instance, in the question, "Does this marriage bring children," if the significator of marriage is in a barren sign, then no, there will be no children at all.

6. Humanity

Signs can be *human* (Aquarius, Gemini, Virgo, Libra, and first half of Sagittarius), *wild* (Leo and second half of Sagittarius), and *bestial* (all the rest). These properties show the behavior of a person. For example, in the question, "Will my new roommate be aggressive," my roommate's planet falls into a wild sign. They will be violent. "How will my mother react if I tell her that I marry Harry?" The mom's significator has got into the human sign—whatever she expresses, she will behave gently.

7. The Quality of the Voice

There are *mute* (Cancer, Scorpio, and Pisces), *loud* (Gemini, Virgo, Libra, and Aquarius), and *half-loud* signs (all the rest). Use this property when publicity matters.

For example, "Will my brother keep my secret?" The brother's significator falls into a quiet sign—he will blab but in a very narrow circle. "Will my podcast resonate? Will it be heard?" The podcast's planet is in a loud sign. Oh, yes, it will become very famous.

8. The Property of the Ascension Rate

The signs can be *of short* (from Capricorn to Gemini) or *long ascension* (from Cancer to Sagittarius). The former shows a rapid ascension, and the latter represents a slow rise. This property is helpful if the question is about the increase rate—"Will my investment grow quickly or slowly?" "Will I climb up the career ladder quickly or slowly?"

As you can see, these properties of the sign are very far from what you find in magazines and newspapers. I want your attention to the fact that the zodiac signs symbolize all the listed properties. Take any sign and see how it works. For example, let's take the following properties:

– Double
– Semi-human, semi-animal
– Fiery (i.e., possessing brute force)

Who do you think it is? It is Sagittarius. It is a dual creature—half-human, half-animal, and brute-forced. Another example:

– A human sign
– Double
– Masculine and
– Airy (i.e., rational)

Who is this? It is Gemini.

The same is true for all the signs. You can check it yourself.

The Table of Sign's Properties

Table 2.8 brings together all the properties of the signs. Bookmark it for quick access.

Homework Assignment №5

Now, let's practice these properties. From now on, we will draw horary charts with exact degrees and minutes of planets and cusps, without cusp numbers—just like in real life. Here is a chart (Fig. 2.6).

Answer the following questions:

– Will Mom keep my secret?
– Will they offer me a long-term or short-term job position?

Predictive Astrology Textbook

Table 2.8: *Sign's properties*

Props.	♈	♉	♊	♋	♌	♍
Gend.	Male	Female	Male	Female	Male	Female
Mode	Card.	Fixed	Mutb.	Card.	Fixed	Mutb.
Elem.	Fire	Earth	Air	Water	Fire	Eath
Voice	½-loud	½-loud	Loud	Mute	½-loud	Loud
Fert.	Modr.	Modr.	Barren	Fert.	Barren	Barren
Hum.	Best.	Best.	Humn.	Best.	Wild	Humn.
Ascn.	Long	Long	Long	Short	Short	Short

Props.	♎	♏	♐	♑	♒	♓
Gend.	Female	Male	Female	Male	Female	Male
Mode	Card.	Fixed	Mutb.	Card.	Fixed	Mutb.
Elem.	Air	Water	Fire	Earth	Air	Water
Voice	Loud	Mute	½-loud	½-loud	Loud	Mute
Fert.	Modr.	Fert.	Modr.	Modr.	Modr.	Fert.
Hum.	Humn.	Best.	Mixed	Best.	Humn.	Best.
Ascn.	Short	Short	Short	Long	Long	Long

– Has one or more hackers attacked my site?

Hint. Find the significators of the quesited in this chart, then look at the signs they are in and pick the *relevant* sign property.

Solution

Let's define the significators first.

– Will my mom keep this secret? Mom is the ruler of the MC, Mercury.
– Next, will they offer a long-term or a short-term job position? The position in the company is the ruler of the 10th house, Mercury.
– Finally, has one or more hackers attacked my site? Hackers are my enemies, the 7th house. The lord of the 7th house is Venus.

Now, let's see what signs these significators are in.

– My mom, Mercury, is in a mute sign. Yes, she will keep the secret.
– My prospective job is in a fixed sign. Yes, it will be a long-term contract.
– The hacker, Venus, is in a solitary sign. It was one person.

Chapter 2. Horary Astrology

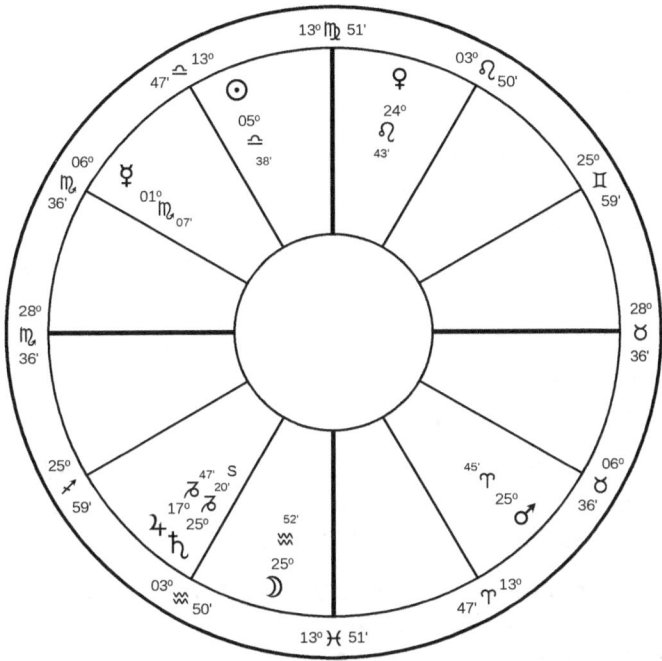

Figure 2.6: *Example Chart For Various Questions*

Object Interaction Techniques: Reception

When a planet enters the domicile of another planet, we say that the lord of that domicile receives the guest planet in its sign. For instance, the Moon in Pisces is received by Jupiter. We pronounce it as

- Jupiter *receives* the Moon *in its domicile.*
- Jupiter *prevails over* the Moon in Pisces.
- Jupiter *disposes* the Moon.

This astrological terminology expresses a simple idea—the ☽ is subordinate to ♃ when she is a guest in his domain.

This subordination is called *reception*. It establishes a connection between two external objects. If planet A is subordinate to planet B, then in the real world, we can observe one of the following:

- Object A *is subordinate to* object B or embedded into it.
- Object A *supports* object B.

– Person A *loves* person B.

Reception by Exaltation

What happens if the significator of object A enters the sign of Pisces—a place of Jupiter's domicile and Venus's exaltation—while Venus signifies object B? Similarly to the previous case, the significator is subordinate to Venus (though to a lesser degree than to Jupiter). We express it as follows:

- Venus *receives* the planet *in the place of her exaltation*.
- Venus *is the dispositor* of planet A *by exaltation*.
- The significator (planet A) *exalts* Venus.

Since the significator sees only the best and exaggerated aspects of Venus (being in the sign of her honor), the relationship between external objects also has a touch of exaggeration:

- Object A is notably subordinate to object B. Still, the power of that subordination is exaggerated or short-term.
- Person A is crazy about person B, but this infatuation is exaggerated and will cool down.

Reception by Triplicity

The same principle applies to the lord of triplicity. We say that the lord *receives the significator in its triplicity*. This kind of reception establishes a mild subordination.

- Object B has some power over object A.
- Object A occasionally tries to support object B.
- Person A has warm feelings toward person B.

Modification of the Celestial State Due to Reception

Now, we are ready to make an important note. As you can see, the lord of the sign has maximum power over the planet in that sign. It forces a guesting planet to follow its rules. What happens if the lord of the sign has a terrible celestial state, say, it is in detriment or fall?

It means that it will, to some extent, force the planet to follow its harmful orders. That makes a planet in a sign slightly worse.

Chapter 2. Horary Astrology

So, Venus in Pisces with Jupiter in Gemini is worse than Venus in Pisces with Jupiter in Cancer. It doesn't mean that the detrimental state of Jupiter transforms the exalted Venus into an evil planet—no way. Even if you're in the house of a criminal authority where you're compelled to speak harshly according to house rules, it doesn't make you a gangster.

Venus is still a very beneficial planet and shows objects in a good state. But the detrimental state of its ruler, Jupiter, slightly worsens Venus.

In most cases, we'll ignore the celestial state of the dispositor unless the context of the question forces us to do otherwise.

Let's say a wife inquires about her husband on a business trip. His significator, Mercury in Sagittarius, is highly debilitated. The husband feels unwell, which makes sense if Jupiter, the dispositor of the husband, governs his work. The husband is drained due to work, giving his all to the project.

However, Jupiter—the husband's project—is in an excellent celestial state. Things are going great with the project. It, to some extent, compensates for the husband's exhaustion. Note that Jupiter has a particular role in the story, so we considered its state.

Negative Reception

Now, let's imagine what happens when the significator enters the place of fall or exile of another planet. For instance, if the significator enters Gemini, the place of Jupiter's exile.

It means the planet is subordinate to Mercury, which acts "against" Jupiter, as its nature is incompatible with Jupiter's. The entire sign of Gemini is infused with the nature of Mercury, which breaks things down into small details, while Jupiter's nature is to enlarge and generalize. If a planet in Gemini acts against Jupiter, it begins to harm him. Jupiter, on the other hand, has no power over the significator.

We express this as:

- Jupiter *receives* the planet *in its exile*.
- The planet *exiles* Jupiter.

In the real world, this creates a repelling effect. We always read receptions in context:

- This diet *harms* the body.
- This employee *hates* their boss.

The reception by fall works on the same principle. Suppose the significator enters the place of the fall (the room of shame) of a particular planet. In that case, the significator sees the negative qualities of that planet under a magnifying glass. It creates a tendency of rejection with some exaggeration.

Let's assume Mercury enters Capricorn, the place of Jupiter's fall. We express it as:

- Jupiter *receives* Mercury *in its fall*.
- Mercury *loathes* Jupiter.

In the real world, we interpret this relation of two significators in context:

- Jane *can't stand* her ex-boyfriend.
- This pasta *triggers* an intense but short-lived allergic reaction.

Influence of the Celestial State on Reception

The celestial state of a planet, experiencing feelings or influencing another planet, matters.

Imagine planet A loves/supports planet B according to reception. But in one scenario, planet A is Jupiter in Pisces, and in another, Jupiter in Gemini.

In the first case, Jupiter is dignified, meaning it will express its love and support favorably for planet B.

Suppose Jupiter in Pisces is the head of the sales department with excellent skills, and planet B is my business. A skilled manager will take my business to a new level.

If Jupiter is in Gemini, it's debilitated, which signifies poor quality or destruction. Despite all its love and efforts to help, it won't contribute much.

For example, the prospective head of the sales department lacks the necessary skills—they cannot manage even a team of three. Despite their tremendous efforts, they are unlikely to help my business. On the other hand, they are unlikely to cause serious harm. After all, they try to organize the sales department as best as possible.

Another example: A rude boy is courting a girl. However, he is so clumsy and rough in his attention that he is more likely to annoy than please the object of his affection.

Now, consider the reverse scenario. Jupiter in Pisces hates/tries to harm planet B. Jupiter will make every effort to cause harm. Still, due to its nobility, it will do so in a civilized manner. For instance, a fired employee is seeking revenge against a former boss. They hire lawyers and take legal action.

It is a completely different story if Jupiter in Gemini represents that same employee. In this case, far from the nobility—they just barge into the office and make a scandal.

So, planets express their feelings according to their receptions and accidental (noble or detrimental) celestial states. We always interpret these combinations of reception and celestial state in the context of the situation, similar to the examples I provided.

At first, it may seem unfamiliar and complex. But with practice, you'll quickly understand that there's nothing complicated about the logical alignment of chart indications with the context of the situation.

The Table of Receptions

Table 2.9 demonstrates the attitudes of a planet depending on the zodiac sign it occupies.

Multiple Receptions Towards the Same Planet

A planet in a sign may have several attitudes toward another planet simultaneously. For example, a planet in Pisces is both in the fall and the detriment of Mercury. A planet in Cancer is in triplicity and the fall of Mars. How do we read such combinations?

Receptions by rulership/exile prevail over receptions by exaltation/fall. The latter prevails over reception by triplicity. Use this rule to understand the total effect of one planet on another.

Here are some examples:

- A planet in Pisces is simultaneously in the fall and detriment of Mercury. It acts against Mercury most intensively.

Table 2.9: *Receptions*

When planet is in	♈	♉	♊	♋	♌	♍
It is in domicile of	♂	♀	☿	☽	☉	☿
It exalts	☉	☽		♃		☿
Day: In triplicity of	☉	♀	♄	♂	☉	♀
Night: In triplicity of	♃	☽	☿	♂	♃	☽
It is in fall of	♄			♂		♀
It exiles	♀	♂	♃	♄	♄	♃

When planet is in	♎	♏	♐	♑	♒	♓
It is in domicile of	♀	♂	♃	♄	♄	♃
It exalts	♄			♂		♀
Day: In triplicity of	♄	♂	☉	♀	♄	♂
Night: In triplicity of	☿	♂	♃	☽	☿	♂
It is in fall of	☉	☽		♃		☿
It exiles	♂	♀	☿	☽	☉	☿

– A planet in Cancer has a negative attitude toward Mars. However, there are still positive aspects due to reception by triplicity. For example, a drug may be harmful to the body, yet it helps maintain mental activity. Still, the overall effect is destructive since reception by fall prevails over reception by triplicity.

N.B.

Although we use expressions like "planet loves" or "planet harms" another planet, these are just metaphors for better understanding.

In reality, planets don't influence each other; they influence us. When one planet acts in discord with the principles of another, it leads to collisions of incompatible elements (like eating pasta that causes an allergic reaction) or encounters between people with opposing feelings. But we label it as "Planet A exiles Planet B; therefore, object A harms object B." It's just a more straightforward way of seeing things.

Mutual Receptions

We will often deal with the following situations:

− Planet A falls into the dignity/debility of planet B.
− At the same time, planet B falls into some dignity/debility of planet A.

Such a type of reception is called *mutual*. We apply what we have learned to both planets A and B, reading the mutual reception in the context of the question.

Let's take a simple example. There are two people. Saturn in Scorpio represents one of them, and the Moon in Capricorn represents the other. Suppose we live in ancient times, and in the context of the question, one of the people is the master, and the other is the servant. Now, let's answer the questions.

− Who do you think is the master, and who is the servant here?
− Does the master beat their servant?
− What is the servant's health?
− Can the servant resist their master?

Let's answer these by reading the mutual receptions. We also use the essential state of the servant's planet since we have questions about their health.

The first person is Saturn in Scorpio. To understand their relationship to the Moon, we will look at the reception table in the column with the ♏ sign.

Then, we find the ☽ in that column. We see that any planet in Capricorn is in the place of the Moon's detriment. So there is no subordination in that reception. That is, the Moon does not control Saturn.

The second person is the Moon in Capricorn. Using the same table, we look for the attitude of the planet in ♑ towards Saturn. We see that the Moon is in the rulership of Saturn. That is, Saturn rules over the Moon. Great, now we know Saturn is the master, and the Moon is the servant.

Now you see how good reception can be for clarifying the significators. Let's answer the following question—does the master beat their servant? We noticed that Saturn exiles or damages the Moon. In the context of the situation, yes, the master beats the servant.

Here is the right place to mention the universal nature of Saturn's dispositor—Mars. It is the planet of violence, so Saturn "inherits" this quality from its ruler. It makes a peregrine Saturn even worse. We use this essential state modification only because Saturn's dispositor fits the context with its *universal* role. We already mentioned this in the section "Modification of the Celestial State Due to Reception."

The next question is, what is the servant's health? This question is about the state of the object. Therefore, we must assess the celestial state of the servant planet. From the table of dignities and debilities (see the section "The Table of Essential Dignities"), it is clear that the Moon is in detriment. It means that the Moon (the servant) feels very bad in Capricorn—in their master's domain. In other words, the servant's health is terrible.

N.B.

Note how we read the detrimental state in the context. We do not say that the servant is a bad guy or it is harmful to anyone, including their master—these claims are contrary to reality.

Can a servant resist their master? The Moon is in the power of Saturn. Moreover, the Moon is weak. So the answer is no. Look at how much information we pulled from the reception. It's impressive.

Reception As a Signification Technique

In the example above, we determined which planet is the master and which is the servant solely through receptions. In practice, we often use receptions to select the correct planet.

The principle is simple. We know from the context what feelings one person has for another or which object is subordinate to another. We know one of the objects; we need to find the other.

For example, a querent's husband is charmed with another person, and it's mutual. The ruler of the 7th house—Mercury—is a planet we know. Who is the other person in that chart? Suppose Mercury is in Capricorn, a place of Saturn's rulership and Mars' exaltation. It means the husband loves Saturn and is crazy about Mars.

Chapter 2. Horary Astrology

Saturn in this imaginary chart is in Pisces; it "hates" Mercury. But Mars is in Gemini—a place where it adores Mercury. We see mutual feelings between Mars and the husband (Mercury). The only object the husband has mutual sympathy with, in the context of the question, is the other person. So, Mars is the other person.

Let's look at a more exciting example. It's known that competitors are getting insider information about my business. I suspect that one of my employees is leaking this information to them.

In the imaginary chart, the ruler of the 10th house, representing my business, is Saturn. I examine which planets, through receptions, harm my business. I expect it to be the ruler of the 6th house, an employee in my department.

However, the ruler of the 6th house is Venus in Capricorn. This planet is fully dedicated to Saturn, loving and supporting it. The employee, I suspect, strongly supports my business. Besides, Venus is in reasonably good condition—in its triplicity.

What other planets could harm Saturn? I see two planets in the chart fitting this condition: Jupiter in Leo and Mars in Cancer. Both planets "hate" Saturn, meaning they harm my business.

But Jupiter doesn't fit because it rules the 5th house. Children, sex, or recreational places can't be the ones stealing information. On the other hand, Mars fits perfectly. Suppose, in my imaginary chart, I observe the following:

- Firstly, Mars is in Cancer and controlled by the Moon. The Moon occupies the 7th house in my imaginary chart, indicating specific individuals in the competitors' company. In other words, Mars follows the orders of these people; he works for them.
- Secondly, Mars is in fall, illustrating a troublemaker. It aligns well with the context. One shouldn't expect high moral standards from someone leaking insider information to competitors.

The last piece is to identify which house Mars rules. Surprisingly, Mars rules my 11th house, signifying close friends. So, one of my close friends works for my competitors and leaks insider information. There's only one person in my close circle with whom I share my business plans. Thus, in a few moves, I identify the suspect.

The simplicity and elegance of horary astrology inspire. Now is the time for your homework.

Homework Assignment №6

Look at the chart (Fig. 2.6 on page 59) and answer three questions.

The first one is pretty simple. Will my brother support me and lend me money?

The second question will be similar to the real one. A man with a question about his spouse came to you. According to him, his wife began to attend spiritual training and recently started to change. He worries about these changes with his spouse. He wants to know who or what influences the wife and the reason for her shifts. And if this influence comes from spiritual trainers, can they be a dangerous sect?

Think about how to solve these questions and give your answers.

Solution

Will my brother support me? Will he lend me money? My brother is the ruler of the 3rd house, Saturn. The querent is the ruler of the 1st house, Mars.

What does Saturn feel about Mars? Saturn is in Capricorn, in Mars' exaltation. Hence, Saturn will help Mars. Yes, my brother will help me.

> **N.B.**
>
> Notice that we use reception for an accurate forecast of the future decision a person will make. You'll be surprised when you see how it works in real life—almost all your predictions will match reality. This just proves that many decisions a person makes are unconscious, influenced by the arrangements of the stars.

Second question: Who manipulates my wife? Who controls her? We have to understand in whose power the significator of the wife is. The wife is the ruler of the 7th house, Venus. She is in Leo, in the rulership of the

Chapter 2. Horary Astrology

Sun. So, the Sun is what controls Venus. But whom does the Sun signify? Which houses does it rule?

The Sun "reflects" in Leo. Let's take a look at the cusps of the houses. Leo is on the 9th house's cusp. This means that the Sun is the lord of the 9th house. It represents religious, mystical, or spiritual places. Yes, spiritual training controls the wife.

Besides, the wife (Venus) occupies the 9th house. And *when a planet is in someone's house, it follows the rules of the lord of that house*. This is another indication that training and its leaders influence the wife.

Does the Sun show bad guys? The Sun is in Libra, in the place of its fall. Yes, these spiritual leaders are bad guys, though not as much as it seems. The wife fell under the influence of a disruptive sect.

See how we got a comprehensive answer with the help of receptions.

Your First Prediction

Well, now it is time for a real challenge. You will make your first realistic prediction. You will only use the techniques that we have covered. You already know enough to make a detailed forecast.

Here is the situation. On February 9, 2009, a famous Russian singer approached me through her agent. She was about to release a new single via YouTube and asked about its future. She asked:

– "Will my single enter the chart and become a hit?"
– "Will the song stay on the chart long?"

It is entirely unclear how to approach the question in such a formulation. But let's restate it so that we can apply familiar techniques to answer.

Let's think about how the song becomes a hit on the chart. Listeners send SMS and vote for the music. It means we need to involve listeners in the question. The single doesn't promote itself.

"Will my single enter the charts and become number 1?" At the very least, the single needs to reach a broad audience. What's the use of a great song that just a few people have heard? So, the first thing we want to know is, **"Will my song reach a large audience?"** And this is something about the *loudness (or voice) property*.

Next, the listeners need to like the song to vote for it. **Will the audience like the song?** It is a simple question to answer. It is something about *motives and sympathies*.

Will the song stay on the chart for long? It entirely depends on the audience's sympathy duration. **Will their sympathy be long-lasting?** It is a question of the audience's *modality* and is easy to answer.

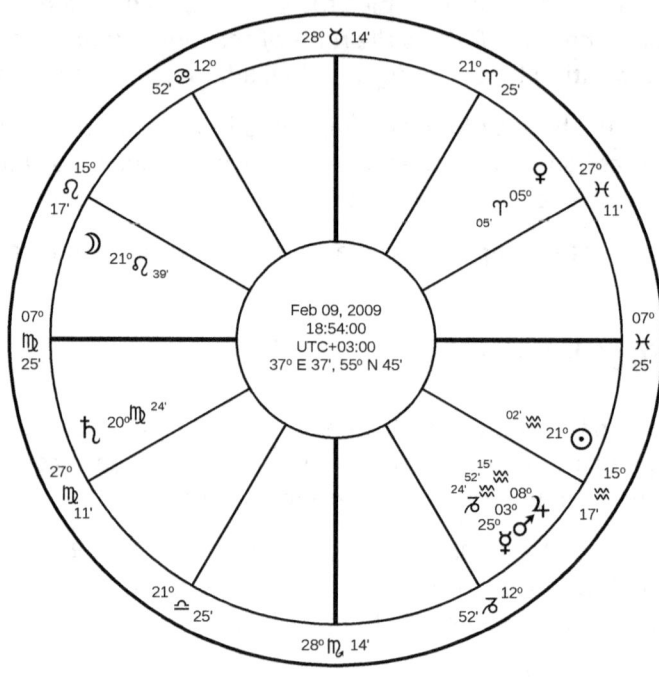

Figure 2.7: *Chart: Will My Single Enter the Chart and Become a Hit?*

So, if a large audience hears the song and votes for it for a long time, this song will enter the chart and become a leader. I want to ask you one more question. If the single enters the chart, **will it rise quickly or slowly?** And this is something about the *ascension rate* property.

So, that is how we restated the initial question. I have highlighted the questioned in bold and the hint about the technique you will apply in italics.

- Will my **song** reach a large audience? There is something about *the loudness property*.

Chapter 2. Horary Astrology

- Will **listeners** *like* **it**? And it's something about the *motives and feelings* of listeners.
- Will the **listeners** keep their sympathy *for long*? That's something about audience *modality*.
- If a **single** enters the charts, will **it** *climb fast or slow*? It is something about the *ascension rate property*.

So, consider this chart (Fig. 2.7), take your time, and answer all the questions. In the next section, I will show you the solution and tell you what happened in real life.

Solution

The first question is "Will my song reach a large audience?" The song is the ruler of the 5th house, Saturn. It is in Virgo—in a loud sign. Yes, the single will be heard.

Will listeners love my song? Listeners are other people, 7th house. The ruler of the 7th house is ♃. What does ♃ feel about Saturn, about music? We look at the receptions here. Jupiter is in Aquarius, ruled by Saturn. It loves Saturn. Listeners will love the song.

Will their sympathy last long? The listeners with their feelings are in a fixed sign. It means that their sympathy will be long-lasting. So, we have a broad audience who will hear and love the song.

So, the music will enter the hit parade. The listeners will vote for the song for a long time. So it will rise to the top of the chart.

Last question. Will it rise quickly or slowly? The song, *Saturn*, is in the sign of a long ascension. It means the single will climb gradually to the top of the chart. So, our prediction is straightforward.

- The song will reach a broad audience.
- It will enter the chart and stay there for a long time.
- It will head the chart (since many people will continue to vote for it)—a logical rather than astrological conclusion.
- But it will be a long climb.

What Happened in Reality

And now. Pa-bam. Here is what happened in reality. After the song appeared on YouTube, it got millions of views on the first day. This single became the highlight of the week. It is how the loud sign, Virgo, worked out.

After this loud debut, it entered the popular radio "Maximum" chart and stayed there for a few months. It is how the reception and fixity of the Aquarius sign worked out.

Despite the bright start, the song climbed to the top for a long time—about a month, until it reached the top. It is how the sign of the long ascension worked.

> **N.B.**
>
> Remarkably, in this chart, we predicted the behavior of an entire group of people—their future choices and behavior traits. This is precisely the case where, in a horary chart, we can see group processes that have not yet occurred but are about to manifest.

See how accurate the prediction we made with just a few techniques. Isn't it impressive? Horary astrology allows you to make incredible predictions with high accuracy. And I hope you enjoyed the taste of this remarkable tool.

Let's take a final look at what we've learned in the previous sections.

- We have discovered how to compare external objects to planets in the chart with the *house rulership technique*.
- We also understood how to find an unknown planet with the *reception technique*.
- We understood how to describe the state of external objects through the *celestial state* of planets and the *properties of signs*.
- Finally, we have learned how to find influences and motives using the *reception technique*.

It is, however, just a small part of the picture. In the upcoming sections of the book, we will elevate our prediction skills to a new level.

Chapter 2. Horary Astrology

Signification Techniques: Derived Houses

We have learned the first of the signification techniques—house rulership. The twelve astrological houses depict the objects in the querent's life, such as money, neighbors, and spouse.

But what if we are interested in the querent's son and his circumstances, such as his health, money, neighbors, or spouse?

In that case, consider the 5th house as a starting point. It will indicate the body and health of the son, serving as his 1st house. Then, his 2nd house (corresponds to the 6th house of the horary chart) reveals information about your son's finances.

You can view each astrological house as a starting point for another object.

For example, we know that the 3rd house represents your brother. However, if you consider it a starting point, then the 3rd house of your brother—his neighbors—becomes the 5th house of the horary chart.

These houses are termed *derived houses*, while the primary houses on the chart are called *radical houses*. We pronounce it as follows:

– The 5th radical house is the 3rd house of your brother.
– The 5th house of the chart is the 3rd from the 3rd house.

Apply the same logic to other houses, and you'll have a much broader list of objects to correspond to the planets.

Remember these two crucial rules.

Rule 1: We prefer the radical house if both the radical and derived houses describe the same object.

For example, the first house represents "me." I have a child who, in turn, has a father (me). Based on that logic, the 4th house from the 5th house (i.e., the 8th house) could also represent my body and health state. However, the 1st house already plays this role and prevails. Multiple houses cannot simultaneously represent the same object. Therefore, we always reserve the 1st house for the querent, the 7th house for the spouse, and so on.

Rule 2: We employ the derived house technique only if the "derived" object explicitly belongs to the "parent object" or if that belonging holds essential meaning in the context.

For instance, my dog's toy belongs exclusively to my dog. The noisy next-door neighbor of my brother disturbs my brother more than anyone else. In this context, it is *his* neighbor who causes harm.

However, suppose the inquiry concerns my daughter's university and the quality of education it provides. In that case, it is not the 9th house from the 5th house. My daughter and hundreds of other students attend the same university—a state institution and the general "place of wisdom" (the 9th radical house). Although we commonly say "my daughter's university," it is merely an expression. The university is not dedicated solely to her in this context.

The less explicitly the "derived" object belongs to a "parent" object, the less necessary it is to utilize the derived house technique.

Consider the importance of this belonging in the context. Suppose you learn from the newspaper that a boy is missing. You wonder if he is alive, where, and when they will find him. Even though he is not your child, you would still use the primary 5th house—the house of children. Why? Because, in general, the 5th house represents children as a class, and you are concerned about a child—a member of this class, regardless of their parental connection.

However, if you were to ask, "Where is the son of my best friend?" then you are specifically interested in your best friend's child, not just any child. This belonging is crucial because you care about your friend's family. In this case, you would look at the 5th house from the 11th, the 3rd primary house of the chart.

In any case, if you have doubts about which house to choose in a specific chart, the chart will provide you with the necessary clues. We will discuss this in more detail when we get to the topic of chart radicality.

> **N.B. on natal astrology**
>
> The natal chart usually shows events regarding close relatives only when they primarily concern the native's life. It could be

a severe illness of a sibling, causing the native to leave work and dedicate time to caregiving. It could be the father's death, resulting in an inheritance for the native, and so on.

Such joint events are usually indicated by derived houses. For instance, the death of a sibling is the 8th house from the sibling, the 10th radical house. We do not interpret the 8th house of the natal chart as "death in general" that the native will encounter in connection to the sibling's departure.

Feel the difference:

- A horary chart belongs to a group process and shapes it. The houses may represent general categories of things that the querent will encounter.
- A natal chart belongs to a specific person and shapes their personal biography. Houses always show things relative to the native themself.

For that reason, the 8th house of the natal chart signifies the death of the native and only theirs. Similarly, the 5th house of the natal chart represents the native's children, not children in general, as the natal chart primarily focuses on the native's life events.

Here are some examples of derived houses in horary astrology:

- Income from renting out a house corresponds to the 2nd house (money) from the 4th (house)—the 5th house of the chart.
- Another country's embassy is the 10th house (authority) from the 9th (of the foreign country)—the 6th radical house.
- My sister's boyfriend is the 7th house from the 3rd, the 9th radical house.
- My sister's boyfriend's money is the 2nd from the 9th—the 10th house.

In practice, you will rarely derive houses more than twice. The longer the deriving chain, the more likely it is to use the primary house.

For example, if the question is about the health of the cousin's best friend's brother-in-law's second cousin, then for the querent, it is already just an individual—the 7th house. The importance of belonging is rapidly disappearing here.

Homework Assignment №7

With all this in mind, let's move on to your homework. Combine what you already know from the previous sections with the new knowledge.

Look at the familiar chart (Fig. 2.6 on page 59), and answer the following questions:

- I want to rent out an apartment. Will I make a lot of money on rent?
- Does the potential tenant have enough money for a long-term lease?
- Could they damage my apartment?
- Will the tenant be loud?

Solution

Will I make a lot of money on rent? Rent money, that is, money from the house, is the ruler of the 5th house, Mars. Mars is in excellent condition, in its sign. Yes, there will be a lot of money.

Does the potential tenant have enough money to pay for long term rent? The potential tenant is the 7th house. Their money is the 8th house of the chart. The ruler of the 8th house is Mercury and it is peregrine. Unfortunately, they do not have enough money for a long-term rental.

Can they harm my apartment? The ruler of the 7th house, Venus, can harm in two ways. Venus can be harmful in itself due to its essential debility. For example, if the tenant smokes a lot, the apartment will smell of smoke. Or, Venus can harm the house by the reception. Say, the tenant is a good guy. Still, they have special needs incompatible with this specific apartment—they will ultimately change something in the apartment with time to suit their needs. Venus is not debilitated and does not harm Jupiter (apartment) by the reception. The apartment will be safe.

Will the tenant be loud? Venus is in Leo—a middle voice sign. They will make noise, but not much.

Signification Techniques: Alternative Rulers

Sometimes, we need to find two objects in the same house. Imagine you received the question: What job to choose? The 10th house describes both positions. Or the woman wants to know about her husband and his lover. They are both described by the 7th house.

Co-rulers of the House

Let me quote a passage from the section "The Lord of the House":

> For example, the cusp of the 10th house falls at 17 degrees of Sagittarius (17° ♐). This means that Jupiter, "reflected" in Sagittarius, influences a particular object in question—let's say, a specific job. Whatever the state of Jupiter is, it determines the state of the job you will get. The 10th house may also include the sign of Capricorn ♑, which follows Sagittarius. This means that Saturn also signifies something related to the 10th house. It may be another job you have, or the private business you run

As you can see, an astrological house often includes multiple signs, through which it determines several planets to the same area of life. And that's what we need—we are looking for other planets, in addition to the house ruler, that are also determined by that house to manifest in the same life affairs.

We will often call the planets that rule other signs within the same house as *co-rulers of that house*. Co-rulers of the house can be excellent candidates for the second object within the same house in question.

Such co-rulers are suitable if a significant part of the sign following the sign on the cusp occupies the house. Suppose the 10th house begins at 20° ♑, includes all 30 degrees of Aquarius, and ends at 2° ♓. In that case, Pisces occupies the last few degrees of the house, where the power of determination is negligible. In this case, Jupiter will hardly manifest itself significantly in the affairs of the 10th house and cannot become its co-ruler.

Planet Inside the House

Let me provide another quote from the section "The Lord of the House."

> "In horary astrology, where we are interested in the fate of a particular position in a company, we prefer the house ruler as the significator of that position rather than the planet in the house. The planet in the house may signify something else within the same area of life, not directly related to the question—for example, social activity, the head of the department in your prospective job, etc."

Suppose we know that one of the jobs is primary and preferable, and the other is an alternative variant (in case something goes wrong with the 1st option). In that context, we can consider the ruler of the house as the main subject in question, while the planet in the house is a backup plan relative to the subject.

In the example above, if we know that the primary job under consideration is a stable office position and the second one is a risky startup, we assign Jupiter to the stable office job and the planet in the house to the startup.

The same principle works for other houses. Suppose there is a primary quesited—a husband, the ruler of the 7th house. And there is some girl with whom he has a romantic relationship. The primary candidate for the girl is the planet inside the 7th house.

How To Choose the Right Co-ruler Among Several

Let's assume we have more than two candidates for the second job role and must know which one to choose. We have two options.

Option 1: We know the preferred job in the question

In this case, the preferred job is the main quesited. By definition, we assign the ruler of the house to it. The same principle applies to other questions—for instance, the questions about a husband and his mistress. The husband is the main querent, and the mistress is a "detail" relative to the husband.

Then, we need to choose the second candidate. We may have more than one candidate in the list:

- One of the candidates is the ruler of the sign following MC, and another is the ruler of the sign following it.
- Two or more candidates are the planets inside the 10th house.

We prefer the planet that is more determined by the house. We use two simple rules to assess the strength of determination:

- The force of determination gradually decreases from the cusp to the end of the house—the closer the planet or the sign to the cusp, the more focused influence they have on a specific object.
- The planet in the house exerts stronger influence on the matter of that house than the ruler of the sign in that house. Morinus called this rule "the position in the degree is stronger than the rulership of that degree in the absence of a planet."

As a particular consequence of these general rules, we have the following:

- The ruler of the sign closer to the cusp is more determined by that house than the other signs' rulers.
- The planet inside the house manifests itself more prominently in the affairs of that house than the rulers of the signs in the house.
- The one closer to the cusp is more determined among several planets inside the house.

We should always consider the context. It may give more significance to one candidate compared to others. The principle here is that the more matches between the properties of one candidate and the actual circumstances, the more willingly we choose that candidate.

Example: Suppose we know the second job is a lawyer's job. One of the candidates falls into the strong dignities of Jupiter or Jupiter itself. According to universal rulership (which we will discuss later in this book), Jupiter signifies lawyers and judges. If one candidate has such a solid connection to legal activities, it's not by chance. It's a hint from the chart to choose this candidate.

Another example: In a question about a husband and his mistress, we know that the mistress recently left the husband, but he continues to pursue her attention. We assign the lord of the 7th house to the husband as the main quesited. Suppose the 7th house includes two planets and the sign of Gemini, which follows Cancer on the cusp.

According to our list, Mercury, the co-ruler of the house, has the slightest chance of becoming the mistress. However, Mercury is the only planet that recently had an *opposition* with the husband's planet (we'll talk about the opposition aspect a bit later in this book). All you need to know for now is that the *recent opposition* between two planets is a *recent separation of two people*. Moreover, you may see that, according to reception, the husband exalts Mercury, while Mercury has no feelings in return.

No other planet in the list of candidates shows the reality as vividly as Mercury does. Therefore, Mercury immediately stands out as a leader and becomes the significator of the mistress.

Option 2: We do not know the preferred job in the question

In this case, we don't know which job to assign to the ruler of the 10th house and which to other planets determined by that house.

In this situation, we will consider each planet determined by the 10th house, including its ruler, and choose the one that best fits the job description.

We will use all available *descriptive techniques* to match the properties of the planets to what we know in reality, for instance:

- If one of the jobs is signified by Mercury, and in reality, one of the options is a statistician job, we'll assign Mercury—the universal ruler of all sciences—to that job.
- If we know that one of the jobs is working abroad, we will prefer the candidate with a connection to the 9th house. It could be a planet that:
  - rules the 9th house or is placed in it
  - is in the power of the ruler of the 9th house or in mutual reception with it
  - has a close aspect, meaning contact, with the ruler of the 9th
- Suppose one of the jobs in question is a choreographer position. In that case, we choose the candidate strongly associated with Venus—the planet of fine arts. Perhaps Venus rules the candidate, or it is in

mutual reception with it, or Venus is in close contact (aspect) with our candidate.
- Suppose the prospective job implies working on two projects in parallel—we prefer the candidate in a double-body sign.
- Suppose the querent recently had an interview for one of the jobs and is expecting an offer. We see that the querent had a contact (an *exact aspect*) with one of the candidates recently—we will prefer this candidate.

We search for all possible connections between reality and each of the candidates and pick those that better describe reality.

It is the area of horary astrology that requires some skills and mastery. Fortunately, situations like that are infrequent in practice.

If There Are No Alternative Rulers

There may be a situation where no planets are inside a house and there are no co-rulers.

- For example, the cusp of the house is in Capricorn. The house also includes the first part of Aquarius. But the ruler of Aquarius (Saturn) coincides with the ruler of the house.
- Another example: the house's cusp falls into the beginning of Aquarius. But the house is so narrow that it also ends in the sign of Aquarius.

What to do in such cases? Where should we look for an alternative house ruler? We can use techniques that we often use in natal astrology to determine the connection of planets with houses.

You already know that each sign, especially the one at the top of the house, is governed by several planets with different strengths. The ruler of the sign has the strongest association with the sign since they share a common nature. A planet exalted in a sign is connected to that sign to a lesser extent. The triplicity ruler is connected even less.

When a sign is on the cusp of a house, it becomes determined by this house towards a particular area of life. The sign reflects its rulers with different intensity.

- The house most determines the ruler of the sign.
- To a lesser extent, it determines the ruler of the sign by exaltation.
- And very slightly, the house conditions the ruler of triplicity.

It means that in cases where we don't have a co-ruler of the house, we can always use the ruler of the house by exaltation. And in its absence, we take the ruler of the house by triplicity.

Let's assume that the 10th cusp falls into the sign of Capricorn. From this moment, Saturn becomes the primary ruler of the house. We cannot take the ruler of the following sign, Aquarius, as Saturn also rules it. Suppose we cannot take Jupiter either—only the first degrees of Pisces occupy the end of the 10th house. Jupiter's connection to the 10th house is minimal. But we can take the ruler of Capricorn by exaltation—Mars. So, Mars will indicate an alternative job related to the 10th house.

Homework Assignment №8

Please revisit the chart 2.6 on page 59. You have two brothers. Do they have a common interest, and if yes, what could it be? The Moon is given to the querent in this question.

Solution

One of the brothers is Saturn, the ruler of the 3rd house. The second brother could be the Moon, the planet inside the 3rd house. However, it is assigned to the querent. So, you can take the co-ruler of the house—Jupiter. It rules the sign of Sagittarius, which occupies a significant part of the 3rd house and is determined to indicate brothers.

So, Saturn and Jupiter represent the two brothers. They are both in Capricorn—under the rulership of Saturn and Mars (Mars rules Capricorn by exaltation). Saturn cannot indicate their common interest as it already shows one of the brothers. However, Mars can.

Thus, we see that the brothers share a common interest. We can observe the same answer through the planetary placement—the brothers are united in conjunction. In the context of the question, they are united by a common interest. Very often, the chart reveals the same answer in various ways.

Now, it remains to understand what Mars signifies. Mars can act as the universal ruler of war or martial arts or as the accidental ruler of the 12th, 1st, and 5th houses.

Chapter 2. Horary Astrology

We can consider these houses as radical (i.e., not derived from the 3rd). This would represent the querent themself and their health (1st house), their secret enemies or severe illnesses (12th house), or their children (5th house).

Alternatively, we can consider these houses as derivatives from the 3rd house of the chart. Then, work and money from it (the 10th and 11th houses of the brothers), or their neighbors (their 3rd house), are what unites them.

Suppose the querent is healthy and has no secret enemies or children. They also mentioned that the brothers are not interested in martial arts. In that case, we are left with two options:

- The brothers are planning a joint business united by the desire for profit (10th and 11th houses of the brothers).
- Or they share a common interest in their neighbor or regular routes (their 3rd house).

Following Occam's razor principle, you understand that the option with a joint business is much more likely and logical, so choose it.

Signification Techniques: Locking of Significators

In rare cases, we may lack the technical ability to find a significator.

For instance, you receive at night: "I'm thinking about switching to a new job. Will the new job be better or worse than the current one?" We need to compare the current and future jobs. For this, we must find two planets conditioned by the 10th house.

The cusp of the 10th house falls into the beginning of Sagittarius. Suppose, however, the 10th house is so short that it also ends in Sagittarius. There are no planets inside the house; there are no co-rulers. You also cannot use the ruler by exaltation because no planet is exalted in Sagittarius. You cannot use the triplicity ruler either. Jupiter, who rules the nocturnal triplicity, is already occupied—he is the primary ruler of the 10th house.

Well-balanced charts are unlikely to put you in such a difficult situation. The chart deprives the astrologer of the opportunity to choose a significator for one reason: **the astrologer is answering the wrong question.**

It is the moment in the judgment when you must stop working on the chart and ask the querent for clarification. For example, you may find out that there is a wave of layoffs in the company where the querent works, and they are apprehensive about being laid off. They plan that if they end up on the street, they will grab the first available job, which hopefully will not be worse than the current one.

But the genuine concern here is about getting laid off. The actual question from the querent is whether the bosses will fire them. It is precisely why the chart left us only with Jupiter—the only ruler of the 10th house, the current job.

Occasionally, you will encounter this behavior in a horary chart. I term this as the chart "locking" the significators, preventing us from utilizing them. This is a logical response from a well-balanced chart—a clear hint to the astrologer that they are answering the wrong question.

The Special Role of the Moon in Horary Astrology

Before we delve into practical applications of what we have learned, I want to emphasize the significance of the Moon in horary charts.

The Moon is the fastest and closest to Earth among all the planets. Its role in shaping daily events is considered crucial. Astrologers often use the expression "sublunary world" when referring the flow of ordinary events.

Horary astrology predicts the development of everyday situations in a person's life. That is why the Moon has the maximum impact on the entire horary chart.

Indeed, let me provide a few examples to support this thesis.

1. Lunar Nodes

Each planet's orbit is slightly inclined to the Sun's orbit. The points where these orbits intersect are called *planetary nodes*. There are Martian Nodes, Venusian Nodes, and so on.

These points do not have inner power; they do not influence the sublunary world, unlike planets. However, if a planet is on its node, such a position affects the planet's strength.

Crucially, a planet's node relates only to that specific planet. The Venusian node influences only Venus, and the Jupiterian node only affects Jupiter.

However, in horary charts, Lunar Nodes influence the entire chart—houses and other planets. Why? Because Lunar Nodes relate to the Moon, which, in turn, influences the whole horary chart. Astrologers mistakenly use Lunar Nodes in natal charts, where they do not hold the same significance, as rightly noted by Morinus.

2. Void of Course Moon and Burnt Path

In horary astrology, we will discuss this essential concept later—*Void of Course Moon*. This is a specific motion of the Moon and only relates to the Moon. But it influences the entire horary chart.

3. Part of Fortune

In the zodiacal circle, there are particular points called *Arabian Parts*. We will delve into them later in this book. It's crucial to understand that there are dozens of such parts, and only one is associated with the Moon—*Part of Fortune*. Ptolemy called this part the Lunar ascendant. And that point, unlike all others, holds a unique role in the horary chart. Why? Because it is linked to the Moon and, through it, affects the entire chart.

4. Universal Role of the Moon

I mentioned earlier that we will rarely use the universal meaning of planets, focusing on their accidental meaning (see the section "Signification Techniques"). An exception here is the Moon.

The universal nature of the Moon is to exercise a transient, changeable influence to give events their final form. In questions where the querent is not directly involved in the context, the Moon defaults to being the universal significator of the flow of events if it doesn't have an accidental meaning. It occurs, for example, in questions about the outcome of a football match. If the Moon does not indicate either team, it shows the game's dynamics.

At the beginning of the book, I also hypothesized about how stars influence a person. The critical point was stimulating unconscious reactions that drive them to act in one direction or another. The Moon universally shows unconscious motives and deep emotions.

In confirmation of my hypothesis, if the querent is involved in the question and the Moon is not occupied by the quesited, the Moon defaults to showing the querent's emotions.

The Moon is the only planet that is never idle. Suppose it doesn't have an accidental role (such as work, money, siblings, or competitors) in the context. In that case, the Moon always interlopes in the chart with its universal role:

- It shows the emotional reactions and motives of the querent.
- Or it shows the flow of events if the querent is not involved in the situation.

So, the main idea of this section is that the Moon always has an active role in the horary chart.

N.B. on natal astrology

Notably, it is not necessary for the Moon to have a connection to the 1st house to start indicating the querent (their emotional side).

In natal astrology, this is not possible. For a planet to reveal its universal significance, it is necessary to be determined by a corresponding house. For instance, the Sun universally signifies fame and recognition, which is associated with the 10th house. Therefore, the Sun should be conditioned by the 10th house to indicate the native's fame in a natal chart.

Similarly, the Moon universally signifies the native's emotions, which are associated with the 1st house in the natal chart. Thus, the Moon must be conditioned by the 1st house to show the native and their emotional side. On the other hand, the Moon is the natural ruler of mothers. Therefore, the Moon should be conditioned by the 4th house to indicate the native's mother. Otherwise, it will show something else.

Homework Assignment

It's time to reinforce the material we've covered. The querent asks, "I am choosing which car to buy—a black Audi or a yellow Ferrari. Which one will give me more positive emotions?" Look at the familiar chart (Fig. 2.6 on page 59)

- **Hint 1**: Examine the impact of each car on the Moon—on the querent's emotions.
- **Hint 2**: When assigning cars to the planets, consider the universal role of Saturn—it indicates things of black color.

Solution

The first car is the ruler of the 2nd house, Jupiter. The second one is the ruler of Capricorn (which occupies the 2nd house)—Saturn.

Saturn shows things of black color. So this is a black Audi. Therefore, Jupiter is a Ferrari (by elimination).

Jupiter and Saturn are both in the Capricorn sign, in detriment of the Moon. That is, they harm the Moon. So, neither car will bring emotional satisfaction.

Signification Techniques: Universal Rulership

Houses do not describe all things. For example, no astrological house represents surgery, sea creatures, or alcohol.

It is where two other techniques are of help. These are

- Universal rulership and
- Arabian Parts disposition

In this section, we will focus on *universal rulership*. As you already know, planets denote entire classes of objects by their universal nature, which is always constant and doesn't depend on planetary positions in a particular horoscope. Let's explore this correspondence. We'll start with Saturn.

Saturn

Saturn denotes things that are:

- Hard and heavy
- Old and decaying
- Restraining and limiting
- Preserving and freezing
- Related to agriculture or history
- Of black color

Examples: slavery, gardening, older men, ruins.

Jupiter

Jupiter shows all things that are:

- Large and spreading
- Fertile (rains, seeds, fruits)
- Religious and teaching
- Noble
- Merciful and just
- Of purple color

Examples: aristocrats, priests, judges, churches, gurus, seeds and fruit trees.

Mars

Mars shows all things that are:

- Sharp, cutting, and burning
- Aggressive and attacking
- Irritating
- Of red color

Examples: spilled blood and cut, fire, nettles, knives, inflammation and allergies.

Venus

Venus shows all things that are:

- Soft, charming
- Sweet and of pleasant smell
- Attractive and bringing pleasure
- Art-related
- Of green color
- Of pink pastel color

Examples: makeup, kisses, chocolate, ballet.

The Sun

The Sun shows all things that are:

- Unique & royal
- Expensive
- Giving life and energy
- Of gold color

Examples: a king in every kingdom (diamond among stones, eagle among birds, lion among animals, president), oranges, gold.

The Moon

The Moon shows all things that are:

- Liquid and soft
- Shapeless
- Ever changing
- Odorless
- Brand new or newborn
- Sea-related
- Appearing at night
- Of white or silver color

Examples: milk, babies, and nourishing; homelessness; a crowd, electorate; octopus and jellyfish; mushrooms; owls.

Mercury

Mercury shows all things that are:

- Mixed, tricky, and fraudulent
- Sarcastic & ironic
- Small and going in large numbers
- Causes of wind
- Grow in a shell
- Of mixed color
- Of gray/sand color

Examples: sweet and sour sauce, cocktails, pizza; scammers, thieves, and liars; comedians; beans, nuts; earthquakes.

It also shows all things that:

- Imitate a man
- Related to articulation & speech
- Servant-related
- Pharmacy-related

Examples: dolls, parrots; virtuosos, fine motor skills; personal assistants; doctors, drugs & medicine.

Mercury shows everything related to:

- Astrology
- Writing
- Calculations
- Commerce

Examples: trade and contracts; mediation, communication, and the internet; documents, books, and magazines.

When Do We Use Natural Rulership?

We use natural rulership when

- There is no specific house for the object.
- When the planet describes an object that the house does not describe.
- When we identify the unknown planet or choose the right significator that better matches reality.

For example, we need to find an older man, not just another person whose age is unimportant, among several persons. We have several planets in the 7th house and the ruler of the 7th house. One of the planets is Saturn. In that case, we may prefer Saturn over the 7th house ruler or other planets in the 7th house, since Saturn naturally shows older men.

Another example. We are looking for the lost passport. On the one hand, it is just a belonging, i.e., the ruler of the 2nd house. On the other hand, all documents, including passports, are shown by Mercury. Since we want to find all possible places where the querent may find their passport, we will use Mercury and the 2nd house ruler. It will increase the number of places to search and give the querent a better chance to discover the right one.

Chapter 2. Horary Astrology

How to Find a Universal Ruler of a Particular Object

Suppose we are searching for a lost camera. What planet is the natural ruler of all cameras? It may be tempting to determine a natural ruler based on how an object is utilized. For instance, a camera can be employed for journalism, and communications and mass media are ruled by Mercury. Alternatively, it can be used to capture enjoyable vacation moments, and fun and joy are governed by Venus. It is tempting to say that Mercury or Venus signifies the camera.

However, the correct approach is to answer the question "What is the main or *universal* purpose of this object?" The camera exists to capture moments—to store them in a picture. Fixation and storage are the realms of Saturn. Therefore, Saturn is the *universal* ruler of the camera.

It will also be correct to compare the planet's universal meaning with the object's property, which is essential in the context. If you are looking for a unique gold ring, not just a ring, then take the Sun as a significator of all golden things together with the 2nd house ruler. The logic is straightforward here.

Homework Assignment №9

With this knowledge, let's move on to the homework assignment. What planet shows:

– Thermometer
– Battery
– Artificial Intelligence

Next task. Please refer to our training chart (Fig. 2.6 on p. 59). The querent left a bookmark in one of their books but couldn't remember which one. Your task is to determine which book contains the bookmark.

– Which planet shows the bookmark? For now, only use the universal rulership.
– If the bookmark conjuncts another planet, it means a bookmark tied to another object. In the context of the question, this is a book.
– Find the planet of the book and describe what kind of book it might be and what it is about. Again, only use the universal rulership.

- Finally, determine whether this is a new book or an old and worn-out one. Recall which technique is responsible for describing the condition of an object.

Third task. Suppose the querent checked the book you indicated but found nothing there. Your task now is to suggest an alternative place for the querent to search. **Hint:** Instead of utilizing the natural ruler of bookmarks, examine the accidental ruler of the bookmark.

- Consider the bookmark as the ruler of the 2nd house.
- Similarly, identify the planet most closely tied to (conjunct with) the bookmark's significator. This planet will indicate the book.
- What is this book about? Utilize the universal meaning of the book's significator.
- Is it a new book or a worn-out one? Evaluate its quality.

Solution

Task 1. The primary purpose of the thermometer is to fix your body's current temperature. Fixation is the natural manifestation of Saturn. So Saturn universally rules all thermometers.

The primary purpose of the battery is to provide energy. Though you may object that the primary objective is to keep the energy, keeping energy *per se* is useless until you apply the battery as a power source. The great source of energy and power is the Sun. So, the Sun prevails over Saturn as a universal significator of all batteries.

Finally, artificial intelligence imitates a human, resolves numerous tasks, and is a handy helper. Mercury rules all these.

Task 2. A bookmark is what saves the page you left off. Saturn universally rules conservation and memorization. Saturn, bookmark, is visually tied to the planet Jupiter. In the context of the question, this is the book where the querent has left a bookmark.

What kind of books can Jupiter describe? These are spiritual books, books on jurisprudence, or purple-colored books, according to Jupiter's nature.

Task 3. This time, we will take Jupiter, the ruler of the 2nd house, as the accidental significator of the bookmark. Again, Jupiter is tied with Saturn—a book in context.

So Saturn shows the book in this approach. What kind of book is it? It is a book on agriculture, history, or of black color.

Is it a new or worn-out book? Saturn is dignified in this chart; this is a new book.

This time, the querent checked all the books on history and black-colored ones and found a bookmark in the black-colored book. However, this book is about wars. It is unsurprising, since Saturn (the book) is in the strong dignity of Mars—the natural ruler of wars.

> ### *N.B. on search questions*
>
> Search questions are the most challenging in horary astrology due to the lack of precise context. Even in my imaginary example where we know the bookmark was left in a book, not just anywhere in the city, we still don't understand what book we are looking for. We can't accurately predict that it will be a black book about wars rather than a black book about knives or a book on the history of agriculture.
>
> We can't technically prefer the interpretation where Saturn shows the bookmark over the one where the ruler of the 2nd house shows it. All these possible interpretation combinations have an equal chance of manifesting.
>
> The only thing left for us to do in search horaries is to consider all possible options, making this prediction the least precise.
>
> If we had a super-specific context, say, the bookmark could be left in either a history textbook or a Shakespearean poem, we would instantly and unequivocally determine that the bookmark is in the history textbook. But, I'm afraid, in such trivial cases, the client would find the book faster than reaching out to the astrologer.

Ptolemaic Aspects

As you know, the dignities and debilities of planets show the condition of an object—whether it is good or bad (in context). However, many objects may have separate aspects or characteristics that can be particularly positive or negative.

For example, a car might be "bad." In the context of the question, it has high mileage and requires maintenance. However, this car has one excellent aspect—very comfortable seats. This compensates for other shortcomings when driving long distances.

Conversely, a job may be "good"—in context, it is prestigious. But it has one negative aspect—it requires working overtime.

Each planet, regardless of its condition, always has particular aspects, some of which are positive, some negative, and some neutral. Technically, these aspects are concentrated in seven places of the zodiacal circle:

- At ±60° from the planet
- At ±90° from the planet
- At ±120° from the planet
- Directly opposite (180°) the planet

Imagine the zodiacal circle refracting the planet's light, focusing it into these seven points. Morinus described this effect as the zodiac concentrating a planet's rays, creating miniature "copies" in these positions— each with distinct traits.

The aspect's position relative to a planet determines its name and glyph:

- *Opposition* (☍), 180°, is self-evident.
- 90° is the angle between the apexes of a square shape; hence the name—*square* (□).
- 120° is the angle between the apexes of the triangle; hence the name— *trine* or *trigon* (△).
- 60° is the angle between the apexes of a hexagon (six-sided figure); hence the name—*sextile* (✶) from the Latin sextus (six).

These aspects are called *Ptolemaic aspects*.

Let's consider an example. Suppose a planet is at 17° ♈,

- Its opposition is at 17° ♎.
- It has two trigons at a distance of ±120°:

- to the right of the planet (against the order of the signs), at 17° ♐ —a *dexter trigon*.
- to the left, at 17° ♌ —a *sinister trigon*.

Event Prediction Techniques: Exact Aspects

Let's imagine you have two planets in the same sign, and the faster planet is approaching the slower one. After some time, the zodiacal degrees of these two planets will coincide.

At this moment, the rays of the two planets mix. It causes a collision of two external objects, each represented by one planet.

For example, if the first planet signifies the reward the querent expects, and the second planet represents the querent, the collision of these two significators will lead to a collision of two objects—the querent and the reward.

When discussing the collision of two external objects, we always talk about an *event*. Here are examples of events (I will italicize the colliding objects):

– My *brother* is coming to visit *me*.
– *Mom* is receiving a *package*.
– My *new book* has been released and is reaching the hands of *readers*.

In events, we always have two significators colliding with each other.

When a planet transits through another, we call such an interaction a *bodily conjunction*. But there are other ways planets can come into contact with each other to mix their rays and produce events.

When a second planet passes through one of the miniature "copies" (aspects) of the first one, the effect similar to a conjunction occurs—the rays of the planets mix, causing the collision of two objects.

We express it like this:

– The Moon *applies to* the sextile of Jupiter, or
– The Moon *performs a trine* with Jupiter.

For example, the querent's planet passes through a favorable aspect of future work—a specific position with high bonuses. The querent passing through a miniature "copy" of the work's significator causes the same blending of rays as passing through the work's significator itself—the querent gets employed.

The only thing we'll add to this event is that, regardless of whether the job is generally "good" or "bad" (e.g., easy or difficult in context), the querent will encounter an especially pleasant aspect of the job—high bonuses.

In practice, we are rarely interested in the specific aspects (facets) of objects when discussing an event. What usually concerns us is the event itself—whether employment happens or not—as well as the nature of the future job: whether it will be difficult or easy in context (that is, whether the work's significator is dignified or debilitated).

Object Interaction Techniques: Close Aspects

A planet acts most prominently in the degree it occupies. However, its influence extends beyond that degree. You can imagine a halo, called the sphere or orb of influence, surrounding the planet. The planet's rays immediately affect everything within this sphere, and the closer to the center, the stronger the impact. The same applies to all seven "copies" of the planet. Thus, when a significator approaches the body or aspect of another planet and enters its orb, their rays start mixing.

When two significators start blending their rays, we refer to this as a connection forming between the objects they represent. We interpret this in context, for example:

– They are constantly *in touch* with their boss.
– Their brother *is tied* to this organization.
– This bookmark *is conjoined* with the book (in context—it lies inside the book; see an example in the section "Homework Assignment №9" on page 91).

We call such planetary interaction a *close conjunction* (when both planets are bodily close to each other) or a *close aspect* (when one planet is closely positioned to the aspect of the other).

We pronounce it as the planet *aspects* the significator, *casts an aspect* to it, or the two planets *form a close aspect*.

Difference Between Exact and Close Aspects

It is essential to understand that exact aspects perform instantly and then disappear. They describe momentary events on Earth—the collision of two objects.

On the other hand, close aspects show the connection or influence of two objects stretched over time. You can think of close aspects as a process.

- The process of marking a book with a dirty bookmark
- The process of how work influences personal life
- A long-term connection with an organization, and so on

Exact and close aspects are essentially different techniques with different purposes. The former identifies momentary events, the latter describes extended interaction. Feel the difference:

- In the question "Will we have sex tonight?" we use exact aspect.
- In the question "Is my husband having sex with another woman? Is he cheating on me?" we use close aspect.

Influence in Close Aspects

When the second significator is close to a planet's particular aspect, we say that the significator closely interacts with the object that the planet signifies—more exactly, it interacts with a particular facet of that object.

For example, the querent's spouse is in contact with the car's favorable aspect—its particularly comfortable seats. This means she often drives the car, *experiencing comfort*. Or the querent is in contact with the job's unfavorable aspect—working late hours. This means the querent stays late at work—it *affects the querent's health*.

Some objects have no favorable or unfavorable properties in the context. For example, a package or a salary does not have positive or negative attributes. However, their significators technically still have aspects or facets concentrated in particular degrees of the zodiac circle, although these degrees do not hold any positive or negative traits of the original object.

If the querent is in close contact with the aspect of the package or salary, it has the same effect as if the querent were in constant close contact with the package or salary *per se*. In this context, it can mean keeping the package or salary with them.

N.B.

We have already discussed the influence of one planet on another through reception. The difference between influence through aspect and reception is as follows:

- Reception indicates a *specific* influence of one object on another.
- An aspect shows the *general* influence of the object in connection with its good or bad qualities.

Feel the difference:

- This flower causes an allergy in John specifically, although its scent is beautiful and most people enjoy it.
- This flower causes tearing in anyone, because despite its beauty, it has a negative facet—sharp burning smell.

Mutual and One-Sided Aspects

Let's consider a close conjunction. The second planet that enters the orb of the first has its own orb and can influence the first planet in return. Look at Fig. 2.8: Planet B is in the orb of Planet A, and vice versa. Such a close conjunction is called *full platic* or *mutual* conjunction.

Now imagine another example: Planet B is in the orb of Planet A, but Planet A is not in Planet B's orb and doesn't experience any counter-influence in return (Fig. 2.9).

We call such one-sided influence of planets a *partial platic conjunction*. Here are examples of such one-sided manifestations:

- Their demanding work is interfering with their relationship, but they cannot do anything about it.
- The dangerous organization suppresses the brother, but he has no way to resist.

Chapter 2. Horary Astrology

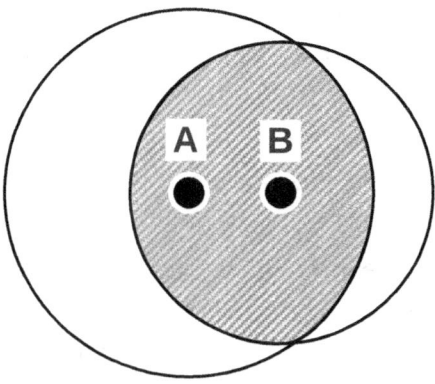

Figure 2.8: *Mutual Aspect*

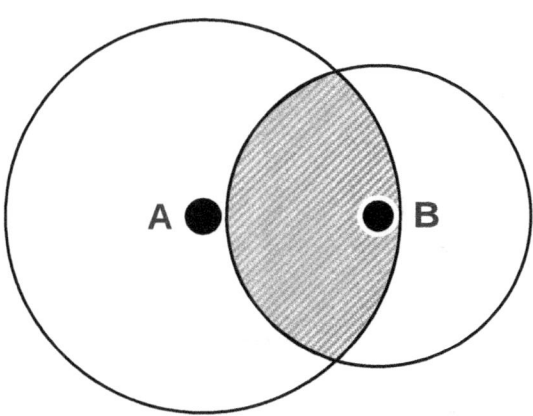

Figure 2.9: *One-Sided Aspect*

The same is true if a planet closely stays within another planet's aspect. For example, Jupiter is at 17° Aries, and Venus is at 19° Sagittarius. Then we would say:

- Venus at 19° ♐ is next to the dexter trigon of Jupiter; she is in the orb of Jupiter's trine (the miniature "copy" of Jupiter at 17° Sagittarius), so she experiences Jupiter's influence.
- Jupiter at 17° ♈ is next to the sinister trigon of Venus, i.e., her miniature "copy" at 19° ♈. Jupiter is in the orb of Venus' trine and experiences its influence.

This was an example of a *mutual trine*. We express this as:

- Jupiter and Venus are in a close mutual trine.
- Jupiter and Venus are in a mutual aspect.
- Jupiter and Venus form a full platic aspect.

Now, suppose Venus is at 27° ♐ (Fig. 2.10). In that case:

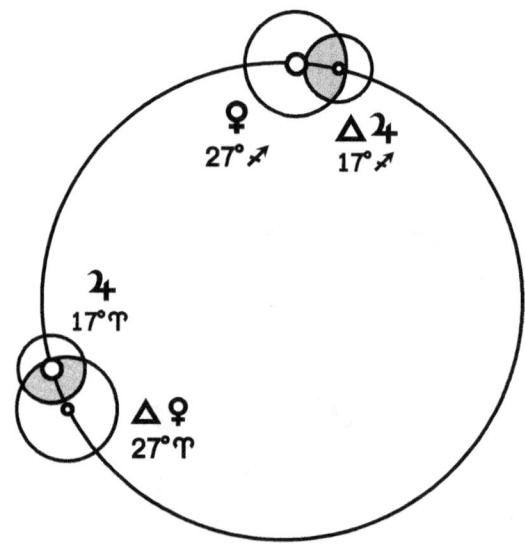

Figure 2.10: *One-Sided Sinister Trine*

- With her sinister trine, Venus would influence Jupiter.
- But Jupiter would no longer be able to reach Venus because it is outside her orb.

We would call this influence *one-sided*. We pronounce it like this:

- Venus casts its trine to Jupiter.
- Jupiter receives Venus' aspect.

- Jupiter and Venus form a partial platic aspect.

The Strength of Close Aspects

When the zodiacal circle refracts the rays of a planet, focusing it on miniature "copies,"[5] these "copies" vary in size. The most significant reflection of the planet is at the point of its opposition. Smaller copies are positioned at 120 degrees, and even smaller ones are at the places of 90 and then 60 degrees.

Morinus proposed the following scheme to assess the strength of an aspect: the stronger the aspect, the less the ray of the planet approaching the Earth deviates from its course. Interestingly, it reminds the real interference picture (Fig. 2.11) of the ray discovered long after Morinus.

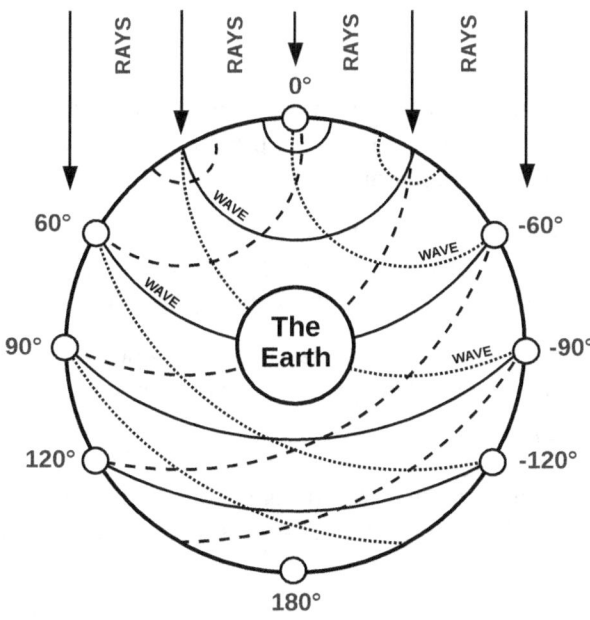

Figure 2.11: *Interference Picture of the Zodiac Circle*

Suppose the light of a planet penetrates the Earth and creates a "copy" of the planet at the opposite point of the zodiac. The ray doesn't deviate

---
[5] In Book 14, Section 1, Chapter 4 of *Astrologia Gallica*, Morinus called this *determination by the ecliptic*.

from its course and reaches the place of opposition with no dissipation. Let's assume 180 degrees (the line from the planet to the point of its opposition) as 100% of the aspect's strength. Any other aspects lose strength as they deviate from this straight line.

For example, 90 degrees is half of 180 degrees. So, the zodiac circle focuses the ray of the planet at ±90 degrees twice less effectively than in the place of opposition. We can call this "the strength of the square is half the strength of the opposition."

By the same logic, a trine is 2/3 of the strength of the opposition, and a sextile is 1/3 of it.

Thus, we can express the strength of aspects as follows:

- Conjunction, opposition—1
- Trine—2/3
- Square—1/2
- Sextile—1/3

These values can be useful when we want to understand the overall impact of mixed influences. For example, my business is experiencing the influence of various factors.

- Brutal competitors exert pressure by the square aspect.
- On the other hand, my business is connected to the noble significator of the government, which legislatively supports my side.

The overall impact on the business is positive since the conjunction prevails over the square. The government protects my business.

Another example:

- Merciless competitors are pressuring my business by close opposition.
- The noble significator of the government supports my business by sextile.

The overall impact is destructive—the government doesn't significantly hinder my competitors who actively disrupt the operation of my outlets. Opposition prevails over sextile.

Do not apply the strength of aspects when you consider just one aspect. Suppose my business is under pressure from competitors, and nothing else supports it. The business significator receives only one adverse aspect—the aspect from competitors. In that case, the square

Chapter 2. Horary Astrology

aspect does not make this pressure less intense than the pressure by the opposition. It is just the pressure, and it is still destructive *per se*.

We only use the strength of aspects when comparing multiple aspects that the significator receives from other planets.

The Effect of Aspect in Connection With Its Form

Often, a planet has both strengths and weaknesses simultaneously. For instance, the Moon may be in its triplicity and at the same time in detriment. Or, it may happen that Venus, while in its triplicity, has an evil ruler, giving Venus some negative traits (see the section "Modification of the Celestial State Due to Reception").

This "duality" is crucial for aspects. The zodiacal circle puts either a debilitated or dignified part of the planet in the place of its aspect.

You can think of it this way:

- Favorable aspects naturally concentrate all the good sides of the planet and mostly dissipate all the bad it carries.
- Unfavorable aspects concentrate all the bad sides of the planet and significantly dissipate its good attributes.

Trine and sextile are favorable aspects, while opposition and square are malevolent.

Let's consider some examples:

Example 1. Let's assume Mars is in the place of its triplicity and detriment. If Mars signifies medicines, we would say that medicines generally have a negative effect. However, they partially help to support mental activity.

Now, consider the square of Mars. All the good in those medicines almost disappears in the degree of square aspect. And all the adverse effects of Mars remain. Such a "copy" of Mars would be destructive.

Now, consider the trine of Mars. Support for mental activity remains unchanged. And all the side effects from the medicines vanish. The "copy" of Mars in the place of its trine becomes constructive.

Example 2. Now, imagine a person signified by Venus in exile. It's better not to encounter such a person on the street. But the ruler of this Venus is a noble planet. This person came into the house of an aristocrat and was forced to behave accordingly. It doesn't make the person noble, but it gives them some manners.

Moreover, the person is surrounded by two noble planets, making their behavior even more refined. It is as if two mentors accompany them, guiding them in etiquette at every opportunity. Of course, this does not change the person's nature, but it gives them enough manners to avoid behaving like a gangster.

Aspects will change the picture:

- The opposition of this Venus washes away all the nobility, accidentally gained by Venus, returning it to a state of pure exile.
- The sextile of the same Venus essentially dissolves the evil nature of Venus, leaving all the acquired manners untouched.

The Effect of the Aspect in Connection with the Place It Falls

Let's move further in our discussions. Since an aspect is a miniature copy of a planet, we need to consider the celestial state of this copy.

It may happen that the "copy" falls into a sign of incompatible nature and ends up in exile. Alternatively, it may fall into its domicile and acquire nobility. We should consider that. Let's look at examples.

Suppose Mars is at 15° Cancer—in its fall and triplicity. It represents medicine that mainly harms but partially helps.

Now, consider the trine of Mars. In this position, the "copy" of Mars is like Mars in triplicity, almost devoid of defects. This medicine moderately helps with scarcely noticeable side effects.

Let's consider the places where the trigon falls:

- Dexter trine of Mars is at 15° Pisces. Here, the "copy" of Mars landed in its triplicity, meaning the medicine now provides even more noticeable assistance.
- Sinister trine of Mars is at 15° Scorpio. The aspect of Mars has landed in its domicile—the medicine now carries a healing effect. Any side effects are almost invisible against the positive impact.

Now, let's consider the opposition of Mars. The opposition retains these medicines' negative aspects, dissipating the positive effects. The "copy" of Mars in the place of opposition is similar to Mars in its fall without the signs of triplicity.

Now, let's consider the sign of the opposition. The aspect falls into the sign of Capricorn—the place of Mars' exaltation. It compensates for the debility of Mars' "copy," causing the effect of the medicine to be useless.

Now, let's look at the square of Mars. Like the opposition, it corresponds to Mars in its fall without signs of triplicity. But the final effect of the square will be different.

- Dexter square falls into 15° Aries, the place of Mars' rulership. Considering that dignity by rulership prevails over debility by fall, the "copy" of Mars has acquired some minor positive attributes. The medicine at 15° Aries has a moderately favorable impact. But since a miniature copy of Mars causes this moderate impact, it is still less than the original positive effect from Mars in triplicity.
- Sinister square falls into 15° Libra—the place of Mars' exile. It makes the falling copy of Mars even more evil. At 5° Libra, the medicine imposes maximum harm to the body.

It's important to understand that in our example, for the medicine to impact the querent, the querent's planet must be close to Mars' aspect within its orb (see the section "Mutual and One-Sided Aspects").

Let's summarize the impacts of these aspects.

- The initial effects of medicines are mainly harmful, though they help
- Trine: medicines help/heal with no side effects
- Quadrature: the medicines are more harmful/less effective
- Opposition: the medicines are useless

As you see, the favorable aspects make the planet more effective, while the unfavorable aspects diminish the planet's effectiveness.

Homework Assignment №10

It's time to get some practice. You've decided to hire an employee for a managerial position. Saturn, representing your prospective employee, is at 10° Libra. Reception shows that Saturn is indifferent toward your business—the employee has no personal motive to support or harm your business. They will simply perform their duties according to their skills.

Consider the scenarios where:

- The employee has no aspect with the planet of your business or is not in conjunction with your company.
- Saturn casts a sinister trine, dexter and sinister squares, and an opposition to your business.

What business impact can you expect from the employee in these cases? Take a moment to think, then continue reading.

Solution

The employee is highly qualified on their own, though not as much as it may seem initially—Saturn is exalted.

Case 1: If the employee has no aspect with or is not conjunct with your business, Saturn's manifestation remains unchanged. A qualified employee working in the company will undoubtedly benefit the industry.

Case 2: Sinister trine. The zodiacal circle effectively places the highly qualified employee in the place of trine, removing any imperfections in their work. The sinister trine is at 10° Aquarius—the place of Saturn's rulership. This further amplifies the positive effect of working with the employee. We expect maximum returns.

Case 3: Dexter square. In the quadrature positions, the zodiacal circle removes all the good in the employee, making them almost useless. The dexter square falls into the sign of Cancer. It is like a miniature copy of Saturn-peregrine falling into its exile—it will start to disrupt (but not as strongly as if Saturn were actually in Cancer). Therefore, despite the employee's good qualifications, they will negatively impact the business.

Case 4: Sinister square. Here, the miniature "copy" of Saturn-peregrine falls into its domicile. It means the employee will be effective (but only to some extent, not as much as if Saturn were in this sign). Ultimately, the employee in a sinister square is still effective, but less than in case 1.

Case 5: Opposition. A large "copy" of Saturn-peregrine is in the place of its fall. The effect is similar to case 3 but with an exaggeration. The employee will have a noticeably negative impact on the business, although they will manage to do something good.

Chapter 2. Horary Astrology

N.B.

Remember, that the force of the opposition is equal to one of conjunction. You can imagine it as if the zodiac circle disposes a full copy of the planet in place of its opposition.

Summing it up:

- No aspects or conjunction: a qualified manager will benefit my business.
- Trine: we expect maximum returns.
- Square: the employee will be more harmful/less helpful for my business.
- Opposition: this manager will noticeably affect my business.

Again, you see the same pattern—the planet manifests itself more effectively in the places of favorable aspects and vice versa.

The Cumulative Effect of Close Aspect and Reception

We have studied in detail how the aspect of one planet impacts the other planet. However, we have not considered receptions that may exist between two significators.

As you already know, a planet in a sign always subordinates to its dispositor. We consider this subordination when the dispositor plays a crucial role in the question.

For example, suppose Venus represents the employee, and Saturn represents the company. Venus in Libra (in Saturn's exaltation) indicates a qualified employee dedicated to the company. This dedication to the job applies to Venus and all its aspects, including the opposition.

The opposition of Venus in Aries is destructive. The "evil copy" of Venus in the employee's 5th house may represent their newborn baby, causing them to lose sleep at night and be late for work.

But since there is a positive reception between the employee and the job, the employee does everything to mitigate the situation—they work overtime.

Therefore, reception modifies the action of the aspect for better or for worse according to the context.

The Orbs of the Seven Planets

Imagine you're watching the sunset. As the Sun sets below the horizon, you begin to see the first stars appearing in the sky—the bright ones, followed by the dimmer ones. At a particular moment, when the Sun is 18 degrees below the horizon, you'll witness all the stars in the night sky (Fig. 2.12).

Ancients believed it was precisely when the upper edge of the Sun's halo (or sphere of virtue, called *orb*) fell behind the horizon, "releasing" the last stars visible to the eye.

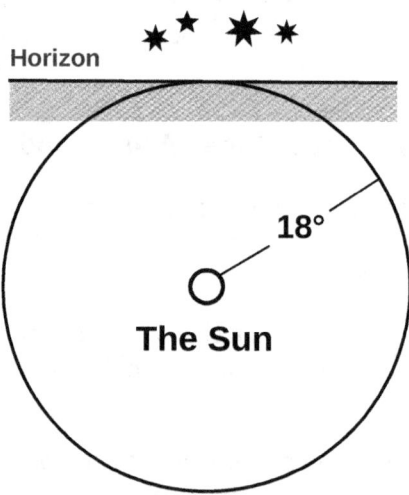

Figure 2.12: *The Orb of the Sun*

Now, imagine yourself observing a bright dot in the sky against the sunset background—that's the evening Venus. It appears before all other stars.

You cannot see Venus in the rays of the sunset if it is positioned very close to the Sun. You can first spot Venus when it is at a distance of 5 degrees from the Sun (Fig. 2.13).

Chapter 2. Horary Astrology

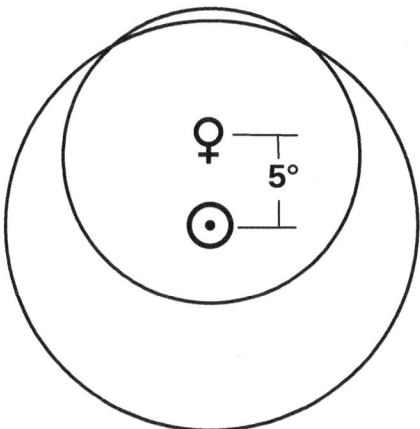

Figure 2.13: *The Orb of Venus*

Morin associated Venus' first appearance with the moment the Venusian orb began releasing itself from the solar halo.

Thus, one can quickly determine the radius of Venus' orb. The Sun must pass 5 degrees away from Venus for the edges of the solar and Venusian orbs to touch. Hence, the radius of Venus' orb is 18 − 5 = 13 degrees.

The radii (also called *moieties*) of orbs for other planets are determined using the same scheme:

- Sun—18°
- Moon—12°
- Mercury—8°
- Venus—13°
- Mars—6.5°
- Jupiter—8°
- Saturn—7°
- First-magnitude stars—6°

When planets touch the orbs of other planets or their aspect for the first time, the influence of these planets is minimal. However, the closer planets get to the centers of the orbs of other planets, the stronger the impact.

In horary astrology, we can confidently adhere to the rough approximation that within 3–4 degrees, any of the planets (regardless of the orb) will immediately influence another. However, remember, this is a simple approximation. For example, the Sun's impact extends much further than Saturn's.

In natal astrology, we consider both significant and weak influences; hence, we will precisely consider the planets' orbs.

N.B.

Please note that some books contain errors[a]. The diameter of the planet's orbs is confused with their radii. For instance, the Sun's orb (36 degrees) is confused with its radius (18 degrees). They erroneously assign half of that radius (8.5 degrees) to the *moiety* (i.e., radius) of the Sun, meaning that the Sun can only hide or combust the stars & planets within that distance.

However, this contradicts the fact that a planet approaching the Sun closer than 17–18 degrees starts to experience the Sun's influence, known as "being under the Sun's beams," and actual combustion occurs when the planet is visually hidden in the Sun's rays—this depends entirely on the size of the planet's orb. Be cautious when reading old books and rely on the astronomical calculations provided by Morinus and presented above.

---

[a] H. Coley. *Clavis Astrologia Elimata: Or the Key to the Whole Art of Astrology New Filed and Polished.* Kessinger Publishing, 1676

Graphical Representation of Aspects and Beholding Signs

We will display the planets' positions in degrees within the current sign on a 30-degree ruler (Fig. 2.14). This ruler will help you determine if there is a close aspect between the planets. For example, in the illustration below, the Moon is visually close to the Sun—the distance between them is less than 3 degrees.

The Sun is at 7° Virgo, which means its aspects are in:

- 7° Pisces (opposition)

Chapter 2. Horary Astrology

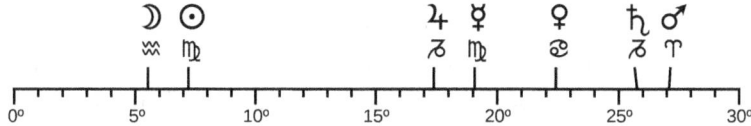

Figure 2.14: *Aspect's Ruler*

- 7° Taurus and 7° Capricorn (trines)
- 7° Gemini and 7° Sagittarius (squares)
- 7° Cancer and 7° Scorpio (sextiles)

As you can see, the Moon at 5.5° Aquarius doesn't fall into the signs of the Sun's aspects, meaning the Moon cannot be within the Sun's orb and form a close aspect with it. We interpret this as:

- The Moon doesn't behold the Sun.
- The Moon is in a non-beholding sign.
- Virgo and Aquarius do not behold each other.

Another aspect in the picture above, between Jupiter and Mercury, is entirely possible. The two planets are close to each other—within 3 degrees—and in beholding signs. Capricorn and Virgo belong to the earth element, meaning there is a 120-degree angle between them.

Thus, Jupiter and Mercury form a close trine.

Aspects on the Borders of Non-Beholding Signs

Take note of aspects occurring on the border of signs. For instance, the Moon is at 29° Cancer, while the aspect or bodily position of the Sun is at 1° Leo. Despite Cancer and Leo not beholding each other, the Moon still falls within the Sun's sphere of influence.

The condition of the Sun (or its aspect) in Cancer differs from the one in Leo. Signs alter the planet's state but do not deny the orb of influence. In other words, the Sun or its aspect at 1° Leo extends its influence over the 30th and 29th degrees of Cancer within its orb.

However, one should approach such aspects with special attention. Context is crucial here.

In horary astrology, a planet's transition into a new sign often signifies a change in circumstances. In our example, the Moon at 29° Cancer is the Moon changing the sign. We interpret this as "when the Moon enters Leo, it will begin to experience the close influence of the Sun."

Suppose the Sun represents a man, the Moon represents the querent, and the Moon's transition to a new sign signifies a move to another city. In this case, we would say, "Once you move to another city, you will immediately engage in a romance with a man." Until then, the sign border is like the distance between cities, preventing the Sun from influencing the Moon.

In most cases, sign borders will manifest in this way.

However, there may be exceptions if the context supports a different interpretation of planets on the sign borders. For example, Saturn is at 29° Cancer and moving backward toward decreasing signs (we will discuss retrograde motion later), and Mars has just entered Leo. Saturn represents the husband, and Mars represents the wife. We know that the two decided to take a break in their relationship—the husband returned to the city where he spent his childhood. The wife moved temporarily to her mother's place.

The planetary positions perfectly reflect the context of the actual situation. The close conjunction of the Sun and Saturn across sign borders indicates that there is still a close connection between the two. However, as the planets move in opposite directions, their distance increases and the connection will break soon. These two will shortly decide to get a divorce. As you can see, we considered close conjunction on the sign borders since the context supported such a judgment. However, the cases like that are more of an exception.

In most cases, you will encounter the first scenario where the sign border prevents one planet from influencing another until current circumstances change (shown by one of the planets entering a new sign).

Homework Assignment №11

It is an actual chart (Fig. 2.15). We will revisit it several times in this book as we explore new techniques to uncover additional details. However, let's begin with the main question.

Chapter 2. Horary Astrology

Querent is considering buying a house. However, there's a suspicious detail. The house is very nice, while the price is considerably low. Finally, this house has been on the market for several years. Querent suspects that something may be wrong with that house, and this purchase could lead to further expenses.

Answer the following questions based on the chart:

- Which planet represents the house, and which one represents the querent's wallet?
- Is the house as good as the querent claims?

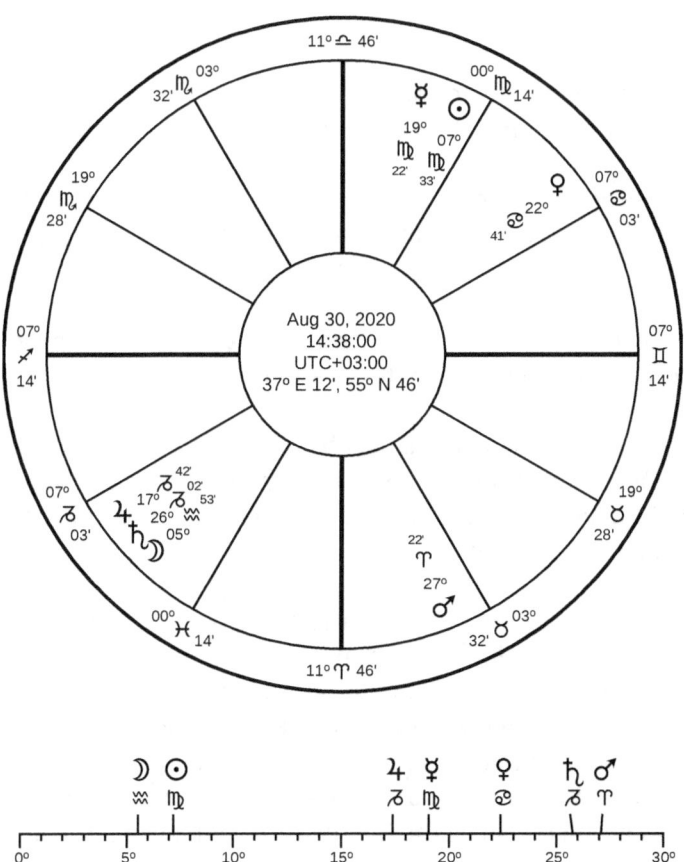

Figure 2.15: *Chart: What Will Happen If I Buy That House?*

- Consider the current reception between these planets as if the house were already in the client's hands, as if you envisioned the future. Does this house indeed pose a threat to the wallet?
- Now, consider the close aspect between the querent and the house. How does this aspect alter the reception (the house's impact on the wallet)—does it mitigate or worsen it?
- Give a final answer. Will the house purchase bring additional expenses/financial loss, or is it financially secure for the querent?

Solution

The ruler of the 4th house, Mars, signifies real estate. The ruler of the 2nd house, Saturn, indicates finances.

Mars is in its domicile. Yes, the house is indeed good, as the querent says. The chart clearly reflects reality. The more precise the correspondence with reality, the more transparent the chart's picture of the future.

Mars receives Saturn in its detriment, indicating that the house, were it to be purchased, would harm the querent's wallet.

Now, let's consider the close aspect between the planets. The square aspect of Mars removes all the positive qualities of Mars, making it almost neutral in the degree it falls. On the other hand, it falls in Capricorn, the place of Mars' exaltation.

However, this miniature "copy" of the exalted Mars is much less noble than the bodily position of Mars in its domicile. In other words, Mars would act more nobly without modification by the aspect—its detrimental reception would be gentler without this aspect. The close square aspect intensifies the negative impact of the house (if it were purchased) on the querent's wallet. Once again, we see a familiar pattern—a close unfavorable aspect makes the hostile reception even more adverse.

Our conclusion is this: purchasing this house (if it happens) will bring additional expenses or financial losses to the querent.

Event Prediction Techniques: Exact Aspects Perfection

Exact Aspects and Events

Exact aspects occur when a faster planet transits through an aspect of a slower one. Exact aspects act like triggers, compelling planets to momentarily release their potential into action according to their current roles, motives, and conditions.

But, as always, the final word belongs to the context. It can override the aspect's effect. So, it's correct to say that exact aspects create circumstances at the moment for two objects to collide, that is, for an event (see the section "Event Prediction Techniques: Exact Aspects").

For instance, let's say a girl plans to go on a date and asks if it will happen. You see an applying sextile between her and her admirer, and your initial thought is to say, "Yes, the date will happen." As planned, both individuals are expected to arrive by metro at the designated place on the appointed day. If it were an applying conjunction with more power to create events (see the section "The Strength of Close Aspects"), the circumstances would further favor the meeting—perhaps they wouldn't have to travel far since they live nearby, and simply walking to the cafe across the street would be enough.

But suddenly, you notice that her suitor's planet enters a terrible condition shortly before the exact aspect's perfection—it goes into the sign of its detriment, ruled by the lord of the 12th house, indicating a serious illness.

The weakest of aspects, the sextile, is unlikely to create suitable conditions and bring the two heroes together if one of them is seriously ill. For the suitor to overcome his illness and go on a date, he must either have a strong immune system or a strong motivation:

- For example, you see that his planet has exceptional accidental strength (we'll discuss planetary strength later in this book). This means the illness won't be strong enough to keep him in bed.
- Or you may see that his planet exalts the girl's planet. This indicates that his desire for the meeting is so great that he will get out of bed in any condition just to see his beloved.

- Or you might see a converging conjunction—circumstances themselves will so favor the meeting that he won't have to make much effort to reach the meeting place.

If we see one, let alone several, such facilitating factors, we would say that the illness won't hinder the date.

In most cases, the aspect brings events to actualization unequivocally. For example, if you're expecting a DHL package delivery, you don't need to look for a courier's special strength or their particular desire to deliver the package to you. Even if an individual courier falls ill, the company will find a replacement. In this context, the presence of the aspect is equivalent to the occurrence of the event—your package being handed to you.

All we care about is whether the aspect will happen or not—whether DHL will manage to deliver your package today or if there are no suitable circumstances, i.e., a delay in the logistic chain.

So, here's the rule: If, according to the context you know or the one you discover on the charts, some special conditions (special desire for a meeting or special strength of aspecting planets to overcome obstacles) are needed for the event to occur, consider these conditions along with the aspect.

Type of Aspect & Event

You already know that reception and celestial state contribute to the final effect of planetary aspect. But that's not all—the aspect type (trine, square, etc.) also shapes the influence the aspect on other significators:

- Unfavorable type (square & opposition) weakens the positive influence of the aspect and strengthens its malevolent effect.
- Favorable type (trine & sextile) does the opposite—it mitigates the negative impact of the aspect and amplifies the positive.

The same logic applies to the exact aspects that trigger events. First, we predict a positive or negative event by primarily looking at the celestial state and reception of significators in the aspect.

For example, suppose the querent's significator meets the dignified ruler of the 10th house. In that case, the prominent company will invite the querent for an interview. Moreover, suppose the ruler of the 10th is favorable towards the querent by reception, and the querent is in a good state (capable of handling the proposed job). In that case, we expect a job offer from such an aspect.

On the contrary, if in a safety-related query, the querent's significator encounters the debilitated ruler of the 7th, who harms the querent by reception, we expect an attack from enemies.

The aspect's type modifies this influence. Suppose the querent's employment happens on a trine. In that case, it enhances the positive effect of the particular job's facet (aspect)—the querent will get the job after the first interview. If the meeting occurs on a square, the querent will still be offered a position, but not as smoothly as in the case of a trine. Perhaps they'll need to undergo several interviews, complete stress tolerance tests, etc.

The most powerful aspect is the opposition, possessing strength similar to conjunction. Therefore, unlike other aspects, the opposition can dissipate the positive effect of the job's significator, for instance, the querent will get the job, but:

- As responsibilities increase, the querent will not be able to cope (all the good qualities of that position will dissipate).
- A company that was a market leader soon becomes bankrupt or turns out to be not as good as it seemed at the time of employment (again, opposition "compensates" all the good traits that the aspect of employment gave to a querent).

In the example of an attack from open enemies, the attack will bring harm regardless of the form of aspect, just because of its nature. If the attack happens on a trine, the querent receives fewer injuries, and the fight is brief. In the case of a square, the harm is more significant. An opposition aspect signifies an attack with potentially life-threatening consequences.

Applying and Separating Aspects

The exact aspect will yet to occur when the faster planet approaches the aspect's place of the slower one. When it reaches that place at some zodiac degree, two planets perform an exact aspect. A moment later, the quicker planet will start to separate from that degree.

Suppose the chart shows that the faster significator is approaching the aspect of the slower one. This means the event will occur in the future. We call the faster planet *the applying planet* in aspect, and the upcoming contact—an *applying aspect*.

If you see that two significators separate from each other, we say that the event has already occurred in the past. In this case, the faster planet is called the *separating* one.

There are often questions about past events, like "Is this person alive?" or "Who is the father of this child?" (see example on page 181) and similar ones.

Aspects Within Signs and Context of the Question

We mentioned earlier (see the section "Aspects on the Borders of Non-Beholding Signs") that a planet changing signs in horary astrology is equivalent to a change in circumstances. Since we make predictions about the development of a situation in a specific context, we look at the exact aspects that planets perform within the signs they are in.

For example, in the question "Will I get a job this year?" you see that the querent (ruler of the 1st or the Moon) forms an aspect with the ruler of the 10th house (work) in 20 degrees. Suppose the faster planet needs 12 degrees to enter a new sign and pass another 8 degrees before it performs the exact aspect. The sign's boundary denotes a significant change in context, which we are unaware of.

It could be a new decision of the querent to start their business instead of searching for a job or something else. Whatever it is, the answer remains the same—"No, you won't find a new job this year."

Exceptions occur when the aspect happens at the very beginning of an adjacent sign (within a few degrees from the boundary). In this case, the chart indicates that getting a job this year is possible only in new circumstances.

For instance, "Yes, you'll find a job if you move to another city," or "Yes, but only if you stop looking for office jobs and switch to searching for remote work." Typically, the ruler of the new sign indicates new circumstances.

Chapter 2. Horary Astrology

Let's assume the sign's dispositor is the lord of the 9th house, representing distant territories or foreigners. The context is that the querent is only looking for jobs in local companies and has no intention of moving anywhere. In these conditions, they won't find a job this year. It would be foolish to discuss options for moving abroad if we know the querent has no plans to leave their home. However, including the search for international companies might be a relevant option.

Then our answer could sound like this: "No, you won't find a job in the current circumstances. But you can look into international companies or consider the possibility of relocation."

This section's key idea is the following: we only consider exact aspects within the current signs of the planets. The exceptions are aspects that happen right beyond the boundary of the neighboring sign.

Cutting Off the Light

In horary astrology, there's a crucial rule. If a significator on its way encounters an unknown planet, it transfers its "power" to that planet. It means that from that moment on, even if the significator reaches the second planet, it won't be able to take action as it's devoid of strength.

Astrologers call such a significator "devoid of light." The moment of transferring the light to the unknown planet is called *abscissio luminis*, meaning "cutting off the light."

Suppose the querent's planet rushes to meet a friend's planet at the local pub. But on the way, the querent's planet encounters another planet that cuts off its light. While heading to the pub, the querent gets an important call and has to cancel the meeting.

Another scenario. While the friend waits at the pub for the querent's arrival, they receive an urgent work call and leave for the office. By the time the querent arrives, the friend is already caught up in pressing matters.

We say that a third planet *interposes* or *intervenes* in the matter. We also use the term *prohibition*:

– Some planet *prohibits* the aspects.
– It acts as a *prohibitor* of aspect.

As always, the context has the final voice in the prediction. As in the example from the section "Exact Aspects and Events," the prohibitor may indicate the querent's illness, preventing them from meeting with the friend on the appointed day.

But if the querent is strong or the illness is weak (we'll discuss the strength of planets later in this book), or if the planets apply in a strong conjunction that's hard to override, or if the querent desperately wants to see their friend, these factors can turn the prohibition into a simple obstacle.

With practice, you will learn to quickly combine the current context with the testimony of the chart based on common sense. The examples and homework assignments I'll provide in this book will train that skill.

Homework Assignment №12

Most computer programs dealing with horary charts display the list of aspects that planets perform within their signs. You can use the astrology software "Olga,"[6] which I created exclusively for horary forecasts or similar apps.

Table 2.10 shows future aspects of the planets. Let me remind you that we use the following symbols to denote aspects:

- ☍ —opposition
- △ —trine
- □ —square
- ✶ —sextile

For conjunction, we use the symbol ☌ .

Table 2.10: *Example of Aspects Perfection*

Date	Aspect
17.06.2023	☿ ✶ ♀
18.06.2023	☽ ☌ ☉
19.06.2023	♃ ✶ ♄
21.06.2023	☿ ✶ ♂
22.08.2023	♀ □ ♃

Looking at this table, please answer:

---
[6] https://morinus-astrology.com/horary-app/

– Is there a future aspect between Jupiter and Saturn?
– Is there a future aspect between Mercury and Mars?
– Who interferes in the aspect between Venus and Jupiter?

Solution

For the sake of simplicity, I will use the expression "planet A meets planet B," indicating that planet A performs an exact aspect or conjunction with planet B.

Nothing prohibits the aspects between Jupiter and Saturn. The first planet that Jupiter will meet on its way is Saturn itself. The first planet that Saturn will meet while waiting for Jupiter is Jupiter itself. There is no other planet that could cut off the light of the significators before their encounter.

On June 17, Mercury will meet Venus before approaching the sextile of Mars on June 21. Thus, Venus interrupts Mercury's light, and by the time Mercury reaches Mars, it is already devoid of light.

Similarly, on June 17, Venus will meet Mercury before reaching Jupiter on August 22. It means that Mercury intervenes in the matter, preventing a direct aspect between Venus and Jupiter.

Translation and Collection of Light

When an interposing planet takes the light of the first significator, it carries this light to the first planet with which it forms an aspect.

Suppose the first planet on its way is the second significator. In that case, the interposing planet acts as a messenger or intermediary. It completes the aspect by taking the light from the first significator and passing it to the second one.

Although we use traditional expressions like "cutting off light" and "translation of light," the rays of the first planet do not disappear or transfer anywhere—it continues to influence the flow of events.

When the intervening planet acts as a prohibitor, its aspect creates an obstacle to the final event we expect. For example, the ruler of the 12th house, encountering the querent's planet, creates an actual obstacle—illness—delaying or canceling the meeting. But this does not negate the desire of both parties to meet—the rays of the significators continue to urge the two people toward an encounter.

When the intervening planet acts as an intermediary, it sets strictly defined conditions for the encounter of the two significators—it initiates the meeting process and concludes it, preventing the two objects from interacting in any way other than through its mediation. This does not negate the action of the significators' rays—they still urge the two parties toward a meeting.

For instance, in a question about the birth of a child, the Moon transfers the light from the ruler of the 5th house (future child) to the querent. In the first aspect, it creates pregnancy, and in the concluding aspect, it triggers childbirth. The Moon here will show special conditions for conception that will subsequently lead to the birth of a child, such as IVF procedure. Meanwhile, the action of the 1st and 5th house significators remains active—they influence the natural processes of fetal development and childbirth, but realize the fact of the mother meeting her child through the Moon.

> **N.B. on transit charts**
>
> It is essential to understand that aspects in a horary chart indicate moments when the necessary conditions for events will occur. Suppose the Moon has 6 degrees left to the first aspect (pregnancy) and another 9 to the second (childbirth). In that case, the actual time the Moon will need to advance by 13 degrees and complete the translation of light is 27 hours. It does not mean that a woman who has not even become pregnant will give birth tomorrow. It shows that a celestial configuration will occur in six months, causing pregnancy, and another nine months later, the birth will occur. The planetary alignment that will trigger the birth of a child in the future is called a *transit chart*—we have discussed this in the section "How The Stars Affect Us."

It may happen that at the time of the question, the Moon has already taken the child's light—it separates from the ruler of the 5th house and applies to the querent's planet—the girl is already pregnant by the time of the question, and we see the approaching birth of a child.

So, the rule is this: if the intervening planet cuts off the light of the significator, look at the first planet it applies to or the one it has just separated. If it's the second significator, we have the translation of light. Otherwise, it's a prohibition.

If the intervening planet is slower than the significators, we say "collection of light" instead of "translation of light." It's just terminology; it doesn't affect the judgment.

As always, the context has the final voice in aspects. Take, for example, a question about the birth of a child. We see that in the first aspect, the Moon sets the conditions for birth—pregnancy. But suppose the Moon is in a barren sign, and its dispositor is debilitated. If, in addition, the Moon afflicts the ruler of the 5th house by a reception and applies to it by a square, we are unlikely to expect an easy conception. Suppose, in addition to what we said, the significator of the querent, her baby, and her spouse are in barren signs. In that case, we are unlikely to expect conception at all.

Now, consider the opposite situation. The woman asking the question is not young. But theoretically, she can still conceive a child. The main significators of the chart (querent, Moon, her spouse, and child) are in fertile signs. Moreover, the Moon is noble, in the dignities of Jupiter—the universal ruler of fertility—favorable to the ruler of the 5th house by reception and applies to it by a favorable trine. Suppose we also know that the querent takes care of her health. Then, we will confidently predict the onset of pregnancy and the future birth of a child, regardless of the querent's age.

Homework Assignment №13

Please review Tables 2.11 and 2.12 of past and future aspects and answer the following questions:

- Is there a transfer of light between Venus and Mars?
- Is there an aspect (direct or through an intermediary) between Saturn and Jupiter?
- Suppose the Sun is your friend, who wants to buy the house, and Mars is the seller. Will your friend buy this house?

Table 2.11: *Example of Past Aspects*

Date	Aspect
28.05.2023	☉ □ ♄
11.06.2023	♀ □ ♃
15.06.2023	☿ □ ♄
16.06.2023	☽ ✶ ♀
17.06.2023	☽ ✶ ♂

Table 2.12: *Example of Future Aspects*

Date	Aspect
17.06.2023	☿ ✶ ♀
18.06.2023	☽ ☌ ☉
19.06.2023	♃ ✶ ♄
21.06.2023	☿ ✶ ♂
22.08.2023	♀ □ ♃

Solution

The first aspect that occurs with one of the significators in the future is the meeting of Venus with the third planet, Mercury, on June 17. We must understand what Mercury is doing—whether it prohibits the aspect or acts as a mediator.

First, let's see if Mercury carries the light of the second significator, Mars, which it took in the past. The last aspect Mercury made in the past was the aspect with Saturn on June 15. So, Mercury carries the light of Saturn, not Mars. That is not what we need.

Then, let's look at it differently. Mercury takes the light of Venus and carries it to the first planet in its way. Who will Mercury encounter in the future? Mercury will meet Mars on June 21. Therefore, Mercury takes the light of Venus and transfers it to Mars. It is a typical translation of light.

Next question. The first aspect that occurs with one of the significators is the aspect of Saturn and Jupiter—a meeting of two significators with each other. It is a direct aspect without the involvement of an intermediary.

Finally, the Moon carries the light from Mars to the Sun. It has already taken the light from Mars on June 17 and is bringing it to the Sun. Yes, the friend will be able to sell the house, but with the help of an intermediary. And they have already found this intermediary.

Chapter 2. Horary Astrology

N.B.

From now on, I assume you will be using computer programs available on the market to calculate the translation and collection of light. It will allow you to spend your valuable time on something other than routine calculations.

Planetary Movements

Only two luminaries—the Moon and the Sun—consistently move in the order signs. Other planets, however, make so-called "loops." They move in the order of signs, then stop, and for a while, move backward (against the order of signs). They then stop again and resume direct movement.

This apparent effect is caused by the circular movement of the planets around the Sun, which we observe from the Earth. At the same time, the Earth also rotates around the Sun.

When a planet moves in order signs, we call it *direct motion*, indicating the ordinary flow of events. When a planet moves against the order of signs, we call this *retrograde motion*.

A retrograde planet can have several meanings, depending on context:

- Someone or something returns to its original place, state, or circumstances.
- Something decreases in quantity.
- If the significator indicates a process, it doesn't go as it should (against its natural course) or will not be completed.

When a planet changes its direction and speed is near zero, we say it is *stationary*. If a planet turns from direct to retrograde, it is the *first station*. If it turns from retrograde to direct, it is the *second station*.

A stationary planet can have different meanings depending on the context:

- An object is immobile (it could be an immovable body, an unsellable item, a wall that is hard to break, or a heavy item that is difficult to move).

- An object loses its ability to act; it is weak (for example, a business where sales have stopped).
- An object changes the direction of its movement (for example, a student changes their mind about leaving the university and decides to return).

For example, a situation may arise where two significators have an applying aspect. At the last moment, one of the significators changes direction and starts moving away from the other. This kind of prohibition is called *refranation*. For instance, the querent is about to get a job. Their planet applies to the ruler of the 10th house, but shortly before the aspect's perfection, it stops and goes backward. At the last moment, the querent decides it's not their dream job and doesn't attend the interview.

A significator often enters a new sign and immediately gets stationary. As you remember, the entry or *ingress* into a new sign signifies a change in circumstances.

For example, the querent enters a sign of its exile and immediately gets stationary. The querent moves to a crime-ridden area where it's unsafe to go outside, so they spend whole days at home. Or, in another context, they move to a country where they feel incredibly uncomfortable and decide to return home.

As usual, we pick the more suitable interpretation that fits the context.

Homework Assignment №14

Let's return to the chart from the section "Homework Assignment №11" (buying a house). This time I'll display letters *R* and *S* next to planets to indicate retrograde movements and stations (Fig. 2.16):

Answer the following questions:

- What does the station of Mars signify?
- What does Jupiter's retrograde movement signify?
- What does Saturn's retrograde movement signify?

Chapter 2. Horary Astrology

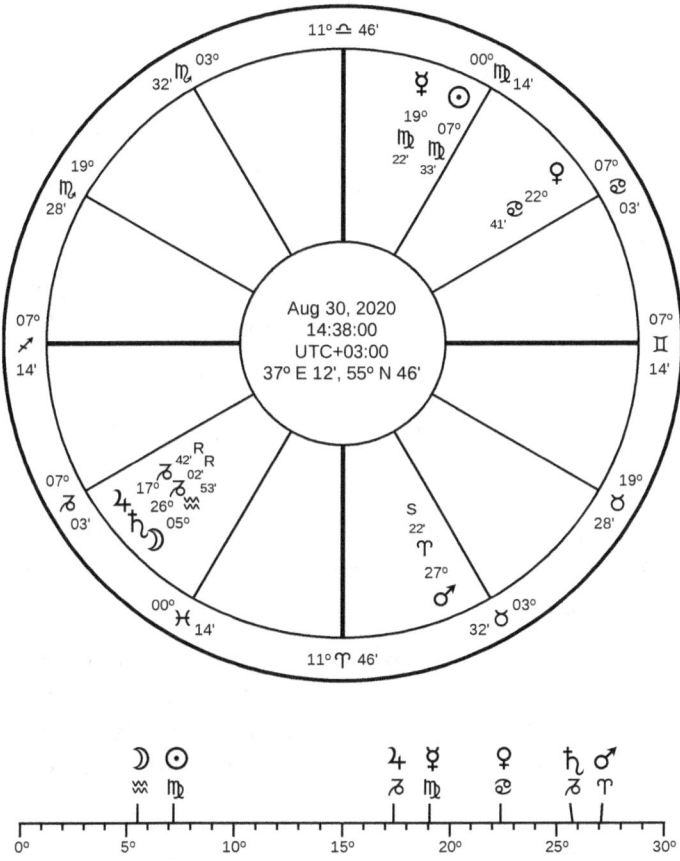

Figure 2.16: *Buying the House: Chart with Planetary Speeds*

Solution

Mars signifies the house. As you recall, this house has been unsellable for several years. At the same time, Mars is stationary. It vividly illustrates the illiquidity of the house. The chart reflects reality.

Jupiter signifies the querent. There are several ways to interpret its retrograde motion:

– The querent returns to the original state (e.g., returning home or following a diet to retrieve the previous shape).

Predictive Astrology Textbook

- The querent returns to dealing with house purchases (meaning they have tried to buy this or another house before).
- The querent decreases in quantity.

The first option is irrelevant to the context. The third option is biologically impossible. The only fitting option in this context is that it was not the first attempt to buy a house. And, indeed, the querent had just been considering other real estate options.

Saturn signifies the querent's money. We have already seen that purchasing the house will cause extra spending of the querent's money.

The retrograde motion of Saturn can mean one of the following:

- Money moves to the original state, but they have no original state.
- Money returns to the original situation, but this phrase lacks common sense.
- Money decreases in quantity. It is a clear sign of additional expenses in the context. It answers the main question "Will there be additional expenses if I buy that house?"

As you can see, the chart has shown us the answer in different ways. As I mentioned in the section "Homework Assignment №8" on page 82, it is normal for the chart to reveal the answer through different testimonies. You also saw in practice that making the right choice based on common sense is easy.

Homework Assignment №15

An Indian man asked me if he could leave the job he hates and move to another country for a new job and life. By default, we give the querent the 1st house ruler, Mars, and the Moon, which shows their emotional state.

Look at the chart (Fig. 2.17) and answer the following questions.

Question 1: Mars was in retrograde motion all this time, but it is turning to direct motion on the cusp of a sign. What does the stationarity of Mars mean?

Question 2: Mars would move further and cross the sign boundary if it were retrograde without a station. In the context of the question, a new sign means a new life in a new country. Look at the state of Mars in a

Chapter 2. Horary Astrology

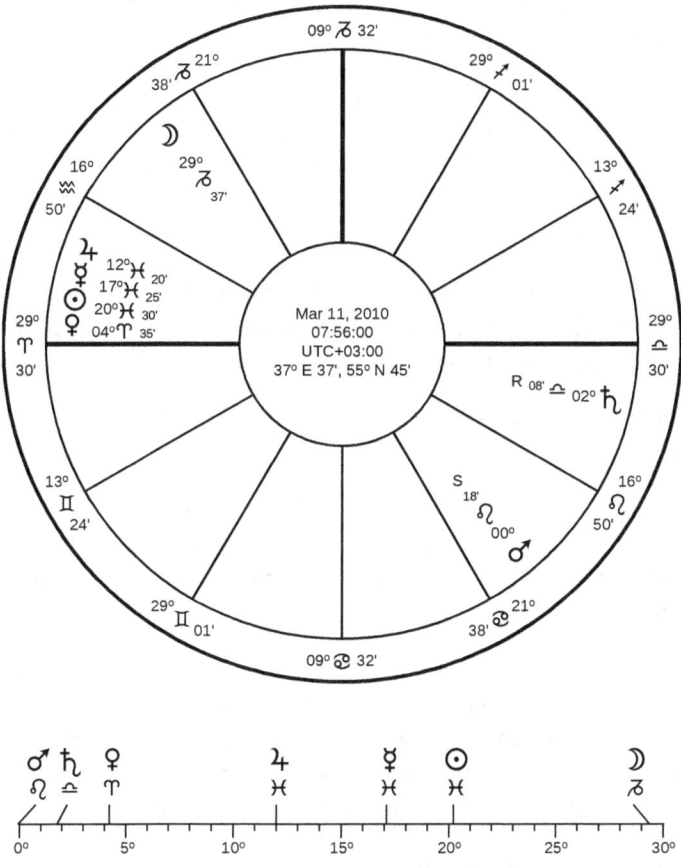

Figure 2.17: *Chart: Moving Abroad*

new sign and answer how the querent would live in a new country. Also, look at whose dignity Mars would fall into and how it reflects reality.

Question 3: In this chart, we have a rather interesting situation. Only the last degree of the sign occupies the 1st house. On the other hand, the next sign, Taurus, is entirely contained within the 1st house. It means that although the 1st house maximally determines the last degree of Aries, which makes Mars the house's primary ruler, this determination is not as strong as if a significant part of Aries were in the 1st house.

On the other hand, all 30 degrees of Taurus are determined to show the querent. It means that the ruler of Taurus and the co-ruler of the 1st house, Venus, shows the querent no less effectively than Mars. For this reason, I suggest including Venus in the analysis.

So, both Mars and Venus show the querent. We expect well-balanced charts to show the same picture in different ways. See what Mars and Venus have in common in their motives. Use reception and knowledge of the context. What is the same object they love or hate so much? Does it reflect the real context?

Question 4: Look at the querent's emotional state—their Moon. How does it feel? If it feels suppressed, who or what is the cause of this state? Look at the Moon's dispositors to answer this question.

Question 5: The last aspect that Venus made was an opposition to Saturn. What does it mean?

Question 6: The Moon changes sign—this speaks more of a change in emotional state than a change in circumstances. How will the Moon feel in the new sign? What will change in the reception of the Moon when it enters the new sign?

Question 7: We see notable dynamics between the querent and Saturn. Venus (the querent) separates from the opposition to Saturn. It is still in close opposition at the moment, but shortly, the close opposition will be gone. At the same time, once the Moon (the querent) enters a new sign, it will meet Saturn by trine. What does it mean?

Question 8: What would you say about the querent's future regarding leaving this job and moving to a new country?

Solution

Question 1: Mars (the querent) is about to change signs, representing a change in life circumstances—he is about to leave his job and move to a new country. But at the last moment, the querent stops and changes direction. He returns to the sign he was about to leave. It means that the querent will soon change his mind. We already have the main answer from the first approach.

Question 2: If Mars had moved further, it would have entered Cancer—a place of its exile and the strong dignities of Jupiter, the ruler of the 9th house. The 9th house shows foreign countries.

Chapter 2. Horary Astrology

The chart literally indicates that if the querent had not changed his mind, he would have found himself in exile in the new country, in the difficult position of an emigrant.

Question 3: Mars and Venus have the same object of love—the Sun. But the Sun does not rule any of the significant houses. On the other hand, both planets hate Saturn, the ruler of the querent's work. The querent himself admitted that he hates his job. It fully corresponds to the context.

Question 4: The Moon feels highly depressed in the sign of Capricorn. It is in the strong dignity of Saturn (work). The Moon feels bad under the power of Saturn—the querent feels terrible while he is at this job.

Question 5: We remember that opposition is the strongest and most destructive aspect. Venus, full of hate for Saturn, opposing it, is the querent, who enters into a confrontation with his boss. Opposition often means a quarrel or conflict.

Note that shortly before the opposition aspect, Venus was in the sign of its exaltation and felt great. The opposition with the boss and strong negative feelings came almost simultaneously. Yes, the querent recently had a major quarrel with the management. It is logical to assume that this conflict triggered the querent to turn to an astrologer.

Question 6: The Moon enters a new sign, ceasing to be in exile. The Moon feels much better in Aquarius. But note that the Moon enters Saturn's sign and feels better there. At this point of judgment, we contradict our previous answer to the 4th question.

The Moon cannot feel bad because of Saturn and improve its state in connection to the same Saturn. So, something else has changed in the Moon's receptions that we haven't noticed before.

In Capricorn, the Moon was in the power of Mars, while in Aquarius, Mars has no power over the Moon. Who is Mars? It is the querent himself, his rational part, firmly determined to move to a new country—Mars is on the very border of signs, ready to enter the dignities of Jupiter, another country. Under the power of such Mars, the Moon is the querent's emotions, which follow his sudden decision to leave familiar places.

But why does the Moon feel so bad about leaving work? Maybe the querent is simply afraid of moving to a new place? Let's check. The Moon in Capricorn is in the place of Jupiter's fall—it sees all the worst that can be in Jupiter through a magnifying glass and rejects it. And Jupiter is the ruler of the 9th house, foreign countries. Yes, emotionally, the querent already anticipates the life of an emigrant, which he does not want to face in any way, and that is why he feels depressed.

As we can see, when the Moon leaves Capricorn, it simultaneously:

- Stops following the sudden decision to leave the country
- Stops feeling the approach of the hard life of a migrant
- It starts to feel much better

All this happens simultaneously with Mars changing its mind about leaving the country and this job. As you see, the chart shows the same picture again and again in different ways.

Question 7: Immediately after that, the Moon makes a favorable aspect with Saturn. It literally means returning to the old job, specifically reconciliation with the boss. All this happens simultaneously with the change of decision to leave the job and move to a new country and is accompanied by emotional improvement.

Question 8: We could answer, "You will change your mind about leaving your job." Instead, we will say, "You don't want to leave your job—you just recently had a conflict with your boss. Soon, your resentment will pass, and you will change your mind about moving to a new country, especially since this move scares you. And for good reason. After all, if you had left, you would have indeed found yourself in a difficult position as an emigrant." That is an example of a sweet and clear prediction.

We often predict the future choices that people have yet to make. As I said, many (but not all) of our decisions are already predetermined.

Descriptive Techniques: the Fixed Stars

You've probably heard of the constellations. It is a group of stars united by similar influences on the visible flow of events. This influence is usually wrapped in the form of legends.

Do not confuse constellations and zodiac signs—they are fundamentally different things. For example, there is the constellation of Ophiuchus, but there is no 13th sign of Ophiuchus. The legends express the essence of fixed stars.

Chapter 2. Horary Astrology

If you take any legend structure, it has a hero who overcomes some difficulties and gains or loses something. The sequence of different battles and results makes up the storyline. The hidden morality of any legend is in between the lines in each scene. Through illustrative examples, the tale shows that this action is right when it leads to gain or wrong when it leads to loss.

Usually, the constellation figure does not show the entire legend but just one scene. Depending on where the fixed star is on the figure, the scene narrows down to a specific action and result.

For example, the star is on the hand. See what the constellation figure does with its hands within the scene—take, give, hold, kill, or heal. The star is on the mouth—what the figure says or shouts at and what it causes.

Hence, you understand the meaning of the star—it is the result of a particular action. If the star is in the center of a figure, look at the whole scene for the final result.

Let's take an example of the star, Antares. This star appears in two legends. According to one of them, the tremendous mortal Phaethon, who decided to equate himself with the gods, stole the chariot of Helios. But he could not cope with the power he received. The Gods then sent a scorpion to stop the arrogant mortal.

According to the second legend, the fabulous hunter Orion equated himself with the gods after a series of brilliant victories. But the gods were angry with the arrogant mortal and sent a scorpion to defeat him.

Both Phaeton and Orion have several scenes in their legends. Moreover, an entire constellation is dedicated to Orion. But we will focus only on one stage of these legends—the final battle between the scorpion and the arrogant mortal. The constellation Scorpio with Antares star in the center focuses on this scene. According to legend, the scorpion hurts Orion or Phaeton, and the great mortal dies.

Let's see which part of Scorpio the star Antares is in. It is right in the center of the constellation. It is called *Cor Scorpionis* in Latin—the scorpion's heart. If the star is in the center of the figure, then we need to see what Scorpio did in this scene and what its task was.

Scorpio destroyed the period of the reign of the great mortal, whose greatness equated with the Gods. Scorpio interrupts the cycle of rulership. And this is what Cor Scorpionis or Antares does. It is a destructive star of the nature of Mars. So, the main result that Antares brings is the completion of glory and reign.

How do we read this in the context of the question? A fixed star produces an effect when it:

- Conjuncts with the significator or the corresponding house cusp within 1 degree
- Fits the context of the question

For example, will my company survive this crisis? The ruler or the cusp of the 10th house conjuncts with Antares. No, this is the end of the company. In the divorce process, you received a question "Will we be able to save the family?" The family's significator conjuncts with Antares. No, you will divorce.

I will not list the meaning of each star. With this algorithm, you can now derive the meaning of any star. I will only give a short explanation of the six more stars with their positions for 2024 that you will need in practice in Table 2.13.

Table 2.13: *Major Fixed Stars*

Name	Notation	Position	Meaning
Regulus	α Leo	0° ♍	Gives great power and social haste
Spica	α Vir	24° ♎	Gives protection
Algol	β Per	26° ♉	Means loss of head, literally or figuratively. For example, someone loses their head because of love. Or the company loses its head, i.e., the manager, because of absorption
Alcyone	η Tau	0° ♊	Brings crying and sorrow due to the loss of a loved one (usually a man)

Continued on next page

Table 2.13 — Continued from previous page

Name	Notation	Position	Meaning
Aldebaran	α Tau	9° ♊	Being opposed to Antares, Aldebaran denotes a new cycle of reign and glory. It is an excellent indicator of the recovery from the illness or the success of a startup
Antares	α Sco	9° ♐	The end of cycle
Vendimiatrix	ε Vir	10° ♎	Creates a divorce and a break in partnership

Homework Assignment №16

A real-life example. The company's CEO asked me where the head of the security department was. They told me that the head of the security department visited their parents in the village for the weekend. But they didn't return to work on Monday.

In the chart, the head of the department was in conjunction with Algol. The last aspect they performed was opposition to Mars. Mars, the ruler of the 12th house, harmed the quesited by the reception. The head of the department was in the 6th house, while the significant "copy" of it (in the place of opposition) was in the 12th house—the house of illness, i.e., in the hospital.

So we know that they are in hospital now. But what happened to them recently? Answer that question based on testimonies you have.

Solution

The head of the department is in conjunction with Algol. Algol blows off their head, literally or figuratively. We always follow the principle of Occam's Razor—the simplest explanation is the correct one. The employee might lose their head figuratively, say from love, and forget about work. But they might lose their head literally. Say, they could get some trauma of the head. It is a more straightforward explanation for their disappearance.

Their significator perfected its last aspect with Mars. As you remember, Mars stands for sharp objects, penetrations, cuts, and spilled blood. Moreover, Mars damages the quesited by the reception. It entirely correlates with our head injury hypothesis.

Combining these indications, we get the following picture. Someone or something signified by Mars (it can be a sharp object or something metallic, since Mars rules iron) has damaged the head of the quesited and caused the blood.

As universal rulership of blood in a watery sign, Mars indicates a large amount of spilled blood. Mars rules the 12th house (enemies or attacks which are not visible to the querent) and, at the same time, is a universal ruler of body penetrators and attacks. At the intersection of these meanings, it shows attacks from behind, causing blood loss. From this, we know that the strike to the head was from the back.

Putting it all together, we get a refined picture.

- Quesited received a blow to the back of the head.
- They lost a lot of blood and are now in the hospital.

That is what I told the CEO. And now, this is what happened in reality. The company's management found out at which railway station the quesited exited and was last seen.

They called the nearest hospital close to that station. Indeed, the quesited was there. As it turned out, the criminals attacked them from behind and hit them on the head with a metal crowbar. They lost a lot of blood and were in the hospital, unconscious, with no documents or mobile phone. They were later released from hospital and recovered shortly afterwards.

See how we can find a person with just a few techniques and give a complete description of recent events.

Signification Techniques: Arabian Parts

Almost any object is described by either a universal or accidental ruler. For example, in the question "Will my marriage be happy?", we must assess the state of the significator of marriage. Accidentally, the ruler of the 7th house shows marriage. Universally, Venus—the planet of love—

Chapter 2. Horary Astrology

shows it. If we have a choice, we always prefer the accidental significator, as it is more determined by houses to influence a particular object, i.e., signify a specific thing.

Suppose we need to separate the marriage from the partner, and the 7th house is ruled by Venus and has no alternative rulers. How can we find the significator of marriage in this case?

The technique of Arabian Parts comes to the rescue.

In this technique, you calculate the arc's length from the relevant house cusp (or the planet). The end of this arc falls into a particular sign, and the ruler of this sign is the significator of the thing in question.

The following formula calculates the arc length: the position of planet A (in degrees) minus the position of planet B (in degrees).

The degree of the zodiacal circle where the arc ends is called the *Arabian Part*. The ruler of that sign—the dispositor of the Arabian Part—is an alternative accidental significator of the object.

Here is an example of the Arabian *Part of surgery*: ASC + Saturn – Mars. It means taking the distance from Saturn to Mars and plotting it from the ASC.

The logic behind this formula lies in selecting appropriate universal significators. Suppose a few hours after you cast the chart, Mars rises on the horizon of your city.

- Mars universally has several meanings: it can signify aggression, burns, cuts, etc.
- Saturn serves as the universal symbol for boundaries, including those of the body.

At the moment of Mars' ascension, you can read other planets, including Saturn, relative to Mars, since Mars dominates the whole chart by being on the ASC. From that perspective, Saturn represents the body's boundary relative to Mars, a natural significator of bodily penetration. At the moment of Mars' (i.e., the operation's) dominance—when it rises and governs the chart—Saturn's position (relative to the local horizon) indicates the position of the body being operated on.

Return to the horary chart and look at that point (relative to the local horizon). It is where Saturn will shortly fall when Mars rises (i.e., when the chart reflects the moment of the surgery happening). This point acts as a precursor to the body being operated on when the time comes for surgery. The same logic applies to other Arabian Parts.

Since we cannot match the external object to an empty zodiac degree, we take a dispositor of the Arabian Part as the significator of that object. However, the dispositor of the Arabian Part holds minimal significance, and we only use it when more suitable significators are unavailable.

For instance, the part of Surgery may fall at 15° Libra, meaning the surgery, whose essence is to penetrate the body, is signified by Venus. But Venus—the planet of love and union—is diverse and much less suitable for that role than Mars. Therefore, we will first prefer Mars as the natural significator of the operation, and only if Mars is unavailable (assigned to another quesited), then we will choose Venus—the dispositor of Part of Surgery.

Here are some examples of formulas for calculating Arabian Parts:

- Saturn + Jupiter − Sun. Saturn represents exiles, the Sun represents publicity, and Jupiter represents noble social status. One can interpret this part as "a social rank at the moment of public exile." It is the Arabian Part of dismissal.
- ASC + DSC − Venus. This part can be interpreted as "the partner (descendant) at the moment of love (Venus) manifestation." It is a part of marriage.
- ASC + DSC − Mars. It has the opposite meaning: the partner at the moment of conflict. It is a part of divorce.

Some of the Arabian Parts are reversed. The last two items in the formula change their places in the night-time charts. For instance, the part of surgery is reversed:

- ASC + Saturn − Mars (in the day-time charts)
- ASC + Mars − Saturn (in the night-time charts)

N.B.

By default, the Arabian Parts show objects in the querent's life. But if the question concerns someone else, the astrologer must apply the formula to the corresponding house cusp. For example, the part of surgery is ASC + Saturn − Mars. The ASC here shows the querent. But if the question is about the querent's son's operation, you need to postpone the arc from the cusp of the 5th house and use the formula: the 5th house cusp + Saturn − Mars. The same logic applies to the rest.

I will only list some of the Arabian Parts—you can find hundreds of them on the Internet. Instead, I will focus on the most important Arabian Part—the *Part of Fortune*. We will use the ⊗ symbol to denote it.

The formula for ⊗ is ASC + Moon − Sun. Suppose you use the Moon as the significator of the flow of events and the Sun as the significator of gold/recognition. In that case, the formula of the Part of Fortune represents (favorable) circumstances at the moment when riches and recognition manifest themselves. That is why it is called Fortune.

You can see that even Lilly often used this part to assess the querent's financial state. But as John Frawley[7] rightly pointed out, this point can indicate the querent's deepest desires. It is a brilliant and logical idea.

Indeed, the Moon shows all the hidden things, and the Sun shows everything notable. The Moon has precise universal meanings regarding the querent themselves. The Moon shows their emotions and desires.

From that perspective, the Part of Fortune is the place (relative to the horizon) where the Moon will shortly appear when the Sun ascends (i.e., when all the hidden things will become notable). The formula ASC + Moon − Sun reveals the deep motives of the querent, which shortly become visible.

Indeed, experience confirms that John Frawley was absolutely right. For example, a girl asks about a romantic relationship with a particular man. Still, the Part of Fortune is in the fifth house. Somewhere deep down, she wants a child from that man.

We have already talked earlier in the section "The Special Role of the Moon in Horary Astrology" about the special significance of the Moon in the horary chart. Part of Fortune is a lunar Arabian Part. Here, the Moon precedes the Sun. Therefore, we will always use this point when assessing the querent's deep desires. At the same time, we will use the

---

[7] J. Frawley. *The Horary Textbook*. Apprentice Books, 2005

rest of the Arabian Parts only occasionally when we cannot find a more suitable significator.

> **N.B.**
>
> In ancient books, you may see that some astrologers used the reversed formula for Part of Fortune. In contrast, others only used the daytime formula. Experience proves that the daytime formula should always be applied at any time.

Example №2: Part of Fortune

Let's revisit the previous chart regarding the Indian man considering leaving his job and relocating to another country (Fig. 2.17 on page 129). We will manually compute the Parts of Fortune and define the querent's deep concerns.

Let me recap the narrative: The querent recently had a conflict with his boss and has an emotionally charged desire to quit his job and embark on a new chapter in a different country. However, the possibility of leaving familiar places scared him.

The Moon is at 29° Capricorn or 299° of the zodiac circle, and the Sun is at 20° Pisces or 350° of the zodiac. ☽ − ☉ = 299° − 350° = −51°. The Moon-Sun arc has a negative length, but that is not a problem.

Now, let's take the ASC and add this negative number to it. The ASC is at 29° of Aries, i.e., 29° of the zodiac. 29° − 51° = −22°. If the final result is negative, just add 360° to it. So the Part of Fortune is in 360° − 22° = 338° of zodiac or 8° Pisces.

On the one hand, its dispositor is Jupiter, the ruler of the 9th house—a foreign country—which is the deep concern in that question. On the other hand, the Part of Fortune is in the 12th house. So, this house determines the deep concern towards fears and exile.

Putting it all together, we see that the client is deeply anxious about the prospect of being an outsider in another country. It perfectly aligns with our earlier findings.

From this point forward, I will incorporate the symbol of the *Part of Fortune* ⊗ in the charts.

Timing Techniques: the Symbolic Timing in Exact Aspects

The zodiac circle has an intriguing property. The number of degrees that a planet must travel to reach the aspect of another planet corresponds to the number of cycles that the luminaries/Earth make before the arrangement of the sky becomes similar to the one we see in the horary chart.

After some time, when the luminaries/Earth have made their revolutions, the significators of the horary chart will:

- Start to rule or occupy the same houses as in the horary chart
- Pass through the places of aspect/bodily positions of the significators of the horary chart
- Pass through the cusps of significant houses of the horary chart

When the significators in their natural motion simultaneously repeat their meanings of the initial (or *radical*) horary chart in several different ways, we talk about the *transit of the planets*, which repeats the patterns of the radical chart. The chart reflecting these transits is called the *transit chart*.

In a transit chart, the planets act not as promissors of events but as momentary agents that reduce the promises of the preceding horary chart into action. Presumably, the planets create "chemical patterns" that cause active actions of a group of individuals, leading to the perfection of events, as described in the section "How The Stars Affect Us."

The number of degrees in an aspect in a horary chart indicates the number of Earth's revolutions around its axis/the Sun or the number of lunar phases that will occur before the moment of the appropriate transit.

For example, if there are 17 degrees left for Mercury to reach the aspect of Saturn in a horary chart, this could mean:

- The number of revolutions of the Earth around its axis (17 days)

- The number of planetary hours (a 1/12 fraction of day/night), corresponding roughly to 17 hours
- The number of phases of the Moon, corresponding roughly to 17 weeks
- The number of cycles of the Moon (approximately 17 months)
- The number of revolutions of the Earth around the Sun (17 years)

In 17 time units, we expect the onset of the transit that will trigger the promised event. Please note that 17 degrees is not the distance from Mercury's position to the current position of Saturn. Saturn doesn't stay in place—it moves away while Mercury approaches it. So, 17 degrees represents the distance until Mercury reaches Saturn's aspect in real-time.

The question is how to understand what time unit 1 degree stands for. We can solve it in 2 steps.

Step 1.

- Take the consequent scale of time units—minute, hour, day, week, month, and year.
- Then, select from this scale the unit that is most realistic in the context of the question.
- Time units to the left and right of the chosen one in our list will show the most optimistic (i.e., fastest) and pessimistic (i.e., slowest) period.

Example: I am expecting a package to arrive this week. My significator makes an exact aspect with it in 3 degrees. Three days fit into the context as the most realistic time. Adjacent units to 3 days are 3 hours and three weeks. Three hours is still a realistic time for delivery, though swift. Three weeks is a long time for delivery that usually takes several days. Thus, we get three intervals—three hours, three days, and three weeks.

Usually, you can quickly identify a realistic, fast, and slow intervals in the context of a question. But this is sometimes difficult to do. For example, you expect a package from China, but you have no idea how long it might take due to the coronavirus.

In this case, use **the 30-degree method**. The aspect within a sign can be 30 degrees at maximum. So the longest possible period is 30 time units.

Start iterating over periods starting from minutes. Ask yourself, "Can an event happen within 30 time units?" For example, is it realistic to deliver a parcel from China within 30 minutes? No. Can a parcel from China arrive within 30 hours via regular mail? No, this is still impossible. Can it be within 30 days? Yes, it is. Once you have found the first possible timeline, use it as an optimistic scale. In our example, the days are the fastest period. So, weeks are realistic, and months are already an extended period.

Step 2.

Once you've identified three periods (short, realistic & long), look at the house and sign the *applying planet* occupies. We have already studied the modality of signs—we apply this property now in determining the time. Use Table 2.14.

Table 2.14: *Determining Time*

Houses	Quick sign	Mutable sign	Fixed sign
1, 4, 7, 10	Realistic	Realistic	Long
1, 4, 7, 10[1]	Short	Realistic	Realistic
2, 5, 8, 11	Realistic	Realistic	Realistic
3, 6, 9, 12	Short	Realistic	Realistic

[1] If the applying planet 1) is in an angle, 2) can act, and 3) wants to meet the applied planet according to reception, angles accelerate time, as they give the planet significant power.

At the intersection of the sign and the house, you will see which period to choose. For example, choose the realistic period if the planet is in the 1st, 4th, 7th, or 10th house and a quick sign. Choose the longest period if the planet is in the 1st, 4th, 7th, or 10th house and a fixed sign.

There is an important note here. Suppose an applying planet can act—it shows a person, group, or organization. At the same time, this planet wants to meet with the applied planet by reception. And suppose this planet is powerful. In that case, we expect such a planet to accelerate the meeting with the other part in real-life situations.

We will discuss the strength of the planets further in this book, but for now, it is enough to know that if the planet is in angles (i.e., in the 1st, 4th, 7th, or 10th houses), it gains lots of power.

So, the angles of the chart point to the short time units if the angular planet can act and has motives to act (according to receptions).

N.B.

If the angular planet is weakened, for instance, when it is combust or on the South Node (we will discuss it later in the section "Accidental Strengthening: Strong Testimonies" on page 217), it loses the power it gains from being in an angle. The angular houses work as usual in that case, indicating the slow time units.

The symbolic timing has an interesting feature. Suppose an applying planet moves faster or slower than its average speed. In that case, the total time until the event occurs is slightly shortened or lengthened. We usually say this as: "The event will happen slightly earlier or later than 17 days." (see the section "Refining the Number of Time Units" for more details).

Table 2.15 defines what we consider an average speed for each planet:

Table 2.15: *Average Speeds of Planets*

Planet	Daily motion
The Moon	12° 30' – 13° 30'
Mercury	1° 00' – 1° 30'
Venus	0° 50' – 1° 10'
Mars	0° 30' – 0° 40'
Jupiter	0° 05' – 0° 10'
Saturn	0° 02' – 0° 05'

However, this feature leads to a critical limitation. If the planet gets stationary before it performs an aspect, its speed will be zero somewhere on its way. The more the slow planet deviates from its average speed, the more this delays the time until the event occurs. But we cannot say anything definitive about timing when the planet's speed becomes zero. It means the symbolic time method is not applicable if the applying planet gets stationary before it perfects the aspect.

In this case, we must use other methods for determining the time, which we will discuss later in this book. The good news is that a situation like that is rare.

Chapter 2. Horary Astrology

Real-Life Example

Let's explore this more with an example. I bought a car but am still waiting to receive it. A dealer delivers a car from another city. My question is "When will my car arrive?" (Fig. 2.18).

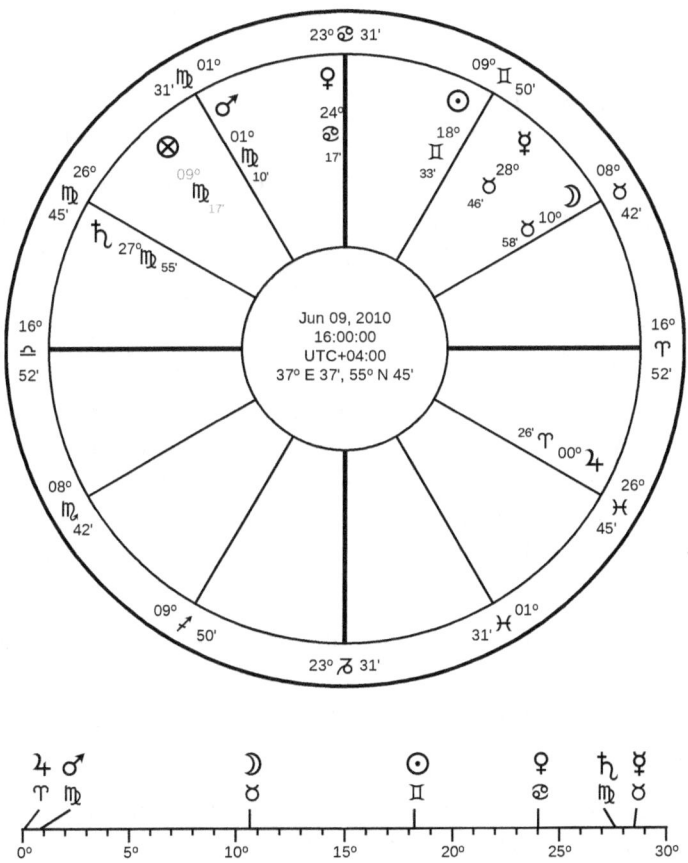

Figure 2.18: *Chart: When Will My Car Arrive?*

If the question were "What is the condition of the car I am going to buy?" I'd look at the 2nd house as if the car were already in my hands. I would see the possible future, were the car bought.

In that case, I need to see when the car goes from the dealer's possession to mine, so I'll look at the 2nd house of the dealer—their item—to see when it comes to my 2nd house or comes to me.

The car, the ruler of the 8th house, is Venus. I need to see when I encounter the vehicle or when the car comes into my possession. The aspect between Venus and me shows the first option, and the aspect between Venus and the ruler of the 2nd house, Mars, shows the second.

The lord of the 1st house, Venus, and the Moon show the querent. But Venus is already occupied by the car, so we cannot use it. So, we will use the Moon instead.

The Moon applies to the sextile of Venus in 14.5 degrees. I expect to receive the car in 14.5 time units without delay or obstacles.

Mars also has an aspect with Venus but through the intermediate planet, the Moon. The Moon has taken the light of Mars in the past, and now it carries it to Venus. The Moon, i.e., the querent, has started arranging car delivery to the garage. And this is true—I have already purchased the vehicle. The Moon must pass the same 14.5 degrees to complete the translation of light.

In my particular circumstances, 14.5 days is the most probable period until delivery. So, my scale is 14.5 hours, 14.5 days, and 14.5 weeks. The Moon is in the 8th house and in a fixed sign. It points to the most realistic period: 14.5 days. I asked this question on the 9th of June, so I expect the car to arrive between the evening of the 23rd and the morning of the 24th.

And so it proved. On the 23rd of June, the dealer called me, and the following morning, on the 24th of June, I received the car.

Looking at the transit chart that day (Fig. 2.19), you see how stars trigger the event on the 24th of June.

– The Moon (me) performs an exact aspect with Venus (the significator of the car in the root chart or *radix*)
– At the same time, Venus (the ruler of the 8th house in radix) falls into the 8th house of the transit chart, repeating its role as the item in the dealer's hands.
– At that very moment, the lord of the transit's 8th house (the car in the dealer's hands) rises above the horizon, becoming visible to the querent.

All three testimonies happen simultaneously, within a couple of seconds. What are the chances for it? They are nearly zero, but this is the way the planets act.

Chapter 2. Horary Astrology

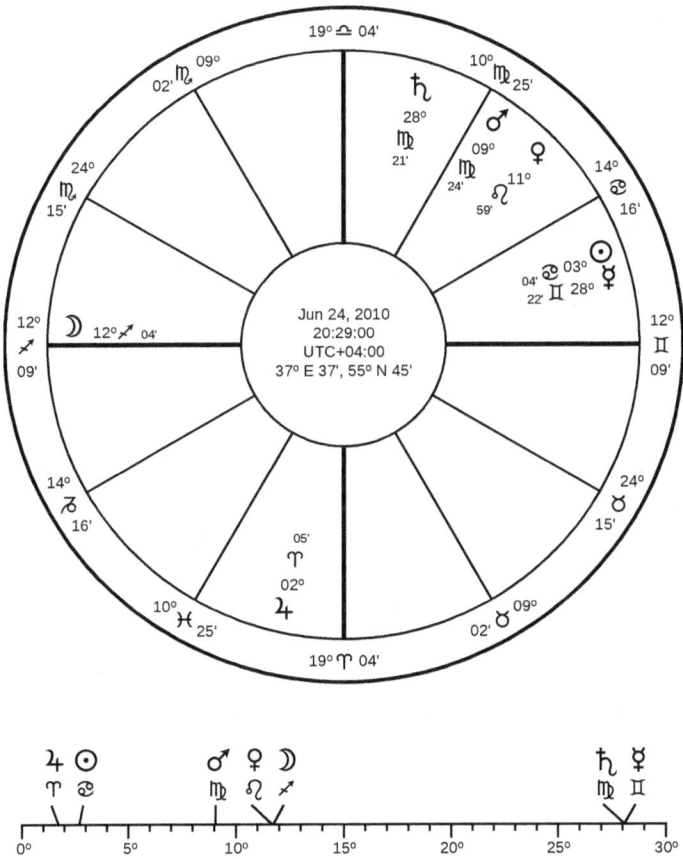

Figure 2.19: *Transit Chart: The Car Arrival*

However, this doesn't mean I'll receive the car at that exact moment. It implies the stars will trigger the event that day through this particular transit. The actual manifestation time, however, depends heavily on external factors like office hours, which can postpone or accelerate the event by several hours.

During the previous two weeks, the stars influenced the whole group participating in the delivery to clear the route from obstacles and delays to complete the delivery process on the 24th of June.

The more you practice with accurate forecasts, the more you will see how the stars arrange the flow of events.

Radicality of the Chart

Morinus wrote in his works that astrological charts serve two functions simultaneously.

- On one hand, they set trends for future events (i.e., contain information about the future). These charts can be used for forecasting.
- On the other hand, they act as triggers, fulfilling the promises embedded in previous planetary configurations, thus partially reflecting the past.

This principle is clearly visible in natal astrology:

- The moment of birth leaves an imprint on a person's body and sets the dynamics of events for their entire life.
- In a specific year of life, the solar return fulfills one of the promises embedded in the preceding birth chart. At the same time, it also sets and refines the course of events for the year ahead.
- In a specific month of the year, the lunar return fulfills one of the promises of the previous solar return, while also setting and refining the course of events for the month ahead.
- On a specific day of the month, the transit chart fulfills the promise of the previous lunar return. And it also shapes the course of events for that day.

The same principle applies in mundane astrology:

- The moment of the "world's birth" (*Figura Mundis*) leaves an imprint on mankind as a global social process (the exact moment is unknown to us).
- In a specific year, the chart of *the Sun's ingress into Aries* fulfills one of the promises embedded in the *Figura Mundis*. At the same time, it sets and refines the course of events for a given country for the year ahead.
- In a specific quarter, the so-called *quarter chart* fulfills the promise embedded in the ingress chart while also refining social processes for the upcoming season.
- And so on, down to the final transit.

Horary astrology is no exception here:

- The moment of formation of a particular life situation leaves an imprint on a miniature group process, determining its future (often, this moment is unknown to us).
- At a certain stage, the horary chart fulfills one of the promises embedded in the preceding formation chart. At the same time, it also determines and refines the future dynamics.
- A transit is a trigger that fulfills the promise of the preceding horary chart, but at the same time, it sets and refines the course of events on that day—we will examine such an example in the section "Transit Chart" on page 280.

Thus, the horary chart contains information not only about the future but also about the past and present state of the situation in question.

As you can see:

- The stars actively "intervene" in individual earthly processes only at specific moments.
- These moments are interconnected—each moment of active intervention follows from the previous one.
- Each such moment reflects the past and sets the future development of the current process.

If an astrologer manages to "catch" such a moment within the current situation, they observe a horary chart that reflects the past and present of the ongoing process.

The horary chart's ability to accurately reflect the current and past state of affairs within a given situation serves as our indicator that we have captured the right moment in time—one that truly determines the future development of the process. In this case, we say that we are dealing with a radical (i.e., root) horary chart, which will point to the subsequent transit, i.e., the future moment of the event's realization in question.

In the following sections, we will train our skills to detect if we catch the right moment, which promises future situation development.

Reflection of the Current Situation in a Horary Chart

If you follow William Lilly's logic closely (Lilly, 1669), you will quickly notice the repeating pattern in his work. Before making a judgment, he always tried to establish a correspondence between the chart's testimonies and the actual circumstances. Sometimes, he even tried to match the state of the querent's planet with the client's external signs.

In any case, the result was the same—Lilly considered only those charts that reflected reality (current and past circumstances within the question). And there is a reason for this. If the chart does not reflect the current & past situation (i.e., does not *focus on the main subject in question*), it was most likely cast at an inappropriate time and is not radical.

In practice, however, the querent often asks about one thing while worrying about a completely different situation, which the chart focuses on. So, the most significant mistake the astrologer can make is to answer the wrong question (even with a radical chart in hands) or consider a non-radical chart.

There are four reasons why the chart may be non-radical or focused on something else.

Reason 1.

The querent's emotional level is often not so great that they understand what worries them. But on the other hand, it is high enough to make them uncomfortable. We call this a *heightened emotional state*.

A person feels a kind of stress but cannot find an explanation for it. The brain does not like situations when it does not understand the cause of anxiety. It starts searching for the reason. We call it *rationalizing*. Eventually, the person comes up with a reasonable explanation for their irritation.

For example, they assure themself that they are worried about whether they closed the door. But in fact, this is a fictitious question. The reason for concern could be an approaching dismissal, fear for a child, or a mild cold. But this is hidden in the depths of the subconscious. That is why the voiced query does not match the actual request.

Reason 2.

Sometimes, a person cannot accept themselves and their real question. For example, a woman likes a man not because he is intelligent and handsome but because he has lots of money. Deep down, she is very interested in whether she can get control of his money. But she cannot accept herself in such a role, so she asks the socially acceptable question: "Will he marry me? Does he love me?" The voiced query here also does not match the actual request.

Reason 3.

If a person is under stress or uncertain, they may ask several questions at once. For example, if there is a high risk of dismissal, a person may be concerned at the same time:

- If they lose their job
- If they can continue paying for their son's education
- Whether their spouse will leave them for someone more successful if they lose their job

In a panic, a person chooses the first question that comes to mind and asks it to the astrologer. It could be "Will I get paid this Friday?" At the same time, their primary headache is the question of whether their spouse will leave them if they lose their income.

And here again, the voiced problem does not coincide with the deep query.

Reason 4.

Finally, a person can ask a question out of curiosity. The chart will not reflect any situation at all.

If the chart highlights the main subject that coincides with the voiced question, it is a strong testimony that we have a radical chart. The more coincidences we find between the testimony of the chart and past/current circumstances of the voiced situation, the bigger the chance we have a highly radical chart.

In the next section, I'll show you how to define what the chart highlights. For now, let's study the principle.

For example, the querent is interested in how their brother is doing. The chart immediately highlights the third house—their brother. We call such a chart a radical one.

Another example. The woman asks, "Will I conceive a child from this man." We expect to see a highlighted 5th house, a child. But the chart shows that the 8th house is in question. The woman is interested in a man's money. It is the case when the querent cannot voice their real question since they cannot afford it.

The chart is still radical, but it emphasizes another issue. From this chart, we can predict whether the woman will receive the man's money. We may answer that question but cannot say anything about her child. The chart is radical for another query.

Another situation. The person asks, "Will I get paid this Friday?" We expect to see a highlighted 11th house—money from work. But the chart shows us the importance of the workplace itself (10th house), the child (5th house), and the relationship with the wife (7th house). It is the case when a person is simultaneously concerned about several related issues.

We don't know which question is the main one. We can concentrate on the 10th house to see if the person will stay in the job. But in reality, the chart may contain an answer to the main question about the wife's feelings and behavior in the event of unemployment.

In such a chart, it is easy to make a mistake. It's not so technical as it is logical—to start answering the wrong question. Such charts can be called *unfocused*.

Finally, you might receive a question like "Did I close the door on my way to work?" The chart highlights nothing. It is a classic fictional question situation. It is a great mistake for a prediction maker to consider such a chart since you do not know what the querent worries about—a closed door, a state of health, fear of losing money, or whether they are trying to test your skills.

Such charts can be called *blank* or *non-radical*.

So let's wrap it up. There are four types of charts and four strategies for approaching them.

First. The radical charts. In these charts, the main subject in a question and the highlighted house are always the same. You can safely apply astrological techniques and make an accurate forecast.

The second type is radical charts but focused on a different issue. Ask the querent's permission to answer the real question. You will almost always hear the exclamation "How did you know this?" But sometimes, you will see the client's shame or passionate denial of real concerns—this is a typical defensive reaction. Start a consultation if the client is ready to hear the answer to the actual question. Otherwise, avoid making a judgment.

The third type is the unfocused chart. If the chart highlights different related topics, consider each of them. But warn the client that only one of the predictions may be correct. In practice, an unfocused chart often contains several answers at once. You can refuse to consult if you do not want to risk the forecast's accuracy.

The last type is blank and non-radical charts. I prefer to refuse consultation in this case. But you can take the client's word on faith. If their voiced question coincides with their deep query, then your forecast will be correct.

Next, I will show you the technical approach to defining the houses that the chart highlights.

How a Horary Chart Highlights a Client's Deep Concern

This technique below isn't found in old astrological books. It's a practical conclusion from 15 years of successful predictions and works well in practice.

The horary chart may highlight a particular topic in question in six ways.

1. Receptions: Remember that receptions reveal feelings. When the querent's planets fall into another planet's major dignities—domicile or exaltation—this planet becomes essential for the querent.

2. The querent's position in the house: When the querent occupies a specific house, that house determines the querent's focus in a particular area of life. It could be the essential part of the question.

3. Part of Fortune: As discussed in the section "Signification Techniques: Arabian Parts," this Arabian Part denotes the querent's deep concern. The house it occupies determines the querent's deep desires for a specific area. Additionally, the dispositor of this part signifies the object of the querent's deep interest.

4. Conjunction with the planets: If the querent or Part of Fortune conjuncts a planet, the querent or their deep concern is connected to what this planet signifies—physically or mentally.

5. Conjunction with house cusp: The same applies to the house cusp. If the querent or Part of Fortune conjuncts the house cusp, the querent or their desires are more closely linked to what that house represents than if they were somewhere in the middle of that house. Note that the significant "copy" of the planet—the opposition—can also conjunct the opposite house cusp and have a connection to it.

6. Past & current circumstances: The chart can also reflect reality not only through the interest of the querent but also through recent events or the current state of significators. Examples:

- The querent has recently found themselves in a difficult financial situation. At the same time, the ruler of the 2nd house, representing the querent's finances, has just entered the sign of its exile. This reflects reality.
- The querent has just had a conflict with their boss. At the same time, their planet separates from the past opposition with the 10th house ruler. Again, we observe correspondence.
- The querent's brother is unconscious. The chart shows the ruler of the third house in station, precisely describing the circumstances.

To accept the chart as radical, at least two correspondences between its testimonies and reality are needed. This is the minimum requirement. The more signs of correspondence, the more radical the chart is, and the more clearly it reflects future events, which will be triggered by the next transit when the time comes.

Example №3: Radicality Assessment

Let's revisit the previous chart about the purchase of the car (Fig. 2.18 on page 145) and assess its radicality. The querent is represented only by the Moon, as Venus signifies the vehicle in the dealer's possession.

We'll compile the list for the highlighted houses in the chart.

Reception: In whose strong dignities is the Moon placed? The Moon is in the domicile of Venus, the ruler of the 8th house, indicating my emotional concern (remember that Venus represents the car in the dealer's hands,

Chapter 2. Horary Astrology

while the querent is represented solely by the Moon). It aligns well with reality. We add the 8th house to our list.

The querent's position in the house: Which house does the Moon occupy? It's in the 8th house (the vehicle in the dealer's hands), indicating the querent is actively involved in acquiring the car.

However, any planet close to the house cusp almost always occupies the sign of that cusp. It means that its dispositor is almost always the ruler of that house. We avoid automatic repetitions and exclude the 8th house as separate points of interest—we have already considered it a step earlier.

Part of Fortune: The Part of Fortune is in the 11th house, so we add this house to our list. Mercury, its dispositor by sign and exaltation, represents the querent's deep desires. It rules the 9th, 11th, and 12th houses.

Since the Part of Fortune is in the same sign as the 11th house cusp, we do not consider Mercury as the ruler of the 11th house to avoid duplication, as we said before. To sum up, we add the 11th house (once), the 9th and 12th houses to our list.

Typically, we do not consider the positions of the planets in the houses when we try to identify their meaning, as they signify numerous things in a specific area of life rather than a particular object.

However, in this particular chart, the placement of Mercury—the querent's deep desire—aligns perfectly with the context. It is inside the 8th house, indicating specific details about the car in the dealer's possession. Since Mercury is the universal ruler of deals and contracts, it signifies documents related to acquiring the vehicle—it fully resonates with reality. We add the 8th house again.

Conjunctions with the planets: The Moon isn't conjunct with any other planets within a 3-degree range.

Conjunction with house cusp: The Moon is conjunct with the 8th house cusp, and it's noteworthy. We add the 8th house to our list again.

There is no automatic repetition here: not every planet in the house conjuncts that house cusp, and not every planet that conjuncts the cusp occupies that house—the Moon could be in the 7th house, say at 7° Taurus.

Our list of highlighted houses is 8, 8, 9, 11, 12, and 8.

The chart emphasizes the 8th house thrice, standing out against the others. The primary concern is the car in the dealer's hands. It perfectly aligns with the voiced question.

Past & current circumstances: Look at the current state of the Moon. It is in exaltation. Yes, at the time of the question, I was truly in a state of anticipation about the new car. This corresponds to reality.

Although the car had not yet been delivered, I was already its rightful owner. Venus (the car in the dealer's hands) is under the dominion of the Moon (that is, me). And this also aligns with the actual circumstances.

Thus, we have found more than two correspondences between the chart's indications and the real situation. The chart is radical.

Homework Assignment №17

I hope you remember the chart on which you made your first forecast. Now I display a Part of Fortune on it (Fig. 2.20). It was a question from the singer: Would her song enter the charts?

Look at this chart and determine which house is vital for the querent and what it can mean in the question.

Solution

The querent's position in the house: The lord of the 1st house, Mercury, and the Moon represent the querent. Mercury is in the 5th house, and the Moon is in the 12th. These houses determine the querent's activity, so we added them to our list.

Receptions: Mercury is in the domicile of Saturn and exalts Mars. Saturn rules the 5th and 6th houses, and Mars rules the 4th and 9th. Note that Mercury is in the same sign as the house cusp. It means that we should not take Saturn as the ruler of the 5th house to avoid duplication.

The querent's co-significator, the Moon, is ruled by the Sun and exalts no one. The Sun rules the 12th house. But again, notice that the Moon is in the same sign as the 12th house cusp. Therefore, we should not take the Sun as the 12th house ruler.

Our list of accented houses at this point is 5, 12, 6, 4, 9.

Chapter 2. Horary Astrology

Part of Fortune: It occupies the 7th house and conjuncts that house's cusp, so we add the 7th house twice to our list. There is no duplication here—it could be in conjunction with DSC from the 6th house.

Jupiter, the ruler of the 7th and 8th houses, disposits Part of Fortune by domicile. Again, Fortune is in the same sign as the house cusp, which means we will not consider the 7th house again.

Venus, the ruler of the 10th house, disposits Part of Fortune by exaltation, so we add the 10th house to our list.

Our list of accented houses at this step is 5, 12, 6, 4, 9, 7, 7, 8, and 10.

Conjunction with other planets and cusps: Neither the querent nor Fortune is in conjunction with other planets. There is no conjunction of the querent with house cusps. However, it is worth noting that Mercury forms close trines (relatively powerful aspects) with the cusps of the 2nd and the 10th houses, and the Moon forms a close trine with the 9th

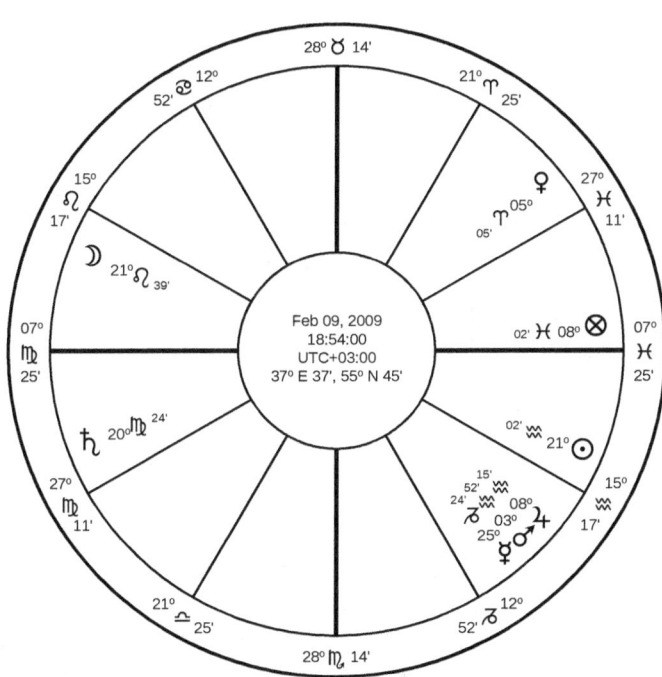

Figure 2.20: *Chart: The Future of the Single With PoF*

house cusp. This suggests that the querent, to some extent, is connected with those houses. We assign additional "weight" to them.

The 7th house is listed twice in our list and is the most crucial in the question, although the 10th and 9th houses also stand out due to the added weight.

While factors such as music, recognition, money, and an upcoming journey remain important for the querent, the 7th house holds much greater significance. The focus is on other people—in this context, the listeners.

– Will **they** like the song?
– Will **they** vote for it?

Remember, I gave you a hint and asked you to look at the audience. Honestly, it was not my idea. It was a hint from the chart itself.

Past & Current Circumstances: The chart contains a planet casting a close aspect to the audience (Jupiter)—Venus. Venus is both the natural ruler of creativity and the accidental ruler of the 10th house—the querent's professional activity.

This crucial detail clarifies that we're examining an audience specifically connected to the singer's creative work—a correlation that matches the actual situation.

Through this analysis, we've accomplished two objectives: first, we've verified the chart's radicality; second, we've identified the ruler of the 7th house (the audience) as the primary subject of the question.

Now you understand the methodology for both validating a chart's radicality and determining its central focus.

The Horary Chart Analysis Algorithm

Earlier in the section "A Simple Algorithm to Make a Prediction," I provided you with a simple algorithm for making predictions. However, it has a weak point. The first step was to reformulate the question to understand the main subject and choose a correct significator. But, as you know, the question voiced doesn't necessarily coincide with what really worries the querent. So, we can easily make a mistake by answering the wrong question.

Now, with the powerful techniques of radicality assessment, the chart analysis becomes much more straightforward. I present to you the horary chart analysis algorithm.

- First, you cast a chart and see which houses it highlights. If they differ from what the querent says, you can advise answering the actual question. You may want to stop a consultation at this point if the client resists hearing the answer. However, if they agree to continue, you will understand the actual context of the question and choose the right significators in that context.
- Next, you compile a list of techniques you will apply to the chosen significators.
- Finally, you use these techniques to get an accurate answer to the actual question.

Let me show you an example of how it works.

Example №4: Flight to Turkey

It is a real story. The girl asks, "Will the flight to Turkey be safe?" (Fig. 2.21).

What do we expect to see? We expect to see the 1st house (personal safety) highlighted. In addition, the 9th house (a long trip and its quantity) can also be a crucial part of the story.

But it doesn't necessarily mean that we'll see what we expect. Let's check our hypothesis and determine what is vital for the querent.

Position in the houses: Venus (the lord of the 1st house) accents the 5th house, and the Moon (co-significator of the querent)—the 9th.

Receptions: Venus is in Mars' domicile and the Sun's place of honor. The Sun and Mars rule the 2nd, 6th, 7th, and 10th houses.

The Moon is dignified (no one rules it by domicile) and exalts Jupiter—the lord of the 3rd and 5th houses.

At this point, the highlighted houses are 5, 9, 2, 6, 7, 10, 3, and 5.

Part of Fortune: It occupies the third house and conjuncts its cusp, so we add the third house twice to our list.

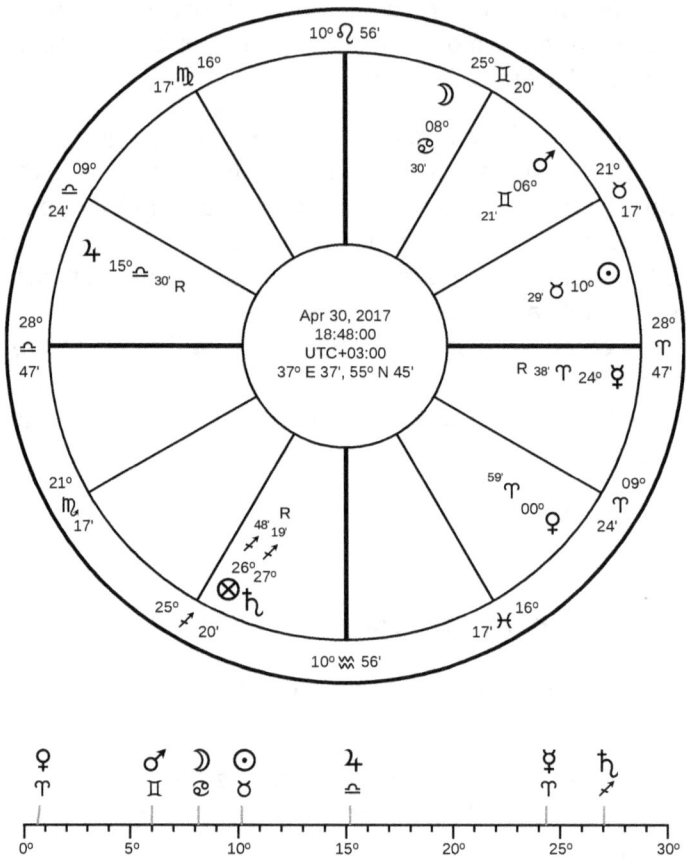

Figure 2.21: *Chart: Will the Flight to Turkey Be Safe?*

Jupiter, the dispositor of ⊗ by domicile, rules the 3rd and 5th houses. Again, since Fortune is in the same sign as the 3rd house cusp, we will not count the 3rd house at this step.

At this point, the highlighted houses are 5, 9, 2, 6, 7, 10, 3, 5, 3, 3, and 5.

Conjunctions with other planets: The querent is not in conjunction with any planets, but Fortune conjuncts Saturn, which rules the 4th house.

Conjunction with cusps: Finally, there is only Fortune that conjuncts the house cusp. We have already counted it.

Chapter 2. Horary Astrology

Look at our list—5, 9, 2, 6, 7, 10, 3, 5, 3, 3, 5, and 4. The 9th house is met only once, and the first house is unimportant. Definitely, it's not a flight safety question. Then what is the real issue?

The 3rd and 5th houses are met three times and stand above the rest. That is, the real question is either about the 3rd or the 5th house. It is either about:

- Siblings and neighbors, or
- Sex and fun

Sound logic dictates that sex and fun are much more related to the trip than brothers and sisters. But we still need to clarify it with the client.

After a couple of questions, it turned out that the girl was going to Turkey searching for sexual adventures. As expected, the querent reacted: "Wow, how did you know that?" It is a classic situation where the querent could not accept her role as a frivolous woman and asked a socially accepted question instead. She believed that if she heard that nothing threatened her on the flights, she would get an indulgence: permission to have a good time.

It is a very typical situation that you will regularly encounter in practice. Since we now know the real question and have received permission from the querent to answer it, we can list the techniques to apply to the ruler of the 5th house. We can find two things about a sexual adventure—whether it will happen and whether it will be great or disappointing.

The first question is resolved through an aspect. We have the key phrase, "Will it happen." It is enough that any planet of the querent contacts Jupiter—the significator of sex. If there is such an aspect, it will trigger an event and fulfill the querent's desire. Sex will take place.

The second question is resolved through essential dignity assessment, since we have a key phrase "Is it good or bad?" We need to see whether Jupiter is in good or poor condition. We can even use the multiplicity property of Jupiter's sign to see if there will be one or more adventures.

Thus, we have three techniques to apply:

- Find an aspect between Jupiter and the querent.
- Assess the essential dignity of Jupiter.
- Look at the multiplicity property of Jupiter's sign.

Predictive Astrology Textbook

These three steps are a clear road-map for us to find an answer in the chart.

Homework Assignment №18

Now, it's your turn to unravel the client's deepest motives. A woman asks, "My boss yelled at me and said he didn't want to see me again. Will he fire me?" (Fig. 2.22).

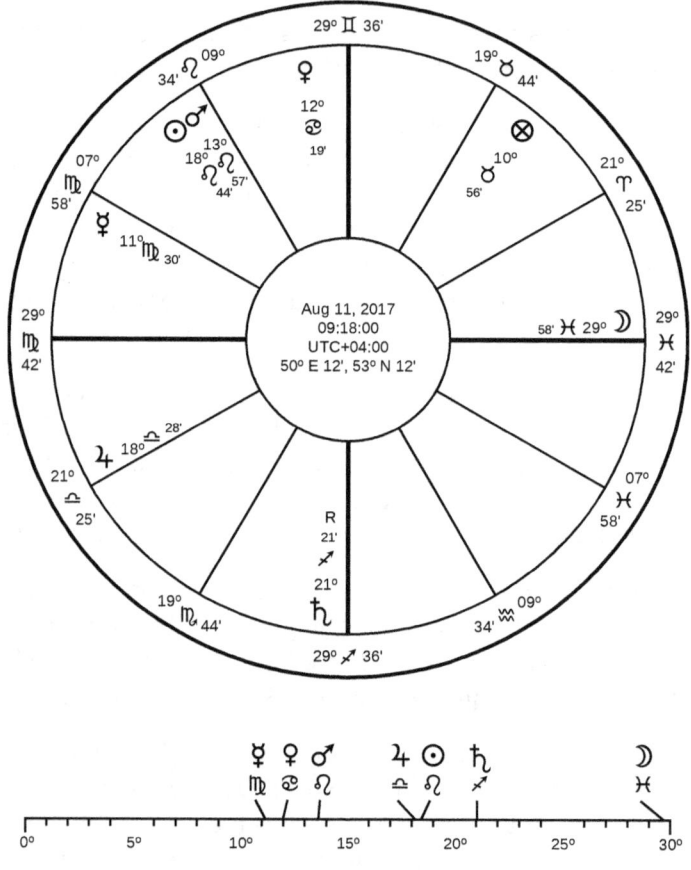

Figure 2.22: Chart: Will He Fire Me?

I will give you two tasks. First, a simple one—indicate the houses that the chart highlights. The second task is more advanced. Look at highlighted houses, and establish what worries the querent.

- **Tip 1:** The 9th house is not in question here. You can safely ignore it.
- **Tip 2:** If some planet conjuncts the relevant house cusp, this planet is interested in (or tied with) that house. When I say "some planet," I do not mean only the querent—it can be any other person. When I say "a relevant house," I imply the house essential for the querent.

These two clues are enough to pinpoint the real question. Use common sense, and you'll be good at giving the correct answer.

Solution

By their positions, the querent's planets emphasize the 7th and 12th houses.

Mercury, the lord of the 1st house, shows nothing by reception in its domain—no one rules it. The Moon, co-significator of the querent, shows the importance of Jupiter and Venus, the rulers of the 2nd, 4th, 5th, 6th, 7th, and 9th houses. Since the Moon is in the same sign as the house cusp, we skip the 7th house at this step.

Venus, the dispositor of part of Fortune, indicates the importance of the 2nd and 9th houses. The Moon—a dispositor of ⊗ by exaltation—is the querent. We could say that the emotional state is essential, but it makes no sense. The emotional state is always crucial; this statement brings no extra information.

Fortune by position highlights the 8th house. Neither the querent nor Fortune is in conjunction with other planets. Finally, the Moon conjuncts the 7th house cusp.

So, here is the list of highlighted houses: 7, 12, 2, 4, 5, 6, 9, 2, 9, 8, and 7.

Although the question concerns work, the chart doesn't emphasize the 10th house. We see the significance of the 2nd, 9th, and 7th houses.

The second part of the assignment is to understand what it could mean. I have already given you a hint that the 9th house is not relevant in this context. That was the first thing I asked the querent.

So, we have two essential characters in this chart. They are Jupiter, the ruler of the 7th house, and Venus, the ruler of the 2nd house.

Logic tells us that in the context of possible dismissal, the 2nd house stands for money rather than lawyers or seconds in a duel. As usual, we use the principle of Occam's razor. The most straightforward explanation is the correct one.

Remember the second clue I gave you: if a planet is at the cusp of a relevant house, then that planet is interested in the affairs of that house. This rule applies not only to the querent but to any planet.

Right at the top of the 2nd house of money, which is essential in the question, we see Jupiter. But look, Jupiter is not just some kind of planet. It rules the 7th house—one of three accented houses.

Jupiter shows other people—partners, lovers, colleagues, strangers, enemies, etc. We can even find out if we are talking about one or more people. Jupiter is in a single sign of Libra—we are speaking about one person. We can even go ahead and check the gender of that person. Jupiter, the masculine planet, is in Libra, the masculine sign. It is a man.

So we see that a particular man, very significant to the querent, is highly interested in her money. Being on the cusp of the second house, he is literally tied to it.

Now, let's generalize what we see. The voiced question concerns the threat of dismissal. At the same time, the chart emphasizes another man who is vital to the querent and is tied to her money. He is not a child or blood relative, not above or below her in the social hierarchy—he can be a partner, a lover, an open enemy, or another male person signified by the 7th house.

What happened in reality? When I first delineated this chart and reached this point, I used common sense. There is a big chance that the voiced question is not random but somehow connected with the actual concern, which the chart reveals. Losing a job can affect the querent's finances and thus threaten her relationship with this man since he is tied to her finances. This means that the man in question is dependent on her money. It is a simple, logical conclusion.

So, I asked clarifying question "Is there a man significant to you who relies on your financial support and whose relationship with you may be affected by your dismissal?"

As expected, I received an exclamation in response: "How did you know?" She indeed had a lover, a gigolo. She feared losing him because she could not pay his rent anymore because of unemployment. It was a classic situation when the querent did not voice the honest question because she did not accept herself as a sponsor-lover.

Her sincere concern was "Will I lose him?" But the inner critic replied, "You shouldn't ask such things." Therefore, a socially acceptable question was born: "Will my boss fire me?"

It is important to note that the chart shows the answer to the real question. This question, as you can see, directly relates to the gigolo. So the main significator is not the 10th house, as you could think, but Jupiter (him) and Venus (her finances). As I said before, the biggest mistake a horary astrologer can make is answering a wrong question.

We don't need to look for events in the form of collisions between two objects. A lover's decision to leave or a deterioration in financial situation are not collisions between two objects.

- The reception shows motives, particularly the lover's decision to stay or shortly leave the querent. Gigolo's feelings will either remain as they are or change to the opposite—indifference or rejection. Hence, we will look at possible changes to the current reception.
- The state of the querent's wallet will either remain the same or change shortly. The celestial state of the significator is responsible for the object's state. Hence, we will look at the possible changes to the current state of Venus.

Therefore, we will apply the following techniques to our significators:

- We will see if the receptions of Jupiter change in the following few degrees of its way.
- We will see if the state of Venus changes in the following few degrees of its movement.

I want to draw your attention to the effectiveness of the chart radicality assessment technique. The querent could have had thousands of reasons to fear dismissal: stopping expensive medical care for her father, lacking a similar position on the labor market, stopping the mortgage payment or paying for her son's education, and so on. The chances of accidentally guessing a far-from-typical situation are close to zero.

We will explore this chart even deeper since we will shortly introduce a new technique—antiscia.

The Planet Interposing the Question

The radical chart reflects reality, including the reveal of external influences, which may be unknown to the querent or hidden by them. Sometimes, you see that the unknown planet affects several significators simultaneously. This is a hint in the chart that you should consider this planet an essential character in the story.

Examples:

- Both significators are in major dignities of the same planet
- Both are connected with it by a close aspect
- The same planet rules one significator and conjuncts another

Suppose the question is "Will he marry me?" The lord of the 7th house, a partner, is in close conjunction with Saturn. At the same time, the querent, the Moon, exalts Saturn. Saturn occupies the cusp of the 7th house and has mutual reception with the lord of the 7th house. Saturn comes into play. The chart suggests paying attention to this planet.

- Saturn relates to the 7th house (other people), representing the other person in the relationship question.
- It has mutual feelings and a bodily conjunction with the partner.
- In addition, the querent is dependent on it.

At this point, asking about the other person's presence in a relationship is appropriate. Don't be surprised to hear something like, "Yes, my partner is married and still cannot leave his family to stay with me."

Signification Techniques: Antiscia

Antiscion (plural form *antiscia*) means the "shadow of the planet." It is a point on the zodiac circle that can be in close conjunction with other planets, their aspects, or house cusps.

We usually consider the most powerful aspect—the opposition—as it most apparently connects antiscion with the planet.

Technically, the antiscion is the point on the zodiac circle to which the celestial sphere's rotation will bear the planet (Fig. 2.23). It will not physically be in that place of the zodiac since the zodiac also moves with the sphere. But the planet "promises" to be at that point *relative to the horizon*.

Chapter 2. Horary Astrology

We will discuss the rotation of the celestial sphere and the primary motions of the planet later in the chapter on natal astrology and primary directions. For now, remember the terminology:

Since the planet "promises" to be at a specific point relative to the horizon, we call such a planet *promissor*.

So, the antiscion is the degree of the zodiac, which signifies the upcoming appearance of the planet. We can think of it as if the planet were connected with that place but has yet to appear.

That is, the planet's antiscion shows the hidden presence of an object that is yet to be discovered. You can imagine a full "copy" of the planet with the same meaning and celestial state located in the place of antiscion and then add the word "hidden" or "secret" to it.

For instance,

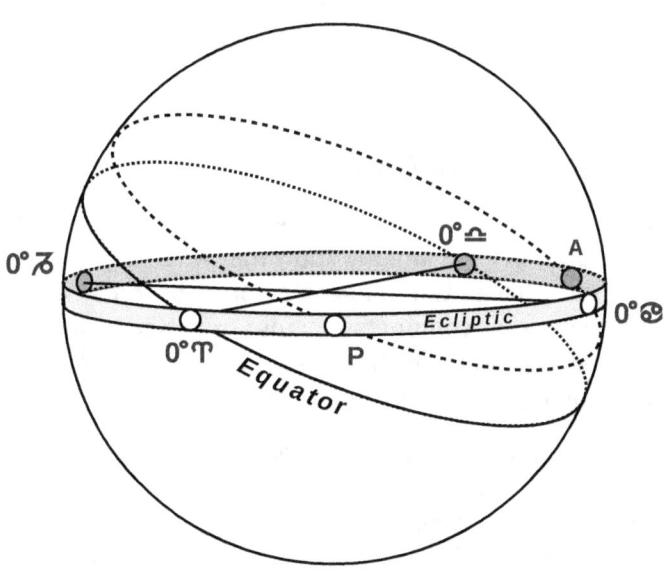

Figure 2.23: *Antiscia*

- The querent is in the 7th house, but its antiscion is in the 8th house cusp. The querent asks about the partner, but secretly, they want their money.
- The husband goes on a business trip, but he secretly conjuncts the alternative ruler of the 7th house—he has a secret meeting.
- My brother is separating from the 9th house lord's antiscion. He recently had a conflict with his partner, which he now kept confidential (the 9th house of the chart is the 7th house of the brother).

How can you quickly find the place of the planet's antiscion? If you draw the zodiac signs on a circle, place the blot where the planet is, and then fold the paper along the Cancer-Capricorn axis, the blot will leave an imprint on the other side of the sheet. It will be the place where the planet's shadow is. If another planet or house cusp is at that imprinted track, the planet is secretly tied with them.

You can quickly calculate the antiscion's degree by subtracting the planet's current degree in a sign from 30. For example, Venus is at 26° Taurus. How many degrees need to be added to get 30? Four. Therefore, the antiscion is at 4 degrees of the other sign. Which sign is symmetrical to Taurus? Mentally fold the zodiacal circle in half along the Cancer-Capricorn axis, and you will see that Taurus coincides with Leo. Therefore, Venus' antiscion is at 4° Leo.

Antiscia and Chart Radicality

We often use antiscia to detect the deep concern of the querent that they deliberately hide. You already know that when a querent conjuncts a planet or house cusp, this planet or house becomes essential. By analogy, if the querent conjuncts a planet or house by antiscion, they are secretly tied to them. This house or planet becomes essential, but the querent would prefer to keep it secret.

From now on, we will expand our arsenal to detect real concerns with antiscia. Let's have some practice and review the previous chart with the woman and her gigolo-lover. But, at this time, we will include antiscia (see letter "A" in Fig. 2.24) in the analysis and see what it brings.

Mercury's antiscion is at 18° Aries, right on the cusp of the 8th house. This house was already accented once by the location Part of Fortune. Now, it has become essential. We have another vital thing in the story—

Chapter 2. Horary Astrology

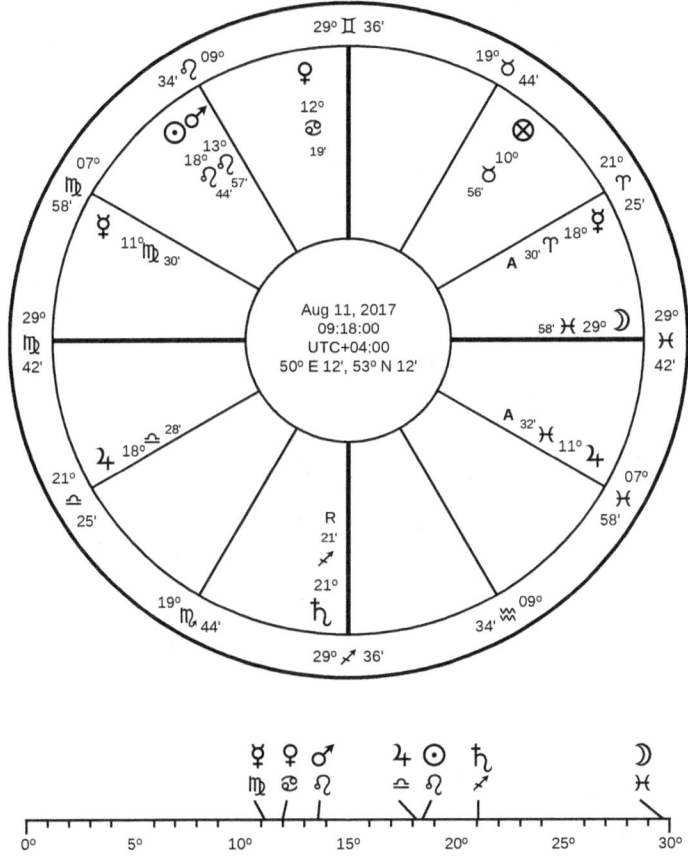

Figure 2.24: *Chart: A Gigolo-Lover (With Antiscion)*

the 8th house, the lover's money. The querent cannot want or need the lover's money; it contradicts reality. We need to read this to fit the context. Deep in her heart, the querent hopes that her partner will have enough money of his own so that he will not leave her, even if she loses her job. However, this is something that she would prefer to keep secret, even from the astrologer.

Now, let's look at the other antiscia in the chart. Jupiter's antiscion is at 11° Pisces, opposite to Mercury, the querent. We have a secret opposition between the querent and her lover. There is a hidden conflict between them, which the client didn't voice to the astrologer. But, we can look at the root of the conflict without even asking the querent about it.

Receptions show feelings, including reasons for frustration and conflict. Mercury expels Jupiter; the querent is disappointed with her lover and his behavior. But why?

As seen from Jupiter's position at the cusp of their 2nd house, the lover only needs her money. Jupiter has no feelings for Mercury or the Moon; he does not fall into any major dignities of these planets. The lover is indifferent to the querent, and money is the only thing keeping him.

At the same time, the woman is emotionally attached to her lover. The Moon (her emotions) is literally tied to the 7th house—the lover. That is, she wants reciprocity but does not receive it. Instead, in response, she only gets the request for money. It is what disappoints her.

We clearly see that picture, and the chart suggests nothing else. So, this is the essence of the conflict that the woman so diligently hides. At the same time, she secretly hopes that her lover will finally have his own money. We saw this a little earlier when we noticed a secret connection of the Moon with the 8th house, the lover's money.

Look at how much new information we have extracted simply by introducing antiscia into the chart.

Example №5: Antiscion in Action

Let's return to the chart from the section "Homework Assignment №11" on page 112 about house purchase. This time, I indicate Mercury's antiscion on the chart (Fig. 2.25). Let me remind you of the story. The querent is considering buying a house. However, there is a suspicious detail. The house is very nice, while the price is considerably low.

Finally, this house has been on the market for several years. The querent suspects that something may be wrong with that property, and this purchase could lead to further expenses.

We have already established that buying a house will lead to additional expenses. Now, let's uncover the secret of the residence.

If we suspect something hidden that will soon manifest, it is time to look at the antiscia. Mercury's antiscion conjuncts the cusp of the fourth house (the real estate in question). So, a particular object signified by Mercury is secretly connected with the house and its illiquidity.

Chapter 2. Horary Astrology

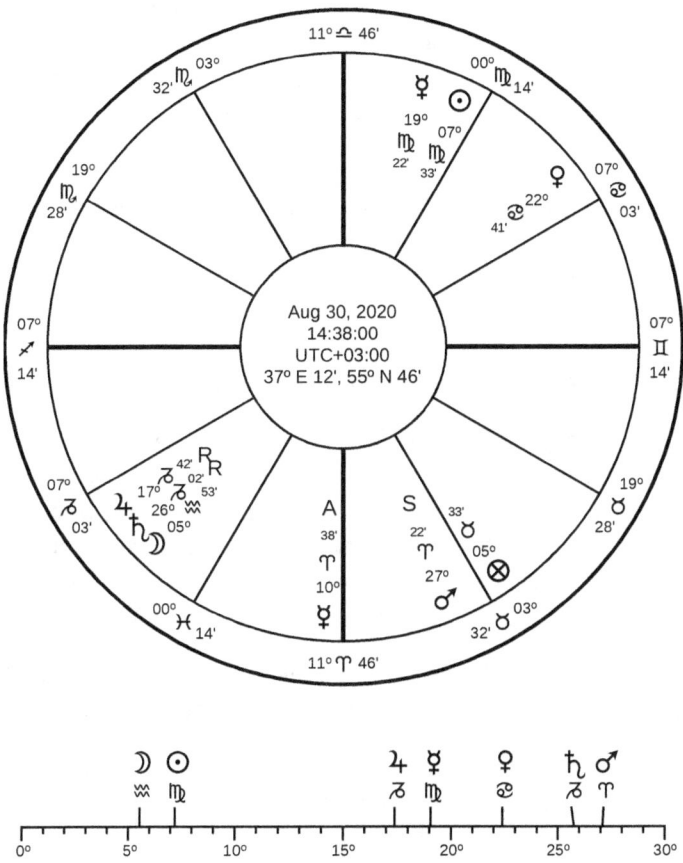

Figure 2.25: *Chart: House Purchase (With Antiscion)*

Who is Mercury? It rules the 9th house and represents distant countries, foreigners, places of wisdom, churches, and long journeys.

Using common sense, we exclude possibilities like "the house is not for sale because it is secretly connected with the library or the querent's trip abroad." It all makes no sense.

However, a person described by the 9th house can be connected to real estate and be the hidden reason for its illiquidity. In the context of the question, there are not many people involved in the transaction—the realtor and the owner of the house, whom the querent has never seen and with whom a meeting was not even planned.

The realtor was neither a foreigner nor a priest. There is only one person left—the owner of the house. Now, let's apply Occam's razor principle. The owner of the house is not just a person, but a person described by the 9th house. Moreover, they occupy that house, i.e., reside in the area described by that house.

- Can being a priest or visiting the church be the reason for potential problems with the contract? No.
- Can being a university professor or studying there be a hidden reason for the problems? No.
- Can the owner's stay in a foreign country affect the sale of the house? No, unless the owner has issues with the foreign country's law.

Of all the options, the last one is the simplest to explain. Suppose the owner has problems with the law in a foreign country. In that case, this thoroughly explains why the house price has dropped so sharply and why the house has been empty and unsold for several years. This hypothesis also explains why buying this house can be risky—if the owner has problems with the law, their property may be seized.

But this is just a hypothesis for now. We need more evidence that the owner is connected with or affected by the local authority.

Now, pay attention to the following. Mercury casts a relatively strong aspect (trine) directly to the cusp of the 6th house. In other words, Mercury is closely connected with the 6th house and what it signifies.

The 6th house is the 10th house from the 9th—another country's local authority. The aspect is remarkably accurate to be considered a simple coincidence. But this aspect confirms our hypothesis in the best possible way.

Look at this, too. The Sun is right at the top of the 9th house—it shows something about the house owner's place of stay. Universally, the Sun rules the governance structure. So, in the 9th house, this Sun shows the authority of a foreign country. It is the second time the chart confirms our hypothesis that the owner is closely connected with the foreign authorities; more specifically—they have problems with the law there.

Now, let's recall the information about planetary orbs. I previously mentioned in the section "The Orbs of the Seven Planets" that when a planet comes close enough to the Sun, it becomes invisible. Specifically,

Chapter 2. Horary Astrology

Mercury completely disappears in the Sun's rays when it approaches closer than 10 degrees to it.

Mercury has just emerged from the zone of total invisibility, known as *combustion*. Throughout this period, Mercury was combust, meaning it was hidden in the Sun's rays. At first glance, the Sun doesn't appear to rule any house. However, considering the co-rulers of houses (refer to the section "Co-rulers of the House"), it becomes evident that the Sun rules the sign of Leo, which occupies most of the 8th house. Therefore, the Sun serves as the co-ruler of the 8th house.

Obviously, we won't interpret the 8th house as the death of the querent—such an interpretation lacks sense. However, the 8th house is the 12th from the 9th—a place symbolizing imprisonment in another country. Thus, the chart paints a rather literal picture: the owner of the house had been concealed in imprisonment for a considerable period and had just been released. It precisely validates our hypotheses.

Now, it's time to unveil the cards.

Sensing something was wrong, the querent hired detectives, who swiftly uncovered that the house owner had legal issues abroad. They had spent an extended period in prison there and had recently been released.

They managed to uncover one additional detail, which I did not observe in the chart. The house owner was released early, having reached an agreement with the investigation, but the charges were not dropped. Shortly after the release, they went on the run and were declared internationally wanted. All their assets, including the house, could be seized.

We cannot extract specific details from the chart without knowing the exact context, such as distinguishing the house owner's recent escape from an early release—it is unrealistic.

Nevertheless, I am excited that it is possible to accurately identify many hidden details using precise techniques and logical breakdown. The likelihood of randomly guessing all these events is close to zero.

It demonstrates that astrology was and remains a mathematically precise predictive discipline, despite the attempts of many modern astrologers to equate it with divination.

Predictive Astrology Textbook

Special Case: The Question on Behalf of the Group

Sometimes, the querent asks a question on behalf of a group of people. If the querent is part of that group (physically or emotionally), we can assign the 1st house to that group.

For example, a woman asks, "Will my husband get this contract?" But she supports him so much with the business that the contract becomes a family achievement, and the question sounds like "Will *we* get this contract?" The 1st house will represent both the woman and her husband simultaneously.

Another example. A man works in the campaign headquarters and asks if their leader will win the presidency. However, the querent is so mentally connected with the leader that his presidency becomes a shared victory. Therefore, the question is whether *they* will win the election. The 1st house will show both the querent, the team, and the leader.

A soccer fan asks, "Will they win the match?" But he is so mentally connected to his team that this is a question of joint victory. The first house shows both the querent and his favorite team.

> **N.B.**
>
> One of the most common mistakes in sports horaries is that the astrologer mistakenly assigns the 1st house to the sports team. The querent is often interested in the victory of a specific team mentioned in the question, without being its active fan.
>
> Therefore, it is crucial that you accept questions from genuine fans or from members of the team itself. For example, one of my students has been predicting football game results for an Italian club for some time—and even received a crate of fine Chianti from them for accurate forecasts.

Homework Assignment №19

Now, let's look at a new chart. It will be your homework assignment (Fig. 2.26).

Chapter 2. Horary Astrology

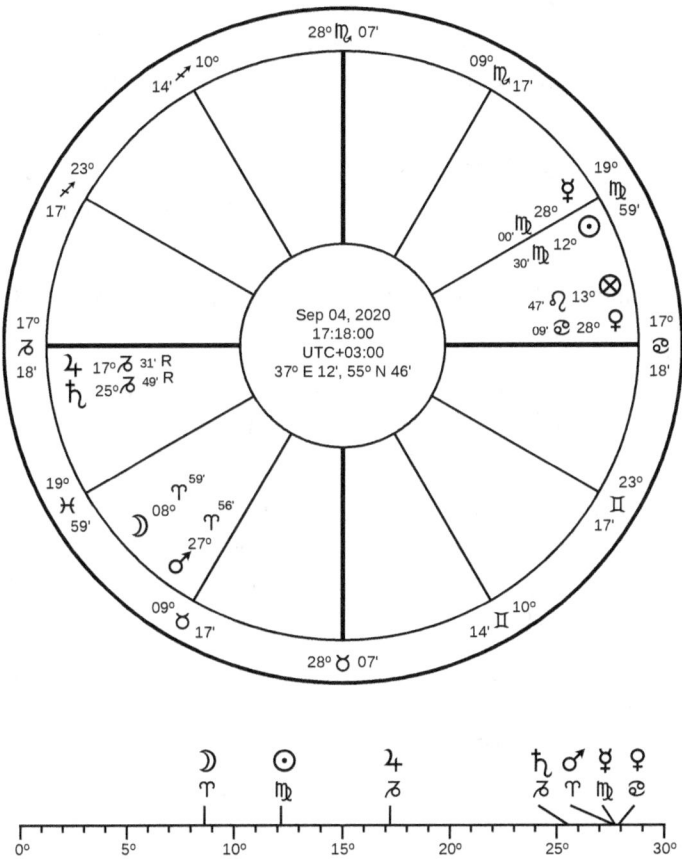

Figure 2.26: *Chart: The Exam*

The mother worries about her son and asks, "Will he pass the exam?" The context of the situation is that if the son fails the exam, he will be expelled from the university and drafted into the army. Since the question concerns the son, we expect the chart to highlight the 5th house. Go through the algorithm to analyze the horary charts, identify the main characters, and create a list of techniques you will apply to the significators.

Solution

By position, the querent's planets highlight the 1st and 2nd houses.

The lord of the 1st house, Saturn, exalts Mars, which rules the 9th and 10th houses. The Moon's dispositors are Mars (by domicile) and the Sun (by exaltation). The Sun does not rule any house in this chart.

The ⊗ is disposited by the Sun, which rules no houses. By position, Fortune highlights the 7th house. The Moon conjuncts the 8th house by antiscion, and there are no conjunctions of querent or Fortune with other planets.

The chart highlights the following houses: the 1st, 2nd, 9th, 10th, 7th, and 8th. It also highlights the Sun two times.

Although the question concerns the son and his fate, the chart doesn't emphasize the 5th house. Instead, it highlights Mars (the lord of the 9th and 10th houses) and the Sun.

As a ruler of the 9th and 10th houses, Mars can be a university or a government structure (that is, an army in context). But Mars universally signifies the military. The chart gives us a hint that Mars is assigned the role of the army. It perfectly fits the context.

So, we cannot say the sun's fate is irrelevant or unimportant to the querent. Nevertheless, the chart doesn't accent the 5th house but emphasizes the 1st house at least once.

It is the case when the querent is mentally connected to the subject of the question and asks a question on behalf of "us": Will *we* pass the exam, or will they take *us* into the army? Often, mothers cannot separate themselves from their children, at least in some cultures. So, we have two essential planets here—Mars, which threatens the querent and her son, and the Sun.

Note that Mars harms Saturn by the reception. The university cannot damage the integrity of the family, but the army can. It is another clue that Mars signifies the army.

The role of the Sun is not so obvious, but we have some clues. The Sun is the natural ruler of gold, which in real life often means a large amount of money. The Sun supports Mercury by the reception. Mercury is other people's money, the ruler of the 8th house. The Sun supporting Mercury may signify considerable funds that fill someone's pocket. At the same time, the 8th house is essential for the querent—the Moon conjuncts it by antiscion.

On the one hand, a woman wants the Sun, i.e., she desires a large amount of money to fill someone's pocket. On the other hand, she is emotionally connected with someone's pocket and keeps this connection secret. A suspicion arises that this is a bribe, but we must clarify this with the querent.

And we come to the next point—we ask the querent clarifying questions. Indeed, the client confirmed that she hopes to offer a bribe if her son fails the exam to save him from unavoidable military service. She also said, "Will they take *us* into the army?" when she talked about her son. It once again confirmed the emotional connection between the querent and her son. So Saturn no doubt shows "us" in question; the querent speaks on behalf of the family.

Since we do not meet any resistance from the querent, we may safely continue judging and compiling the required techniques. The real question is whether we (our family) will face harmful contact with the army (Mars).

The question is "Will object A collide with object B?" The aspect shows such collisions. If there is a Saturn-Mars aspect, the threat potential (shown by Mars' negative reception) will be realized. If there is no aspect, then the son will remain untouched.

Three Ways How the Chart Shows the Future

With practice, you'll notice that the horary chart shows the future by repeating the same three patterns, depending on the type of question asked. For the sake of simplicity, I decided to classify these patterns and give them their names.

- The horary chart shows the "snapshot of the future" if the question is about the prospective state of objects.
- It presents a "short movie" with the shift of circumstances if the question concerns upcoming changes in the object's state.
- It unfolds a "full movie" if the question is about the collision of two objects.

Let's discuss it in detail.

1. The Snapshot of the Future

When we receive the question about the prospective state of the object, the chart shows us the "photo" of the *future circumstances* with the *current position* of the planets.

In questions like "What is the condition of the house I am planning to buy?" we look at the planets' current positions as a snapshot of the future. We examine the current state of the ruler of the 4th house as if the house were already in the querent's possession.

In the question "Will I get sick from this food?" we analyze the current state and influence of the ruler of the 2nd house as if the querent has already consumed the food.

In the question "Will he return?", the boyfriend's significator is retrograde, indicating a backward movement. Initially, we were supposed to find an aspect between the querent and her boyfriend, but the chart answers by illustrating the current state of the boyfriend's planet, which perfectly fits the context as the response to the main question. It shows him as retrograde, moving backward, revealing *the future circumstances* by *his current state*.

2. The Short Movie

Often, we are interested in future changes in the state of an object or a shift in its motivations/influence, for example:

- Will they continue to love me, or will they fall out of love?
- Will my mother stop interfering in my relationship with my girlfriend?
- Will finances be improved?
- Will I be fired from my job?

The chart reveals an answer by showing the immediate ingress of the significator into a new sign. Ingress of the significator within the following 3–4 degrees means:

- Upcoming change of reception: If occurring, indicates a shift in feelings or one's influence on the planet
- Shift in celestial state: If occurring, reflects a change in the object's condition (financial or health status)
- Change of location: May indicate job change, relocation, or similar transition

Suppose the significator needs 5, 6, or more degrees to ingress an adjacent sign. In that case, circumstances will remain unchanged—the querent will stay on their job, love will continue as before, and so on.

We allow significators to advance only 3-4 degrees ahead to see what happens next as if we were watching a short movie.

3. A Full Movie

In most cases, an event involves a real-life encounter between two objects.

- "Will I get this job?" The event is a meeting between the querent and prospective employer
- "Will she conceive a child?" The event of conception is a meeting between a mother and her child

The perfection of the exact aspect between significators indicates the encounter of these two objects. It can be a direct aspect, translation, or collection of light. Remember, if the context demands, we must additionally find the potential for this aspect—the main character's motive and the power to act.

In this scenario, the planets can advance until they leave their signs. We watch them until the end of the story—the perfection or not of the aspect, as if we were watching a full movie.

The default option

Sometimes, situations arise where the event is either extremely unlikely or almost inevitable. Be careful with these cases: absence or presence of the exact aspect may mean nothing.

For example, a querent has to take an exam today but doesn't know the subject. However, they ask, "Will I pass the exam?" The probability of passing the exam is negligible. The default option here is the answer, "No, you won't pass it." even if we have an aspect between the examiner and the querent with a positive reception from the examiner to the querent.

For the chart to show us the answer "yes," rewriting the default option, it should show the outstanding indicators for passing the exam, such as:

- The examiner is blinded (e.g., burned by the rays of the Sun)
- Simultaneously, according to the reception, they are delighted with the querent
- Simultaneously, the querent is in their place of exaltation, demonstrating exaggerated excellencies
- At the same time, the examiner applies by trine to the querent

The simultaneous occurrence of such indicators is as likely as passing an exam without preparation. However, if this happens, one can expect a miracle—successfully passing the exam.

Another example: A close friend of the querent is in a coma. Doctors talk about imminent death. The querent asks, "When will my friend leave?" The chart does not show any aspects between the quesited and their death, but this does not mean that the friend will wake up. It implies that everything is going according to the doctor's prognosis.

Please pay attention to such cases.

Short Examples

Let's consider a few imaginary examples. They will help you understand the logic behind choosing the right approach to the chart.

Suppose I am buying the house. We've almost reached a deal with the seller, but I'm worried they might change their mind. My question is "Will the deal happen, and when?" We may have two options here:

Option 1. Suppose the querent is Venus in Gemini, and the seller is Mercury in Libra. We see an excellent mutual reception between the two parties. It reflects the current situation—the parties have almost reached the deal. In that case, we need to see what will happen next and how the situation will unfold as if the chart showed a short movie. We allow the significators to advance for 3–4 degrees ahead and see what happens next:

- Planets do not change their directions or signs. Nothing prominent happens. The deal will happen because it is the default option—parties have the agreement, and nothing prevents the deal. We do not need an applying aspect here. We look for timing using the long-term aspects (see the following section).

- The querent shortly gets stationary and moves backward. They will change their mind, and the deal will not happen.
- The seller enters Scorpio in a few degrees and changes their attitude to the reverse. They will shortly refuse to sell the house.

Option 2. Suppose the querent is Venus in Gemini, and the seller is Mercury in Aries. The querent wants the deal, but the seller actively refuses it and moves backward (away from the querent), which contradicts the current situation. Hence, the planet's *current disposition* shows us *a picture of the future*, as if we were looking at a snapshot of the prospective seller's motive. It clearly answers the question "Will they change their mind?"—yes, they will.

Another example. I found the house online and asked, "Will the deal happen, and when?" I have not yet met the seller and have not negotiated the price.

First, we need to see the possibility of the deal—an applying aspect between the querent and the buyer. At the minimum, I should call or write an email with my proposal.

Moreover, we need to ensure the house is available for sale and that the advertisement is up to date. We must see that the lord of the fourth house is not afflicted—not in station or hidden by the Sun's rays. Suppose the online resource lists only the available property; nothing can be wrong with the house. In that case, we do not impose these requirements on the significator of the property. See how we interweave the context of the situation with what we look at in the chart.

Then, we allow the significators to advance up to 30 degrees ahead in their signs to perform or not perform the exact aspect. The intermediate planet, i.e., the realtor, may come to the stage, collecting or translating the light. Or the prohibitor, signifying another buyer, can cut off my light. We look at the chart as if we were watching a long movie.

A Real-Life Example

Sometimes we need to test all possible strategies—the "short/full movie" strategy, and the "snapshot of the future" approach—to answer a question properly. Here's an example of such situation.

Predictive Astrology Textbook

A young lady recently approached me having just discovered that the man she believed to be her father might not be her biological father. She has identified two other men as potential fathers and asks, "Who is my biological father?" (Fig. 2.27).

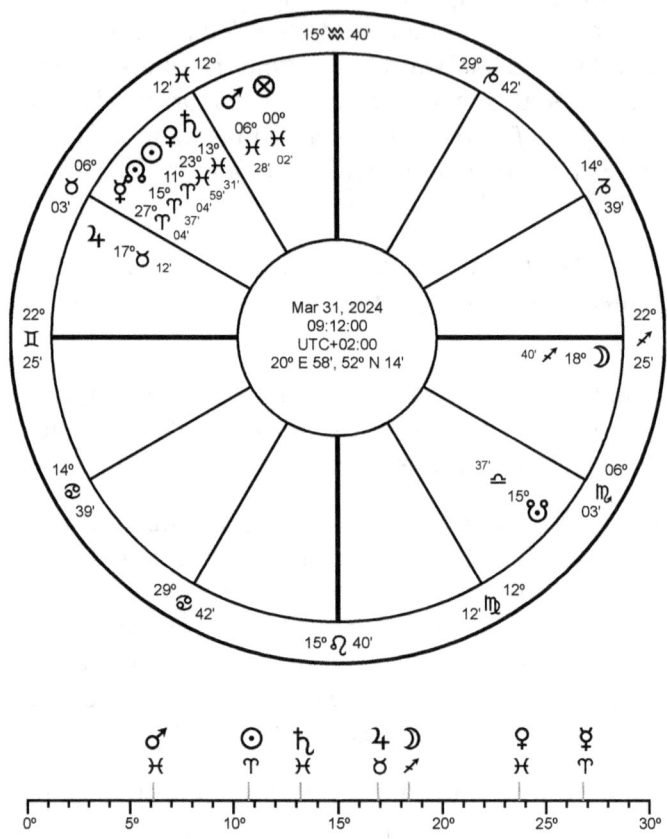

Figure 2.27: *Chart: Who is My Biological Father?*

Initially, I expected the chart to highlight the fourth house, the house of fathers. But there's only one indication supporting this hypothesis—Mercury (the querent's thoughts) exalts the Sun—the ruler of the 4th house and a natural significator of fathers.

In reality, Jupiter, the lord of the seventh house, is emphasized twice. It rules both:

- The Moon (emotions)

Chapter 2. Horary Astrology

- The Part of Fortune (the querent's deep desires)

Thus, Jupiter becomes the main subject of the question. The seventh house represents other people, confirming we're investigating another individual. While the ruler of the fourth house (her current father) matters, it's not as prominently highlighted as Jupiter—another (unfamiliar) person.

The only logical explanation for this scenario is that the primary question would be: "Could this unknown person (Jupiter) be my father?" Thus, I need to find a biological connection between Jupiter and the querent.

How can the chart show a biological connection with Jupiter?

- **A past conception**—this is an event, a past aspect between the querent and Jupiter. This is part of the *"full movie"* strategy. But such an aspect is absent.
- **Genetic inheritance**—this is the influence of one person over another, the querent being under Jupiter's influence by reception. This is part of the *"snapshot of past circumstances"* strategy. But we cannot use this reception to establish paternity, as we utilized it to assess radicality.
- **A genetic connection**—this is a close connection of two people, a close aspect (or antiscion conjunction) between the querent and Jupiter. This is also a *"snapshot"* strategy. But such a connection is also absent.

Thus, Jupiter is not the father.

We know there was another candidate for fatherhood, which we can find either through:

- The seventh house (as the second individual), or
- The fourth house (as an alternative significator of fathers)

Saturn is the co-ruler of the seventh house (it rules Capricorn, which occupies a significant portion of the seventh house). Mars is the co-ruler of the fourth house—its large "copy" in the place of opposition at 6° Virgo falls right into the fourth house. This is equivalent to the planet itself being in the fourth house. This technique of Morinus is known as *"accidental rulership of the opposite house."*

Between these two planets, Mars is more important to the querent because Mercury (the querent's thoughts) is ruled by Mars, and none of the querent's significators are concerned with Saturn. However, this second candidate (Mars) is much less relevant to the querent than Jupiter, as it is highlighted only once. Indeed, the girl didn't believe the second candidate could be her father—she was more concerned about the first person.

Let's check the connection between the querent and Mars:

- A past conception—this is a past aspect, but it is absent
- Genetic inheritance—the querent is in Mars' dignities. But we cannot use this, as we utilized this reception to identify the second candidate for fatherhood
- A close genetic connection—a close aspect or antiscion conjunction is also absent

The Sun, the ruler of the fourth house, is the only planet strongly connected to the querent. Mercury was previously combust (burned) by the Sun and first emerged from combustion when it was 10° away from the Sun—exactly at the moment of entering Aries, the first sign of the zodiac symbolizing life.

This simultaneous appearance of Mercury and its entry into Aries, under the Sun (the natural significator of life-giver), perfectly indicates birth under the Sun's influence. Moreover, throughout her life (shown by Mercury in Aries), Mercury has remained in the Sun's rulership and exaltation, maintaining an unbreakable genetic connection with the Sun.

Thus, without any doubt, the Sun—the man who raised her—is her biological father.

Unfortunately, I never received feedback from the querent regarding this prediction; nevertheless, I am confident enough in the result to include this prediction in the book.

Choosing the Right Timing Technique

We have three primary timing techniques in horary astrology:

- Symbolic timing in exact aspects, which we discussed earlier
- Symbolic timing in long-term aspects, and
- Symbolic timing in ingresses, which we will discuss in the next two sections

The choice of timing technique depends on how the chart depicts future events.

Suppose the chart shows the answer by a "full movie" pattern. In that case, we employ the symbolic timing in the exact aspects discussed earlier in the section "Timing Techniques: the Symbolic Timing in Exact Aspects." Suppose you received the question "When will my brother visit me?" The translation of light between the querent and brother will perfect in 3 degrees, corresponding to 3 days. The brother will manage to buy the air tickets and fly in 3 days.

If the chart shows the answer by a "short movie" pattern, then we employ:

- The symbolic timing in ingress
- The symbolic timing in exact aspects (between alternative significators)
- The "long-term aspect" technique

Suppose you receive the question "Will my financial situation improve within a year, and if so, when?" Within the "short movie" pattern, the significator of money enters its domicile in 2 degrees, giving a positive answer: "Yes, the situation will improve within the year." But that does not mean it will improve precisely in two months or two weeks. It could improve in 6 months. The timing lies somewhere else.

For instance, the chart may show us that the co-ruler of the querent, the Moon, is debilitated, and by reception, the ruler of the 2nd house bothers them. But after 18 degrees, it leaves the sign of its exile and simultaneously stops worrying about money. Given that financial improvement is inevitable, this is an excellent indicator that the expected improvement will occur in 18 weeks (within the year). Thus, we employed *the symbolic time in ingress*.

Alternatively, another scenario could be that the ruler of the 1st house makes an aspect to the noble ruler of the 11th house, indicating a significant bonus from the company in 6 degrees. Since financial improvement is inevitable, this aspect is a precursor to a substantial income. Then, we calculate what 6 degrees corresponds to—six months or six weeks—and make the final forecast. Thus, we employed the *symbolic timing in exact aspects* of alternative significators that are important in the question.

Don't worry—in the clear radical chart, the testimony where you can find indications of timing lies on top of the picture—you will not contemplate for long.

N.B.

Usually, the querent does not ask, "Will my financial situation improve? If so, when?" Typically, the client asks, "When will my financial situation improve?" In this case, we first need to establish whether it will improve by the "short movie" strategy and then proceed to answer the question "When." Also, in practice, clients often are not concerned about the exact date—they inquire about timing to comprehend that the uncomfortable situation will end within a reasonable time frame (usually months or years), i.e., it will not last forever. If the girl desperately looks for marriage, the answer "You will meet your husband in 1 year" or "You will meet him in 1.5 years" would equally mean "You will not be alone." And that is the answer to the sincere question. In such cases, the chart may not provide specific time frames. Be ready to face such cases.

Please note that if the default option, the reality of the context, or other testimony of the chart suggests that the collision of the objects is inevitable, but there is no perfection of an exact aspect between corresponding significators, we use the "long-term aspect" technique described below.

Timing Technique: Long Term Aspects

Suppose you know from the context or other chart testimonies that the encounter of two objects is inevitable, but there is no aspect between corresponding significators. In that case, you can use the "long-term aspects" technique. Allow the significators to advance as many degrees as needed until they finally perform the exact aspect.

The significators will likely encounter prohibitors—other planets—or change signs on their way. However, this should not concern you. You are not answering whether the event will happen; you already know that the event (the meeting of two planets) is inevitable. You are simply seeking an indication of the timing. The number of degrees in the aspect will signify the number of time units until the event.

The term "long-term aspects" doesn't imply a long time. Instead, it indicates that other events and changes of circumstances (other aspects and changes of signs) will occur before the applying planet performs the final aspect.

In "long-term aspects," we cannot define time units as with regular aspects (see the section "Timing Techniques: the Symbolic Timing in Exact Aspects") since the applying planet can change signs and houses on its way.

Therefore, we set the time units based on common sense and knowledge of the context. For example, a girl asks, "When will I meet my husband?" You observe her significator aspecting her husband's planet in 65 degrees.

- Could it be 65 years? We dismiss this—it contradicts reality.
- Could it be 65 months or 5.5 years? Yes, this is a realistic time frame.
- Could it be 65 weeks or 15 months? Yes, this is also quite possible.
- Could it be 65 days? Two months is a reasonably short period, especially if the girl has been searching for a husband for the last two years. Most likely, the chart would have shown us a simple applying aspect performed in 2 degrees. So, the default option is to reject this time frame. However, suppose the chart shows us an exceptionally powerful position of the girl's planet with a strong reception (desire for marriage), and you know that she goes on dates every day. In that exceptional case, we will choose the option of 2 months.

You might have two options—65 weeks or months before meeting—that is normal. You can honestly answer, "I expect you to meet your husband in 5 years, but I do not exclude the option of 1.5 years."

However, you can look for clues in the chart. For example, the applying planet moves in a fixed sign most of the time, so it is logical to prefer a longer period.

As I said before, a radical chart does not confuse the astrologer with controversial testimonies. The chart may show the same period in two ways, which could be a clue. For example, the girl's significator meets the husband's significator in 65 degrees. On the other hand, the Moon enters the domicile of the husband's planet or enters the 7th house (literally, moves to its territory) in 5.5 degrees.

Both testimonies indicate the same period—65 months or 5.5 years. So you have no other options. Be prepared to see such synchronization in radical charts.

Prohibition of Long-Term Aspect

As the applying planet moves towards the second significator in a long-term aspect, it encounters various obstacles (aspects with unknown planets and changes of sign)—these are all indicators of accompanying events and changes in circumstances before the applying planet meets the second one.

It may turn out that the applying planet will stop on its way. As you remember, a planet's station is either a loss of motion or a decision change. If this happens with the applying planet, then we say that the meeting process is interrupted—either because the querent changes their mind or because they lose the opportunity to act due to future circumstances that we do not yet know. In any case, the turn of the applying planet prohibits the long-term aspect.

Another situation may occur—the applying planet may disappear in the rays of the Sun somewhere on its way. Suppose the Sun is not the second planet to which the fast significator is heading. In that case, something unknown hides the applying planet. The future obstacle will prevent the planet from approaching another significator. The effect will be the same—the prohibition of the aspect.

In practice, you very rarely encounter a situation where you predict the date with a long-term aspect technique and find the aspect prohibited. But even if you come across such a situation, do not panic. The chart can show you the event in other ways.

Suppose, in a death-related question, there is no direct aspect between the quesited and its death. At the same time, a long-term aspect between the two significators is prohibited.

In addition to the exact aspect, other ultra-specific testimonies may indicate approaching death.

- The quesited may shortly become stationary. The number of days until stationarity will indicate the time until departure.

- The quesited may set below the horizon, literally completing their life path. Then, the number of degrees until the conjunction with the cusp of the 7th house will indicate the time.
- The quesited may enter combustion or the place of its fall, indicating the departure time.

If you see such indications, the chart shows you the time through ultra-specific testimonies instead of the general aspect.

Secondly, even if you do not see such specific indicators, you can substitute the accidental significator in the long-term aspect with a universal one.

- Take Saturn—the universal significator of death—instead of the ruler of the 8th house.
- Take the Sun—the universal significator of life—instead of the person in question.

You will almost certainly overcome the prohibition. However, I'll again emphasize that if the chart forces you to seek an answer through such complications, you will likely answer the wrong question. Soon, you will see that radical charts are crystal clear, showing several simultaneous bright indicators pointing to the same time, so you won't have to contemplate long.

Several Long-Term Aspects

You may have several long-term aspects pointing to the same event. In a marriage-related question, the Moon meets the husband's significator in 23 degrees. The ruler of the 1st house meets the alternative significator of the husband—the Sun, a universal ruler of all men—in 18 degrees.

Twenty-three degrees and eighteen degrees do not correlate. The chart does not provide us with any other clues. In this case, we follow simple logic.

Concurrent obstacles (aspects and sign changes) encountered by the applying planet symbolize accompanying events and shifts in circumstances. Here, the two aspects represent potential scenarios for meeting the husband, each unfolding through distinct events and circumstances.

Like water seeking the path of least resistance, the aspect with fewer obstacles is more likely to manifest. Therefore, we prioritize the aspect with fewer accompanying aspects and sign changes.

Example №6: Part-Time Job

Here is an example of how we can use a long-term aspect to clarify the date of the event.

The head of the department gives their employees contacts of clients for personal assistance once a month, meaning the employees have a private part-time job in addition to their primary work. However, this month, the boss did not give staff contacts. One of the staff asks, "When will I get a private part-time job again?" (Fig. 2.28).

We begin to follow our algorithm—cast a chart and look for the principal houses in question. But first, let's think about what houses we expect to be essential.

The querent wants to meet with clients. These are other people, 7th house. Also, the querent wants to receive money from these clients. It is the 8th house. So, the chart may highlight both the 7th and 8th houses.

Let's check this assumption. The Moon, co-significator of the querent, exalts Jupiter. The exact Jupiter disposits Part of Fortune—the deepest desires. The querent desperately wants something that Jupiter signifies. Jupiter rules the 7th and the 8th house—the client and their money.

The chart is radical; we can create a list of techniques. What technique should we use? We are looking for an event that involves meeting two external objects—the querent and the customers or the querent and the customers' money.

The meeting of two objects is an aspect between 2 significators of these objects. So we are looking for an aspect between the querent and Jupiter.

There is an exact indirect aspect between these planets in the chart. The third planet, the Sun, will bind the querent and clients—it took the light of the Moon and carries it to Jupiter. This means the querent will not find a future client themselves—the Sun will help them. As you remember, the Sun shows all the kings and bosses. In the context of the question, this is the head of the department where the querent works. It is they

Chapter 2. Horary Astrology

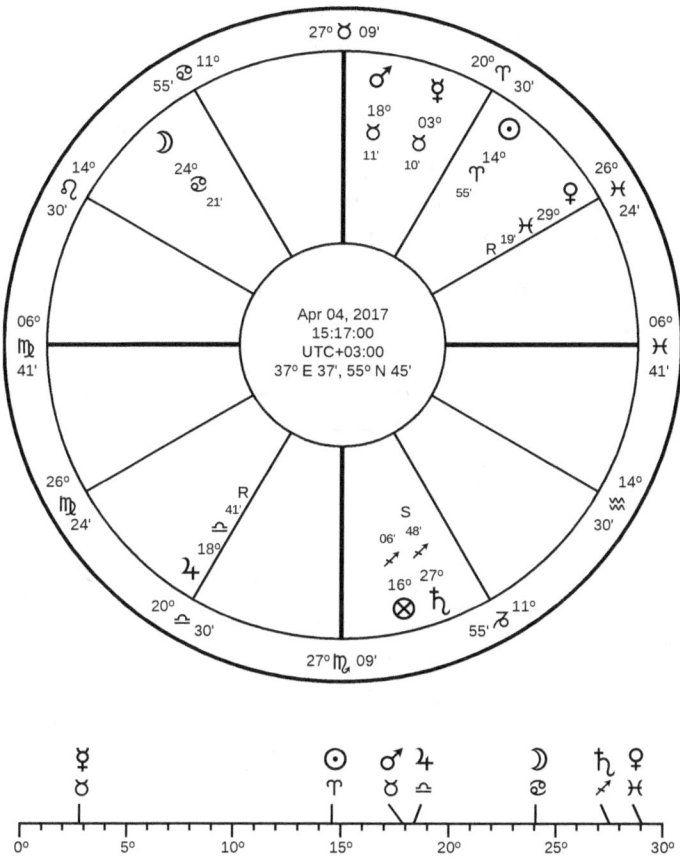

Figure 2.28: *Chart: When Will I Get a Private Job Again?*

who will bring the querent and the future client together. The aspect will perform in 3 degrees.

Which time scale should we choose—fast (that is, days), medium (weeks), or long (months)? The Sun (boss) is the applying planet. We will look at the Sun's position. The Sun is in a fast sign and the 8th house. It indicates an average time scale of weeks. So, the boss will bring the client in roughly three weeks.

Remember that the degrees in the long term may well correlate with those of the exact one. If this is the case, we can use it to clarify the timing.

Look, the Moon will meet Jupiter in 24 degrees in the long-term aspect. Three degrees correlate with 24 degrees, indicating the same period—about three weeks or 24 days.

Finally, our forecast looks like this: You will get the next client in around three weeks (24 days to be exact). Indeed, on April 28 (exactly 24 days later), the querent got the new private contract. We made the forecast with an accuracy of up to one day. Isn't it beautiful?

Let's look at the transit that occurred on that day for educational purposes (Fig. 2.29).

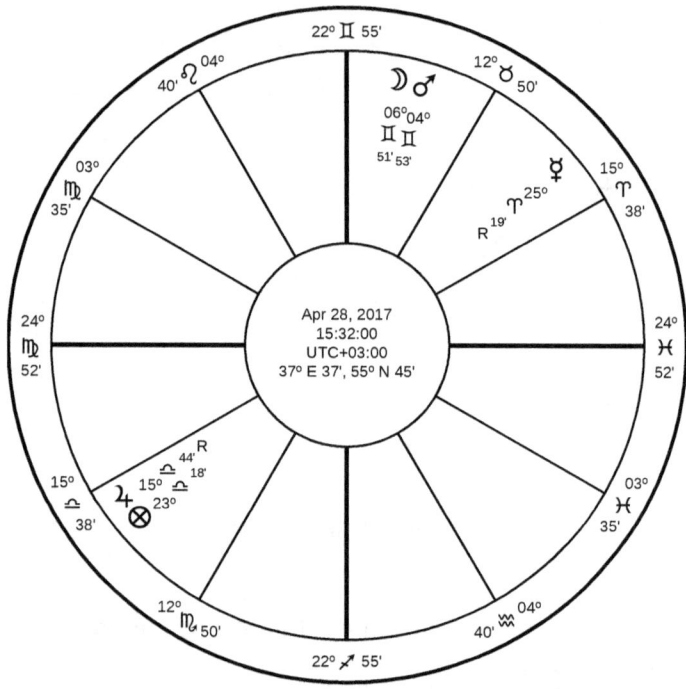

Figure 2.29: *Transit Chart: Getting the Job*

On that day, the Moon—the fastest of the planets and the universal significator of the flow of events—was closely conjunct with Mars. For several hours, Mars had become the ruler of the 8th house, symbolizing other people's money. At the same time, the Moon was temporarily taking on the role of the flow of events related to other people's money due to the close connection with Mars.

Chapter 2. Horary Astrology

At a particular moment during this period, the Moon's square had just passed through 6° 41' Pisces, the cusp of the 7th house of the horary chart. It connected the appearance of another person (the client), promised by the preceding horary chart, with their money (Mars) at a specific minute.

Simultaneously, another square of the Moon had passed through the 1st house of the horary chart, connecting the querent with someone's money within that minute.

During this minute, there was a particular second when Jupiter—the ruler of the client and money in the preceding horary chart—had just passed strictly along the cusp of the 2nd house. At that moment, it connected the promised client and their money with the querent's wallet.

In addition, Jupiter had strengthened its role as the client since it was also ruling the 7th house at that moment.

This configuration lasted for a very short time and then disintegrated. However, several factors manifested simultaneously and connected the chart's promise with the current moment. Even with all the desire, you can hardly guess such a successful combination. However, it occurs 24 days after the horary chart, and we knew in advance that it would happen.

You can see how the degrees in the aspects in the horary chart indicate the period (in this case, 24 complete rotations of the Earth around its axis), after which a suitable transit will occur that will fulfill the chart's promise.

Example №7: Film Release Date

A girl starred in the film and was looking forward to its release on TV. The film should be released within a week or two, but the girl wanted to know the exact date (Fig. 2.30).

Let's check the chart's radicality. We hear, "When will the film reach the audience?" The audience is the 7th house. Since the querent participated in the film, we can assign the 5th house to it. The film is the result of the querent's creativity.

One can argue that the film is the audience's entertainment; it is the fifth house from the 7th, i.e., the 11th house of the chart. But I expect more personal interest, like when *my* creative work reaches the audience,

Predictive Astrology Textbook

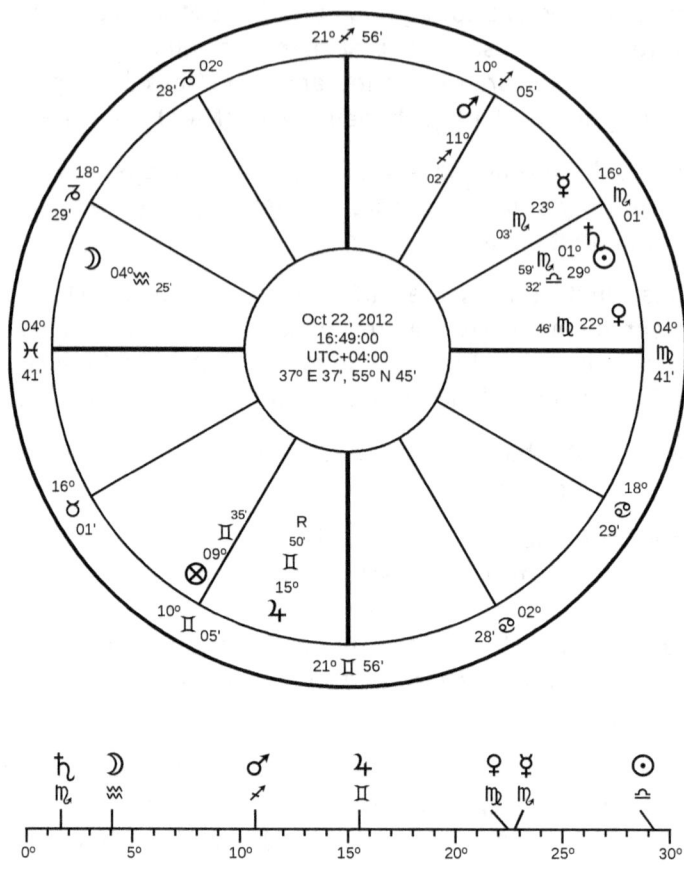

Figure 2.30: *Chart: When Will the Film Be Released on TV?*

rather than when the audience gets *its* fun. Following Occam's razor principle, I'll stick to the 5th house.

So, we expect the chart to highlight the 7th, 5th house, or both.

And yes, Jupiter (the querent) is captivated by Mercury, the ruler of the 7th house, audience. The same happens with the parts of Fortune, the querent's deep desires.

It is a question about the encounter of two objects—the movie and the audience. To answer, we need to find the aspect between the Moon and Mercury and then apply the symbolic timing technique to that aspect.

Chapter 2. Horary Astrology

But the Moon doesn't perfect the exact aspect with Mercury.

In that case, we can use the long-term aspects since we know the film will be released sooner or later. We will advance the Moon, ignoring prohibitions until it meets Mercury. After 20 degrees, the Moon will finally reach Mercury's square aspect.

The movie will be released in 20 units of time. Now, we need to understand the time units in context. We use common sense here. We know the film is due out in a week or two.

- Twenty degrees cannot be 20 hours; it is too early.
- It cannot be 20 weeks. It is too late.
- It can be 20 days. It perfectly fits the context.

Our forecast will sound like this: "The film will be released on TV in roughly 21–22 days." The film was released on November 12, precisely 21 days after the question was asked.

For educational purposes, let's examine the transit that occurred on November 12, fulfilling the promise of the horary chart (Fig. 2.31).

The Moon, the film significator in the preceding horary chart, conjoined with the momentary ruler of the 7th house for several hours, establishing a connection between the promised movie and the current audience.

At a specific moment during these several hours, the Moon formed an exact conjunction with the ruler of the 7th house. Such precise conjunctions occur several times a month. However, on November 12, the momentary conjunction of the Moon with the audience happened at 4° 33' Scorpio. This position is noteworthy because, at the moment of conjunction, the two planets cast a powerful trine to 4° 41' Pisces, the ASC of the preceding horary chart.

You can interpret this quite literally—the audience, momentarily connecting with the promised film, became visible to the querent, who observed the moment of the film's release.

The simultaneous occurrence of such a combination is extremely rare.

But there is one more coincidence. Right at the moment of the audience's conjunction with the film at 4° Scorpio, the audience significator of the preceding horary chart, Mercury, was passing strictly along the cusp of the 5th house. It means that the audience, as promised by the horary chart, finally encountered the film at that exact moment.

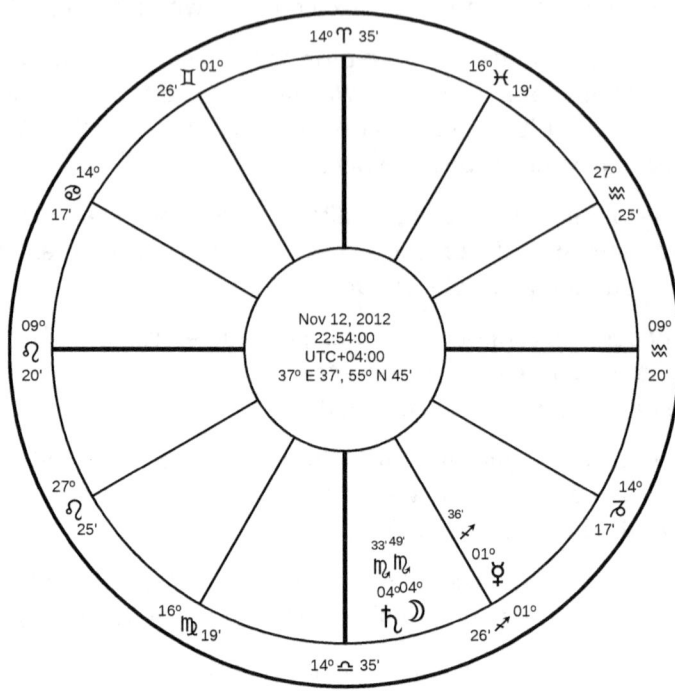

Figure 2.31: *Transit Chart: Film Release*

We have three independent testimonies of the conjunction of the film with the audience, all happening simultaneously.

The probability of such a concurrent occurrence is nearly zero. Yet, it happened on November 12, precisely 21 days after the question was asked.

As I mentioned earlier, the exact moment of the transit does not coincide precisely with the moment of the event. In the real context, many different constraints exist, such as the broadcast schedule, prime time, weekdays or weekends, and so on. All this affects the final time of the event.

However, the transit indicates the peak moment around which the promise of the horary chart will be realized. In the evening transit, we certainly should not expect the morning broadcast. The film was released a few hours before the transit moment, which is quite expected.

Chapter 2. Horary Astrology

Example №8: Job Search

Here is an example of a chart with two long-term aspects, of which we need to choose one.

A girl lost her job recently and is currently in an active search. She has very little money and is ready to accept any offer. She wants to know when she will find a new job (Fig. 2.32).

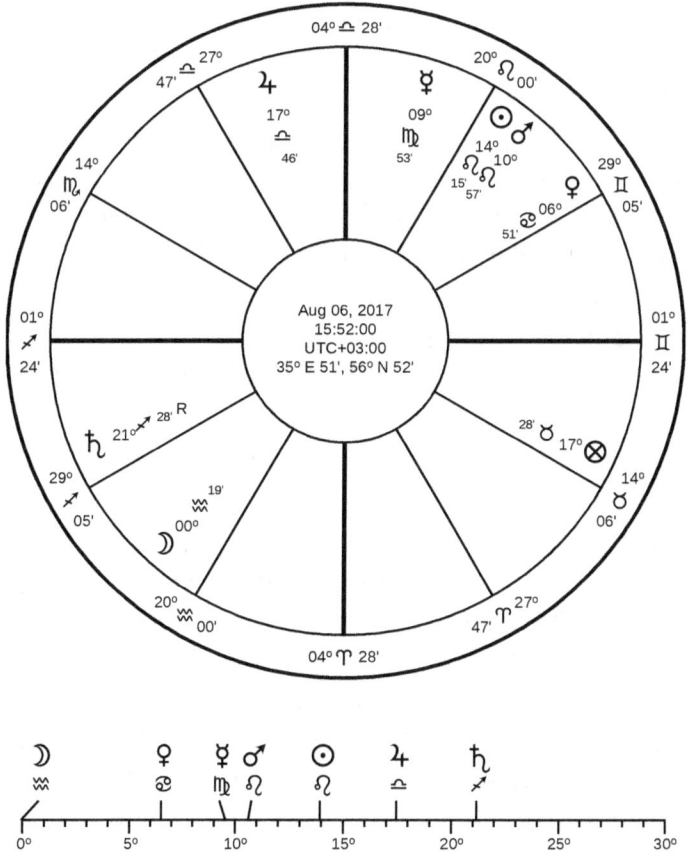

Figure 2.32: *Chart: When Will I Find a New Job?*

As always, we start by checking the chart's radicality. Since the question concerns the job, we expect the chart to highlight the 10th house. Let's test this hypothesis.

Indeed,

- Jupiter (the querent) is in the 10th house and is captivated by its lord.
- Venus, the ruler of the 10th house, also rules the Part of Fortune (the deep concern).
- In addition, the Moon has just entered Aquarius, which occupies the most part of the 2nd house—she just started to worry about her financial state. It also perfectly reflects reality.

We can proceed directly to compiling a list of techniques we will be using. Finding a new job represents an encounter between the candidate and her future workplace. Therefore, we must find the aspect between Jupiter or the Moon (the querent) and Venus (the future work).

We will first look for perfection in the exact aspect. There are no exact aspects between the querent and work, but this is not a problem here. The market is active, and the girl is young. Sooner or later, she will find the job. We can use a long-term aspect technique.

We have two aspects here. The first one is between the Moon and Venus. And the second is between Jupiter and Venus. Both give different time units—40 and 13. Moreover, these time units do not agree with each other.

Forty hours is not 13 days. 13 days is not 40 hours, etc. So, what should you choose?

As I mentioned earlier, we choose the long-term aspect, where the faster planet has fewer obstacles on the way. When I say obstacles, I mean the number of other aspects and new sign ingresses the applying planet performs before it meets the second planet.

In our case, Venus is the faster planet in the Jupiter-Venus pair. Before meeting Jupiter, Venus will collide with Mercury. In the Moon-Venus pair, the Moon is more rapid. Before it meets Venus, the Moon meets Mars, the Sun, Jupiter, and Saturn. After that, it enters a new sign. Only after that does it reach Venus.

The path of Venus to Jupiter is much easier—it has fewer obstacles. We will choose this aspect, which gives us 13 degrees. Since the aspect occurs on quadrature, the girl will look for work for a little longer than 13 time units.

What are these units of time?

- The girl is young, full of power, and actively looking for a new job.
- She needs money and is ready to take on the first opportunity.
- The market is full of opportunities, and many job offers are available.

In this context, 13 months or weeks is a very long time. Thirteen hours is too short. Thirteen days is quite realistic. Venus is in the house of average speed and a fast sign. It points to the realistic time scale. Since we have a square aspect, the girl will find a job in a little longer than 13 days, about two weeks.

So, our forecast is "the girl will find a job in 2 weeks." Exactly two weeks later, she found a new job.

Timing Technique: Symbolic Timing in Ingress

This technique is relatively straightforward. Let's assume that a change in certain circumstances is inevitable in the context of the question. Simultaneously, the adjacent sign effectively describes the new circumstances. In that case, the number of degrees the significator passes before entering the neighboring sign will correspond to the number of time units until the circumstances change.

For instance, a person living in a dry region asks, "When will the rainy season finally come?" The ruler of the 1st house, signifying the querent's local area, moves into a moist sign in 7 degrees. We know that the rainy season will inevitably come. Therefore, we can interpret these 7 degrees as the duration of the remaining period of drought.

- Could it be seven years? Highly unlikely.
- Could it be seven months? That may be exceedingly long.
- Could it be seven weeks (around two months)? Yes, it is the most expected timeframe in this context.
- Could it be seven days? No, it is too early for the rainy season.

The significator moves 7 degrees in a fixed sign. That corresponds to a longer time scale—7 months.

Often, we use symbolic time in ingresses to clarify the time in the aspect between the main significators. In the same question about rains, the significator of the local area makes an aspect with Jupiter—the universal significator of fertility and rains—in 1 degree. So we expect rain to occur in 1 unit of time. Jupiter is in Pisces, and we expect heavy rain.

Simultaneously, after 7 degrees, the Moon (querent) enters the moist sign of Cancer—a place of Jupiter's exaltation. In 7 time units, the querent will find themselves in a wet environment with lots of water. Both testimonies point to heavy rain in 7 days or one week.

A change of sign also signifies a shift in reception. If it is inevitable in the question, you can apply this technique. For example, a girl asks, "When will I find a new man?" But the chart shows (and the girl confirms) that she has just broken up with her previous boyfriend. You see a separating opposition and a recent change in the boyfriend's reception—he recently left the girl. A new man is not even in the question—her Moon is in a highly suppressed state and captivated by the ex-boyfriend. The sincere question is, "When can I finally forget him and find peace of mind?"

We understand that the pain of separation cannot be eternal. After 9 degrees, the Moon leaves the sign where she is captivated by this guy and feels so depressed. She has 9 degrees left to overcome the painful dependency and improve her emotional state.

It cannot be nine years or days. Realistic options are nine weeks (around two months) or nine months. The Moon moves through a fast sign, so it refers to weeks.

Example №9: Investment Payback Date

Here's an example of symbolic timing in ingress.

Some time ago, the querent invested substantial money in a mutual fund. Recently, they applied to the bank to pay their dividends. However, they are concerned that the bank might delay the payment. "When will the bank return my dividends?" (Fig. 2.33).

As always, let's begin with a radicality assessment. We expect the chart to highlight the querent's money (2nd house).

Indeed, Mars, the ruler of the 2nd house, dominates by exaltation over Jupiter (the querent) and the Part of Fortune (their deep desires).

Mars is in excellent condition, which aligns with reality—the querent invested a substantial amount. But note that Mars is not moving anywhere; it is in the station.

Chapter 2. Horary Astrology

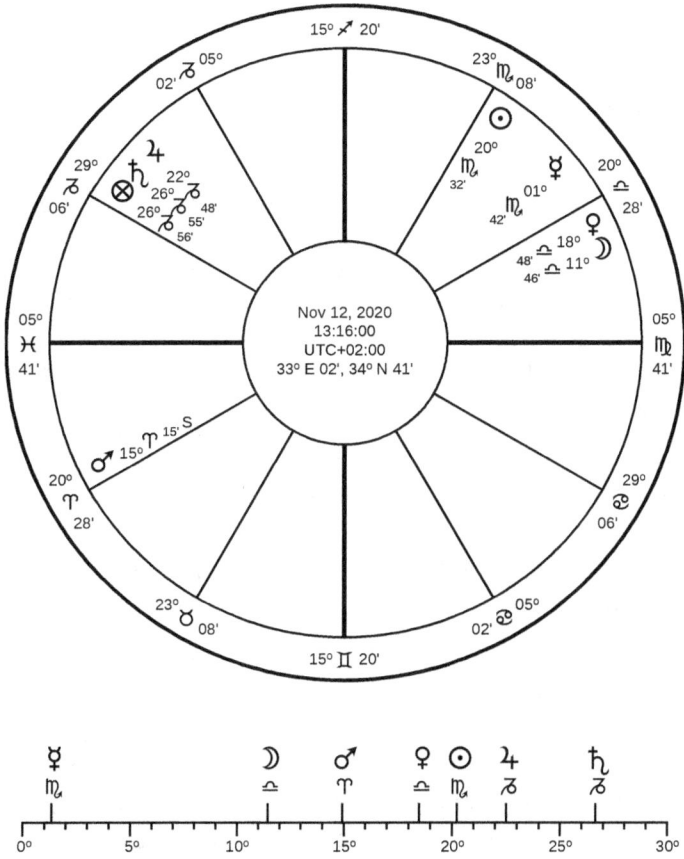

Figure 2.33: *Chart: When Will the Bank Return My Dividends?*

This means that the querent's finances are "frozen," and they cannot access them. The only logical explanation is that they invested all their money and don't have savings for everyday expenses.

Indeed, in a conversation with the querent, it turned out that all their savings are in the mutual fund, and they currently have no free funds. Hence, there is a worry that the bank might delay dividend payments.

The querent's contact with stationary Mars is not the best indicator of money return. It is more of an indication of the querent's attempt to use frozen finances. Still, stationary Mars will hardly produce any effect.

What could be an indicator of the bank returning the money then?

- We cannot look at the real-time when Mars will leave the station as it's more of a period than an exact moment.
- We cannot look at Mars' entrance to the next sign where it gains dignity (improving financial condition) as Mars already has the maximum dignity.

The only thing left is to find a separate significator of dividends in the chart that either adds to the querent's pocket (i.e., makes an aspect with the ruler of the 2nd house) or reaches the querent itself (i.e., makes an aspect with the querent).

There aren't many options that can indicate dividends transferred to the querent by the bank:

- It could be the 2nd house of the bank or the 8th house of the chart—money currently owned by the other party but soon transferred to the querent.
- It could be the 2nd house from the 2nd, i.e., the third house of the chart (literally, dividends from the querent's investments).

Both houses are ruled by the same planet—Venus. Moreover, this Venus is crucial for the querent—the Moon is captivated by it. In addition, Venus occupies the 7th house and conjuncts the 8th. It is at the disposal of the bank. It fits perfectly into the context. The chart didn't even allow us to choose between the 3rd and 8th houses, showing us the only correct significator of dividends. It is expected behavior of the radical chart.

Venus is in excellent condition, which indicates a significant payout. Indeed, the querent confirmed that they expect a substantial amount.

We have two equally possible aspects between Venus and the querent's account:

- Mars has taken the light from Venus, and now the Moon is approaching Mars to collect that light. The querent initiated the process of receiving dividends to soon complete it. This aspect completes in 3.5 degrees.
- The Moon is taking the light from stationary Mars and will soon pass it to Venus. The querent will take additional actions and complete the receipt of dividends. This aspect completes in 7.6 degrees.

Both options are possible, but we need to choose one. It is where *symbolic timing in ingress* comes to the rescue.

Jupiter (the querent) leaves the sign where they are so concerned about money in 7.2 degrees. It aligns entirely with the second time frame. In the context of the question, the bank should return the money within 1-2 weeks. It implies we are talking about days. We forecast that the querent will receive money in 7-8 days.

The money arrived in the bank account after eight days.

Example №10: Dismissal

Here's another example of the symbolic timing in ingresses technique.

A querent works at a factory. The management has announced an upcoming wave of layoffs, and they ask, "Will I lose my job? If so, how soon?" (Fig. 2.34).

As usual, let's check the chart for radicality. We expect the chart to highlight the 10th house. Indeed, the ruler of the 10th house, Jupiter, controls the Moon (the querent's emotions) and the Part of Fortune (deep desires).

Yes, keeping the job is essential to the querent. We can proceed to compile a list of techniques that we will apply.

It is not a question of the collision of two objects but of an approaching change in circumstances—losing the current job. What can firmly indicate an upcoming job change?

- The querent changes sign in the following 3–4 degrees
- The job changes its state (i.e., sign) in the following 3–4 degrees

What additional factors may accompany a job change if strong testimonies show them?

- The conjunction of the querent or the job with a corresponding star, such as Vindemiatrix or Antares
- The querent's presence at the end of the 10th house indicates leaving that place
- Additionally, we can check for the immediate applying aspect between the querent and the dispositor of Part of Dismissal (see the section "Signification Techniques: Arabian Parts").

What strong indicators will suggest no job loss?

Predictive Astrology Textbook

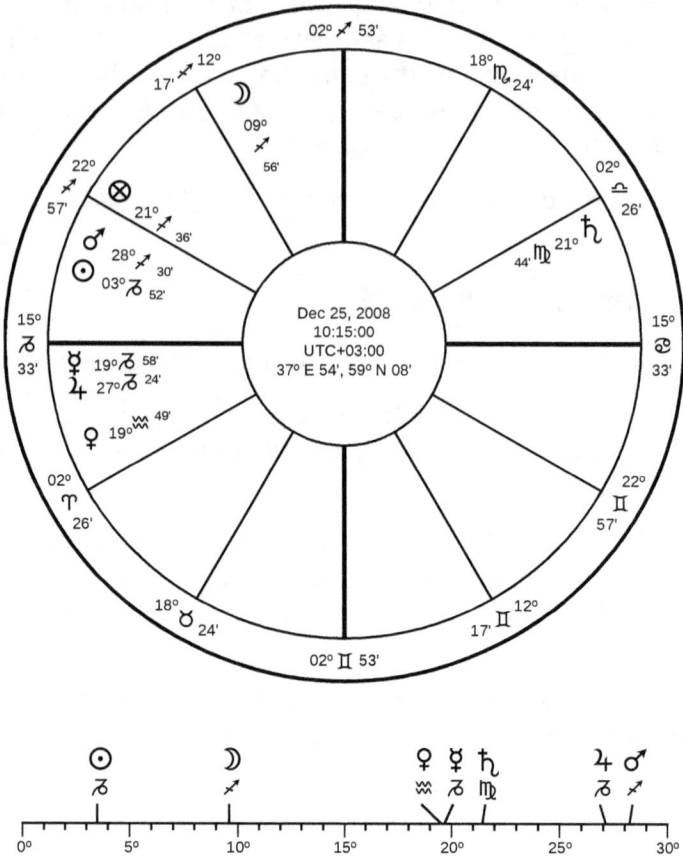

Figure 2.34: *Chart: Will I Lose My Job? If So, How Soon?*

- The absence of the querent exiting the sign in the following 3–4 degrees
- Simultaneous absence of the job exiting the sign in the following 3–4 degrees

What additional indications will tell us that nothing will happen?

- The querent is stationary, meaning they are not going anywhere
- The management highly values the querent and does not want to let them go

Since the question is crucial and the chart is radical, we expect that it will provide an answer through strong indicators and support it with additional reinforcing signs.

The chart shows a primary indication of job loss: Jupiter, the ruler of the 10th house, is changing signs, so the querent cannot retain their position.

As expected, the chart provides us with several supporting indications:

- The Moon, co-significator of the querent, is at the very end of the 10th house. The querent is about to leave their job.
- The Moon is on Antares, symbolizing the end of a significant cycle, i.e., job loss in this context.

Yes, job loss is inevitable. But look at the surprise the chart has in store for us. Saturn, the ruler of the 10th house, is stationary. Literally, the querent never leaves; they stay where they are. Moreover, Jupiter, the employer, adores the querent and is unlikely to part ways quickly. It contradicts the vital indications of job loss.

Usually, radical horary charts do not behave like this—all their indications are highly coherent. However, the chart is radical, and we have found several simultaneous indications of job termination. Therefore, we have no choice but to find a logical explanation that accommodates these contradictions.

From the context, we know that the querent fears losing their job, i.e., losing income. The position of the Part of Fortune confirms this. The 11th house is no less important for the querent than the 10th. The fact that both the 10th and 11th houses are shown by one planet makes sense. Changing social position (job termination) is equivalent to income cessation. Jupiter's ingress to the adjacent sign signifies both phenomena equally.

Note that Jupiter, entering the new signs, gains dignity rather than loses it. Currently, it is debilitated, but it will soon become peregrine. It implies that the position and salary will not just change; they will improve.

It may seem incredible, but the chart shows a promotion that will happen in connection with organizational rearrangements, not job termination. However, before reassuring the querent, I want to deviate from the main significators and find additional promotion indications.

For instance, looking at the querent's income would be appropriate. Mars, the ruler of the 2nd house, is about to change signs. Oh yes, this is what I wanted to see. But how exactly does the querent's financial situation change? Mars enters Capricorn—its exaltation. It becomes much better. The querent's financial state will improve.

Great. I have several independent confirmations of the promotion. Yes, the querent will lose their current position, but they will gain another, higher one.

Now, we can answer when the querent leaves their position and gets promoted. We usually determine the time when the querent asks for it, as in this case.

We see that the Moon leaves the house of the current job, and Jupiter changes its condition in a few degrees. We also see Mars entering Capricorn in a few degrees. This only means that the querent will soon change their position. It doesn't necessarily mean it will happen exactly in a few weeks.

However, we have time sync here. The Moon leaves the 10th in 2.5 degrees, and the lord of the 10th house (current position) also changes its state at 2.5 degrees. It is no coincidence. We have timing here. 2.5 degrees show time until the event. *This is exactly where we utilized the ingress timing technique.*

The question is, how long is it? 2.5 days? 2.5 weeks? Or 2.5 months? All three options are possible in the context. Jupiter is in the fast sign, and the Moon is in the average one. We don't even have any clues from the chart. We need more information.

Remember I told you that we can use the Arabian Parts if we need more information? It's time to do it. The part of dismissal falls at 15° of Libra. Venus, the dispositor of this part, is the significator of leaving the current position.

The Moon (i.e., the querent) performs an immediate aspect with Venus. It makes perfect sense. The first event that the querent will face in the context of the situation is leaving their position. And it will happen in 11 units of time.

So, we have three clear indications of the same event: 2.5 degrees, again 2.5 degrees, and 11 degrees. They should correlate with each other.

Indeed, 11 degrees refers to 2.5 as 11 weeks to 2.5 months. Check it yourself. One month is 4.5 weeks. 2.5 months is 11 weeks.

The querent will step down from the position in 11 weeks. Remember that symbolic timing has a level of accuracy. When the event happens in the next few hours, a deviation of several minutes is possible. If the event occurs in days, an error of several hours is allowable. If the event occurs in several years, the acceptable accuracy is plus/minus months.

So, we forecast that the querent will stay with the company and get a promotion, which will happen in roughly 11 weeks. And so it happened. After ten weeks and several days (just about 11 weeks), the boss transferred the querent to a new position with much better conditions.

Supplementary Timing Techniques

Transit Time

I already mentioned in the section "Timing Techniques: the Symbolic Timing in Exact Aspects" that symbolic time in aspects has a limitation. We cannot apply it if the applying planet makes a turn on its path.

In this case, we look at real-time aspects when the significator reaches the second planet in real-time.

The future station of the planet often symbolizes an event we are looking for—loss of mobility, business suspension, or someone's death. We cannot count the degrees until the station, but we can consider the real-time when the significator stops.

Later on, we will examine such a chart.

Freezing the Significator

Two aspecting planets often have similar speeds—while the first planet catches up with the second, the second significantly moves ahead. But if we "freeze" the second planet and do not allow it to move, then the path in the aspect will be much shorter.

This technique resembles secondary progressions in natal astrology. We usually do not use it in horary charts. However, exceptional cases exist when "freezing" the second significator leads to the only correct answer.

For example, Mercury is catching up with Venus. Their contact will occur after 17 degrees, symbolizing the querent's presentation at a conference.

However, we know the presentation will be scheduled tomorrow or the day after tomorrow, and the querent is interested in the exact day of the presentation. Seventeen degrees do not align with reality: it cannot be 17 hours—it's too early. It cannot be 17 days—it's too late.

But if we "freeze" Venus, Mercury will reach it after 1.5 degrees—that perfectly aligns with the context.

Another example: We expect an inevitable improvement in the querent's financial situation due to the expected bonus. The ruler of the 2nd house enters its domicile in 9 degrees. Simultaneously, the querent encounters the dignified ruler of the 11th house—a financial bonus at work—in 20 degrees.

Mercury and Venus are involved in this aspect. We do not know what to choose—whether it is 20 degrees until receiving the bonus or 9 degrees until the improvement in the financial situation.

But as soon as we "freeze" Venus, Mercury will catch up with it in 2 degrees. Now, 2 and 9 degrees point to the same time frame—two months or nine weeks. Freezing the significator resolved the contradiction in the chart.

Please use this technique solely to eliminate contradictions in the chart. It is not the primary technique for determining time. The real-life example of this technique is given on page 277.

Aspects to House Cusps

An aspect to the cusp of a corresponding house alone cannot be the primary indicator of event timing. However, it can refine the timing established by other techniques. For example, if symbolic timing in an aspect suggests that moving abroad will occur in 9 units of time, but you also observe that the querent makes an exact aspect to the cusp of the 9th house (long-distance travel) at 1.5 degrees, these values do correlate—1.5 degrees and 9 degrees correspond to 1.5 months or 9 weeks. Thus, the aspect to the cusp clarifies the timeframe: the event will occur in 9 weeks, not 9 days or months.

Refining the Number of Time Units

As I mentioned earlier in the section "Timing Techniques: the Symbolic Timing in Exact Aspects," symbolic timing has an interesting feature. If an applying planet moves faster or slower than its average speed, the total time until the event occurs is slightly shortened or lengthened.

One way to express this idea mathematically is to introduce a simple proportion: if the speed v' differs from the average speed $\bar{v}$ by a factor of n, that is $v' = n\bar{v}$, then the time until the event changes according to the inverse formula $t' = t/n$.

Therefore, if we know the deviation $\Delta v / \bar{v}$ of the speed from the average in percentage terms, we can say that $n = 1 + \Delta v / \bar{v}$, hence

$$t' = \frac{t}{1 + \Delta v / \bar{v}} \qquad (2.1)$$

I will show how to apply this formula in Example №7 on page 212.

Example №11: Lockdown

Here's an example of the transit timing technique.

A girl lives in Baku city. The coronavirus is spreading around the world. She asks, "Will there be a lockdown in our city? If so, when?" (Fig. 2.35).

In such a statement, it is challenging to understand what exactly worries the client.

- It may be the loss of her own business due to a lockdown
- It can be the lockdown itself and the restriction in movement it will cause
- Maybe there is something else that we don't know yet

Let's see what the chart suggests. Remember that the chart reflects the querent's psychic reality. There is an excellent chance that we will see what worries her.

Saturn rules the Part of Fortune and the lord of the 1st house. It signifies the main subject in question. It rules the 5th and 6th houses.

The 5th house is irrelevant. The 6th house shows misfortune, which is primarily related to servile work. You may often hear that the 6th house

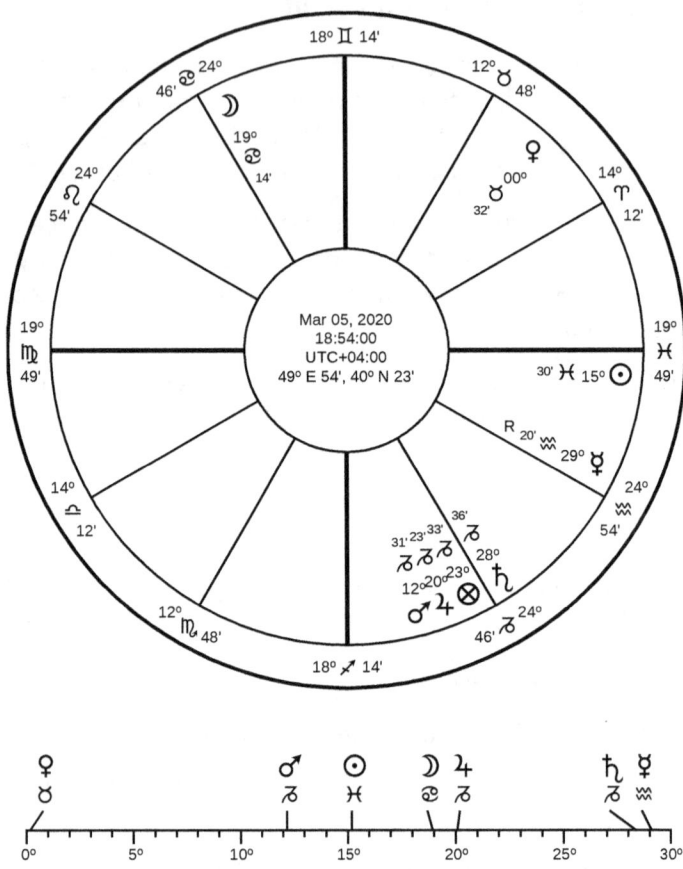

Figure 2.35: *Chart: The Dates of Lockdown*

shows illness. Still, the 12th house determines planets for severe diseases, like coronavirus, rather than the 6th. Saturn universally signifies restrictions and limitations, particularly the lockdown and restriction on free movement.

With that universal role, Saturn perfectly fits the context. There is no need to consult the client additionally. The chart is radical, and we can go straight to the list of techniques.

What techniques can we apply here?

- It could be an aspect of the querent and Saturn—the client facing a lockdown

Chapter 2. Horary Astrology

- It may also be the entrance of the querent into the sign of Saturn—the client entering the restricted environment

Both options are possible.

- We may move the planet a few degrees forward to see if it will enter the sign of Saturn.
- We also may ensure an exact aspect between the querent and Saturn.

Let's start by moving the planets a few degrees forward. The Moon (the querent) doesn't change the sign. It remains where it is. The querent's second planet, Mercury, is in retrograde motion. It has already entered the sign of Aquarius, which Saturn rules.

Moreover, before this ingress, Mercury was in Capricorn, the sign of Saturn. The querent cannot enter the period of difficulty and restrictions if she is already there. So the ingress doesn't show the upcoming lockdown and restrictions.

Let's now turn to the aspects. There are no aspects between the querent and Saturn. At first glance, this means that there will be no lockdown. But is it?

Let's look at additional details—is there anything prominent that happens to the querent in the following 3–4 degrees other than the entrance in the new sign? See, Mercury is retrograde. Very often, this means that things are not going as usual but rather against their ordinary course. But this is understandable—a pandemic is spreading, and the querent's life is not going as expected.

The question is, what will happen to Mercury in the following few degrees? Is there anything remarkable about its movement? Mercury is now at 29° Aquarius. But look, in just 1 degree, it stops completely. It is an outstanding event. The querent is about to stop, that is, to lose the ability to move. And it is something that should happen very soon. It clearly indicates the upcoming "freeze of movement," i.e., the lockdown.

We found the answer not via ingress or aspect, as expected, but via other testimony—the querent (or the territory where the girl lives) losing the ability to move.

In addition, Saturn, which plays the role of restrictor here, is on the 5th house cusp, which signifies places of pleasure, like restaurants, cafes, cinemas, etc. Now we understand why the Part of Fortune lies right on the cusp of that house. The possible unavailability of these enjoyable places is a deep concern of the querent, which makes perfect sense. Saturn's position limits these areas, which aligns with what we found.

So, a lockdown will happen.

Let's now look at the timing. When exactly will it happen? Since we know the event will occur, we can apply long-term aspects. Mercury cannot meet Saturn in the long-term aspect since there is a point of obstacle in its path—stationarity. But the Moon will meet Saturn in 9 degrees.

In the context of the situation, it cannot be nine years or nine months. The hours do not fit either. No one will declare a lockdown at night. The only remaining options are nine days or nine weeks. Given the rapid spread of the virus, two months seems unrealistic.

Moreover, the chart provides a hint. It is a *transit time till Mercury's station*. Mercury's real-time motion will stop in about a week, so we are talking about days before the querent loses her ability to move freely across the city.

Thus, nine days is the most plausible of all possible time frames. So, our forecast is, "In 9 days, on March 14, a lockdown will happen in the city of Baku."

This horary chart perfectly demonstrates how we can predict social phenomena that personally affect the querent without using mundane astrology techniques.

According to Wikipedia, "The Operational Headquarters under the Azerbaijan Cabinet of Ministers conducted the measures on social isolation that applied countrywide from March 14." Exactly as we predicted, in the period of Mercury's station.

Example №12: Power Supply Restoration

Here is an example of aspects to house cusps and refining the number of time units.

A female astrologer asked herself, "When will the electricity be restored?" Some time ago, the electricity in her house was cut off, and she was experiencing discomfort.

Chapter 2. Horary Astrology

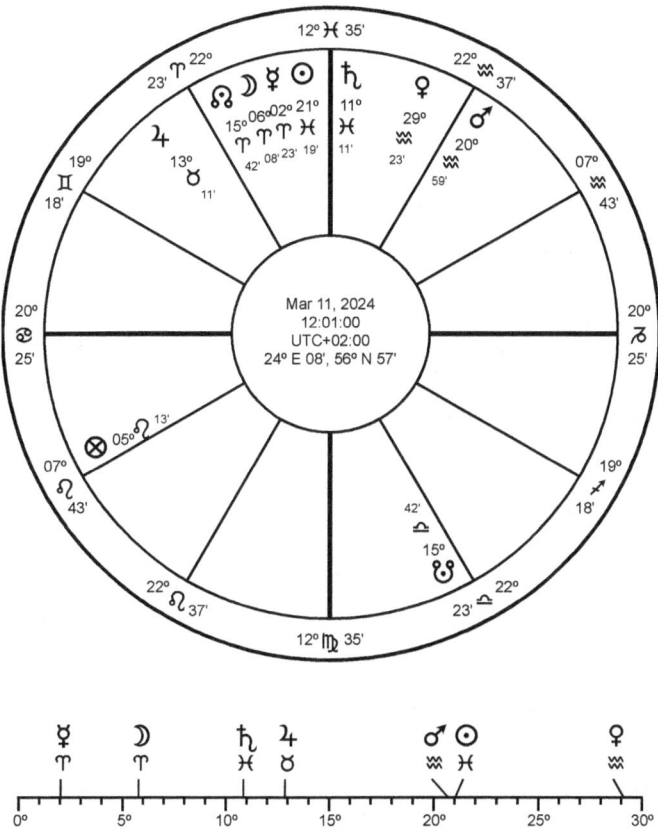

Figure 2.36: *Chart: When Will the Electricity Be Restored?*

First, let's check the chart for radicality. There is no specific house for electricity, but it has a universal significator—the Sun. The Sun represents the source of energy and light, including electricity. I expect the Sun to be significant for the querent. And indeed, the Moon (the querent) exalts the Sun, and the Part of Fortune (the querent's deep desires) is in the Sun's power. The Sun is highlighted twice—the chart is radical.

What technique will we use to determine the timing? We are dealing with an event—a future meeting between the querent and electricity. Therefore, the timing will be indicated by symbolic time in the aspect between the Moon and the Sun. However, the Moon does not perform an exact aspect with the Sun within the sign.

This is not a problem. Since we know for sure that the electricity will eventually be restored, we can consider long-term aspects, ignoring light prohibition and the Moon's transition into a new sign. The Moon will make an exact aspect with the Sun after 48.5 degrees.

What time unit should we choose? We need to apply logic and contextual understanding. If we are talking about 48 hours, it likely indicates a significant power outage in the area. Given that the woman lives in Europe, she would have already received a notification if that were the case. But there was none. Therefore, we are likely dealing with a localized power outage. This leaves us with only one option—48 minutes.

Moreover, the Moon traverses most of its path to the Sun through the fast-moving sign of Aries—this suggests a short timeframe until the event. But that's not all. The chart provides a direct indication that we are dealing with minutes, not hours.

- The Sun, highlighted in the chart, rules the 2nd house.
- The Part of Fortune (the querent's deep desires) is conjunct the cusp of the 2nd house.

The 2nd house is clearly significant in the context of the question. It represents the querent's vital resources. In the context of electricity consumption for daily needs, electricity becomes an essential resource for normal living. Thus, the emphasis on the 2nd house makes logical sense.

Now, observe this—the Moon will make an exact trine to the cusp of the 2nd house in about 1 degree. Often, such closely approaching aspects indicate that "the event is moments away." Literally, the querent is on the verge of coming into contact with their vital resource (electricity in this context). As I mentioned earlier, this aspect alone does not indicate the exact timing of the event, as an aspect to a cusp is a relatively weak indicator. However, it can refine already known timing. So, on one hand, we have 48 units of time until the event; on the other—the event is imminent. This finally clarifies that we are dealing with the fastest possible timeframe—minutes.

Thus, our answer is that the electricity will be restored in 48 minutes. Since we are discussing such a short timeframe and attempting to predict down to the minute, it would be good to account for the actual speed of the aspecting planet to refine our answer. Here, we apply formula (2.1) on page 209.

The Moon, throughout its path, is roughly 20% faster than its usual speed. This means the deviation $\Delta v/\bar{v}$ is 20%, or +0.2. Then, according to formula (2.1):

$$t' = \frac{48}{1 + 0.2} \approx 41$$

Thus, the event should occur approximately 41 minutes after the question was asked. And indeed, the electricity was restored 42 minutes after the question was posed.

Homework Assignment №20

Now, it's your turn to predict the date of the event.

I assume you have chosen software to calculate various aspects (collection/translation of light and long-term aspects). I use the "Olga" astrology software,[8] which I created specifically for horary astrologers. Still, you may choose something else that suits you better.

So, here's the situation: A girl is in the last month of her pregnancy. The question is, "When will I give birth?" (Fig. 2.37). Your task is to determine the exact day of the child's arrival.

We exclude the situation of premature birth or miscarriage. There are no accidental injuries of the 5th house or its ruler in the chart (we will discuss accidental damage further in this book). Therefore, we assume that the birth will proceed as planned. So,

- Ensure that the chart highlights the 5th house.
- Check if the exact aspect is perfect between the mother and the child; if yes, find the timeframe.
- If there is no perfection of the exact aspect, look at long-term aspects—we know that the girl will give birth sooner or later.

---

[8] https://morinus-astrology.com/horary-app/

Predictive Astrology Textbook

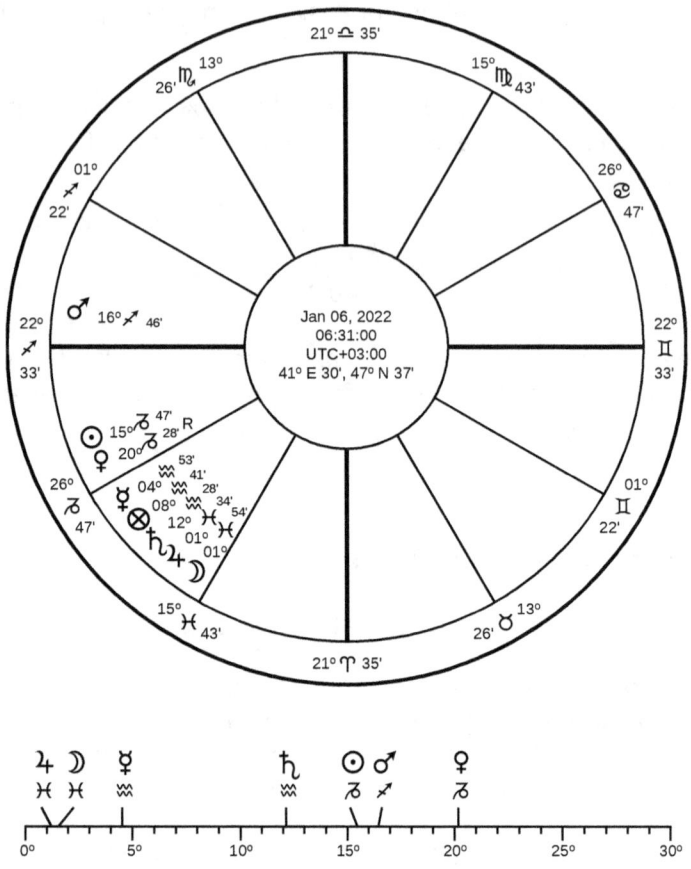

Figure 2.37: *Chart: The Exact Day of the Child's Arrival*

Solution

- Venus, the ruler of the 5th house, controls both querent planets (Jupiter and the Moon) by exaltation. Yes, the querent is wholly concerned about the child. The chart highlights the 5th house.
- There are no aspects between Jupiter and Venus or between the Moon and Venus here. But that's not a problem. Since birth is inevitable, we can move on to long-term forecasting techniques.
- Venus cannot reach Jupiter; on January 29, it gets stationary before making an aspect with Jupiter. A stationary state acts as an obstacle for the faster planet. However, the Moon (the other querent's

planet) calmly reaches Venus and completes the long-term aspect in 18 degrees on sextile.
- Eighteen degrees in the context of the question equals 18 days; there are no other options here. We expect the onset of easy childbirth without delays, precisely 18 days from the moment of the question.

We forecast that childbirth will occur on January 24. And so it was. The girl gave birth to her daughter precisely on January 24.

Accidental Strengthening: Strong Testimonies

According to its celestial state, a planet becomes accidentally benefic or malefic. However, it can manifest its goodness or badness with different intensities, which we call "strength."

For instance, you may have noticed that a stationary planet indicates an object losing mobility or activity. It doesn't inherently make the object good or evil, creative or destructive; it simply makes it less apparent.

Thus, we differentiate the planet's state from its power to act. Your best friend may be the most supportive person in your environment, but lying in bed with a temperature, they are of little help now.

The evaluation of accidental planet strength is only occasional. Typically, we use this assessment to determine if a character can overcome an opponent. These scenarios could involve sports competitions, legal proceedings, or questions such as "Will they overcome an illness to come to the office?"

More often, our interest lies in identifying apparent signs of accidental weakening that could restrict the significator from its intended action. We seek very pronounced signs of weakness but nothing beyond that.

Several factors contribute to a planet's strengths or weaknesses, each of which we will discuss in detail. The first factor is the planet's position in the house.

Position in the House

In astrology, a planet's placement in angular houses strengthens it, while placement in cadent houses weakens it.

As a planet moves away from the cusp of a house, it loses even more of its strength. For example, a planet on the cusp of the 4th house will manifest itself more strongly than a planet in the middle of the 4th house. However, this manifestation will still be stronger than if the planet were in the 11th house.

Remember that a planet's position in a house is the location in the sector of the celestial sphere, not of the zodiacal circle (Fig. 2.1 on page 29).

For instance, consider the previous chart (Fig. 2.22 on page 162). Visually, the Moon occupies the 7th house, but you see the projection of the Moon on the zodiac circle.

The Moon is typically situated slightly above or below the zodiac circle. As you see in the picture below (Fig. 2.38), although its projection is still above the horizon, the Moon has already set below the horizon, indicating that it has exited the area of the 7th house.

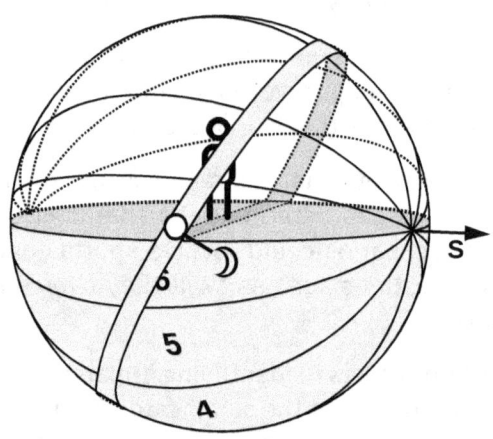

Figure 2.38: *The Moon on 3D-Sphere*

Ancient astrologers didn't bother calculating the precise positions of planets in the celestial sphere. They made an approximate assumption: if a planet is closer than five equatorial degrees to the cusp, it is already in that house. This rule wasn't arbitrary; astrologers found through practice that if a planet is close to the cusp, it begins to influence that house.

And it makes sense. The Moon, which is close to and below the horizon, still conjuncts the horizon within its orb. It influences the matters of the 7th house through its cusp, although it is physically in the 6th.

Such a Moon will still make the 7th house highly significant in assessing chart radicality. But this doesn't make the Moon strong. The strength of the 7th house extends from the western horizon and above, while the Moon is still below the horizon, as seen in the illustration.

If the cusp of the 7th house were to strengthen the Moon through her projection onto the zodiacal circle, this would mean that the 7th house enhances the Moon through an ordinary conjunction along the zodiacal circle. This would also extend the principle to any aspect of the Moon that falls on the cusp of the 7th house—the Moon casting an aspect to the DSC would become stronger. It would make the Moon in the 6th house, beholding the descendant, more potent than the Moon that doesn't behold it, which contradicts experience.

Therefore, when choosing an astrological program for calculations, choose one that considers the actual positions of planets in houses, not the positions of their zodiacal projections.

It is essential to distinguish between the actions of houses (determining a planet's influence on a particular area of life) and the strengthening/weakening of a planet.

For instance, a planet in the 12th house may indicate a specific person among secret enemies. However, a planet in the 12th house is weak. It does not imply that a particular person who acts covertly against a querent is inherently weak.

A planet in the 12th house is either weak or related to illnesses/hidden enemies. We interpret only one property within the context of the situation.

Example №13: Football Match

Let's consider an example of the accidental strengthening of a planet due to its position in a house. A football fan asked, "Will our team win this match?" (Fig. 2.39).

As I mentioned in the section "Special Case: The Question on Behalf of the Group," when a fan asks questions, we attribute the fan and their

Predictive Astrology Textbook

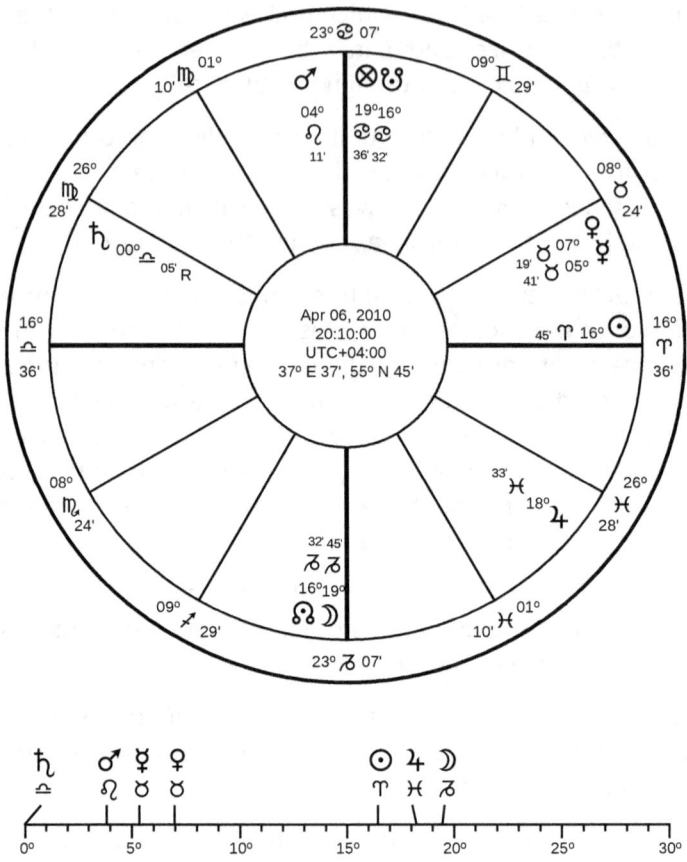

Figure 2.39: *Chart: Will We Win?*

team to the 1st house, as if the question were from the collective—will *we* defeat our enemies? What technique will we apply? We will assess the accidental strengthening of our team and the enemy team and see who is stronger.

The ruler of the 1st house, Venus, is positioned at the top of the 8th house, but this does not weaken her because, if we consider her position in the celestial sphere, she is still in the 7th house physically. Mars, our opponents, is also in an angular house.

Chapter 2. Horary Astrology

However, Mars is much closer to the cusp of the angular house than Venus, which is right at the end of the 7th house. Venus is significantly weaker than Mars.

Mars has no apparent weaknesses, such as stationarity, combustion, or conjunction with the node (we will discuss these testimonies later). Our opponents are more powerful.

Furthermore, the Moon, which indicates the natural course of events in such horaries, inclines by reception towards Mars. You can interpret this literally—the game's dynamics will favor our opponents.

Notice one more thing. The Moon has just made a precise aspect with the cusp of the 7th house, and after that, it does not encounter any planet. It resembles a picture of the future in which the flow of events has just been connected by an aspect and supporting receptions to our opponents, but nothing happens after that.

So, we expect to see something similar—a bright goal or a series of goals early in the game, after which both teams will "stagnate."

And so it was. The opponents scored a goal in the first minute, after which there were no bright moments. The favorite team lost 0–1.

Important: Please pay attention to an important detail. In horary astrology, where the position in the house is part of the answer, we cannot use the position of the querent in the house for determining radicality.

For example, if we see that our planet is in the 1st or 7th house, it means we are interested in our strength or the strength of our opponent. But on the other hand, this immediately makes our planet angular, that is, strong. We cannot say any player interested in the opponent's strength automatically becomes strong.

We need to choose whether to use the position of planets in houses to assess radicality or strength. If we prioritize assessing radicality, we immediately deprive ourselves of the ability to evaluate the strength of planets based on their positions in houses.

The same goes for receptions. If we are interested in our opponent, we expect to see the ruler of the first house in our opponent's power as testimony of radicality. On the other hand, this automatically means that our opponents have control over our team. Therefore, we leave the reception to assess who has control over whom during the game—it's an additional strengthening factor, although not as strong as the position in houses. We cannot use the reception to assess radicality.

Therefore, we cannot ensure the question is crucial to the querent. We must take the client's word that they are fans of this particular team.

Lunar Nodes

The Moon is usually positioned slightly above or below the zodiacal circle because its orbit is slightly inclined to the plane of the zodiac. The points where the Moon's orbit intersects the zodiacal circle are called *Lunar Nodes*.

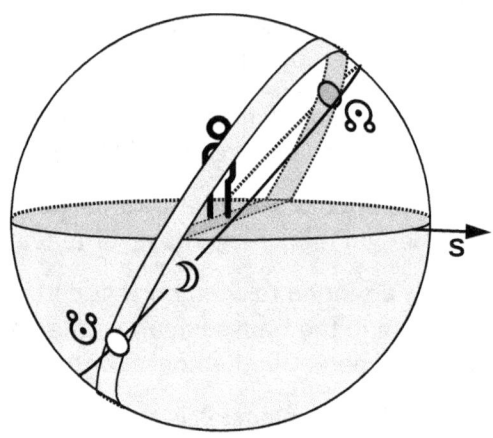

Figure 2.40: *Lunar Nodes*

Such nodes exist for every planet except the Sun. In astrology, there is a rule: if a planet is on its node (strictly in the plane of the zodiacal circle), it becomes slightly stronger in its manifestation.

However, this increase in strength is so insignificant that astrologers typically do not consider it. But with the Moon, things are different. In the section "The Special Role of the Moon in Horary Astrology," I mentioned that the Moon plays an exceptional role in horary astrology—it governs the overall flow of events. Therefore, the Moon's conjunction with its nodes signifies an intensification of the flow of events. If the Moon has not yet conjoined its nodes, it will soon do so since it is very swift in motion—about 14 degrees per day. So, we can consider a Lunar Node as a promise for the upcoming intensification of events.

Thus, if any other planet conjuncts with the Lunar Node, we say that the planet is where the flow of events will soon manifest very vividly.

The node where the Moon transitions from the southern celestial hemisphere to the northern is called the *North Node* ☊, or the *dragon's head*. It symbolizes the bright manifestation of accompanying supportive events. The opposite point is called the *South Node* ☋, or the *dragon's tail*. It denotes the bright manifestation of opposite events or obstacles.

When a planet or the Moon conjuncts the North Node (within 3 degrees), it portends:

- An increase in the volume of the object represented by the planet;
- An increase in the strength of the object's manifestation due to accompanying circumstances.

The reverse effect occurs if a planet or the Moon conjuncts with the South Node.

- We expect a decrease in the volume of the object.
- Or we anticipate a bright flow of obstacles, reducing the strength of the object's manifestation.

As you recall, the location of a planet or the sign within a house conditions them to manifest in a specific area of life. The same applies to the North or South Node.

If the North Node occupies a house, we expect accompanying events in a particular area of life that will bring favorable results. Conversely, the South Node in a house brings disruptions and failures.

Remember two important rules:

- We only consider the conjunction of nodes with the main significators or the node's positions in relevant houses.
- We either focus on the North or South Node in the context of the question, but not both simultaneously.

Short Examples

Let's explore how the nodes manifest themselves through examples of familiar charts.

In the horary chart from the section "Homework Assignment №11" on page 112, the querent was purchasing a very suspicious house. We established that the deal would result in financial losses. Additionally, we learned that the house owner had legal issues in a foreign country. Now, take a look at the position of the South Node (Fig. 2.41). It is in the 1st house, causing obstacles and disruptions in the querent's life. It, in itself, is an additional indication against buying the house.

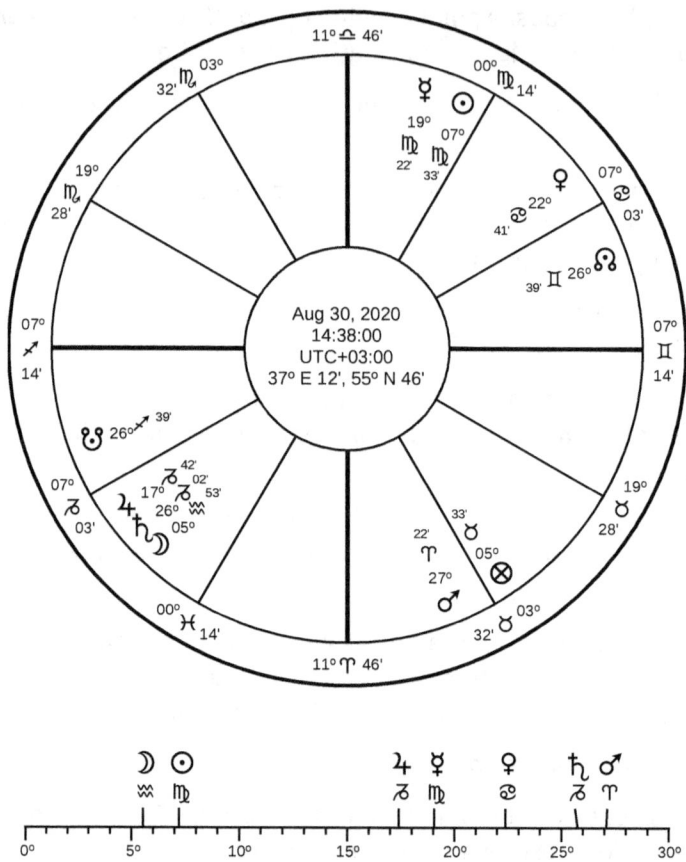

Figure 2.41: *Chart: House Purchase (with Nodes)*

In the horary chart from the section "Example №7: Film Release Date" on page 193, a girl asked, "When will the movie be released on TV?" We observed that the audience is the main significator in the story. Look at the North Node (Fig. 2.42). It is very close to the audience, so there will

Chapter 2. Horary Astrology

be many viewers. Indeed, the movie circulated on a national channel, which once again reflects the radical nature of the chart.

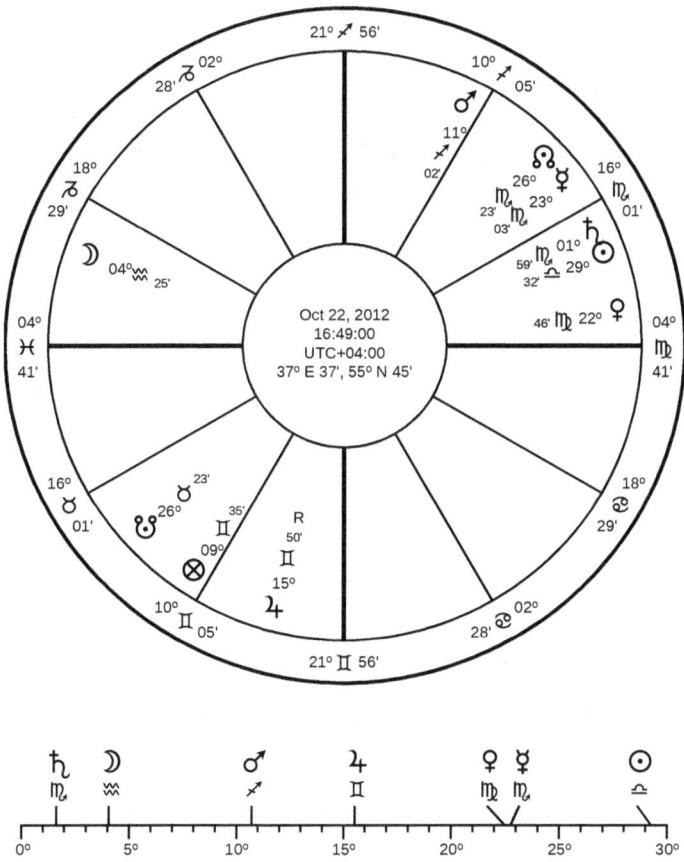

Figure 2.42: *Chart: Film Release (with Nodes)*

In the horary chart from the section "Example №10: Dismissal" on page 203, the factory management announced the start of a wave of layoffs. The querent asked if they would keep their job. We predicted their promotion due to staff rearrangements. Look at the placement of the nodes in this chart (Fig. 2.43).

We can interpret this in two ways.

- The South Node is in colleague's house, meaning the layoffs will affect them rather than the querent.

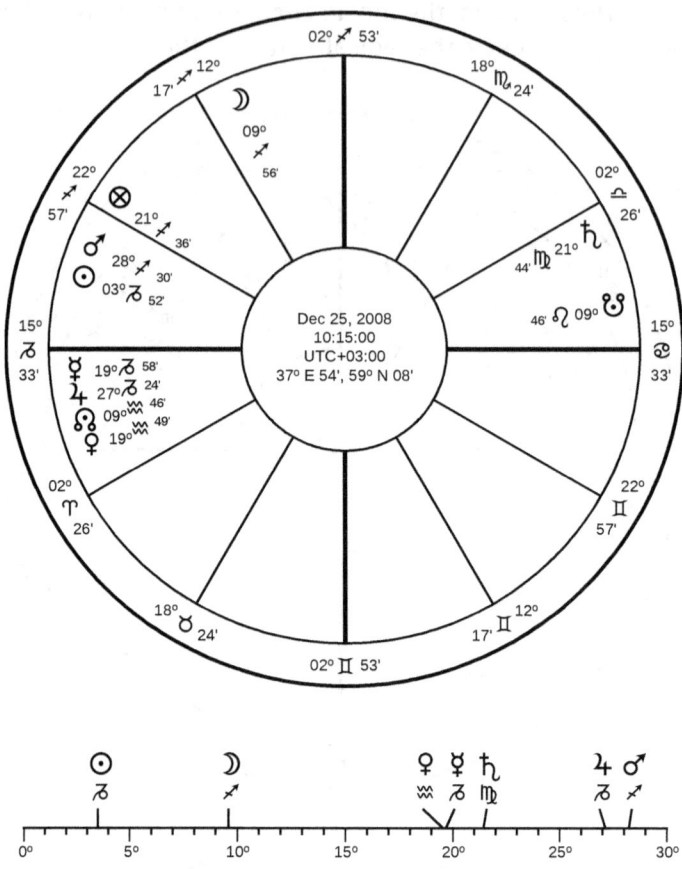

Figure 2.43: *Chart: Dismissal (with Nodes)*

- The North Node is in the querent's house. The querent will face the accompanying circumstances that will help them retain their position in the company.

Both interpretations equally support the chart's indications regarding the upcoming promotion.

As you can see, the nodes often complement the overall picture or assist us in determining the radical nature of the chart.

Combustion

I mentioned in the section "The Orbs of the Seven Planets" that when a planet comes close to the Sun, it disappears in its rays. We call this the *planet's combustion*.

For a planet to disappear in the Sun's rays, it must approach at a distance equal to the difference in the radii of the Sun's orb and the planet's orb. For example, the Moon's orb is 12 degrees, and the Sun's is 18 degrees. Hence, the Moon must be within 6 degrees of the Sun to become combust.

You may encounter a different definition of planetary combustion in William Lilly's works (Lilly, 1661). A planet is combust if it stays within 8.5 degrees of the Sun and is in the same sign.

But this assertion contradicts observable phenomena. For instance, Saturn disappears much earlier in the Sun's rays than Venus—they cannot both be combust at the same 8.5° distance from its center.

Regarding the position of a planet in the same sign as the Sun, Lilly did not provide any arguments to support his claim, nor did he cite the predecessors on whose authority he relied. The Sun obscures a planet in an adjacent sign just as effectively as one in the same sign, since the influence of its rays extends beyond sign boundaries. On this point, I side with Morinus regarding the conjunction.

A combust planet signifies:

– The object is hidden or invisible within the context of the question.
– The object is weakened and unable to manifest due to external factors.
– The object is, literally or figuratively, "burned."

We often use combustion in the question of death because a significator, which becomes invisible at one moment, signifies a person who stops manifesting themselves due to death.

When the planet lies within the Sun's orb (18 degrees), it is still visible but not as brightly. It signifies an object that experiences heavy obstacles in manifesting itself. We call such a planet *under the Sun's beams*.

N.B.

Crucially, when the Sun itself signifies the object in question, combustion becomes the sole means of close connection with that object. For instance, in the query "Whether I will keep my house during the divorce?" the Sun, the ruler of the 4th house, is in close conjunction with the querent. This indicates a positive answer. This does not imply the querent is combust, deceased, or incapacitated.

A planet's rare position on the ecliptic and in conjunction with the Sun (within 16–17 angular minutes) is called *cazimi* (Coley, 1676). They believed that the planet in cazimi receives all the power of the benefic Sun and becomes maximally strong.

But here, I also agree with Morinus, who ignored the cazimi for three reasons:

- When the Sun plays a supportive role in the horary question, any close conjunction (not limited to 16 angular minutes) indicates strong support from the object it signifies—and the closer, the better. As accidental ruler of the house, the Sun is neither better nor worse than other accidental rulers of that house; it cannot provide support through conjunction only within 16 angular minutes and not provide it within 20 angular minutes from conjunction.
- When the Sun occupies Aquarius, it is debilitated. Its conjunction with a planet becomes maximally detrimental. The Sun's debilitated celestial state cannot become dignified and supportive for a planet simply because it approached the Sun within 16 minutes. Thus, the Sun in Aquarius will suppress the closely conjoined planet, not support it.
- If the Sun hides the planets in its rays, it makes them invisible, that is, unmanifested. Moreover, the closer to the exact conjunction, the stronger the Sun combusts the planet. If this is the case, why should the planet suddenly emerge from the Sun's rays, manifest itself, and become maximally strong at the point of cazimi? It contradicts logic.

Example №14: Missing Person

You have already seen how combustion works in the section "Homework Assignment №11" (the question of purchasing a suspicious house). The house's owner has just emerged from combustion by the Sun—the ruler of the 12th house in a foreign country—and is currently under the Sun's beams. Based on these factors, we determined that the homeowner has just been released from prison but is still hiding.

Here is another example of combustion.

A businessman who was familiar with the querent disappeared about two weeks ago. The querent asks, "Is he alive? And where is he now?" (Fig. 2.44).

Let's start with the assessment of radicality. The missing man is neither a friend nor a relative. We expect the chart to highlight Saturn, the ruler of the 7th house.

Indeed, the Moon (representing the querent's emotions) is under the influence of Saturn. Simultaneously, the Part of Fortune (indicating deep concern) exalts Saturn. Yes, Saturn is significant for the querent.

Let's address the first question and determine if there are any signs of recent death in the chart. I already mentioned that a planet entering combustion and losing its visibility is one of the signs. The second is the previous contact of the querent's significator with death. We will examine both these testimonies.

In this chart, Saturn is close to the Sun, indicating that it recently entered combustion. It is a sign of recent death. One might object that the Sun represents the querent, so the chart shows the close connection between the querent and Saturn, not combustion.

But this is not the case. First, the querent is not connected with Saturn in this context; on the contrary, they are very concerned about the missing person. Second, since the querent themself is not part of the question, and it is the Moon, not the Sun, that reflects the querent's motives, we can assign the Sun to an external factor that recently affected Saturn, leaving the Moon for the querent.

Predictive Astrology Textbook

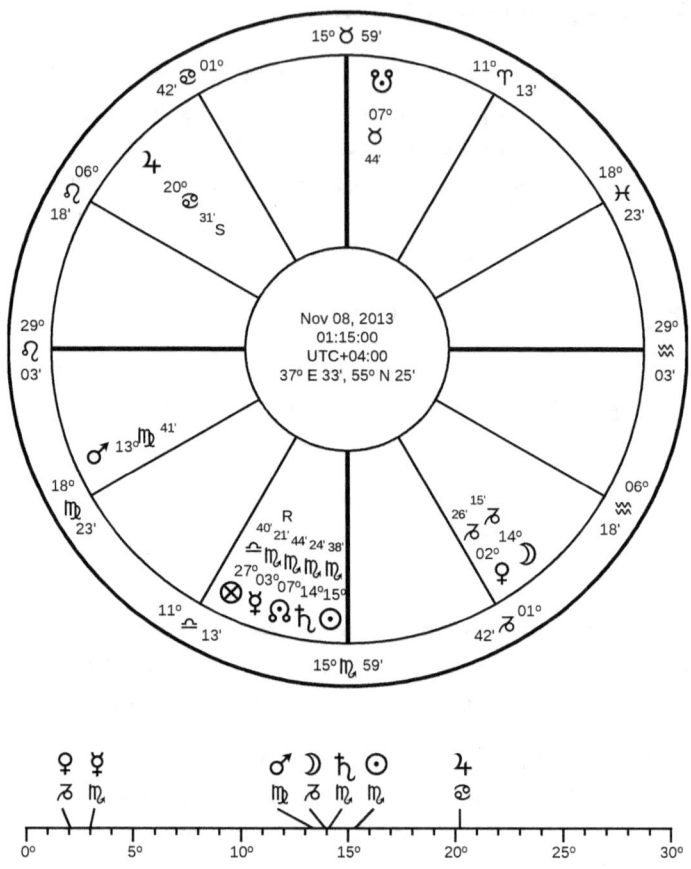

Figure 2.44: *Chart: Is He Alive? And Where Is He Now?*

N.B.

Note that when you assign one of the querent's planets to the quesited, you need to consider whether this violates the radicality of the chart. In our case, we can safely "remove" the Sun from the querent without compromising the chart's radicality.

So, we have one testimony of past death. But that's not enough to conclude such an unexpected tragedy on one factor alone. I would like

Chapter 2. Horary Astrology

to see at least one more sign of recent departure. You can refer to he section "The default option."

The combustion is not necessarily an indication of death. It could be a sign of the disappearance of the man in general. Since death is not a default option here, combustion may show the general disappearance of the person. That is why my initial thought is to examine whether this combustion is somehow related to death. I want to find contact with death that occurred immediately after or simultaneously with the recent combustion.

Since Saturn's orb is 7 degrees, it became invisible when the Sun approached it at a distance of 18 − 7 = 11 degrees in the past. At that moment, the Sun was at 1°45' Scorpio, and Saturn was at 12°45' Scorpio. Notably, the afflicting Sun was at 28°15' Aquarius by antiscion at that moment—precisely at the cusp of the businessman's 1st house. If combustion indicates death, it happened secretly, fitting perfectly into the context. At the same time, there is nothing secret about the disappearance itself—everyone was aware of the missing person due to the publicity. This is the first logical connection between combustion and death.

Immediately after entering combustion, Saturn made a conjunction with Mercury, the ruler of the businessman's 8th house. These two events occurred one after another, further reinforcing the connection between combustion and death.

The synchronicity in time observed in this chart strengthens our concerns. Since the moment of combustion, Saturn has traveled approximately 1.5 degrees. On the other hand, the past contact with death, which immediately followed combustion, occurred 10 degrees ago. It corresponds to 1.5 weeks ago or ten days ago. And this again fits into the context—the businessman disappeared about two weeks ago, and death happened later. So, we have three testimonies that support past combustion as an indication of recent death.

But that's not all. Earlier in the section "The Planet Interposing the Question," we discussed a planet intervening in the question. It applies to our case. The chart highlights Mars in three ways:

- Combustion occurred under Mars' influence.
- Death (Mercury) is under Mars' influence.

- Mars has mutual reception (i.e., connection) with death.
- In addition, Mars rules the essential part of the 8th radical house (death in general), and its opposition afflicts the businessman's 1st house.

Mars universally indicates violence and spilled blood, and such a strong connection with death suggests possible violence.

But let's consider one more thing. We examined what happened with Saturn at the moment of combustion while establishing if combustion was related to death. Now, let's see what aspect Saturn had in the past relative to the current moment. What was its last contact?

Saturn's last contact was the completion of the past aspect with Mars. The Sun took the light of Mars and then transferred it to Saturn. The afflicting Sun, representing the occurrence of past death, is also the mediator between violence and the businessman. Moreover, the Sun completed the light transfer about 1.5 degrees ago, confirming our correlation—1.5 weeks or ten days ago. It definitively confirms the contact of the quesited with violence, which occurred on the day of death ten days ago.

Where is the quesited now? He is at the bottom of the chart in a watery sign, which can be interpreted literally—at the bottom of a lake, river, or well.

So, our conclusion is grim. The man was killed ten days ago, on October 29. His body is at the bottom of a river, lake, or well.

I do not know whether the querent reported the results of this horary chart to the police. However, shortly after this conclusion, the police found the body of the murdered man at the bottom of a lake with a gunshot wound. Examination confirmed that the death occurred on October 29.

Station of the Planet

The station is a relatively strong indicator of immobility. Typical examples where we interpret station as immobility in context include the following:

- Business has come to a halt (sales and revenues have stopped).
- A house has ceased to be liquid.

- A person has fallen ill or died.
- And so on.

It speaks to the object's significant weakness: its inability to manifest itself in the context of the question.

In some cases, stationarity can be interpreted as a property of the object that does not necessarily make it weak—for example:

- The significator of barriers is stationary in the question "Will the barrier withstand external pressure?" It indicates that it is challenging to move (break) the barrier.
- The significator of a heavy object is stationary. It underscores the radical nature of the chart—this object is indeed challenging to move.
- The significator of a person in the question "Will they change their mind?" is stationary. No, they will insist on their opinion.
- The significator of the person in the question "Will they go away or will they return to me?" is about to change direction. They will change their mind. We observed a similar configuration in the question of an Indian man asking about moving abroad.

You have already seen the section "Homework Assignment №15," where the stationarity illustrates a change in decision. In the next section (Example №15: Permission From Authorities), I will show you how stationarity denotes the inability of the significator to manifest itself.

Accidental Strengthening: Moderate Testimonies

As you have seen, the positions of planets in houses, stations, combustions, and conjunctions with nodes strongly indicate whether a planet is reinforced or weakened. We also have moderate testimonies of accidental strengthening or weakening of the significator. Let us explore each of them.

Retrograde Motion

Retrograde motion does not inherently strengthen or weaken the object. However, sometimes retrograde motion indicates that things are not going as they should—against their natural course. If the significator denotes a process, retrograde motion can indicate its interruption. In these cases, we speak of a moderate accidental weakening of the planet.

Example №15: Permission From Authorities

Here is an example of the station and retrograde motion of the planets. A girl works for a company and is about to start a significant project. The company must obtain permission from the authorities to commence this work. The question is "When will we obtain permission?" (Fig. 2.45).

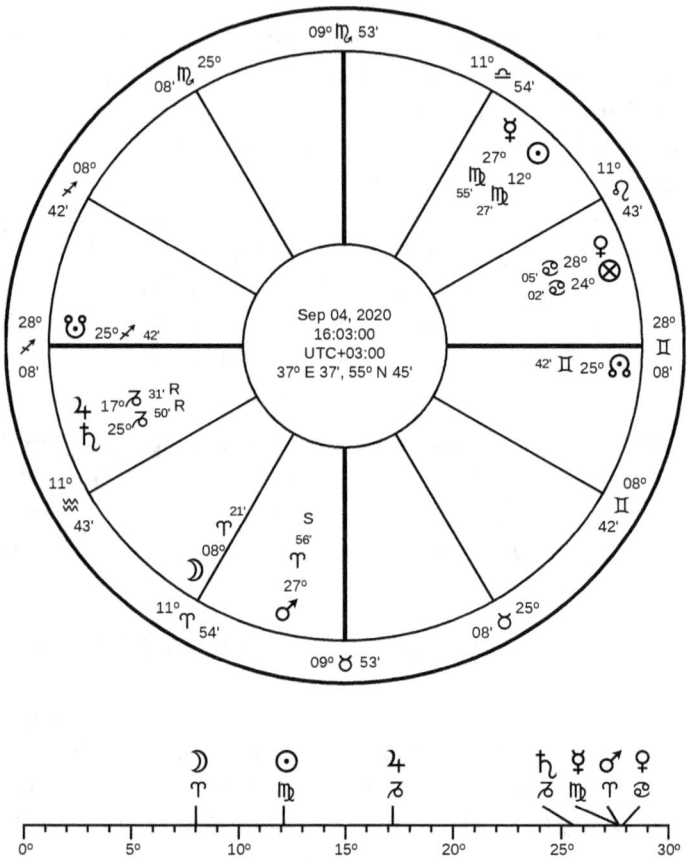

Figure 2.45: *Chart: When Will We Obtain Permission?*

Authorities' regulatory documents are often indicated by their second house. It represents their power (resources), with which they endow the company, granting it certain exclusive rights.

Let us begin by assessing radicality and compiling a list of techniques. Since the querent is asking on behalf of the company, the 1st house represents both the company and the querent herself (see the section "Special Case: The Question on Behalf of the Group"). We expect the chart to highlight Mars, the ruler of the 11th house.

Indeed, the querent (Jupiter) is focused on Mars, being in its place of its exaltation. The querent (Moon) deeply cares about this Mars, as she is in its domicile. Moreover, the Part of Fortune (representing the querent's deep desires) is in the 7th house of the client—the start of project work is essential to the querent. All this perfectly reflects the context—the chart is radical.

What techniques will we use? Since the question involves the interaction of two entities—the querent and the regulatory documents—we will look for an aspect between Jupiter and Mars. If none is found, it is not a problem. Given that the project will eventually proceed, and the question concerns only the timing of obtaining permission, we can apply long-term aspect techniques.

Jupiter and Mars do not form exact aspects, so we proceed to long-term ones. However, we cannot apply them either, because Mars will station and turn before reaching Jupiter. The chart technically closes off the answer to us. But why?

Observe that Mars is currently stationary. It does not move. Mars governs both regulatory documents and the operations of governmental structures. Here, we see that these structures are "frozen" and are not issuing documents. This is not a depiction of the current moment—government agencies are presently operating normally. Thus, this is a "snapshot" of a future state.

But how is this possible?

At the time, the world was experiencing the second wave of the coronavirus pandemic. Theoretically, this could have led to a second lockdown in the city. However, few people—including the querent—believed this possibility. Yet the chart clearly indicated this outcome, and we have further testimonies supporting it.

Consider another point: Jupiter itself—representing the querent and the company—is retrograde and about to station. The future-state snapshot reveals that the company's operations will deviate from their normal course, suggesting an impending suspension of activities.

Moreover, the South Node conjuncts the ASC, indicating that external circumstances will obstruct the company's operations. This supports our hypothesis about an upcoming lockdown restricting business activities.

Now examine Saturn, the universal significator of limitations, placed directly in the 1st house, the company's position. This shows that external limitations will certainly be imposed on the company's operations. Saturn's retrograde motion suggests these won't be the first lockdown restrictions affecting the company.

The company would clearly be unable to commence the project as planned due to the second citywide lockdown.

This prediction proved accurate. Shortly after the question was posed, the city's mayor implemented a self-isolation regime, including business operation restrictions that remained in effect until January of the following year.

Remember that when discussing the chart's radicality, I mentioned it indicates the next developmental stage within the given context. Our analysis assumed the company's normal operations amid the current city's activities. The chart revealed that *within this specific context*, the project would not advance. This interpretation does not suggest permission will never be granted or that the project is permanently canceled.

Sooner or later, authorities will lift the lockdown measures, and the company may revisit this project. However, this would constitute a different context, potentially prompting new questions like "Will our client withdraw from the project after transitioning most employees to remote work?"

Close Aspects and Receptions

We have discussed in the section "Object Interaction Techniques: Close Aspects" that the zodiacal circle places "copies" of planets in the degrees of their aspects. These "copies" can be constructive or destructive. Suppose the significator falls within the orb of such a "copy." In that case, we say that the significator experiences the influence of the planet's aspect or "receives" that aspect. This influence can be supportive, in which case we speak of the strengthening of the significator due to the external factors indicated by the aspecting planet. Alternatively, the

Chapter 2. Horary Astrology

influence can be harmful. In this case, we speak of the weakening of the significator due to conflicting factors.

Let me remind you how we evaluate the effect of an aspect:

- We assess the celestial state of the aspecting planet. It can be accidentally dignified, debilitated, neutral, or of mixed nature (for example, in fall but simultaneously in triplicity and having a noble dispositor).
- We evaluate the form of the aspect. Favorable aspects efficiently "concentrate" all the good the aspecting planet has, while unfavorable aspects efficiently concentrate all the bad. Favorable aspects from debilitated or neutral planets have no essential effect or harm slightly, while favorable aspects from planets of mixed nature help.
- Add to this the dignity/debility of the planet's "copy" in the degree of the aspect. Suppose Venus's aspect falls into Taurus or Pisces. It amplifies all the good the aspect concentrates and diminishes all the bad. But if Venus's aspect falls into Aries, the effect will be the opposite.
- Add to the aspect's effect the effect of reception of the aspecting planet. If it is in the significator's dignity, the aspect's positive effect increases, and the negative impact is almost nullified. If it rejects the significator by reception, think the opposite.

Let's assume Venus in Capricorn indicates a new place of residence in the question "How easy will my life be in a new country?" Suppose Venus receives an aspect from Mars in Taurus.

Mars in Taurus is debilitated, and there's nothing good in the degree of Mars's bodily position. But we are not considering Mars itself, but its "copy" in the place of the trine.

The trine transmits all of Mars's good qualities and suppresses all its bad ones. In a debilitated Mars, there's nothing good, so we don't expect anything supportive in the place of the aspect. However, we also don't expect explicit harm from this aspect—the trine significantly suppresses all the evil the debilitated Mars creates. The trine from such Mars doesn't help or harm significantly.

But the almost neutral "copy" of Mars falls into the place of its exaltation, which means the aspect starts to help. Of course, the effect of the exalted "copy" of Mars is not as strong as if Mars itself were in Capricorn. Still, we expect a positive impact from such an aspect.

Now, let's consider that Mars is in the domicile of Venus and strives to help her. Therefore, the miniature "copy" of Mars will also strive to help Venus. It makes the positive effect of the aspect even more noticeable.

If Mars didn't have a close aspect to Venus, we would say that the malefic planet is trying to help Venus, but this produces a mixed effect. It's like a criminal with terrible manners trying to court a beautiful girl. On one hand, he protects her from enemies, but on the other, he inadvertently harms her with his behavior.

The presence of a close trine aspect, which falls into Mars's exaltation, makes Mars's influence effective. It's as if we removed the criminal's bad manners and enhanced his defensive strength against enemies (demonstrating his best aspect).

In most cases, we don't need to identify the sources of harm or support; it's enough for us to assess the situation. Our answer would be, "You will not encounter obstacles" or "Circumstances will favor you."

Usually, we identify the sources of assistance or hindrance in questions like "What is blocking my business from growing?" or "Where to expect assistance from?"

Multiple Aspects Received by the Same Significator

The significator may receive several close aspects simultaneously, some favorable, while others unfavorable. To understand the cumulative effect, consider the following:

- Conjunction and opposition are stronger than trine, which is more vital than square and sextile.
- The applying aspect is stronger than the separating one, indicating that the influence will increase over time.
- The closer the aspect, the stronger the impact.

Let's provide examples:

- There are two aspects—a helpful trine and a harmful square. With equal strength of support and damage, the trine prevails. We expect moderate assistance, although with obstacles.
- There are two squares—one significantly harmful, the other almost neutral. All else being equal, we expect a weakening of the significator due to external obstacles.

- There are two aspects—a separating conjunction with a benefic planet at a distance of almost 3 degrees and an applying trine from a malefic planet, which neither helps nor harms, at a distance of 0.5 degrees. We do not expect significant assistance or harm from external factors.

Reception without a close aspect acts much weaker than reception with a close aspect. A single aspect strengthens or weakens a planet, but not as strongly as stationarity, house placement, or other significant factor. However, if a planet simultaneously receives several favorable or unfavorable aspects, it significantly strengthens or weakens that planet.

Note on Natal Astrology

Since we do not know the specific meanings of planets in a natal chart, we cannot assert aspects as someone's influence on a particular object within context. The planets in the natal chart are sources of all potential positive or negative life events in a specific area of life. Notice the distinction:

- In a horary chart concerning illness, the ruler of the 12th house indicates a specific disease regardless of its celestial state.
- In a natal chart, the malefic ruler of the 12th house indicates a potential future illness, exile, or attack of secret enemies. Conversely, the benevolent ruler of the 12th indicates something that will bring relief from such afflictions.

Therefore, we assess the impact of received aspects differently in the natal chart:

- If a significator represents something positive in life, adverse influences from the received aspect will diminish the significator's constructive effect.
- If a significator represents something destructive, such as illness, job loss, conflicts, or wounds, unfavorable aspects it receives will strengthen its detrimental effect.

The accidentally benefic/malefic significator, which promises a whole spectrum of "good" or "bad" events, becomes more "malevolent" or "benevolent" due to the nature of the aspect it receives. Thus, in natal astrology, we regard close aspects not merely as accidental strengthening factors, but primarily as elements that *alter the celestial state of the significator* for better or for worse.

The same relates to the receptions.

Example №16: First Reaction

Here is an example of a close aspect in action.

Before writing the book, I considered how the readers would react (Fig. 2.46). Since the audience and its reaction to the book are the main subjects of concern, I expect Saturn, the ruler of the 7th house, to stand out in that chart.

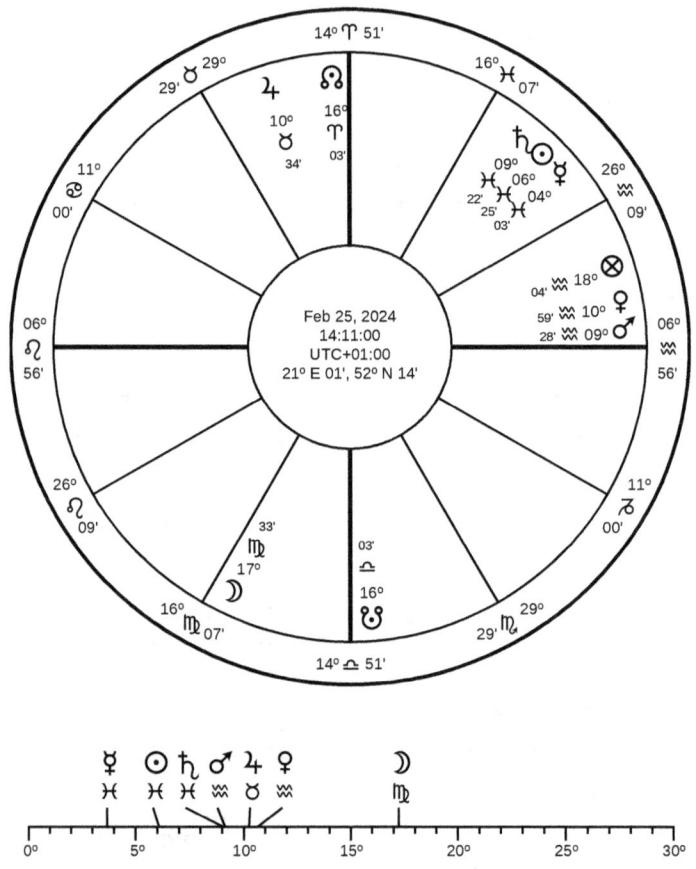

Figure 2.46: *Chart: Future of This Book*

And indeed, the Sun (the querent) is conjunct Saturn (the audience). You can interpret this as the querent being mentally connected to the

Chapter 2. Horary Astrology

readers. At the same time, the Pars Fortune (the querent's deep concern) is in the 7th house. Yes, the audience occupies the querent's thoughts; the chart is radical.

Where is the book here? What planet signifies it? We have two options.

- The book is the product of my creativity and hobby, ruler of the 5th house, Mars.
- Alternatively, we could consider the book as knowledge associated with the 9th house, as if the question were, "How will the audience perceive this knowledge?" In this case, we would choose Jupiter for the book.

Both variants are feasible in this context. However, I expect the chart to give me a clue—it will highlight either Jupiter or Mars as significant planets for the querent.

Mars is not highlighted in this chart, but Jupiter is. Indeed, Jupiter controls the Sun (me and my thoughts). At the same time, the Moon is on the cusp of the 3rd house, meaning its significant "copy," at the degree of opposition, is on the cusp of the 9th house. The querent is emotionally tied to the 9th house by the opposition.

Universally, Jupiter signifies supreme knowledge, which perfectly intersects with its accidental role. So, no doubt, the book (in terms of knowledge) is Jupiter here.

Since the question concerns the audience's feelings and motives, I must consider Saturn's relationship to Jupiter. Jupiter receives Saturn in its domicile—an excellent indicator that the audience will like this book (the knowledge it carries).

But look at the remarkably close conjunction of debilitated Mercury with the querent. Since this is a conjunction, we do not modify Mercury's influence and say that this contact is detrimental to the Sun.

But who is Mercury? It rules the 9th house of the audience—the system of their beliefs. Now, we need to find a reasonable explanation for these indicators in the context of reality. How can one's system of beliefs hurt me?

This book will likely reach the astrologers. It is no secret to me that precise forecasts contradict the beliefs of many modern astrologers, as described in "the section Refutation of Modern Astrologers' Arguments against Accurate Forecasting." This book and examples of accurate forecasts may trigger a wave of criticism, which will hurt me or affect my reputation. It could be a reasonable explanation for such a prominent conjunction.

But for now, it's just a hypothesis. I want to find more evidence to stick to this version.

The 3rd house of the chart traditionally shows waves of criticism. In ancient times, it was called the house of "rumors and gossip." Is there any connection between Mercury and the 3rd house? Oh yes. Mercury is the ruler of this house, which shows criticism *per se*.

So, the book's release will evoke great love from the audience and a wave of criticism. This understanding easily explains the Moon's position, which initially surprised me.

It has been some time since the publication of the first edition of this book,[9] which included this forecast. And now I can summarize the results. Indeed, almost all reader feedback was divided into two parts—either very positive or extremely negative.

It is not surprising that the negative feedback mostly came from astrologers who have been practicing astrology for a long time. Moreover, none of the astrologers I approached agreed to give a positive review of the first edition. At the same time, I received a lot of positive feedback from readers. The forecast turned out to be accurate.

Affliction/Strengthening of the House

As you know, the house determines any celestial object it includes to manifest in a specific area of life. In particular, the South/North Nodes in the house create an intense flow of obstructive or supportive events in a specific area of life.

Likewise, if a debilitated planet occupies the house, it will manifest itself in its affairs. More precisely, it will create obstacles and disruption in the area of life to which the house corresponds. A benefic planet will act in the opposite manner.

---

[9] This book was first published as a two-volume set titled "The Mysteries of Medieval Astrology."

Chapter 2. Horary Astrology

In these cases, we speak of the strengthening or affliction of the house itself. Suppose the ruler of the house is dignified, but the house is afflicted. In that case, the ruler will still create positive effects but with significant obstacles due to the house affliction.

It is evident that when nodes or planets closely conjoin a house cusp, their influence on specific matters within that life domain becomes more pronounced. The closer they are to the cusp, the more intensive their supportive or disruptive effects on the primary subject.

Following the same principle, malevolent stars occupying a house will afflict it, while benevolent stars will strengthen it. The stars have a very limited orb, making their general position within a house relatively insignificant for influencing life areas. However, when stars conjoin a house cusp (within 1 degree), their effect on specific matters becomes notable.

Remember that not only the planet's body but also its large "copy"—the aspect of opposition—can occupy the house. You may recall the horary chart from the section "Example №14: Missing Person." Mars, the natural ruler of violence and accidental co-ruler of the 8th house, signified a violent death at the intersection of "violence" and "death." Mars was in the 1st house, but its opposition was in the 7th house, the body of the quesited. Thus, Mars affected his body by the opposition, which is another indication of violent death afflicting the quesited.

For this reason, the planet in the house always has a connection with the opposite house. For example, a planet in the 6th house opposes the 12th house of diseases.

Thus, the planet in the 6th house will always manifest itself as an illness. Hence, the thesis that the 6th house is associated with diseases is not a random assumption. It holds true if we consider the planet in the 6th house, but this does not apply to the ruler of the 6th house.

When falling into the house, less powerful aspects (trine, square, sextile) affect it much less. Therefore, for a planet to significantly support or afflict the house by a weaker aspect, it must cast that aspect close to the cusp of the house. In that case, this aspect becomes significantly influential.

We use the following terminology:

- The house is afflicted/strengthened by the bodily presence or aspect of the planet.
- The house is afflicted/strengthened by the star on its cusp.
- The house is afflicted/strengthened by the South/North Node.

Example №17: Exhibition

Here is an example of a house affliction. The querent has a jewelry business and plans to participate in a jewelry exhibition. Their previous experience with such events has been negative. The querent asks, "How will this exhibition go? Will there be any obstacles?" (Fig. 2.47).

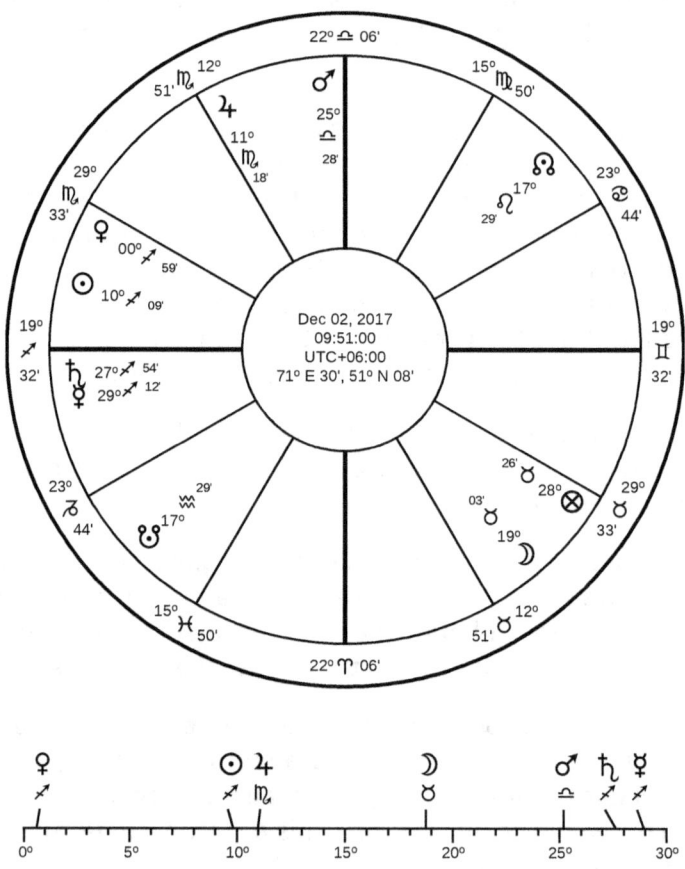

Figure 2.47: Chart: How Will This Exhibition Go?

Chapter 2. Horary Astrology

The 10th house of "Social Activities and Recognition" represents the performance of the stand showcasing the business. I expected the chart to highlight Venus, the ruler of the 10th house. Indeed, Venus controls the Moon (the querent's emotions) and the Part of Fortune (deep desires). Venus is highlighted at least twice—the chart is radical.

Now, let us consider the techniques we will use. The question contains the phrase "How well will it go," which clearly requires a description of the future state of the exhibition. We will examine Venus's current celestial condition as if observing a snapshot of the coming moment. However, the question also includes "What might hinder," which refers to external influences on Venus or the 10th house. This requires assessing accidental afflictive factors. We must determine whether anything significantly weakens Venus or the 10th house and, if so, name these factors.

We begin by evaluating Venus's celestial state. Since Venus is neither benefic nor malefic, the stand's performance will not be exceptional—unless suppressed or enhanced by external factors.

Venus's neutrality results from being in Jupiter's domicile. Thus, Jupiter (i.e., the querent themselves) is responsible for the stand's average performance. This makes perfect sense, as the querent personally crafts the jewelry and represents the business.

We can interpret Venus's state as indicating the quality of the presented jewelry. We have an additional reason for this interpretation: Venus *universally* signifies items of beauty and, *accidentally*—the stand's operation at the jewelry exhibition. Venus assumes an ultra-specific role at the intersection of these meanings—the exhibited jewelry.

Its average state literally denotes jewelry of average quality. Therefore, we should not expect exceptional results from the exhibition under normal booth conditions.

Let us now evaluate Venus's accidental dignity. It is significantly weakened due to its placement in the 12th house. Thus, the 12th house represents external factors hindering the stand's normal operation.

Venus is under the Sun's beams, meaning the Sun largely obscures the booth from visitors. The Sun gains additional significance through its conjunction with the star Antares, the heart of Scorpio. As you may recall, Scorpio brought downfall to the great mortal who displayed exceptional qualities before the gods. The essence of this star is to destroy what was once great. In this context, it conceals the finest jewelry that the querent presents to visitors.

But what does the Sun signify? It rules Leo, which occupies a significant portion of the 8th house, making the Sun the co-ruler of this house.

However, the 8th house does not fit the context as a hindering factor for product demonstration. It neither represents the native's death (which is irrelevant here) nor the 11th house from the booth that would hide the stand from visitors. The eighth house remains insignificant in this context.

The Sun's position in the 12th house reveals an ultra-specific detail within the 12th house's significations. Since we've established that the 12th house describes afflictive factors, we now have a double confirmation of this influence.

Let us now examine the 10th house and assess its condition. Is there anything afflicting it? Indeed, Foramen—one of several blinding stars—is positioned directly on its cusp. This provides further evidence that the booth will be obscured from visitors' view.

Additionally, we find debilitated Mars located precisely on the 10th house cusp, disrupting all booth operations. But which house does Mars rule? Significantly, it also governs the 12th house.

We have three distinct astrological indications that 12th house influences will hinder the exhibition—specifically by obscuring the stand from visitors' view.

Let us now examine potential 12th house significations. In this context, it cannot represent:

- The querent's secret enemies
- Illnesses or health matters
- Imprisonment or captivity
- Exile or foreign displacement

The 12th house's meaning here relates more to the exhibition environment than to the querent personally. As the third house from the 10th (the exhibition stand), it represents the immediate surroundings. What nearby exhibition elements could reduce visibility? The most plausible interpretation is an unfavorable physical location within the hall.

This interpretation proved accurate: on the exhibition day, organizers placed the querent's booth in the hall's most remote and poorly-lit section. Consequently, few visitors reached the location, resulting in commercial failure.

Example №18: Failed Prediction

A persistent issue I have observed among astrologers is their tendency to demonstrate only those cases where their forecasts proved correct, while disregarding numerous instances where the same techniques failed to align with reality.

In scientific terms, this practice is known as **cherry-picking**—a data manipulation tactic where only facts that support the desired viewpoint are selected while opposing ones are ignored.

To maintain rigor, any forecasting method that cannot demonstrate statistically significant and reproducible results should be discarded as unreliable.

As a practitioner committed to honest analysis, my goal is to test astrological techniques transparently, without selective reporting. Below, I present a horary chart where my prediction proved incorrect, acknowledging the failure as part of the validation process.

Immediately after finishing the first edition of my book, I approached several publishers, hoping to secure a contract. Simultaneously, I questioned whether any publisher would give a positive response and when that might happen (Fig. 2.48).

I expect the publisher (7th house) to be the central subject of this question. However, Jupiter, ruler of the 7th house, is only highlighted once by Part of Fortune (a significator of my deep desires) in the 7th house.

This alone is not enough to consider the chart radical. But I see that Mercury (my thoughts) is in the 8th house, indicating the publisher's resources. This aligns with reality, as I want a publisher with substantial marketing capabilities.

Although this chart fails to emphasize any single house at least twice, it retains radicality through the emphasis on two thematically connected houses, with each receiving singular emphasis. I classify such charts as

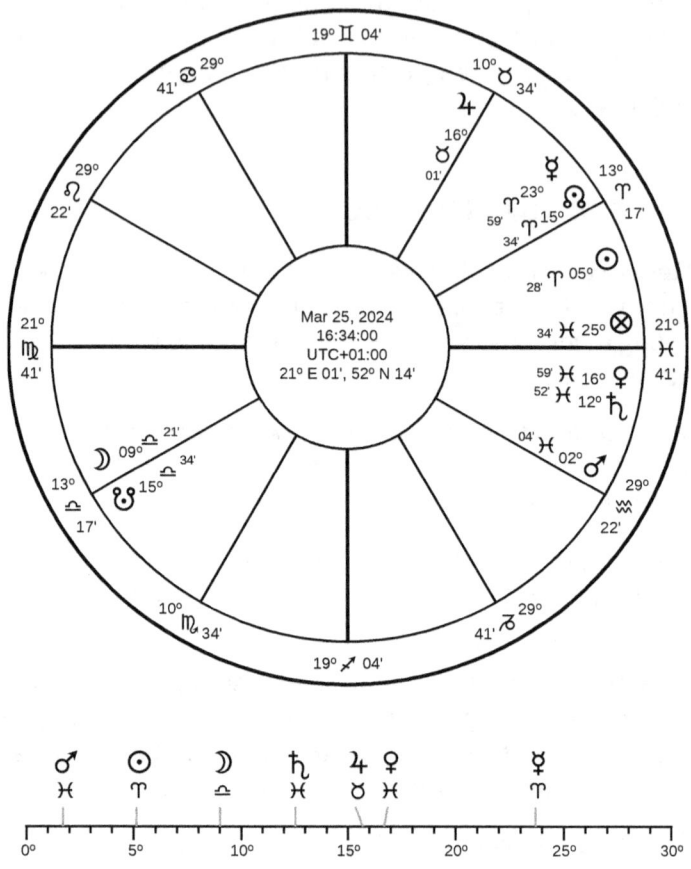

Figure 2.48: *Chart: When Will I Get a Contract With the Publisher?*

"unfocused" (see "Reason 4" in the section "Reflection of the Current Situation in a Horary Chart" for more details).

The publisher (Jupiter) looks favorably toward the Moon, so I will receive an agreement. Looking at the North Node in the publisher's 2nd house and the noble Sun within the publisher's 1st house, I conclude that it will be a major publisher.

However, the timing interests me. When will I receive the offer? There are no applying aspects between me and Jupiter. But this does not mean there will not be an offer. Based on the reception, the publisher wants to work with me, so I will receive an offer sooner or later.

In this case, I can apply the long-term aspects method. Mercury has no aspects with Jupiter, but the Moon reaches it in 37 degrees. The context implies that publishers typically consider requests for several months. So, 37 degrees likely refers to 37 days rather than 37 weeks.

The chart immediately hints at it. Note Venus (co-ruler of the querent, who also strongly desires contact with the publisher) is 5 degrees away from the cusp of the 7th house.

Such contact alone is not sufficient for a positive response (since contact with the cusp produces events to a lesser extent than contact of the querent with the significator of the quesited). However, contact with the cusp can undoubtedly refine the timing.

Venus will touch the 7th cusp in 5 units of time, corresponding to 5 weeks or 37 days. Thus, I expect the first positive response in 37 days from the time of the question.

Yet, there was something in this chart that greatly troubled me.

Note the movement of the querent. Mercury turns retrograde and immediately combusts. This can be interpreted in two ways:

- I will change my decision to work with this publisher and encounter difficulties because of it.
- I will become stationary—losing any chance to get my book to readers. Simultaneously, I will become invisible to readers. This means the publisher will not distribute the book, which looks pretty odd.

Of course, this made me reconsider the horary from a different perspective. I notice that Venus, also highlighted in the question, signifies my wallet. From that perspective, I can look not at the North Node in the 8th house (influential publisher) but at the South Node in my 2nd (significant financial loss due to a contract with this publisher).

Again, I had no idea how such an interpretation was possible at the moment of the question. But formally, this negative option of events unfolding remained.

So, I awaited the developments. Nothing happened after 37 days, and even after 40 days, I received nothing. However, after 42 days, a British publisher contacted me with an offer to publish the book, requesting a substantial investment in their marketing activities in advance.

Recalling my horary chart, I quickly investigated and found that this publisher solicits publication fees, retains copyright indefinitely, and does not effectively apply principles for publishing authors' works.

Of course, I declined. In this sense, the horary proved entirely correct. It showed both—the change in my decision and the potential problems I would encounter. However, I was mistaken about the timing. I expected a letter from the publisher in 37 days but received it in 42 days.

Every mistake is a wonderful opportunity to understand where exactly I was wrong. I considered 37 degrees as 37 days, based on Venus's support, which connected in 5 degrees (5 weeks) with the cusp of the publisher's house. And I considered Venus to be the co-ruler of the querent correspondingly.

In reality, Venus' actual role was money, which I was requested to invest. Its aspect to the descendant doesn't have any logical sense regarding timing.

In that case, we refuse the synchronicity of timing. Hence, we can use the Moon-Jupiter aspect alone and consider the Moon's actual speed to refine the time units. The Moon's speed turned out to be 10% slower than its average. This means the deviation $\Delta v/\bar{v}$ is minus 10%, or -0.1. Then, according to formula (2.1) on page 209:

$$t' = \frac{37}{1 - 0.1} \approx 41$$

I received the letter 42 days after the question was asked. This timing fits well with reality (considering slight errors due to differences in time zones, weekends, and other minor factors). As you can see, horary astrology continues to work flawlessly.

If you use reliable forecasting techniques and the prediction does not match reality, the error lies with the astrologer—you either use the wrong technique or attribute incorrect significations to the planets (as in this example).

Treat your mistakes as your allies, helping you quickly refine your forecasting skills.

Chapter 2. Horary Astrology

Example №19: Money Transfer

This is the forecast my student from Australia made. It demonstrates how the dynamics of house affliction and the applying aspect to the house cusp can determine the time until the event.

The querent and her husband bought a new house and simultaneously sold their old one. The money for the new house had already been spent, and the money for the old house was supposed to come at the end of January. However, the financial gap was so large that the querent asked the realtor to contact the buyer of the old house and request to transfer part of the total amount—25,000 Australian dollars—to cover moving expenses.

It was during the New Year holidays, and the buyer was out of reach. The querent asked the question "When will the 25,000 dollars arrive in my account?" (Fig. 2.49).

This chart highlights the second house since both of the querent's planets are in the second house of money. The buyer who is supposed to transfer this money is also essential in the question.

Indeed, Venus controls the Part of Fortune (the querent's deep concern), and Jupiter, the querent's wallet, strongly depends on the buyer (i.e., Venus) through receptions, which fits perfectly into the context.

The first thing that comes to mind is to see if the wallet's state improves shortly. But Jupiter does not change its state; it is at the beginning of a fixed sign. The second thought is to check if the state of the second house itself improves.

A debilitated Mercury severely afflicts the second house. Since Mercury rules the buyer's money, it means that "the lack of the buyer's money" (Mercury is detrimental) is the cause of the querent's financial problems.

Thus, we can see what will happen next with that affliction: when Mercury leaves its place of exile, it will stop harming the 2nd house. This will occur in approximately 4.5 degrees. We know that affliction is not eternal in this context and will cease sooner or later. Thus, we have a symbolic timing in ingress: the state of the second house will improve in approximately four units of time—the lack of money from the buyer will no longer harm the querent's bank account.

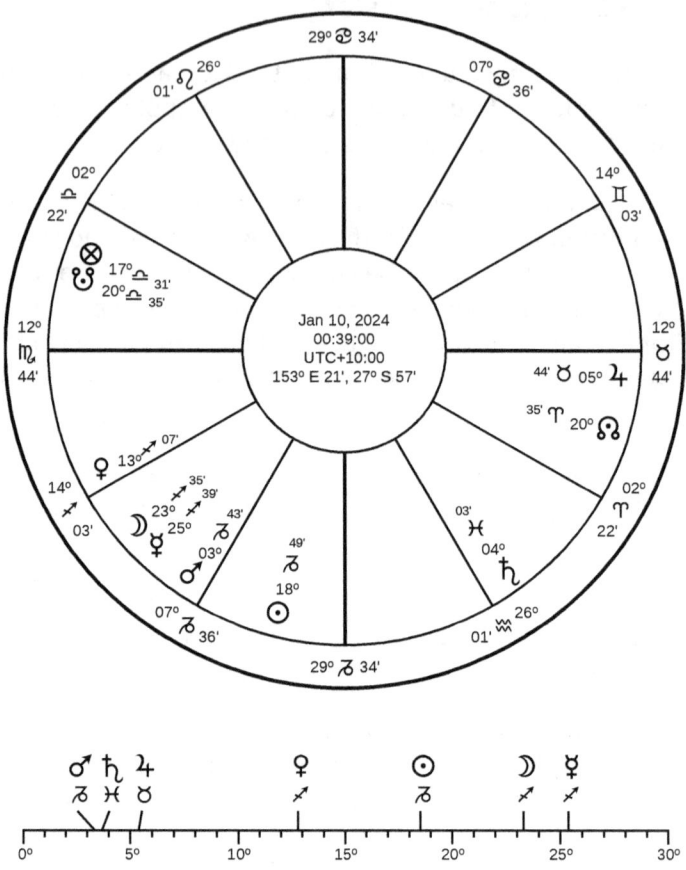

Figure 2.49: *Chart: When Will I Get $25,000?*

Mercury in this chart is slow, moving about one-third slower than its average speed. So, we must increase the number of degrees shown by Mercury by about $1/0.7 \approx 1.4$, as explained in the section "Refining the Number of Time Units," which gives us approximately seven units of time.

Simultaneously, Jupiter will conjunct the cusp of the 7th house in 7 degrees, meaning it will become maximally strong. For the wallet, this means maximum usability. So, in 7 units of time, it will be possible to pay from this account without any accidental difficulties. Again, we use the dynamics of accidental strengthening and an applying aspect with the cusp to determine the timing.

The Moon, representing the querent's emotions, is entirely absorbed by Jupiter—the wallet and its state. But 7 degrees later, the Moon will leave its place of worries. In 7 units of time, the question of lack of money will be off the table.

Finally, Venus (the buyer who should transfer the 25,000 dollars) conjuncts the cusp of the second house. Quite literally, the buyer's hands reach out to put money into the querent's pocket. This conjunction with the cusp happens in 1 degree, that is, in 1 unit of time.

As you know, we often observe a correlation of terms in well-balanced charts. One degree and seven degrees correspond to one week or seven days. My student announced to her family that the money should arrive seven days after the question was asked, that is, on January 17, 2024.

And so it was. My student attached the incoming transfer receipt as proof of the forecast's accuracy.

The important note here is that the house cusp acts as an active player in the applying aspect. Since the cusp is just a point in space that falls into an empty zodiac sign, it means that 14° Sagittarius is an active point. It demonstrates what we discussed in the section "The Lord of the House."

The Position of a Planet Relative to Luminaries

We use the terms "oriental" and "occidental," meaning "eastern" and "western," respectively, to refer to the planet's position relative to the luminary (the Moon or the Sun). To understand this, mentally rotate the celestial sphere so that the luminary is conjunct with the cusp of the 4th house. Planets found in the eastern hemisphere are termed "oriental to the luminary," while those in the western hemisphere are termed "occidental."

A planet oriental to the Sun or occidental to the Moon gains slightly more strength.

Pay attention to the Moon—it can gain strength even when occidental to the Sun. The Moon universally signifies the ever-changing flow of events. If the question pertains to the future development of a situation and the Moon is occidental to the Sun (i.e., waxing), it slightly favors any upcoming changes. If the inquiry concerns maintaining the status quo, then a waning Moon supports preserving the current state.

Accidental Strengthening: Weak Testimonies

A Planet Void of Course

A significator's exact aspects with other planets, as it transits the current sign, indicate events that happen with that significator within the present context. If the significator lacks future exact aspects before leaving the sign, its movement is termed "void of course."

N.B.

Please do not confuse the significator changing its current sign (indicating a shift in current circumstances) with the void state. The significator that stays within 3–4 degrees from the border of the adjacent sign and is about to leave the current sign is the planet, changing its current condition, not keeping it.

Given the Moon's crucial role in horary astrology, representing the querent or the overall flow of events within a given situation, a "void of course" Moon suggests an absence of significant accompanying events as the situation unfolds within the context.

The void Moon does not negate the situation's outcome. Instead, it reduces the intensity of accompanying events as the situation progresses toward the resolution.

However, if an intense sequence of events is anticipated within the context, the void Moon could be considered an affliction, as seen in the horary chart from the section "Example №13: Football Match," which concerns a football game lacking exciting moments.

However, the void Moon often maintains the status quo and can act as a fortifying or protective factor. For example, in the horary discussed in the section "Example №16: First Reaction," where I evaluated readers' reactions to this book, I anticipated an impending wave of criticism. The Moon, reflecting my future concerns about criticism, was void. This scenario is beneficial—criticism will not lead to significant developments, negating the need for a response action in the context of reader reactions.

While the void Moon can influence the intensity of the process, its impact on the outcome is relatively minor. After all, the main significators—not the intensity of the process—ultimately reveal the question's resolution.

The Elevated Planet

Planets can have varying elevations in their orbits relative to the Earth's center (see the Fig. "Planetary Cycles" on page 471). The closer a planet is to its apogee (the maximum distance from the Earth), the stronger it becomes. However, this is a minor factor that strong indicators, such as combustion or conjunction with a node, can easily override.

Planets can also have different elevations above the local horizon. The higher a planet is above the horizon, the stronger it is, while the lower it is below the horizon, the weaker it becomes. These factors are also minor.

Indeed, imagine one planet is at maximum elevation above the horizon, within the 9th house. In contrast, another planet is slightly lower but precisely at the Midheaven (MC). Such a disposition does not necessarily make the first planet stronger overall than the second. The angle significantly strengthens the second planet, while the falling house weakens the first planet much more than their altitudes relative to the horizon do the opposite.

So, you can follow a simple rule: a planet above the horizon has a slight advantage over a planet below the horizon, all other things being equal. It is worth noting that the nocturnal planets (the Moon and Venus) are more effective above the horizon at night, while diurnal planets (all the others) are more effective during the day.

A planet may have different elevations relative to the celestial equator. The more a planet deviates from the equator (i.e., the closer it is to 0° Cancer or 0° Capricorn, where it has *maximum declination*), the stronger it becomes. However, this is also a very minor indicator. Please refer to the section "Different Coordinate Systems" in the Appendix for a deeper understanding of planetary declination.

A planet may have different elevations relative to the ecliptic (the plane of the zodiacal circle). Here, the reverse rule applies: the closer a planet is to the plane of the zodiacal circle (i.e., to its own node), the stronger it becomes (see the Fig. "Lunar Nodes" on page 222 as an example).

In practice, weak testimonies are rarely necessary in horary astrology and are typically used in mundane forecasts.

Special Forecasting Techniques

Now, you have a complete set of tools for predicting future events. With them, you can forecast the development of almost any situation.

For example, if the querent is interested in income from long-term investments, evaluate the condition of their 2nd house as if you were looking at its state in the future. If the client is curious about how their financial situation will change shortly (due to short-term trading or a risky operation), look at the ingress of the ruler of the 2nd house into a new sign—is there an ingress, and if so, what condition does it lead the significator to?

If you are asked about the outcome of a legal dispute in the question "Will we defeat our opponents?" assess who is stronger—you or your enemies. You can also look at the judge—whether they might take a bribe or have a personal preference toward one of the parties, finding a favorable interpretation of the law if such an option exists in the context.

Only a few special forecasting techniques may seem non-obvious, and I want to discuss them separately in this chapter.

Death Questions

In inquiries regarding the departure of the quesited, we apply the standard rule—the contact between the quesited and the significator of death (i.e., an exact aspect between the two significators) indicates an upcoming departure.

However, other signs also indicate approaching death:

Chapter 2. Horary Astrology

Station

The immediate entrance of the quesited's significator into stationarity symbolizes an impending loss of mobility. I want to note right away that death inquiries apply not only to people but also to animals and even to collectives of people, such as a company facing bankruptcy. Stationarity for a business would mean the cessation of its activities.

The Setting of the Planet

Traditionally, the rising of a celestial body signifies the birth of the thing it represents, while its setting signifies its disappearance or death. Therefore, we speak of imminent departure if the significator is within a few degrees above the western horizon.

Be attentive. In computer programs, you will observe planets and house cusps projected onto the zodiacal circle, not their actual positions above the horizon. Visually, a planet may appear above the horizon but be already below it, or vice versa (we discussed this earlier in the section "Position in the House" on page 217).

Therefore, choose a computer program that calculates the actual positions of planets above the horizon. The planet's coordinate, called altitude, should be within 3–4 degrees, no more. You can learn more about altitude and other celestial coordinates from the section "Different Coordinate Systems" in the Appendix.

Entrance into Combustion

The combustion of a planet signifies that the object is hidden. In the context of death, it represents the quesited who has ceased to exist. At the same time, entrance into combustion signifies the moment of disappearance. If the significator is within a few degrees of entering combustion, we speak of an impending death. I provided you with an example of entering combustion in the section "Example №14: Missing Person."

Recall what we discussed about the default option in the section "3. A Full Movie" on page 179. Typically, the body resists death, and we need to see clear indicators to predict departure. Exceptions include situations where a person is terminally ill or on the front lines of a war, where the chances of survival are minimal. Therefore, under normal conditions, we require the presence of several simultaneous factors indicating death, for example:

- Contact between the querent and death, along with notable weakening of the quesited (such as conjunction with the South Node and a killing star, such as Algol or Antares);
- Simultaneous entrance into combustion and stationarity;
- And so on.

However, if death in the context of the question is almost inevitable or if no attempt is made to save the quesited, then we only need one of these indications to judge the impending departure (see the section "The default option").

Example №20: Death

Here is an example of a classic death horary. The querent's cat was sitting on the windowsill of the top floor during a thunderstorm. Suddenly, there was a loud clap of thunder nearby. The querent turned around and saw that their cat had disappeared. The querent asks, "Where is my cat?" (Fig. 2.50).

Let's start traditionally with determining the radicality of the chart. We expect the chart to emphasize Jupiter, the ruler of the 6th house of pets.

We see only one indication that Jupiter is essential to the querent—the Moon (the querent's emotions) is under Jupiter's influence. The cat and its location are not the main subject of the question. What is the querent most concerned about?

Venus (the querent) and the Part of Fortune (the deep concern) are in strong dignities of Saturn—the accidental ruler of the 4th house (the bottom of the chart) and the natural significator of death. Relative to the top floor, the 4th house is the base level, the place in front of the house where the cat could have fallen out of the window. On the intersection of these meanings, Saturn has an ultra-specific role—death from falling from a height—that logically fits into the context.

The chart suggests that the querent is more concerned about the cat's possible death from falling out of the window than its whereabouts.

Chapter 2. Horary Astrology

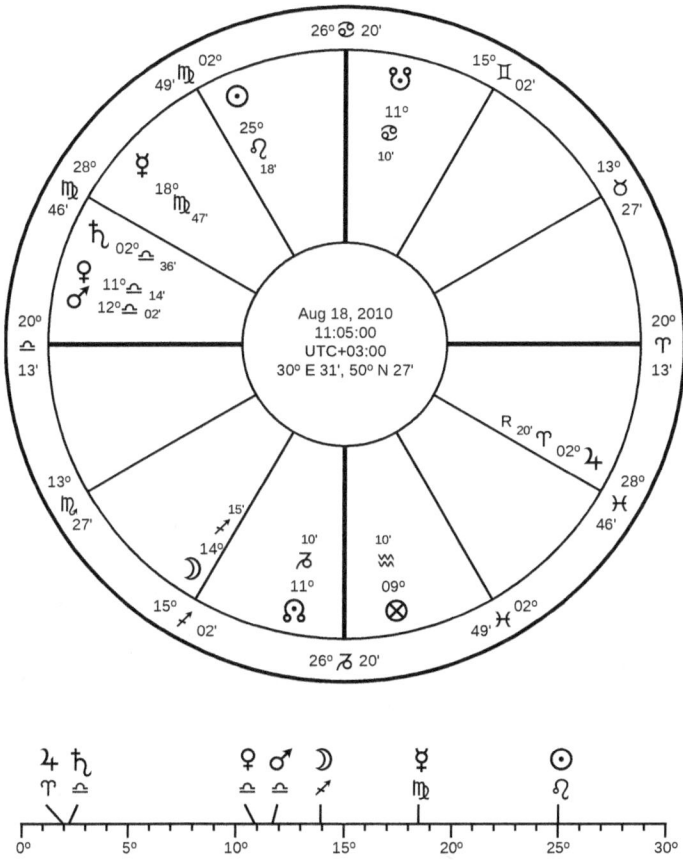

Figure 2.50: *Chart: Where Is My Cat?*

Look at Jupiter—it has just entered a stationary position and turned back. Simultaneously with the past station, it formed an exact opposition with Saturn. This opposition is particularly evil, as the "copy" of Saturn, positioned in the degree of opposition, is detrimental. We see two coherent indications:

– The cat has just experienced a fatal fall.
– The cat has just lost signs of life (ability to move).

Just before these events occurred, Jupiter was in Pisces, its domicile—the cat was at home a few moments ago. This alignment adds further weight to our unequivocal prediction. Indeed, the querent soon discovered the unfortunate cat's body beneath the window.

Example №21: Date of Departure

Here is an example of predicting the timing of a person's departure. The querent recently learned that their brother is in the terminal stage of cancer. All this time, he had concealed his condition from relatives and confessed only when his departure became inevitable. The querent asks, "How much time does my brother have left to live?" Doctors say it is a matter of months (Fig. 2.51).

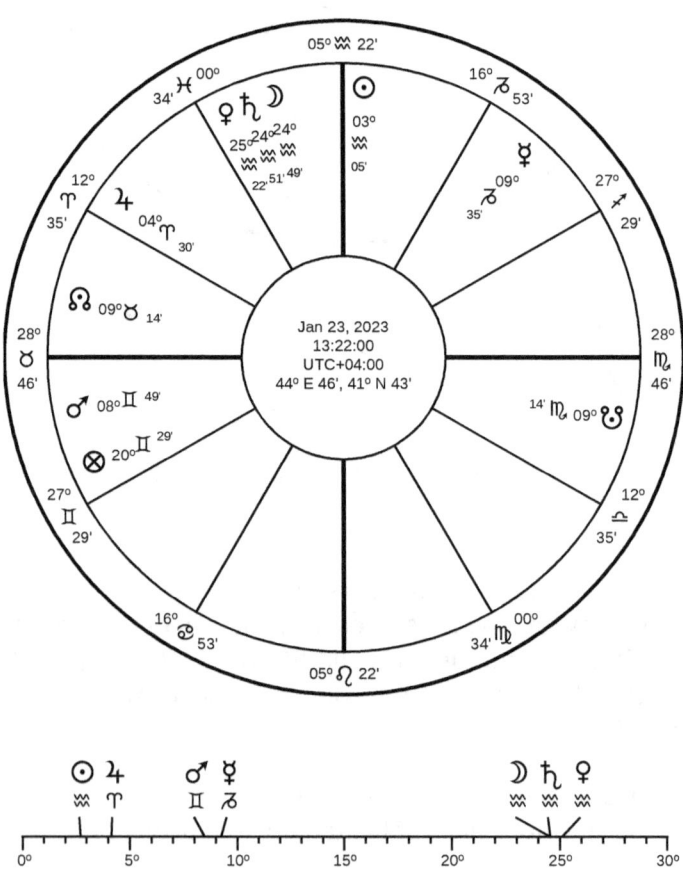

Figure 2.51: *Chart: How Much Time Does He Have?*

Chapter 2. Horary Astrology

Let us start by checking the radicality. We expect the chart to highlight either the brother (the Moon, ruler of the 3rd house) or his death (Saturn, ruler of the 10th house, the 8th from the 3rd). Knowing that Saturn is also the universal significator of death, I find the coincidence of Saturn's accidental and universal roles not accidental. So, Saturn should be highlighted first and foremost in the chart. Let us check it out.

Venus (the querent) is under the influence of Saturn and simultaneously in close conjunction with it. Saturn is twice accented.

It perfectly reflects reality, and the chart is radical.

All that remains is to find the aspect between the brother and death and determine the timing. But look, the Moon immediately encounters death. Such a noticeable proximity indicates the imminent onset of death.

Let's refine the timing. Since we have already used the main significator of the brother (the Moon) for timing, we can now turn to the alternative ruler of the 3rd house to clarify "immediate departure."[10]

The co-ruler of the 3rd house is the Sun. It rules the last part of the 3rd house, symbolically—the final part of the brother's life. The fact that the Sun is in a debilitated state and under the influence of death reflects the last part of the quesited's life in the terminal stage of illness. The fact that the Sun is on the threshold of the 10th house (the brother's house of death) confirms the correctness of choosing the second significator to assess timing.

We know that death is inevitable, so we can bring the Sun to Saturn through a long-term aspect. The Sun will reach Saturn in just under 24 degrees, which is just under 24 hours in the context of imminent departure. So our forecast is "your brother will depart tomorrow midday."

The quesited departed from this world in the middle of the next day, unexpectedly for the whole family, as the astrological forecast—although given—was not believed and seemed unlikely.

---

[10] We have seen the similar picture of an imminent event shown by a 1-degree aspect in the section "Example №12: Power Supply Restoration."

Search Horaries

Questions regarding the search for missing items or individuals are among the most complex. This complexity arises from the lack of specific context. All we know is that the item is *somewhere*. And that's all we have. So, if you find that the significator of the item is in the 9th house, it could equally mean:

- The item is far away, on the outskirts of town.
- The item is on the upper floors of a building.
- The item is in a library or a bedroom.
- And so on.

There is often no clue as to which of these options to prefer. Therefore, searching for a missing object involves considering all possibilities. You propose different options for finding the item to the clients until they hopefully locate it.

The Houses in Search Questions

Below are some examples of particular meanings of houses in search questions (Table 2.16):

Table 2.16: *House Meanings in Search Questions*

№	Meaning	At home	Outside home
1	Querent's location	Entrance, querent's room	A place near the residence
2	Dining area, storage place for essentials	Kitchen, pantry, wardrobe, querent's clothing or car	Food courts, warehouses
3	Communication nodes	Hallways in the house	Distribution hubs, post offices, sorting centers, communication rooms, primary schools

Continued on next page

Chapter 2. Horary Astrology

Table 2.16 — Continued from previous page

№	Meaning	At home	Outside home
4	Parents' residence, underground spaces	Parents' room, basements	Underground spaces
5	Places of joy/children	Children's room, leisure areas (favorite couch, etc.)	Restaurants, bars, cinemas, and other leisure areas
6	Places of small animals and servants	Pet's favorite spot, storeroom	Doghouse, servants' quarters, utility room
7	Other people's places	Spouse's room, room opposite the querent	House opposite the querent's residence
8	Places of "parting with matter"	Toilet, bathroom	Public toilets, trash bins, waste disposal sites
9	Places of higher knowledge and prophecy	Library room, meditation space, upper corridors, bedroom (place of dreams)	Churches, monasteries, libraries, universities, scientific centers
10	Official places, elevations	Home office, living room, attic	Hills, mountains, business offices, government institutions
11	Places of friends	Guest room	Homes where close friends live
12	Places of large animals	Stable, barn, cowshed	

N.B.

You can consider each house as the area adjacent to the previous one. For example, the 2nd house is the one next to the querent's room (adjacent to that room), the 6th house is the area adjacent to the children's room, and so on.

This table only illustrates some of the particular meanings of houses. For instance, if the missing item is in the 9th house and closely aspected by Venus—the natural ruler of adornments—or is in its domicile, the item may be in a jewelry box in the bedroom.

Houses can also indicate the direction in which to search for the missing item. The first house points to the east, the 10th to the south, and the 11th and 12th to the southeast. Opposite houses indicate opposite directions.

Alternatively, houses denote the object's proximity to the querent. Angular houses suggest that the object is somewhere nearby. The logic here is that significators in angular houses manifest more prominently. In the context of a search, they are easier to find. Contrarily, cadent houses make objects less accessible for quick discovery. Often, this is interpreted as the item being farther away from the querent.

We can use only one of these factors in a question:

- Either the house's meaning (location),
- An indication of directions, or
- An indication of proximity to the querent.

Suppose a lost phone is in the 10th house of a business office. It does not inherently mean that every office is close to the querent's residence.

Typically, we use the direction of search or indication of proximity when we have no idea where to look for the item. It can be helpful when asking questions about a missing person.

Zodiac Signs in Search Horaries

We actively utilize the elemental qualities of the signs where the significator of the missing item falls.

- If the planet is in an earth sign, the item is on the floor, at the bottom, or underground.
- If the planet is in an air sign, the item is in an open space—in a field, on a windowsill, or on an elevation.
- If the significator is in a fire sign, the item is in a warm and dry place, for example, near a heater or stove.
- If the planet is in a water sign, the item is in a moist place or near water.

Close and Exact Aspects in Search Horaries

We often use close aspects to describe surrounding objects that are in close contact with the missing item. For example, suppose the Moon casts a close aspect to the significator of the loss. In that case, the item is located near a mirror, next to a pond, near a silver object, or a toy if the Moon rules the 5th house. As you can see, we have dozens of different search options.

We also use conjunctions (bodily and by antiscion) of the missing item with another planet to find the thief. Suppose the significator is in conjunction with the ruler of the 6th house—one of the project team members took the missing documents.

Past aspects help understand with whom the item last interacted. If it occupies the 7th house but was last in contact with the ruler of the 5th, you might have left your item in a restaurant, but a staff member (another person) kindly picked it up and is keeping it.

The diversity of search options makes these horary questions the most complex. Having some context is beneficial—the search becomes much more manageable. For example, if the querent knows that the passport is in the bedroom, we concentrate on signs rather than houses. If the significator is in an earth sign, at the bottom, or on the ground—the first thing to do is check under the bed. The task becomes simplified right from the first step.

In practice, you will only be able to resolve some search horaries. But the good news is that if the horary chart straightforwardly points to the item's location, your description will be so accurate that it will produce a "wow" effect.

I had a funny incident when I was at a barbecue with friends. One of the guests misplaced an expensive camera. Then they turned to me for help, knowing I was an astrologer. It attracted everyone's attention—all the guests started watching what would happen next. After studying the horary chart for a while, I pointed to a bag on the floor in the pavilion. I said the camera was in that bag under a red makeup pouch.

Imagine the guests' surprise when the querent reached into the bag, pulled out a red makeup pouch, followed by the camera.

Significator of the Missing Item

We usually give preference to the planet's accidental meaning. This means that we choose the ruler of the 2nd house for the querent's missing item or the ruler of the 4th house for the brother's missing wallet. But sometimes, the chart perfectly describes the loss through universal significators.

For example, we are looking for a missing gold ring. The chart shows Venus in the strong dignity of the Sun—a combination of "jewelry" and "gold." Venus in Leo much more accurately describes the missing golden ring than the ruler of the 2nd house. We consider such coincidences as meaningful and prefer universal significators in such cases.

Example №22: Search Question

The querent lost a thermometer in their apartment. The question is "Where is my thermometer?" (Fig. 2.52).

Let's start with determining radicality. I expect Jupiter, the ruler of the 2nd house, to be prominent in this chart. Indeed, the Moon and the Part of Fortune, indicating the querent's concern, are in strong dignities of Jupiter.

Jupiter is the accidental significator of the lost thermometer. But let's see if the chart suggests a universal significator, which would pinpoint the item more accurately.

The essence of a thermometer is to fixate the current body temperature. Fixation is Saturn's function. Saturn is in the strong dignity of Mercury, the natural significator of quicksilver. Saturn in Virgo indicates something

Chapter 2. Horary Astrology

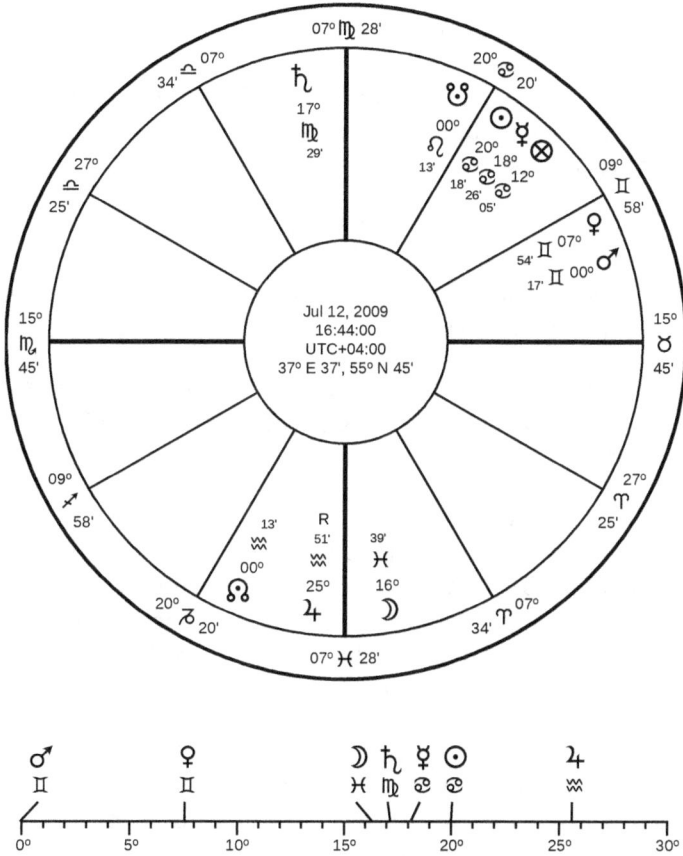

Figure 2.52: *Chart: Where Is My Thermometer?*

that fixates with quicksilver. The customer is looking for a mercury thermometer.

Saturn in dignity of Mercury would better indicate the thermometer than Jupiter. Moreover, Saturn directly relates to the 2nd house—it rules a significant part of it, being its co-ruler. Without a doubt, I would prefer Saturn to find the lost thermometer.

Where is Saturn located? It is inside the 10th house. This could be the upper floors, attic, home office, or room for official receptions. But the querent lives in a small apartment. The most suitable option here is a home office. There is a small desk with a computer in that apartment. Our first thought is to check the thermometer around the desk.

Saturn is in an earth sign, meaning it is on the ground or at the bottom. It could be the floor under the desk or the bottom of a drawer in the desk. We have at least two search options.

Mercury casts a close aspect to the thermometer. We cannot say that the thermometer is next to quicksilver; it makes no sense. But Mercury also rules various documents and office supplies—precisely what we usually keep in a desk drawer.

Finding the thermometer in the desk drawer seems more straightforward. Therefore, according to Occam's razor principle, we prefer it and start searching in that place.

The querent described the situation further: "The pull-out drawer in the desk, where there are many papers and stationery, was the permanent place for the thermometer, but I had already looked for it there without success. However, the chart indicated that it was there! I decided to look again carefully and found it! The thermometer was in another corner of the same drawer, covered with papers."

If we had initially preferred Jupiter as the accidental significator of the thermometer, we would have reached the answer through a longer path. Jupiter is in the 3rd house—in the corridor or the house's communication hub. We would have first searched for the thermometer in the corridor, then turned our search to "communication" places—a PC with Internet access and phone locations. And we would have looked for the thermometer on the surface, uncovered, as it is in an air sign. After exhausting these possibilities, we would have considered the thermometer in Aquarius not as a position in an air sign, that is, on the surface, but as the location in the dignity of Saturn—the natural ruler of safes, boxes, and drawers. And in one of the scenarios, we would have reached the desk drawer.

But look at how long our path would have been. The more precise the significator describes the loss, the more explicitly it indicates its location.

Not all search horary charts are as straightforward as this one. Be prepared to review dozens of options before finding the right place.

The advantage of search horaries is that you have a limited number of options, excluding places where the item cannot be found.

For example, even on the longest route through Jupiter, you won't search for a thermometer in the bedroom, kitchen, or bathroom, which makes the search process much more efficient.

Relationship Questions

It is one of the most common questions—I will provide several horary charts showing different nuances.

Technically, receptions represent emotions and feelings. We could answer questions like "How does my partner feel about me right now?" and "How will our relationship develop?" by evaluating the current receptions between the querent's and quesited's planets, as well as their immediate changes (ingress into a new sign within 3–4 degrees).

But here lies one problem. Suppose we assign the ruler of the 7th house to the partner. In that case, we will see only one feeling—love, friendship, indifference, or rejection. However, in reality, a person can experience a spectrum of emotions.

For example, your partner may feel sexual attraction but have no intentions for a long-term relationship. We do not want to miss such a picture.

However, we cannot track such an emotional spectrum with just one reception between a pair of planets. Therefore, we need more significators to denote partners that reflect the full spectrum of their feelings.

Gender Planets

For this purpose, we involve Venus, the universal significator of all women, and the Sun, the universal significator of all men.

Some may argue that Mars is the significator of men, not the Sun. However, Mars primarily represents brute force and warriors as carriers of that force. The Sun, in turn, symbolizes the governing and creative power—the leader of the hierarchy—which is attributed to the male principle in families (at least in patriarchal communities).

In relationship questions, we assign Venus to women. As the universal ruler, she shows the social archetype of a woman in a particular society. The celestial state of Venus shows how well the woman corresponds to that archetype. It includes the expression of sexuality, flirtation, and similar traits. For example, dignified Venus shows a woman full of virtue, an "ideal woman" in a specific culture. It could be a faithful wife with a meek temperament according to domestic common standards. A debilitated Venus would indicate a woman who clearly does not fit this socially accepted ideal.

Some men may prefer a woman who fits the social archetype, while others may prefer a revolutionary woman who disregards accepted norms of the "right girl." The man's attitude toward Venus will show this aspect of his feelings.

We apply the same scheme to the Sun—it will show how well a man corresponds to what is commonly called the "ideal man" in a particular culture, including the expression of sexuality, masculinity, care, problem-solving skills, and so on.

The rulers of the 1st and 7th houses reveal the personalities of the two partners. This includes their sense of humor, habits, personal views on things, and everything unrelated to their gender roles.

In relationship questions, the Moon shows the querent's emotions in their pure form. For women, this often includes an expression of care for the partner.

Receptions between these significators demonstrate the full spectrum of feelings between partners. For example:

- The ruler of the man is delighted with Venus but indifferent to the woman's personality: The man perceives her only as a mistress.
- The Sun rejects the woman's Moon: Her emotions hurt the man's pride. Perhaps the woman is overprotective of the man, which can be especially true if the Moon is in the man's house, acting like an invader on his territory. Even with the best intentions, if a woman repeatedly tells a man how to dress to avoid catching a cold, it might eventually lead to rejection from his Sun.
- Venus has warm feelings towards the ruler of the man but rejects his Sun. The woman likes the guy's intellect and sense of humor. Still,

Chapter 2. Horary Astrology

she doesn't see any masculine charisma in him and doesn't find him sexually attractive. He is a close friend to her, but nothing more.
- And so on.

Regular Patterns

Below, I will provide a list of frequently occurring patterns in relationship questions:

- One partner's planet is located in the other partner's second house. The second house signifies the close circle of trusted individuals one can rely on. This configuration may indicate a partner's desire to enter the circle of trusted individuals, that is, to be closely accepted.
- Negative reception between a pair of planets of the same person. Usually, this indicates that one part of the person wants one thing while the other part requires something contrary. For example, Venus rejects the Sun, and the ruler of the woman hates Venus for it. At the same time, the ruler of the woman is delighted with her partner. The woman has no warm feelings and sees that her coldness in response to the man's courtship leads to his distancing. But she is not ready to lose such a wonderful friend, so she criticizes herself.
- Conjunction of two planets of the same person means the partner has no internal conflict. For example, the Sun and the ruler of the man are conjoined, and both reject the woman. The man has no disagreements between the ruler of his house and the Sun—he does not pose the question as to whether to leave but lose her as a mistress or keep the sex but continue enduring her reproaches. He has made a clear decision to leave the woman.
- One partner's planet occupies the opposite partner's house or is conjoined with its cusp. It can indicate a greater interest in the partner or pressure on them. In this case, clarification from the querent is required.
- The woman is concerned about her Venus but indifferent to her partner. It signifies that the woman feels lonely and needs her current partner for comfort. It often happens after the breakup of previous relationships.

Betrayal

Regarding betrayal, we must find connections between the partner and another planet.

- A conjunction (bodily or by antiscion) of the partner with the unknown planet indicates "planetary coitus," i.e., the sexual connection of the partner with someone else.
- Reception between the partner and an unknown planet indicates sympathies on the side, but it does not yet prove infidelity.
- Finding an external planet in the partner's house is a moderate indication that a third party is on the partner's territory. If there is a mutual reception with that planet, it is a strong indication of betrayal.
- It often happens that the querent is in the dignity of the partner's lover, or the partner's lover is in the dignity of the querent. It does not indicate love between competitors but dependence. It also suggests that both sides either know or suspect each other's existence.

If the question is not related to cheating, but you see that querent or quesited is conjoined with an unknown planet, there is a high chance of you witnessing betrayal.

Special Cases

If the question involves choosing between two partners, we look for the alternative ruler of the 7th house as described in the section "Signification Techniques: Alternative Rulers." Then, we compare the receptions/past contacts of the three parties with the feelings/past events in the story that the querent describes. This way, we determine which planet represents which partner. In this scenario, we do not use the gender planet for the partner.

In questions about same-sex relationships, we also exclude the gender planet.

Example №23: Relationship Models

Relationship horaries allow us to analyze the reasons behind current feelings if we consider them as projections of early childhood experiences with parents onto the current partner. Here's an example of such analysis.

Chapter 2. Horary Astrology

A girl has been dating a wealthy and successful man who values his freedom and is unwilling to commit. He is popular with women and recently ended another relationship with the mistress. He is currently abroad on business, and the girl is waiting for his return, secretly hoping he will eventually agree to marry her. The querent's question is, "How will our relationship develop?" (Fig. 2.53).

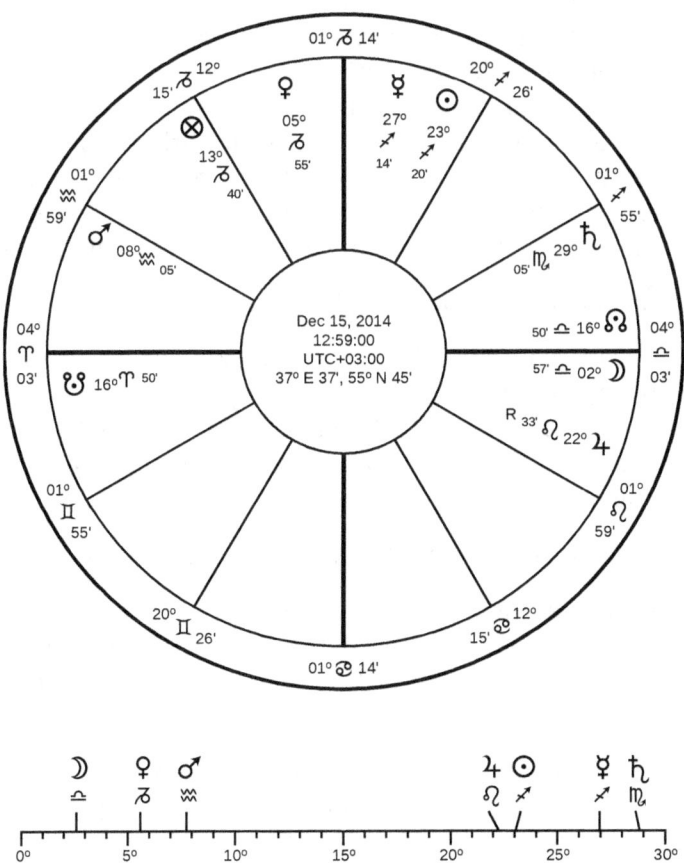

Figure 2.53: *Chart: How Will Our Relationship Develop?*

Traditionally, we will begin by checking the chart for radicality, comparing the querent's current feelings and other circumstances with what the chart reflects. The querent gets the ruler of the 1st house, Mars, the Moon, and Venus, the universal significator of all women.

But Venus also rules the 7th house. Since we cannot deprive the man of the primary significator, we will assign Venus to represent the man's personality. The girl will be left with only Mars and the Moon. We will also assign the Sun to the man.

Now let's compare the querent's feelings with the receptions in the chart:

- The querent's emotions (Moon) are under the influence of Venus. Yes, the girl is emotionally attached to this man.
- Both the Moon and Mars, as well as the Part of Fortune (deep desires), are under the influence of Saturn—the dispositor of the Part of Marriage. The girl passionately desires to start a family with this man.
- Both Mars and the Moon reject the Sun. The girl is very disappointed with how the man behaves, contrary to the expected model of male behavior. Indeed, we can hardly expect much enthusiasm from a woman if her man constantly cheats and refuses to marry her.

Additionally, we have a reflection of known circumstances:

- The Sun (the man) is in the 9th house. We know that the man is currently indeed abroad.
- Mercury (the outsider planet) is separating from the Sun, although they were recently conjunct. We know that the man recently had a relationship with another lover.

The horary chart perfectly reflects reality, and we can consider it radical.

Let's now consider the man's feelings. His Sun is indifferent to all the querent's planets. He shows neither proper care nor takes on expected commitments. And this is precisely the planet that disappoints the girl so much.

But Venus tells us a different story. On the one hand, Venus exalts Mars—he is in love with the girl and is not ready to let her go. Venus even seems open to starting a family, judging by its positive reception towards Saturn. But look—Venus rejects the Moon. The Moon represents the female care from the querent's side, which deeply affects the man.

Indeed, the querent excessively showers the man with her care, as seen from the Moon's position on the cusp of his house (we have discussed this in the section "Regular Patterns"). So, we see the reason—the girl's care repels the man. But let's investigate it even further and answer why it happens.

Chapter 2. Horary Astrology

The Sun and the Moon have two more universal roles—they signify the father and mother. We can temporarily assign them these roles to see each partner's original childhood relationships with their parents. Childhood expectations or fears in relationships with parents often lay the foundation for models of relationships with partners.

First, let's examine the relationship model that the man is trying to reproduce.

Model of the Man: Overfeeding Mother

Let's look at the guy. Temporarily, the Moon represents his mother. What did his mother do in his childhood? She pressed him (the Moon pressing on the boy's ASC). What is the pressing Moon filled with? Love and care for Venus. That is, the mom suppressed his male space, meaning she didn't allow him to make his own mistakes with her hyper-care. She deprived the boy of his freedom to experiment with the world in childhood. It is an act of symbolic castration of the psyche. It causes a wave of rebellion in the child against the mother and her care (Venus rejecting the Moon) and a solid desire to pave his way in life.

Indeed, at 47, this man has achieved a lot. And it's understandable why—his whole life, he has been trying to prove that he can achieve everything on his own, without his mom's help. The childhood trauma gave him tremendous energy for success, for moving towards independence, and for constantly defending his freedom.

On the one hand, any approach to a family is an approach to memories of stifling love and care from a mother. On the other hand, the need for care has not disappeared anywhere; it is inherent in all people.

Since the brain fears everything unknown, the man will prefer the familiar, though painful, relationship model. He needs women of a particular type who can accommodate his psychological reality, that is, fulfill the role of "overfeeding mother" in his life, from which he must constantly flee. That is familiar, i.e., the safest scenario, which the man will follow.

Our querent turned out to be one of those women. But to understand why such a man entered her life, we need to look at her childhood story.

The Girl's Model: The Rejecting Mother

Again, let's look at the primary relationship with the mother—these are the ones that set the tone for relationships with the world. You see that the Moon hates, or rejects, the querent. Moreover, it is in opposition to the ASC. It's as if the mother rejected the little girl in childhood.

Right away, after I told her this, the girl proved that starting from age four, the mother regularly left her for long periods. It stimulated resentment and a lack of love in the girl's heart. This trauma was reinforced multiple times—the mother regularly left her daughter.

Children are incapable of understanding why their parents leave them or show coldness. Children assume the reason is within them, that they misbehave, so their parents reject them. Such children not only justify but also fiercely defend their parents. Moreover, they try in every possible way to "redeem" their love and attention using all available means.

Therefore, the only familiar scenario for the girl is a relationship with a man for whom she tries to be perfect but receives rejection in return.

Suppose such a girl meets a guy who showers her with attention. In that case, it will trigger maximum anxiety and rejection. After all, such a relationship system is unfamiliar to the brain. And the brain avoids anything unfamiliar as potentially life-threatening. That's why she chose a man who familiarly rejects her love and care (Venus rejects the Moon).

Indeed, the querent later confirmed that whenever men appeared in her life who offered her warmth and family, she felt anxious.

The Interweaving of Two Models

So we see how two people have perfectly found each other.

- The man found a girl who exhibited hyper-care, from which he would constantly run away.
- The girl found a man who would seem close but at the same time constantly disappear or go to other women.

Each of the heroes of this story feels maximally familiar and safe in these relationships. The two have formed perhaps not the most harmonious but a very stable couple.

Chapter 2. Horary Astrology

Even without astrology, it is clear that these relationships will not transition to marriage—this is a zone of discomfort for both partners. However, the chart confirms this logical conclusion.

- Venus remains in the same sign, rejecting the Moon and continuing to dream of marriage theoretically.
- The querent's planets also do not change signs, and the reception remains unchanged. The girl will still love this man and be satisfied with the bits of attention he is willing to give her.
- The South Node in the first house weakens the querent—the girl is unlikely to go to a psychologist to change her mental reality.

Everything will remain as it is. The relationship will not break apart or transition into another phase.

Example №24: Relationship Development

Here is an example of astrological prediction of relationship development. The girl recently started dating a guy from her office and asked about the future of their relationship (Fig. 2.54).

As usual, we will start with the radicality assessment. First, look at the lord of the 1st house, Saturn, which is in the 8th house (a circle of trusted people). Does the girl want to be a trusted person for that guy? Yes, it is possible if she is not there yet, i.e., if he still considers other girls around.

We need to ask a clarifying question about the guy to make the correct interpretation of Saturn's position. The querent proved that the guy is trendy among the girls in that office and constantly flirts with others.

It is precisely the option here. Saturn in the 8th house represents the desire of the girl to be the only trusted and loved person in a close environment of that guy.

Then look at her Venus. As a woman, she stays opposite the 7th house cusp with a negative feeling toward its lord. She is very upset about that guy. And now we know why—she doesn't feel trusted in that relationship.

Does she admire his behavior as a "right man"? No way, none of her planets loves the Sun. Indeed, it is strange to expect enthusiasm if your partner flirts with others. It completely corresponds to the reality. We consider the chart as radical and move on to the prognosis.

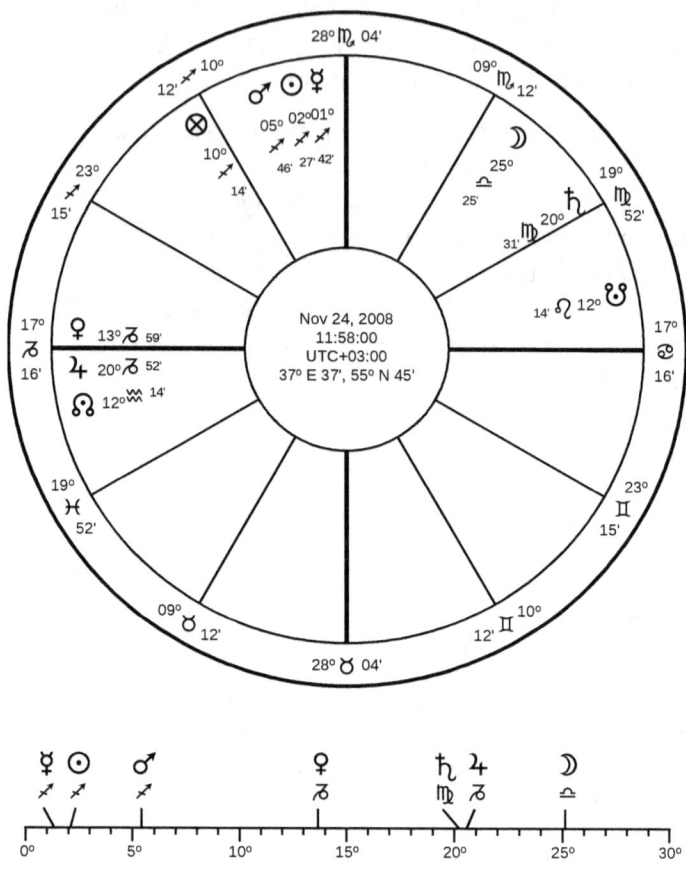

Figure 2.54: *Chart: Relationships No. 2*

Since the question concerns a prospective change of feelings, we first need to estimate the partner's current feelings and then let their planets pass 3–4 degrees to see if they change their attitude.

First, we assess the man's current feelings for the girl. His Moon is full of passion for the girl. It is in the sign of Venus and exalts Saturn. Great.

The Moon is in the place of the Sun's detriment. The guy "rejects" or "hates" his own behavior as a man. But why? What is prominently happening to the Sun?

It is in conjunction with two other planets. The conjunction or "planetary coitus" of two planets in the relationship question almost always means

Chapter 2. Horary Astrology

the coitus of two persons. We are nearly sure that the person has sex with two other girls, and he hates hiding it from the querent. On the other hand, he cannot leave these two girls since Mercury and Mars are applying to the Sun, not separating from it.

Well, we have discovered some hidden details about the current situation. But what will happen in the following few degrees? Nothing prominent happens with Saturn or Venus. But look at this:

- The Sun will eventually conjunct Mercury. The guy will bind himself with another girl.
- At the same time, the Moon shortly leaves Libra, the place where it is so passionate for the querent.

We have two coherent indications that the guy is dropping his current relationship and moving to another.

The timing is typically shown in the relationship question when explicitly asked. Nevertheless, *if we have a prominent coincidence of timing indicators, we can consider them.* It could be, for instance, 1 degree and 7 degrees until the same event, which shows one week or seven days.

In our case, Mercury needs to pass 2.5 degrees for the actual conjunction with the Sun, and the Moon needs to pass 4.5 degrees to change its feelings for the querent.

2.5 and 4.5 do not correspond to each other. But if we apply the "freezing the significator" technique, Mercury will move one degree to conjunct with the Sun. We discussed this technique earlier in the section "Supplementary Timing Techniques."

One degree and 4.5 degrees correspond to one month and 4.5 weeks. It is a remarkable correlation. Hence, the chart shows the timing, even if it was not part of the question.

So we know the guy will turn to another girl one month after the question was asked.

And so it proved. Indeed, the guy was involved with two other girls all this time. On the 24th of November, he moved into the house of one of those girls, and a few days later, the querent found out about it.

What is interesting is that the guy did not know about this forecast, and the result of this forecast could not influence his actions. But I not only predicted his own "free will" but also the exact date when his "free will" would transform into action.

Transit Chart

Sometimes, we can get extra details from the transit chart, which, as I said before, realizes the promise of the preceding horary radix.

On the 24th of November (Fig. 2.55), the Moon was in Scorpio (the place of the querent's exile). Around 10 AM, the transit chart's descendant coincided with the horary radix's descendant, when the 1st and the 7th houses repeat their radical roles. This immediately replaced the Moon's meaning of "the guy who is still in love" from the horary chart with the current meaning of "guy who hates" (the Moon was captivated by Venus but now rejects it).

But look at what was happening right at that moment. Mercury, i.e., another girl, is immediately rising on the ASC of the querent, meaning the other girl appears in the querent's life that day.

The Planet Interposing the Transit and Radix

Simultaneously with opposition to its radical position, the Moon makes an exact aspect with Jupiter. After that, it will enter Jupiter's sign. Ascending Mercury will also shortly transit through Jupiter. Thus, Jupiter will be the main influence throughout this day. This may not be by chance but because Jupiter already plays an important role in the situation and now only reflects in the radical chart. Let us check it.

Jupiter indeed intervenes in the preceding horary chart. The last aspect the Moon formed before leaving the sign of passion (from the querent's perspective) was with Jupiter. This means Jupiter was the final event the guy encountered before changing his decision to pursue another woman.

The same Jupiter ascends in the horary chart, meaning it soon became visible to the querent.

Moreover, both the guy's and his new girlfriend's planets are in the sign of Jupiter—they both depend on it. No doubt, Jupiter relates to the guy's new relationship with another girl. What does it signify?

Chapter 2. Horary Astrology

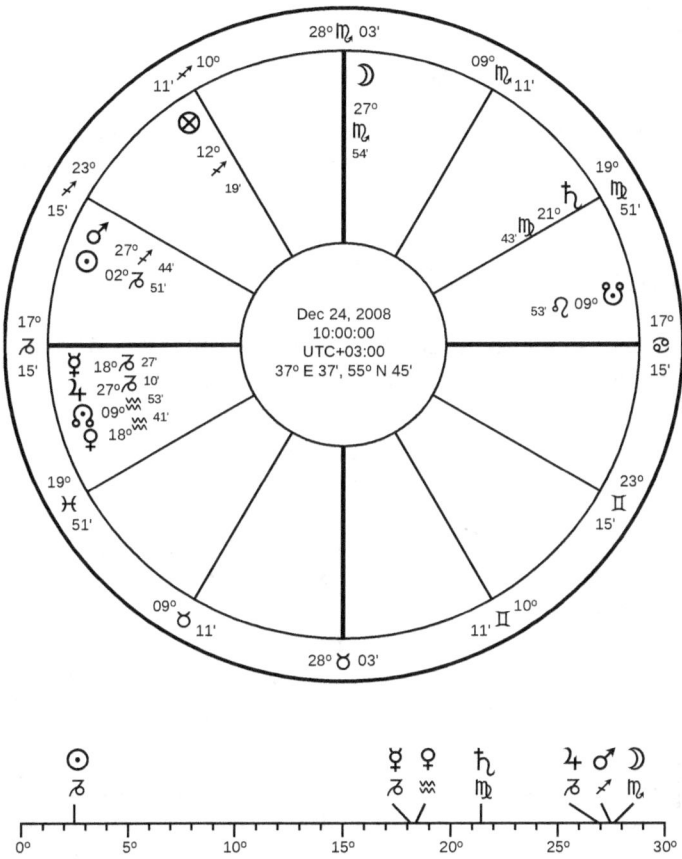

Figure 2.55: *Transit Chart: Relationship*

Jupiter rules the 11th house in the horary, the 5th house of the guy—his child. At the same time, we know that the guy has sex with two other girls. It is easy to conclude that Jupiter's most probable role is the pregnancy of one of those girls. It caused the guy to change his mind and move to another girl.

The horary chart supports this idea. Jupiter's antiscion falls into the 11th house cusp, which enforces their role as the quesited's child, which is hidden but is about to appear. That is what antiscia do.

The transit chart also supports this idea: Jupiter rules the 11th house of the transit chart, and the Part of Fortune occupies that house. Since there is no querent for the transit moment, the ⊗ signifies the hidden things followed by their short appearance (we discussed it in the section "Signification Techniques: Arabian Parts").

Indeed, the querent shortly knew that the guy's new girlfriend was pregnant, which is why he dropped his relationship with the querent.

Example №25: Betrayal

Here is an example of a horary question about betrayal. The man asks if his close friend is sleeping with his wife (Fig. 2.56).

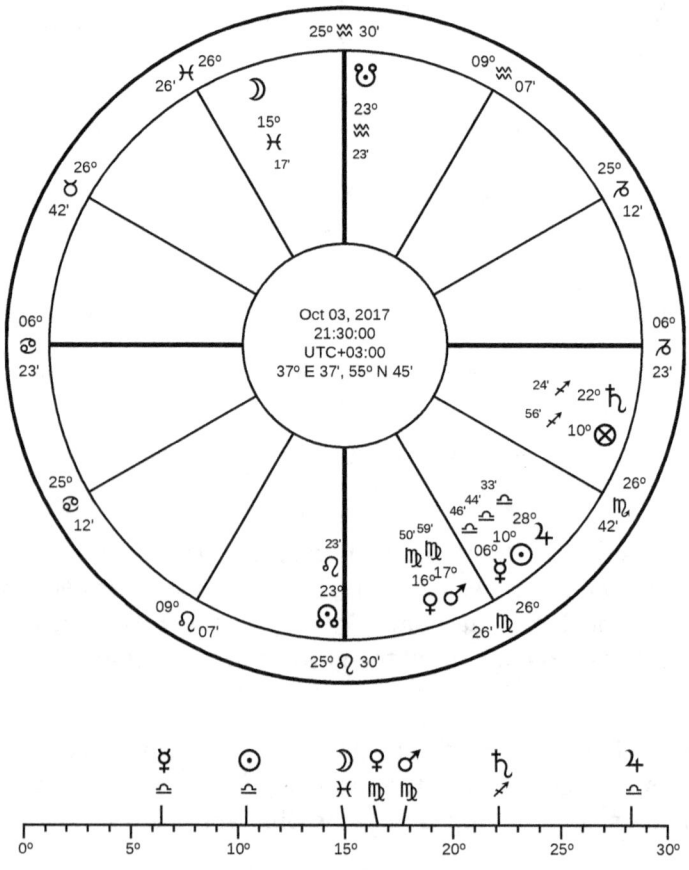

Figure 2.56: *Chart: Betrayal*

Chapter 2. Horary Astrology

Let's begin with a radicality assessment of the chart. I expect the chart to highlight the wife and the friend.

- Indeed, the Moon (the man's feelings) and the Part of Fortune (his deep concern) are under the influence of Jupiter, the ruler of the 11th house, i.e., his friend. Yes, the querent is worried about his friend.
- At the same time, the querent's Sun is under the influence of Venus and Saturn (his wife's planets)—yes, the chart is radical.

Now, let's examine the feelings between the wife and the best friend.

- The close friend (Jupiter) is in the dignity of Saturn and Venus—the close friend loves the querent's wife.
- This feeling is mutual: Saturn, representing the wife as an individual, is under the influence of Jupiter. She loves the querent's friend in return.

That is a warning bell, but it is just a warning. The fact that two people have mutual feelings does not inherently mean they are sleeping with each other.

To confirm betrayal, we must observe a close conjunction, i.e., "coitus," of two planets. This could be a bodily or antiscion conjunction, but there is no such connection in this chart.

They flirt with each other and may even have a little romance, but there is no sexual relationship between the wife and close friend. We could end our consultation here. But we can continue to delve deeper into this chart and uncover some hidden details. So, let's proceed with our prognosis to the next level.

Look at the wife's Venus. As a person, she loves Jupiter, but as a woman, she rejects him—Venus occupies the place of Jupiter's detriment. The querent's wife sees Jupiter as a good family friend and loves him in that sense. However, she is entirely unwilling to cross boundaries and translate affection into a sexual context. Why is that? What is prominently happening to Venus that forces her to reject Jupiter's attention, except for high moral standards?

Venus is conjunct Mars. As you already know, if a planet (especially the gender planet) is conjunct a third planet in relationship questions, it almost always indicates sexual relations with another person. So yes, the wife has a lover, signified by Mars. And it is another man, not a close friend of the querent. What a surprise!

The chart provides additional evidence for this secret connection:

- Saturn (i.e., the wife) is in her 12th house, indicating that she is hiding something from the querent, and now we know her secret.
- Moreover, Saturn's antiscion conjuncts the 7th house cusp (the wife's ASC). She is concealing something at home, in her territory, which will soon be revealed. And now we know what she is hiding. In the context of the question, it also implies that the lover visits her home rather than the wife visiting him.

Let's take our prognosis to the next level and see what happens next. The Moon will soon oppose the pairing of Venus and Mars. It suggests that the querent will catch their spouse with a lover having fun.

Where will this happen? We already know that the spouse invites their lover to the house. So it means that the querent will catch them both when they return home—there are no other options in this context.

Opposition in a relationship question always means conflict or divorce. Both conflict and divorce fit the picture's context. But how do we differentiate between these meanings? Let's find a clue from the fixed stars. If the primary planet on the stage conjuncts a fixed star that fits the context, it provides additional details to the picture.

The Sun (the querent's planet) is conjunct Vindemiatrix, the star of divorce. It immediately clarifies the meaning of opposition—a conflict leading to divorce.

Who will initiate the divorce? The Sun—the querent's planet—contacts Vindemiatrix; hence, the querent will initiate the divorce, not the spouse.

What about the timing? It was not part of the question, but if we find a notable coincidence of timing indicators, we can consider them.

- The Moon will reach this couple by opposition at 2.5 degrees, which denotes 2.5 time units.
- On the other hand, when the Sun advances 2.5 degrees, it will come to 13 degrees of Libra—a degree where Venus's antiscion opposition is. It means that in 2.5 degrees, the Sun will unexpectedly oppose Venus.

We have two consistent indicators of the same event with coinciding timing. Hence, the chart indicates the timing, even if it is not explicitly part of the question. We use a standard timescale of weeks, months, and years in relationship questions. Hence, 2.5 degrees may indicate 2.5 weeks, months, or years. Let's clarify the time unit.

- The Moon is the applying planet in the first aspect. It is in the sign of average speed and quick house. This combination of fast and average speeds gives us the average time unit, i.e., months.
- The Sun is the applying planet in the second aspect. It is in the quick sign and the house of average speed. Again, the combination of average-fast speeds gives us the average time unit, i.e., months.

So we know the husband will catch his wife with her lover when he returns home in 2.5 months. It is challenging to specify the exact date, so we indicate the approximate time, like "after 2.5 months" or "at the end of November." This is an acceptable level of accuracy for us.

So, our prediction includes the following details.

- The close friend does not sleep with the wife.
- The wife has another lover.
- 2.5 months later, at the end of November, the man will return home and catch his wife with her lover.
- Shortly after that, he will file for divorce.

The last three items on the list were not part of the question and would upset the client, so the only answer given to the man was, "Your friend doesn't have sex with your wife."

I discussed this prognosis in detail during the astrology lecture and recorded it on camera at the beginning of October. So, all the students of that lecture were expecting the results.

And so it proved. Indeed, at the end of November, precisely on the 26th of November, the man returned from a business trip earlier than expected and caught his wife with her lover. It was not his friend, but an unknown guy. Shortly after that, he filed for divorce, and on the 15th of January, they officially divorced.

The Transit Chart

For demonstration purposes, let's examine the transit that triggered the event. In hindsight, knowing that the querent discovered their wife with her lover on November 26th, let's revisit that date and find the transit that realized the promises of the horary chart (Fig. 2.57).

Predictive Astrology Textbook

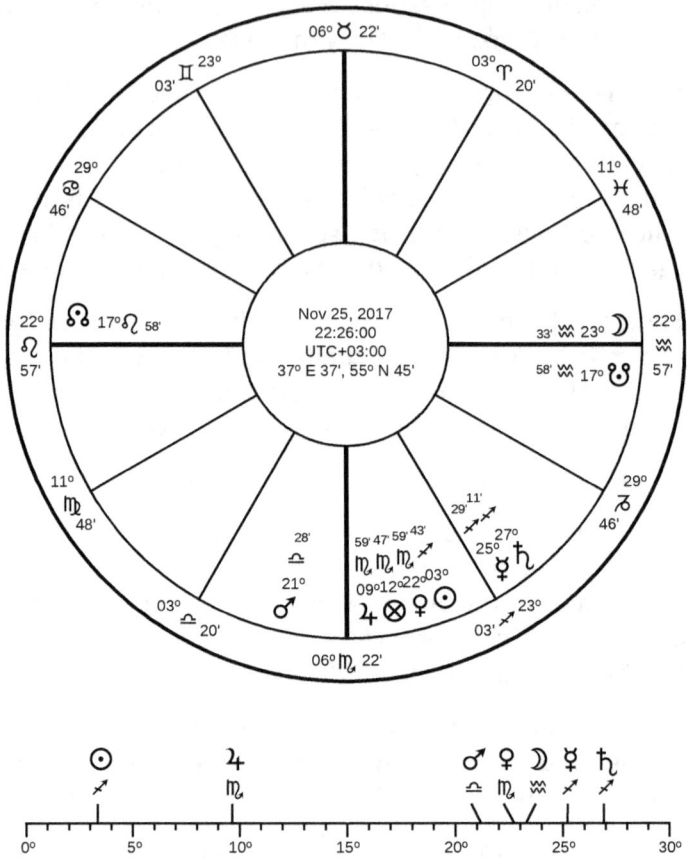

Figure 2.57: *Transit Chart: Betrayal*

Searching for the corresponding transit during the day is always a tedious manual process of checking every minute to find the moment that best reflects the preceding horary chart.

Here is that moment. Here, Saturn has taken rulership of the 7th house, just as in the radix, emphasizing its role as the wife, while the Moon, which signified the man in the horary, entered the wife's room at this exact moment.

At the same time, Saturn (the wife) was in conjunction with an unknown planet, Mercury, in the 5th house of physical pleasures and sex. This exactly reflects the promise of the preceding horary chart.

Simultaneously entering the 7th house, the Moon immediately aspected this pair, who were blissfully spending time in the 5th house. We see a literal picture of the moment—the husband catches this couple engaged in lovemaking.

Also, note that the transit chart repeats the promises of the radical figure through other planets. You remember that Mars and Venus represented the couple in the radical figure. Look at the transit chart—the Moon (husband) makes a precise aspect to Venus, which is in mutual reception with Mars.

The same picture—the husband catches the two. And again, a repetition of this happening directly on the wife's territory—Venus with Mars casts a precise aspect on the 7th house cusp.

Also, note that the Moon casts an unfavorable aspect to its place of detriment. That is, it strikes Venus, which is already debilitated. It reflects reality—one can only imagine the anger the husband confronted his wife and her lover. By the way, the lover from the radical figure (Mars) is also debilitated at the moment of the transit, which makes sense.

See how many repetitions there are of what the preceding horary chart promised. Most importantly, a particular moment gathered all these indications together.

Move the time forward by a few minutes, and the exact aspects to the cusps will begin to dissipate. Move the time forward by half an hour, and the close aspects of the Moon will start to dissolve. Move the time forward by an hour—the cusps will change signs, and the planets will exit their respective houses. As you can see, the transit is the momentary peak of the realization of the potential of the preceding horary chart. As one moves away from this moment, the potential for realizing the horary chart promise gradually diminishes.

The Planet Interposing the Transit Chart

The Part of Fortune shows everything hidden that will soon become evident (we discussed this in the section "the section Signification Techniques: Arabian Parts"). Here, this point is conjunct Jupiter, which will soon manifest itself.

At the same time, the ruler of the 1st house of the transit chart and the gender planet of the man—the Sun—is under the influence of Jupiter.

The chart of the moment conditions the husband to take further steps in the direction indicated by Jupiter.

Jupiter is the main character in the story for that day (and for the next stage of development of the whole story). But what does Jupiter mean in this chart? It cannot be the querent's friend from the previous radix—they are not in any way connected to the discovered infidelity. So it must be something else. Let's check if it signifies divorce. After all, divorce was already seen in the preceding chart.

The Part of Divorce falls at 24° 26' Sagittarius, exactly where Mercury—the accidental ruler of the lover in the transit chart—is located. We read this quite literally: divorce is connected to the discovered lover.

Now let's see who the dispositor of the Part of Divorce is. The Part falls in the sign of Sagittarius, ruled by Jupiter. Yes, Jupiter is indeed divorce, just as we assumed. So, the decision to pursue divorce is the main trend for that day (and for the months to come).

You see the exact behavior of the heavens—the transit charts, on the one hand, realize the promise of the preceding radix. On the other hand, they set the direction of further story development as promised by the preceding radix.

Summary of Chapter 2

The information provided above is sufficient for predicting the development of any particular life situation. I want to summarize some fundamental principles to follow:

Before Judgment

1. Make a list of significators that you believe the chart should highlight. Prepare a list of techniques you will apply to these planets in advance. Only then can you begin to examine the chart. Mistakes made by astrologers often derive from the absence of a clear plan for reviewing the chart and instead searching for "something interesting to catch the eye." They may predict by applying random techniques to random planets, labeling it a "personal vision."

2. If you encounter something in the chart contradicting reality, resolve this contradiction logically—find out what the querent is hiding from you. Suppose a simple rational explanation cannot resolve the contradiction. In that case, the chart does not reflect reality and most probably does not contain the answer. In such cases, postpone judgment. The mistake of astrologers is to ignore such contradictions and work with any chart, even if it does not provide an answer. Not every horary moment "intervenes" in the situation development; not every horary chart is radical for the subsequent transit that realizes the promise of the radix.

During Judgment

1. Always rely on logic; avoid relying on intuition. The gravest mistake of an astrologer is to consider astrology as divination or to rely on psychic abilities. Astrology is the elder sister of mathematics, the most exact of sciences.

2. Follow Occam's Razor principle—choose the most straightforward and logical explanation from all possible variants in the context. Suppose the ruler of the 9th house interposes the question, and you know that the querent has been preparing for university admission for six months. In that case, it is a university, not a sudden long journey to the astral plane. The mistake of astrologers is to indulge in absurd fantasies, tailoring the answer to what the querent wants to hear or to their own "intuitively grasped" image of the future.

3. Always prefer the planet's accidental meaning to its universal one. Pay attention to the intersections of the planet's universal and accidental meanings—the significator can take an ultra-specific role, such as "fatal falling from a height" in the horary from the section "Example №21: Date of Departure." Astrologers often make the mistake of assigning universal "psychological" roles to the planet. Seeing Saturn as the ruler of the 1st house in a relationship question, they might immediately conclude the querent's solitude. But that's not the case. Saturn may be in a perfect celestial state, surrounded by the ruler and co-ruler of the 7th house, representing a close sexual connection with two other lovers. The accidental role prevails over the universal one.

4. Always correlate newly discovered indications of the chart with the current context. The indications must logically and non-contradictorily reflect the current situation. Astrologers' mistake is inventing nonexistent details of current circumstances (including dubious claims about the objectives of this incarnation) based on newly discovered details.

Chapter 3

Natal Astrology

One of the main problems in natal astrology is the diversity of interpretations of the same testimony. The same planet can indicate different events that will occur throughout your life.

It doesn't mean we can't make accurate forecasts from a natal chart. It only means we need a different approach than the one commonly practiced in contemporary astrology.

We should follow Morin's approach and systematically discard all of the planet's significations with little chance of occurring in a particular period of life, retaining only the most expected ones. By applying such a filter sequentially to a specific year and then to a certain month and day, we can not only specify which specific event will occur but also pinpoint the exact date of its occurrence.

This chapter teaches how to accurately forecast crucial life events based on the birth chart. We start our journey by discussing the main differences between natal and horary astrology.

Roles of Planets in the Natal Chart

The Diversity of Roles of the Same Planet

A horary chart describes the development of an ultra-specific situation. You might ask, "When will my friend John come to visit me?" In this question, the ruler of the 11th house of friends becomes the significator of your friend John. From this moment on, it can only denote John and no one else.

In the natal chart, the ruler of the 11th house represents all the friends you will ever meet. It also means your father's death (as the 8th from the 4th), earnings from a particular job, tax returns, and so forth. Moreover, the ruler of the 11th house may also rule the 3rd house, representing your brother, sisters, and neighbors. Therefore, the ruler of the 11th house can no longer denote one specific object as in horary.

So, the first significant difference is that a planet has multiple roles in the natal chart. For example, in my natal chart, Venus signifies:

– All my potential spouses
– A whole class of illnesses
– Secret rivals who plot intrigues behind my back
– My finances

When it comes to illnesses, there's nothing good about such a Venus, but when considered as a significator of spouses or money, Venus brings a lot of good into my life. The same planet in its different roles can be both constructive and destructive. We'll talk about this later.

You remember that several planets can denote the same thing in horary astrology. For instance, in relationship questions, the querent is shown by the ruler of the 1st house, the Moon, and the Sun or Venus. Similarly, multiple planets in the natal chart signify the same object.

So, we have a more complex picture in the natal chart:

– A particular planet has several roles simultaneously.
– A particular role is "distributed" among several planets. There is not just one planet for marriage or lawsuit. It is always a set of planets.

Changing Roles Over Time

Each planet in the natal chart can fulfill only one role at a time, determined by a specific period of your life.

For instance, Mercury may represent income, friends, and long journeys. Meanwhile, Venus might symbolize my brother, friends, or income. Suppose these two planets interacted and overlapped in significance in

Chapter 3. Natal Astrology

2016–2017. During this time frame, they shared a common connotation—friends and income. Their celestial state and the form of aspect they perfect portend something good.

Further prognostic techniques reject the significance of income and confirm the one of friendship. It also pinpoints the exact year when something good happened to my friend—2017.

The following technique narrows this significance to specific details: both planets show not just a friend but a friend who is getting married. It also narrows down the time of the event—between November 26 and December 23 of that year.

The final technique proves the correctness of this significance and clarifies that the marriage will happen on November 27.

Let's assume I'm a student, and in 2017, I had only two friends—Max and Peter. Max had been in a long-term relationship while Peter lived with his mom, and his personal life wasn't going well. By combining the promise of the chart with the specific context, I conclude that it's Max, not Peter, who will get married on November 27, 2017.

As you can see, I start with the natal chart, which promises all possible events throughout life. Then, I select the planet's unique significance (my friend) within a specific time frame. After that, I move to the planet's ultra-specific role (my friend, who is getting married) in a particular month, overlapping it with the context.

The main idea of the scheme is to discard the irrelevant meaning of the planets in the natal chart as I approach a specific date.

As you see from this imaginary example, our task as astrologers consists of two things:

- Using astrological techniques, we need to determine what object the planet indicates in a particular month and year—whether it's your friend, income, or the death of a father. And if it signifies your friend, what specific event will it bring—whether it is your best friend's marriage or injury?
- Then, logically combining these meanings with the current context, we can predict a particular event—the marriage of your friend Max in November 2017.

Therefore, questions from many clients like "Tell me, what does the Sun signify in my horoscope?" are meaningless. The right question is, "What will my Sun signify in my chart on September 2021 in that particular circumstance?"

Celestial States of the Planets

Precursor of the Event

In horary astrology, when questioning the future state of an object or circumstance, we examine the current state of the planets as if the chart were a snapshot of the future (see "Three Ways How the Chart Shows the Future" on page 177). For instance, in a question about the profitability of long-term investments, we focus on the 2nd house ruler, as if it showed the prospective finances after the investment period ends. The ruler's current celestial state indicates prospective profit or loss.

This same principle applies in natal astrology, where the positions of planets at birth are considered significators of future circumstances.

For example, if the ruler of the second house is debilitated, it suggests future financial hardship. Conversely, the ruler of the second house in excellent condition indicates future wealth.

Since multiple planets signify the same thing (money), some planets portend poverty, while others, wealth. When a particular planet manifests, the financial condition starts to change according to the state of the significator. During periods when none of the financial significators are active, the native's financial state changes randomly, influenced by external factors. But it returns to its determined course when the financial significator comes to the stage again.

Therefore, planets in natal astrology act as precursors of future significant events. For example:

- If the rulers of the 7th house is dignified, it will bring new love or support from a partner at an appropriate time.
- If the ruler of the 7th house is debilitated, it will create conflict—a fight with an enemy or divorce (if the querent is in a relationship by then).

Chapter 3. Natal Astrology

- If the ruler of the 7th house is in a moderately unfavorable condition, once it comes to the stage of life, it will start creating obstacles in relationships. And if there are no relationships by then, it will have no effect. As always, the context has the final say in the forecast. If the current circumstance doesn't allow the event to happen, the event won't happen.

Regarding unfavorable houses, planets act in reverse.

- If the ruler of the 12th house of illnesses is in terrible condition, it will create the most severe illness possible with dire consequences.
- However, if the ruler of the 12th house is in an excellent state, it acts against the 12th house. According to its favorable nature, a dignified planet cannot create evil things. On the contrary, it can relieve the course of the disease or even stop it entirely (if the native is ill by the time this planet manifests). Even if such a planet is determined to cause an illness (if strongly conditioned to diseases by the 12th house), it will realize a short-lived disease with a favorable outcome.

Thus, planets in the natal chart act as precursors of future events: they either portend to realize what the house signifies or contrary—to hinder or even nullify the circumstances of the house:

- Accidentally beneficial significators produce the good in favorable houses—money, career, family. Malefic significators produce maximum harm in unfavorable houses—severe illnesses, violent death, etc.
- Accidentally beneficial significators act against unfavorable houses and mitigate or nullify their harm—they liberate from prisons, relieve illnesses, and save from death. Malefic significators act against favorable houses—they ruin financial savings, hinder career growth, etc.

So, our task as astrologers, when looking at the chart, is to understand the following:

- In which area of life will the planet most easily manifest itself?
- What it will do in this area of life—create, destroy, or hinder.

Close Aspects

In horary astrology, close aspects show favorable or unfavorable influences on the subject from the other planets. For example, there might be a beautiful house, but it is hard to sell because it receives opposition from the debilitated ruler of the 6th house (the neighboring area of the house). The house itself is lovely, but directly opposite it is a park where homeless people frequently reside. This unpleasant detail confuses customers and hinders sales.

In natal astrology, we cannot interpret close aspects as the influence of specific circumstances on a particular object, as in horary. Remember, planets, in the absence of context, act as precursors of events rather than the significators of particular objects.

Consequently, when a malefic planet receives an unfavorable aspect, its negative effect intensifies. A favorable aspect can mitigate the negative promise of such a planet.

N.B.

When I say "favorable/unfavorable" aspect, I imply the cumulative effect due to the celestial state of the aspecting planet, the form of the aspect, and the sign it falls into, as discussed in the section "Object Interaction Techniques: Close Aspects."

For example, imagine the ruler of the 12th house (illness, imprisonment, exile) receives a favorable trine from the noble ruler of the 11th house (friends and allies). Whenever the native falls ill, encounters legal trouble, or needs to leave the country, friends come to the rescue. As a result, illnesses pass more quickly, time spent in prison shortens, and forced immigration is easier to cope with due to the generous help of friends.

Without knowing particular details, we regard close aspects as factors shifting the significator's celestial state for better or worse.

Thus, the debilitated planet in the 7th house may deny marriage, but favorable aspects help reduce the denial effect to minor relationship obstacles.

The Dispositor of the Planet

In horary astrology, we sometimes consider the dispositor of a planet as a factor that changes the condition of the significator. For instance, in a query concerning the husband's well-being, we might observe that he feels terrible—his significator is in exile. The dispositor of the sign it occupies is the cause of this detrimental state. Let's presume that the husband's dispositor governs his 10th house—his project, to which he devotes himself so passionately that he is left depleted.

However, if the dispositor is in excellent condition, indicating that the project is highly successful, this state of affairs uplifts the husband and makes him feel better. The scenario would be markedly different if the dispositor were debilitated.

As you can see, in certain instances, provided the context supports it, the celestial state of the dispositor can impact the condition of the significator.

In natal astrology, we lack such specific contexts. Hence, when examining the chart in a broader sense, we always consider the condition of the dispositor as a factor that influences the celestial state of the significator. For example, the ruler of the 10th house in Sagittarius with Jupiter in Pisces will yield greater success than the same ruler of the 10th house in Sagittarius with Jupiter in Gemini.

The significator's dispositor may represent the surrounding circumstances within which the significator operates. We'll refer to this principle as *"the planet always manifests itself through its dispositor."*

Receptions

In a horary chart, we say that a planet in a sign depends on the ruler of that sign, which, in the context of the question, means that Planet A loves, protects, or desires what Planet B signifies.

The context of the situation primarily drives this dependence. For example, if the ruler of the 2nd house (the querent's car) is under the control of the 7th house, we cannot say that the vehicle loves or cares for the querent's spouse. We can say that the spouse controls or drives the car.

In natal astrology, however, we lack a specific context, so we cannot choose a definitive meaning for the reception. Nevertheless, we know that the state of the dispositor of a planet reflects on the planet itself, as we have just shown above.

This means that if the ruler of the 2nd house is under the control of the ruler of the 7th house, the state of the ruler of the 7th house will affect the finances in the broadest sense. For example, if the ruler of the 7th house is debilitated, conflicts and lawsuits will negatively impact the finances. Conversely, a successful marriage or partnership will strengthen the financial situation if the ruler of the 7th is dignified.

This will be especially true if, in addition, the ruler of the 7th house casts a favorable aspect to the ruler or cusp of the 2nd house, adding even more of its beneficial essence to the realm of finances.

However, wherever a planet signifies a person, we can generally read receptions as in horary astrology—the person desires what their dispositor represents. For example, Morinus wrote that in his horoscope, the ruler of the 1st house is in place of Jupiter's exaltation, which imprinted in him a natural inclination to rise above others.

Similarly, suppose the significator of the brother is under the control of the ruler of the 10th house. In that case, we can read this as "the brother exposing himself to mortal dangers" since the 10th house is the 8th house of the brother. The state of the ruler of the 10th house will tell us how dangerous these threats are, whether they indicate an early death or a miraculous escape from death at the last moment.

Technical Side of Reception

I want to explain more explicitly how receptions work. To understand it, you can recall that a planet is "reflected" in the signs it rules. Consider Jupiter—it reflects in Pisces and Sagittarius, meaning it directs its rays to Earth from its current position and simultaneously from the signs of Pisces and Sagittarius.

Now, suppose Venus is in Pisces. This means that Jupiter's rays from Pisces are mixed with Venus's rays. Since Pisces emanates part of Jupiter's total influence, we can say that eventually, Jupiter mixes its rays with Venus's nature. So, Jupiter's rays reaching Earth are now mixed with the essence of noble Venus. The influence of noble Venus makes Jupiter's impact more beneficial.

In horary astrology, Venus's noble influence will improve the brother's condition if Jupiter signifies a brother and his state. This means Venus "helps" or "supports" Jupiter—we read this supportive effect in a context. For the same reason, a debilitated Venus in Virgo will unlikely help Mercury.

On the other hand, we can consider Jupiter's effect on Venus. Since Jupiter and its condition influence Pisces and, through that sign, Venus, a debilitated Jupiter in Gemini makes the sign of Pisces harmful, reducing Venus's nobility.

In horary astrology, we would say that if Venus in Pisces signifies a respectable person, then Jupiter in Gemini and Pisces both indicate a criminal area where the person is located. This does not deprive the person of nobility but worsens their well-being compared to if they were in a prosperous neighborhood.

Universal Benefics and Malefics

As you've seen in horary astrology, planets sometimes manifest not as accidental significators but as universal ones. For instance, in search horaries, we often prefer natural significators of lost items to the ruler of the 2nd house. In relationship questions, we assign the Sun and Venus as the main characters of man and woman according to their universal significance.

Occasionally, in the natal chart, planets take on universal significance. For example, Saturn during a specific period may represent loneliness according to its universal nature. Venus—the planet of love—may bring new romance in a particular year, even though, accidentally, it may denote long journeys.

Although Saturn governs boundaries and structure, it also represents decay, aging, dirt, restricted circumstances, illness, death, slavery, imprisonment, etc. Its destructive significations outweigh its constructive ones. The same applies to Mars.

For this reason, two planets—Saturn and Mars—are called *universal malefics*, while all other planets are considered *universal benefics*.

Since the natal chart lacks an ultra-specific context, we cannot predict in advance whether a planet will manifest as an accidental or universal significator in current circumstances. But we know that any planet in the natal chart will manifest its universal qualities sooner or later. It means that, to some extent, any planet contributes its universal qualities to its significance in the natal chart.

Therefore, Saturn and Mars are initially considered more destructive planets than all others. It means that when assessing a planet's celestial state, we also consider whether it is universally malefic or benefic, something we have never done before in horary astrology.

For example, Venus peregrine, without any aspects from other planets, is considered neutral—it neither creates nor destroys matters of the house it occupies or rules. Under the same conditions, Saturn peregrine is already a destructive planet—according to its universal nature, it delays marriage in the 7th house and creates financial constraints in the 2nd.

House Rulership

House Meanings in Natal Astrology

In horary astrology, we search for planets that correspond to pre-known objects. If the question concerns the mother, we examine the ruler of the 10th house (the 7th house from the 4th house of fathers in patriarchal societies). While the 4th house generally denotes all ancestors, we prioritize the more specific 10th house for the mother because we know the person whose significator we seek. Similarly, we would prioritize the 7th house for the grandmother (the mother of one's mother) over the broader 4th house of ancestors.

In natal astrology, it's the opposite. Our task is to understand, looking at a planet, what exactly it will signify in a given period.

For instance, let's consider Venus to be prominent this year. In a natal chart, Venus may rule multiple houses. It could govern the 8th and 10th houses while occupying the 7th house. Each house has specific meanings; for example, the 10th house may represent the mother, boss, or spouse's property, while the 8th house could signify a colleague's lawyer or a spouse's finances, among other things. The more ultra-specific meanings we associate with each house, the more roles Venus can take on, making it more challenging to pinpoint the correct one.

Chapter 3. Natal Astrology

As discussed in the section "Changing Roles Over Time," we consequently filter the planet's roles starting from the most general, then reducing it to a particular one, and then further to an ultra-specific role. We need to begin filtering from the planets' most general roles for that purpose.

Therefore, we adhere to general house meanings in natal astrology when delineating the chart.

- For instance, the 10th house generally represents the native's actions and undertakings (more correctly, it shows the native in their actions and their results). But in particular, it can signify the mother, the spouse's property, or the teacher's finances. However, at least in the initial step of chart delineation, we will ignore these specific meanings.
- The fourth house generally indicates the native's family roots (including mother, father, and grandparents) and lands. We prioritize the fourth house for ancestors over the 10th house of mother or the 7th house of grandmother. The shorter the list of broad significations to examine, the greater the chance of finding the right one.

In the first step, we know the general meaning of the planet, and then we narrow it down to a specific object.

For example, Venus rules the 8th, 4th, and 7th houses. However, two special techniques of natal astrology—*primary directions* and the *lunar return chart*—emphasize the 4th house, rejecting all the rest. So we know Venus indicates one of the parents (without specifying exactly who). Then, we seek a way to identify a relative within a native's family.

For instance, we may observe that Venus is a feminine planet and separates from the native. In the general context of the native's life, we know their mother left them when they were a kid. We also see that in other prognostic charts, like lunar return, Venus conjoins with the Moon—the natural ruler of mothers. And so, with many coinciding testimonies, we pronounce that Venus represents the native's mother in a given period of their life.

Notice that we didn't use the special meaning of the 10th house (as a house of mother) as we usually do in horary astrology. We focused on the 4th house—the house of ancestors—and then narrowed down the meaning of its ruler to a specific person.

Thus, houses are more generalized in natal astrology. Here's a list of house meanings in the most general sense.

1. Life in general, state of health, moral and mental qualities.
2. Wealth, goods of acquired estates.
3. Siblings.
4. Parents, successions.
5. Children, bodily pleasures.
6. Servants, subordinates, domestic animals.
7. Marriage, open enemies, lawsuits.
8. Death.
9. Religion, journeys.
10. Action, profession, dignity, fame.
11. Friends.
12. Sickness, imprisonment, exile, secret enemies, hardships.

Derived Houses

The natal chart typically reflects events involving close relatives only when they significantly impact the native's life.

- It could be a severe illness of a brother, causing the native to leave work and dedicate time to caregiving.
- It could be the father's death, resulting in an inheritance for the native, and so on.

Derived houses usually indicate such joint events. For instance, the death of a brother is the 8th house from the brother, the 10th radical house. Unlike in horary charts, we do not interpret the 8th house as representing "death in general" that the native will encounter in connection with the brother's departure. The 8th house of the chart signifies the death of the native and only his.

Similarly, the 5th house of the natal chart represents the native's children, not children in general, as the natal chart primarily focuses on the native's life events.

Position in the House

You know that any stellar object in the house is conditioned by that house to manifest in a specific area of life. In particular, an astrological house determines the planets and degrees of the zodiac that it contains to influence particular objects.

We have also discussed that the influence of a planet in a house is far stronger on the affairs of that house in general than the influence of the house's ruler, which tends to affect specific objects within a given area of life.

For this reason, when searching for an accidental significator of a house that influences the corresponding area of life, we prefer a planet in the house over its ruler. We phrase it as follows: "A planet in the house is more determined to affect the affairs of the house than its ruler."

Therefore, unlike in a horary chart, whenever possible, we prefer a planet in a house (and its primary "copy" in the degree of opposition) rather than the ruler of the house as a brighter significator of the house's affairs.

The List of Techniques

As you've understood, all natal astrology methods fall under "signification techniques." We're clarifying a planet's role at a specific period in life. I'll list these techniques and explain with appropriate argumentation why they appear the way they do.

Delineating a Natal Chart

In the section "How The Stars Affect Us," I referred to physicists' theories that the current positions of the planets in the sky alter the biologically active composition of the atmosphere, which in turn affects the neuron activity in the brain. I agreed to call this specific atmosphere composition a "chemical pattern."

I also described that, according to modern research, the human brain experiences incredible activity at the moment of birth, during which there is intense formation of neural connections.

I hypothesize that the biologically active composition, formed at the moment of birth, influences the formation of neural connections. Thus, the planetary configuration at birth creates a specific neural imprint, which we can express as the "deep nature of a person." Unconscious motives manifest at different periods, pushing a person to be in the right circumstances at the right time, ultimately leading to life events.

Therefore, the first technique, which everything starts with, is *delineating the natal chart*—it examines the root imprint (the *radix*) for basic destiny patterns embedded there. A natal chart indicates thousands of events, but not all occur, and some will occur only once. We will look for indications of consistently recurring events, which we can call the life scripts. It will help us to understand in what general context or life the events of a particular year will unfold.

Primary Directions

The postnatal spike of neural activity continues for several hours after birth. During this period, the Earth completes a full rotation on its axis, and the celestial sphere completes a rotation relative to its initial position at birth.

As the celestial sphere rotates, the moving planets form new "chemical patterns," which I believe additionally shape the primary imprint at birth. From a celestial geometry perspective, this appears as the rotating celestial sphere overlaying its initial position at birth.

In their daily (or *primary*) motion, the moving planets and their aspects approach the planets and house cusps from the natal chart. This process resembles the formation of exact aspects in horary astrology. The only difference is that in horary charts, we focus on the secondary motion of planets (their slow movement along the zodiac circle), whereas in natal charts, we observe fast aspects associated with the rotation of the celestial sphere.

It is not surprising—the burst of neural activity with intense neural connection formation lasts only a few hours after birth. It is unlikely that an aspect occurring 15 days after birth would significantly contribute to shaping a person's "inner nature."

As you've seen in horary astrology, the aspect's distance measures the time until the appropriate transit occurs, fulfilling the chart's promise. The same rule applies to the natal chart. The distance in fast aspects measures the number of years until an appropriate transit occurs, replicating the same "chemical pattern" as at the time of the fast aspect formation. This transit will trigger the event.

Thus, by examining primary aspects (also called *primary directions*), we can see which specific part of the natal chart becomes active in a particular year of life. Astrologically speaking, through primary directions, we establish what specific roles the planets will take on when it's time for them to manifest.

Primary directions are the royal predictive technique[11]—they order the prospective events seen in the natal chart into a sequence. As I mentioned earlier, not all the promises of the natal chart will come true:

- Some events will occur 150–170 years after birth. But people do not live that long.
- Some events prohibit each other. Suppose that a person's inner nature inclines them toward solitude in 1998. Following this inner call, they isolate themself on Mount Athos for five years. No matter how strongly the birth chart suggests having children in 1999, it simply will not happen—by that time, the person will be leading an ascetic lifestyle.

I do not know a better technique for arranging events into a sequence in time than the primary directions. It is the most precise as far as I have time to observe.

Primary Directions & Spindle of Ananke

Here, I want to refer to Greek mythology. There is a beautiful legend about the goddess of inevitability, Ananke. The goddess constantly spun a spindle while her first daughter wound thread from it, the second measured it, and the third cut it off. I see a direct analogy with primary directions:

- The ball of wool is the variety of events visible in the natal chart.
- The thread is the ordered sequence of events in time.
- The rotation of the celestial sphere by the *Primum Mobile* (the force of inertia) is the spinning of the spindle.
- The length of the thread is the number of degrees in the rotation, indicating the timing of the events.
- Cutting the thread signifies the final event—end of life. It occurs when the significator of life approaches the point of death, called the *abscissor* (from the Latin "abscissio"—"the cutting off," from which the word "scissors" is derived). Another name for that killing point is *anaereta*.

---

[11] M. Gansten. *Primary Directions. Astrology's Old Master Technique.* Wessex Astrologer Ltd, 2009

Revolutions of the Planets

Primary directions indicate that a suitable transit will occur in a specific year of life, triggering the event. Suppose, in the horoscope, Venus signifies

- Conflicts with bosses relative to professional activities
- Conflicts with parents relative to the 4th house, and
- Money acquired through disputes relative to the 2nd house

Now, imagine that this planet, in its primary motion, forms an unfavorable aspect with the rulers of both the 4th and 2nd houses 140 minutes after (which corresponds to 35 degrees of rotation of the celestial sphere).

The aspect points to the transit that will activate the negative role of conflicts with parents regarding money. Thus, we anticipate conflicts with parents over inheritance. It means that approximately 35 years after birth, a suitable transit will occur, triggering a court hearing with the parents.

Shortly before the final transit, Venus returns to its original position. Suppose it enters the house of conflicts and simultaneously rules the 2nd and 4th houses, fully repeating its natal role.

We say that the planet participating in primary directions, shortly before the final transit, *actualizes its natal role*. The native's body will react sensitively to this moment—this establishes in them a tendency toward conflicts and disputes with parents in the near future.

There will be a clash of interests and everyday tensions between the native and their parents. This will gradually escalate until it culminates in a day when both parties find themselves in court on a suitable transit. This initiating constellation is called planetary *return charts* or the *charts of revolutions*.

Thus, the revolution chart sets up and intensifies the conditions necessary for the realization of the final transit. Had there not been a prolonged conflict between the querent and their parents over inheritance, the transit could not have led to any event, as the issue of inheritance and disputes over it would not have even arisen in the context of the current year.

Solar and Lunar Returns

The Sun serves as the center for all planets. Therefore, when the Sun returns to its original position at birth, it refreshes its roles and the roles of each of its satellites. In particular, at the moment of solar return, Venus will also refresh its meanings—it can either confirm or negate its role of "conflict with parents" in the solar return chart.

The Moon, as the traditional companion of the Sun and the second luminary in the sky, possesses the same property. At the moment of its return to the natal position, it refreshes the meanings of all planets in the horoscope, including those of Venus.

Traditionally, astrologers call charts of solar revolutions *solar returns*, while charts of lunar revolutions—*lunar returns*.

Solar returns occur every year, unlike the returns of Saturn or Jupiter. Therefore, astrologers primarily rely on solar returns to confirm or refute the promise of the preceding direction for a specific year of life.

When the solar return confirms the promise of directions, it sets conditions necessary to realize the promise. However, the event may occur in any month of the year. Within a year, the Moon will return to its natal position several times, refreshing the meaning of all planets in the radix. If, in some lunar returns, Venus, promising a court case with parents, repeats its conflicting role, then in the corresponding month, we expect the onset of the final transit and the beginning of a court hearing.

> **N.B.**
>
> We may have several months when the event is possible. In one of the lunar returns, Venus will particularly vividly repeat its role. Most likely, it will be the month of the final transit's occurrence. In any case, there is an additional technique called *primary directions derived from revolution charts*—it allows specifying in which of the possible months the event will occur.

In rare cases, no lunar returns may confirm Venus's conflicting role. At the same time, Venus's return may also deny her conflicting role for that year. It means that although the solar return will trigger activity around inheritance, it will not lead to a court case in any of the months of the year.

So, there is a rule: For the event to occur,

- The solar return must set up the necessary conditions in a particular year
- The lunar return must intensify these conditions in a specific month of the year, and
- The suitable final transit should trigger this potential on a specific day of the month

Astrologically speaking, the solar return must confirm the promises of the preceding direction, and the lunar return must confirm the promises of the preceding solar return. The final transit should repeat these promises in many different ways at a particular moment.

Therefore, planetary revolutions, primarily solar and lunar returns, serve the following functions:

- They prove or deny the promise by the preceding directions.
- They specify in which month of the year the promised event will occur.
- Finally, they contain additional ultra-specific details describing the expected event. In other words, solar and lunar return serve as additional signification techniques.

Final Transit

When the solar and lunar return charts both prove the central event of the year, we can calculate the primary directions from the solar and lunar return charts to find a short interval of a few days when we anticipate the event.

After this begins the most routine part. Within the specified interval of a few days, we manually cast transit charts for every 3–5 minutes, searching for the moment that most vividly reflects the promises of the preceding solar and lunar return charts.

Looking back and comparing known events with the transits during which they occurred, you'll notice that the transits reflect event details quite well. However, this only works retrospectively.

In practice, predicting minute circumstances of an event from a transit chart in advance is nearly impossible, as we don't know the ultra-specific context of the day when the event will occur. We can't synthesize the chart's indications with the current situational context as we would in a horary chart—the context is unknown beforehand.

Therefore, in practice, transits serve a different primary purpose—they indicate the day when the event will occur.

Transits: Cost and Value

As a practicing astrologer, I find the value of transit charts rather questionable. You expend tremendous effort to predict the exact day of an event. Yet ordinary life circumstances might accelerate or delay it by a day or two.

For the overwhelming majority of forecasts, predicting the season—or at most the month—of an event will suffice. Greater precision rarely justifies the effort required.

Nevertheless, I will provide examples in this book demonstrating how to pinpoint exact event dates in natal charts.

Delineation of the Natal Chart

Four Types of Determination

To better understand the role a planet can play in a horoscope, it is important to examine how a planet's action is conditioned or *determined* by various external factors.

1. Determination by kind of things. Each planet possesses specific attributes, such as elemental qualities and the orb of virtue. A planet can be dry or moist, hot or cold. It can be malefic or benefic *per se*. Additionally, a planet has a particular mode of action; for instance, Saturn tends to slow down processes, Mercury binds various elements, and the Sun governs.

However, with regard to different types of objects, planets begin to signify specific things through analogy.

For example, the Sun generally acts as the governor. But in the human world, it signifies kings (presidents for countries, bosses for companies, etc.); in the animal kingdom, lions; among birds, eagles; among metals, gold; and among bodily organs, the heart and cognitive functions of the brain.

As you can see, a planet's general mode of action takes on specific forms due to the objects it influences. This conditioning of planetary action is called *determination by kind of thing*.

2. Celestial determination. When a planet falls into a sign of a similar or adverse nature, receives favorable or unfavorable aspects from other planets, or when its dispositor becomes dignified or debilitated, the planet accidentally gains or loses dignity—that is, it becomes an accidental malefic or benefic.

Exalted Mars will show a noble warrior among people or immunity among bodily functions. While debilitated Mars will indicate a robber in the human world or an autoimmune response among bodily functions.

As you can see, the planet's celestial condition further specifies its action according to its disposition. This conditioning of planetary action is called *celestial determination*.

3. Terrestrial determination. But even in this case, the planet's action is general and the same for everyone. Relative to a particular horizon, planets fall into various houses, which force them to manifest in specific areas of life.

For example, Mars in the second house will manifest in the financial sphere, but still according to its universal nature. Exalted Mars will gift money as an accidental benefic, but with sudden spending, according to its nature. On the other hand, debilitated Mars will result in financial losses due to unforeseen expenses, a trial, or a robbery.

That same Mars in the eighth house will manifest in matters of death. Exalted Mars will pose a threat of violence, but save from it. Detrimental Mars will bring violent death. And if the seventh house also determines Mars to war, it will bring death at the hands of an enemy.

As you can see, considering the current terrestrial horizon, planets begin to signify specific things. This kind of conditioning of planetary action is called *terrestrial determination*.

Chapter 3. Natal Astrology

4. Determination by context. Finally, the same planet in the identical horoscopes of two individuals will signify different things. If two babies were born at the exact same moment—one in the queen's chambers, the other 100 meters away in a peasant's house—then Mars in the seventh house for them would be completely identical from an astronomical perspective.

But for the prince, Mars signifies a victorious war with the conquest of neighboring lands. At the same time, for the peasant, it means a fight with the neighbor over the ownership of the chicken coop.

As you can see, the context gives the planet an ultra-specific meaning. It is the final and most important type of conditioning of planetary action. It is called *determination by context*.

When delineating a chart, we must remember all four determinations to articulate the specific event we anticipate. It's an astrologer's mistake to focus solely on the first type of determination or to overlook the fourth.

In practice, we always assess a planet's meaning at the intersection of all four types of determinations. If we see that a planet is conditioned in multiple ways to signify the same thing, it will almost invariably denote precisely that thing rather than another.

For example, Mars, by analogy, signifies aggression. Relative to interaction with others, it indicates battles and wounds. Its placement in the 7th house of confrontations further emphasizes martial signification. If Mars is additionally debilitated, this further reinforces its role in such matters. And if the native comes from a troubled family background and lives in a crime-ridden neighborhood, Mars will almost certainly manifest as clashes, fights, or assaults—with much less likelihood of showing anything else.

You'll soon see that an astrologer's key skill is logically synthesizing possible meanings to find common patterns, while focusing on the most likely one.

Celestial Determination

Mechanics of Celestial Determination

You already know that to assess a planet's celestial state, we look at its compatibility with the zodiac sign it occupies, close aspects from other planets it receives, and the state of its dispositor.

Morinus described the mechanism of celestial determination in great detail (see Book 21 of *Astrologia Gallica*). He believed that the primary driver of all processes on Earth is the neutral and uniform radiation of the *Primum Caelum* (Primary Heaven).

Initially, the primary radiation contains the nature of all planets and all possible elements. However, sections of the sky filter some of its qualities or *determine* this radiation to manifest specific features.

Thus, as the rays of Primum Caelum pass through the degrees of the planets, they further carry the nature of these planets. We may say that planets *determine* the primary heaven to their nature. This particularly shaped form of the *Primum Caelum* with the specific degrees on the sphere, determined by planets, is imprinted in the human body and perceived by the native throughout life.

The zodiacal circle itself also refracts or *determines* the neutral radiation of the *Primum Caelum*, penetrating that sign. We said earlier that the zodiacal signs "reflect" their rulers—they not only share the planet's nature but are also sensitive to its condition. *Primum Caelum*, passing through Pisces in a favorable house with Jupiter in Sagittarius, will produce good deeds. In contrast, passing through Pisces in the 12th house with Jupiter in exile, *Primum Caelum* will produce evil, such as causing blood or liver diseases (according to the nature of Jupiter).

Since each planet occupies a particular degree of the zodiacal circle, that degree determines the *Primum Caelum* in two ways: through the intrinsic nature of the planet (*determination by planet*) and through the zodiac sign to which that degree belongs (*determination by sign*).

So, if the Sun is at 17° Pisces, which reflects Jupiter's nature, then 17° Pisces resembles a conjunction of the Sun with a small copy of Jupiter. This *per se* is a good combination (not considering Jupiter's actual celestial state), as the Sun and Jupiter are benefics. Thus, the 17th degree of Pisces *per se* determines the *Primum Caelum* towards a Solar-Jovian nature, making this degree favorable (unless Jupiter is heavily debilitated and signifies something bad).

By the same logic, the Sun at 10° Aquarius represents a mixture of the nature of the Sun and the nature of Saturn. These two rays are emitted from 10° Aquarius to the center of the Earth without influencing each other. However, their combined effect will be destructive, since these two planets have diverse natures.

It is like two people in a boat rowing in different directions without interacting with each other. The overall effect will be disastrous—the boat will rock and capsize. Therefore, the Sun in Aquarius becomes an accidental malefic, and 10° Aquarius with the Sun in it determines the *Primum Caelum* to create troubles. In this evil form, this degree is imprinted in the native's body and will be perceived by them throughout their life.

We can extend similar reasoning to the degrees of each planet's aspects and antiscia, since the zodiac circle creates nine copies of each planet in degrees of their aspects and antiscia.

N.B.

Morinus detailed the scheme of the origin of the 12 aspects, which I have included in a separate Appendix (the section "C"). He called it *determination by ecliptic*.

Therefore, each of the 360 degrees of the ecliptic, including the locations of the planets, determines the *Primum Caelum* to produce beneficial or destructive effects.

Reading the Celestial State

Let's focus on the bodily positions of the planets. The celestial condition of each planet determines what precisely it will do relative to a specific astrological house, i.e., a particular sphere of life:

- Will it create good things according to a favorable house or destroy them, and to what extent?

- Will it create evil things according to an unfavorable house or mitigate/protect from them?

Table 3.1 provides a general idea of the planet's action according to its celestial state. We will consider whether the significator is universally malefic (Saturn and Mars) or benefic (all the rest). Remember that the 6th, 8th, and 12th, together with the 7th house (regarding conflicts), are unfavorable.

Notes on the analogy between the beneficence and maleficence of a house and a planet: A malefic planet often has a direct analogy with a detrimental house. For example, Mars—associated with injuries and violent death—has an analogy with the 8th house of death.

Therefore, even in an excellent celestial state, Mars in Aries retains this connection by analogy—it creates threats of violent death instead of preventing it. However, due to its noble celestial state, this same Mars in Aries reduces the effect of violence or saves from death at the last moment. As you see, the analogy with the house prevails over the celestial state.

Sometimes, if the dignified malefic in the unfortunate house has a very strong analogy with it and has no other beneficial support (through favorable aspects or reception), it may signify "pure evil." An example is Mars in Aries in the 7th house: the planet of wars has an apparent analogy with the house of wars. Without a beneficial dispositor or aspect that can soften it, Mars can signify "pure war" in its pure Martian state.

In contrast, benefic planets often have a direct analogy with the favorable houses. For example, the Sun—associated with fame and success—has a connection with the 10th house of fame.

Therefore, even in a debilitated celestial state, the Sun in Aquarius retains this connection. It does not forbid fame but instead creates it.

However, due to its debilitated celestial state, this same Sun brings bad fame or fame through hardships and misfortune.

In contrast, Mercury has no direct analogy with the 5th house of bodily pleasures. Thus, Mercury in Pisces cannot create something that it does not possess by analogy. On the other hand, since it is a natural benefic in a favorable house, Mercury will not forbid pleasures. In sum, it will produce nothing. We will discuss it later in the section "Coincidence of the Planet's and the House's Natures."

Table 3.1: *Celestial States of Planets in Houses*

Planet	State	Favorable House	Unfavorable House
Benefic	Good	Effectively produces the good things of that house.	Effectively mitigates the evil of the house, or cancels it.
Malefic	Good	Produces good things of this house, but through hardships, deprivation, or vicious ways.	Does not cancel the evil of the house. Instead, it creates a malevolent event either in a mild form or with subsequent rescue.[12]
Benefic	Neutral	Produces things of average quality, quantity, or duration.	Does not create nor cancel the evil of the house, only mitigates it.
Malefic	Neutral	Does not produce, nor cancel the affairs of the house. Instead, it hinders their manifestation.	Does not protect but instead creates the evil.
Benefic	Bad	Either gives nothing or gives through hardships, deprivation, or in an unreliable or ineffective way.[13]	It does not protect from evil. On the contrary, it may create one.

Continued on next page

---

[12] This happens because a malefic often has direct analogy with an unfavorable house
[13] This happens because a benefic often has direct analogy with a favorable house

Table 3.1 — Continued from previous page

Planet	State	Favorable House	Unfavorable House
Malefic	Bad	It does not produce the good things but rather cancels them. And if it creates them, it is through misfortune.	Effectively produces evil things, making them even worse.

Example №26: Aspects of the Planet

Let's see how it works. Look at Venus in my natal chart (Fig. 3.1). By its position in the 12th house, it is most strongly determined to manifest itself in the 12th house matters—diseases, secret enemies, imprisonment, or exile.

But how will it operate within the framework of the 12th house? Let's assess Venus' celestial state.

- It's a natural benefic in its triplicity, making it a moderately noble planet.
- Its dispositor, Saturn, is detrimental. It worsens Venus' condition, but not so much as to cancel its moderately noble state.[14]

Now, let's assess how close aspects from other planets alter this picture.

Venus receives a close sextile from the Moon. Although a sextile is a weak aspect, its proximity to Venus and the fact that it is an applying aspect make it the most influential.

- The Moon is a natural benefic and peregrine, making it a favorable planet overall. The Moon has no maleficent qualities except that it rules the unfavorable 6th house. This doesn't cancel its overall noble condition but adds a small portion of badness.
- The aspect from the Moon is favorable, meaning it places all the good things from the Moon and holds back most of her bad qualities in the

---

[14] Strictly speaking, a debilitated Saturn worsens the sign of Capricorn in which it is reflected. Since Venus is at 17° Capricorn, this degree radiates the noble nature of Venus and, to a lesser extent, the nature of debilitated Saturn. These two rays do not affect each other but influence earthly processes. Therefore, "Saturn worsens Venus" means that Venus' effect at 17° Capricorn will somewhat worsen due to Saturn's influence.

Chapter 3. Natal Astrology

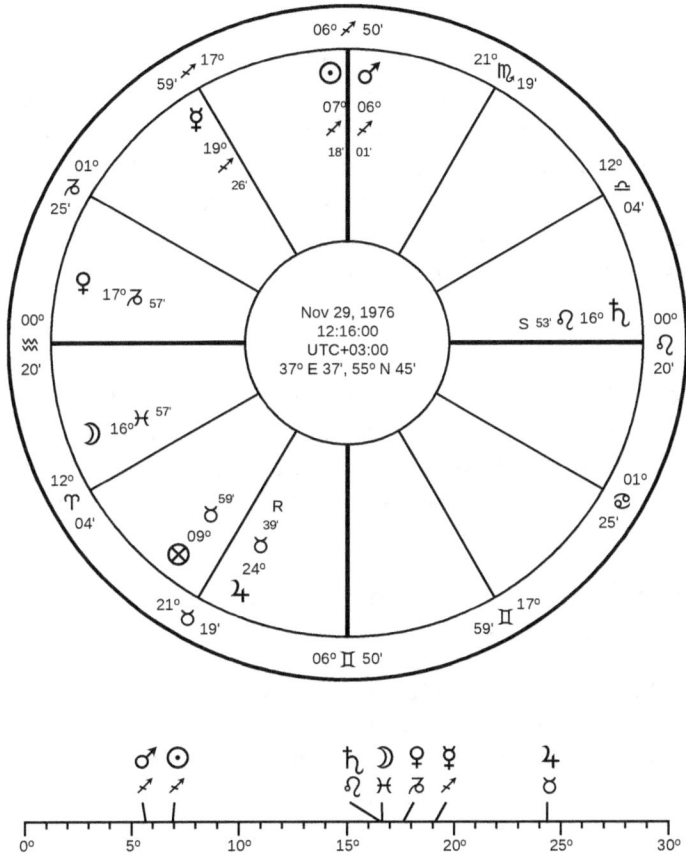

Figure 3.1: *Alexey Borealis. Rectified Figure*

degree of her sextile. Since the Moon has a small portion of badness, sextile aspect brings this badness practically to zero. So, we can say that the "copy" of the Moon in the degree of her sextile is generally favorable. However, note that this "copy" has landed in the sign of the Moon's exile, thereby making the sextile of the Moon moderately destructive.

- Finally, let's consider reception. The Moon exalts Venus. This means the Moon, and therefore its "moderately bad copy," will strive with all means to assist Venus or protect it. It compensates for the adverse effect of the aspect, making the Moon's sextile useless—it doesn't change Venus' celestial condition in any way.

> **N.B.**
>
> An aspect does not modify a planet's universal nature, which can be benefic or malefic. For example, the square of Saturn in Aquarius diminishes all the beneficence Saturn has in its domicile, leaving an almost neutral copy in the place of the aspect. But this nearly neutral copy *still possesses the nature of Saturn*, which we consider naturally malefic. Hence, a Saturnian copy in place of its square is no longer neutral but slightly harmful.

The second close aspect that Venus receives is Jupiter's trine. Although the trigon is a relatively strong aspect, it is separating. In addition, Venus is far from it, almost at the edge of Jupiter's 8-degree orb. Hence, the influence of this aspect on Venus's celestial condition is negligibly small, so we can disregard it.

So, close aspects do not change Venus's celestial state—it remains a moderately noble planet.

Important Note: In addition to considering the effects of close aspects, it is always worth examining their dynamics. If a planet were to cast a close aspect on Venus and this aspect were applying, the negative influence of this aspect would intensify over the years. In contrast, if the aspect were separating, the negative impact would diminish with age. The same reasoning applies to favorable aspects.

If a planet simultaneously receives favorable and unfavorable aspects, we should consider the sequence in which the exact aspects will occur. If this sequence ends with an exact unfavorable aspect, all the good created by the favorable close aspects will be undone by the adverse aspect, the reason for which can be understood from the nature of the aspecting planet.

For example, suppose the significator of money receives a favorable close aspect from Jupiter, and an unfavorable one from Mars. If we move planets forward, then Mars's exact aspect is the final one.

In that case, according to Mars in the 5th house, the native will regularly lose all the financial benefits received from Jupiter through irrational expenses such as bodily pleasures, luxury, or gambling.

Chapter 3. Natal Astrology

In my case, Venus does not receive such a mixed influence, so we do not consider the dynamics in close aspects.

The last thing we need to examine is the dispositor of Venus—Saturn.

Saturn is a malefic planet in a debilitated state. This automatically makes the signs of Capricorn and Aquarius harmful.

However, since Saturn rules the ASC, the most vital favorable house of life, this somewhat mitigates Saturn's negative influence on other areas of life.

Nevertheless, Saturn's stationarity, its intrinsically malefic nature, and its debilitated state harm everything in the signs of Capricorn and Aquarius, including Venus.

Since Venus is not in its fall or detriment and does not receive unfavorable aspects, the debilitation of its dispositor cannot turn Venus into a source of evil but can diminish its beneficence.

Thus, Venus's moderately benefic state is reduced to barely benefic or almost neutral. We say that *intrinsically beneficial* Venus becomes an *accidentally neutral* planet.

Since Venus' neutral celestial state contradicts the evil nature of the 12th house, Venus cannot produce diseases or secret enemies, at least by its bodily position. However, Venus has "copies" in the degrees of its aspects. These copies inherit the meaning of the 12th house, where Venus resides. Unfavorable aspects easily accumulate the evil part of Venus (significance of 12th, enforced by Venus' dispositor, Saturn, that naturally rules diseases and imprisonments and accidentally creates evil), and reject all the favorable essence that Venus possesses. Such aspects can easily produce illnesses and imprisonment as well as secret enemies among young ladies.

Let's consider Venus' aspects. I'll provide a brief comment on each aspect's action in the Table 3.2.

Table 3.2: *Alexey Borealis: Aspects of Venus*

Aspect	Degree	Comment	Effect
Sinister ✶	17° ♓	Accumulates Venus's noble qualities in the place of her exaltation.	Highly favorable
Sinister ☐	17° ♈	Accumulates a slightly unfavorable copy of Venus (due to her connection with the 12th and 8th houses) in the place of her exile.	Notably destructive
Sinister △	17° ♉	Accumulates Venus's noble qualities in the place of her rulership.	Highly favorable
☍	17° ♋	Accumulates a slightly unfavorable copy of Venus without any changes.	Slightly harmful
Dexter △	17° ♍	Accumulates a favorable copy of Venus in the place of her fall.	Moderately harmful
Dexter ☐	17° ♎	Accumulates a slightly unfavorable copy of Venus in her domicile, though Venus's position in an unfavorable house moderates the effect.	Moderately favorable
Dexter ✶	17° ♏	Accumulates Venus's moderately noble qualities in the place of her exile.	Slightly harmful

As you can see in my horoscope, only one point associated with Venus in the 12th house is most capable of actualizing that house's evil. It is 17° Aries. This point is called the *promissor* of disease, exile, and secret enemies.

Chapter 3. Natal Astrology

The rest of the aspects, including Venus's bodily position, are either little capable or not capable at all of actualizing the evils of the 12th house. It is elementary to verify in practice.

Although we will discuss primary directions in detail further, I want to demonstrate how they work right now. Think of primary directions as applying aspects in horary astrology: We have two significators, ASC (the body in natal astrology in health-related questions) and Venus (illness). Venus may apply to ASC in different ways, such as conjunction, trine, etc. But one of them—we expect it to be sinister square—should produce illness, while others do not.

Let's list the primary directions of all Venus's aspects to the ASC that were performed before 2024 (Table 3.3).

Table 3.3: *Alexey Borealis: Direction of Venus' Aspects*

Primary Aspect	Age	Time	Event
ASC ☌ ♀ (Sinister)	3.8	March 1980	Nothing
ASC ✶ ♀ (Sinister)	23.3	October 2000	Nothing
ASC ☐ ♀ (Sinister)	31.7	February 2009	Acute kidney disease occurred during the winter between 2008 and 2009
ASC △ ♀ (Sinister)	41.9	April 2018	Nothing

We have seen confirmation of Venus's action with an accuracy of a few months. Remarkably, according to its second determination, Venus among the diseases indicates kidney disorders.

The Position of the Aspect and Its Dispositor in the Houses

When considering planetary aspects, especially in revolution charts—which reveal specific details of upcoming events—it is important to assess not only the celestial state of the planetary aspect but also its terrestrial determination. Let us consider this through an example.

Example №27: Terrestrial Determination of Venus's Aspect

In my horoscope △♀ at 17° Virgo is a moderately harmful aspect (see Table 3.2). But which area of life does it affect? It influences 7th-house matters, as it is located there.

Is there a connection between Venus and the 7th house? Yes, there is.

On one hand, Venus is the natural ruler of love, and its specific aspect manifests in matters of love and marriage. Therefore, this aspect could bring a romance (according to Venus's nature and the 7th house), but with a subsequent breakup (due to a particular unfortunate aspect affecting my love affairs).

On the other hand, Venus accidentally rules the 8th and 12th houses. Is there a connection between them and 7th house? Yes, the 7th house of battles can logically be linked to death (8th house). In that case, we might expect death at the hands of an enemy, most likely a woman (given Venus's nature).

Alternatively, the 7th house of conflicts could be logically tied to other people's money (the 8th house represents money in transactions). Thus, the same aspect might bring financial disputes.

Which of these two accidental roles is more likely?

Consider the dispositor of 17° Virgo—Mercury. It is in the 11th house. This means △♀ will express itself either through friends or through professional income of a Mercurian nature. Friends do not fit well within a narrative about death in battle or financial conflicts. However, professional earnings align well with a possible monetary dispute.

Thus, this aspect may bring:

- An unhappy romance (the most likely meaning)
- A conflict over money and earnings (a less probable scenario)
- Death by an enemy's hand (a highly unlikely scenario)

Note that I am not just analyzing the terrestrial determination of the aspect and its dispositor, but also:

- Logically combining multiple indicators (celestial and terrestrial states of the aspect and its dispositor), seeking common themes
- Prioritizing possible interpretations based on their likelihood

Let us test the validity of these conclusions.

If I direct this Venus aspect, as a *promissor of conflict*, toward Mars—the natural significator of conflicts and a planet tightly conjunct the ruler of the 7th house of conflicts—I should more likely encounter a financial dispute rather than a mortal threat or new heartbreaking romance.

Such a direction exists and will manifest in my life: the conflicting Venus aspect reaches Mars, pointing to April 2011. Indeed, that year, I completed a significant freelance project and received substantial money from the client. However, in the same summer, a group of criminals threatened me. They took away this money, and the police could not do anything about it.

As you can see, a major confrontation over other people's money with the loss of my income occurred as expected—the terrestrial position of the aspect and its ruler played a decisive role in the event.

Example №28: Planet-Trendsetter

Let's look at another planet as an example—Saturn in the 7th house (Fig. 3.1 on page 317). It is a natural malefic in a poor celestial condition. Not only does its celestial state contradict the favorable 7th house, but also its nature—Saturn, according to the *first determination by kind of things*, is responsible for loneliness among possible human relationships.

Such a Saturn will not produce either partnership or romantic relationships. On the contrary, it will actively hinder them. I do not expect specific events from Saturn, such as "loneliness," as loneliness is not an event. Saturn lacks the speed to create fast-happening divorces and conflicts—it is stationary. Instead, I expect such a Saturn to create a consistent isolation background due to the native's behavior (note that Saturn rules the 1st house).

And that's precisely how it was—for most of my life, I lacked stable, long-lasting relationships due to my character. My further efforts and psychotherapy improved the situation over the years. However, I've had three official marriages, all of them late.

I want to clarify that I don't have a total "ban" on happy family life, even with such an unfavorable Saturn. The same signification of love affairs is "distributed" among different planets. Besides Saturn manifesting in the 7th house, the Sun rules it with two co-rulers, Mercury and Venus. They or their favorable aspects are capable of creating marriages.

It is especially true for Venus, as apart from its accidental rulership of the 7th house, it also governs romantic relationships according to the *first determination* (see the section "Four Types of Determination").

Allow me to demonstrate this to you. The most favorable aspect of Venus, capable of producing the happiest marriage in my life, is a sinister trigon of Venus in its domicile at 17° Taurus as you know from the Table 3.2 on page 320. All other aspects, including the bodily position, are less beneficial.

Hence, we may expect a marriage with a most stable and long-lasting relationship to happen when this trine comes to the native in primary motion.

We can easily verify that hypothesis. The sinister trigon of Venus approached the ASC in April 2019. I filed for marriage registration in April 2019, and my third and final marriage happened in May 2019, just in time, which proves the correctness of our delineation.

This example demonstrates what I wrote earlier. The same planet (in my case, Venus) can signify different things in the horoscope. On the other hand, the exact significance (love & marriage) is "distributed" among several planets.

Summary

From this section, it is essential to note the following:

- A planet in a house manifests itself more brightly in the matters of that house than its ruler. Examples: Although I have had disease incidents, my life is generally healthy because of the moderately dignified Venus in the 12th house. Although I'm happily married now, for the first part of my life, I haven't been able to manage healthy relationships because of debilitated Saturn in the 7th house.
- The planet's celestial state determines its actions regarding that house—whether it produces things, hinders them, or cancels them. Examples: In my natal figure, Venus generally acts against diseases (although it can episodically bring them by its negative aspect), and Saturn acts against 7th-house matters.

If the planet in the house operates against that house (denies the good things or mitigates the bad ones), the aspect of that planet or other house rulers still may produce corresponding events.

A scarce situation is needed for a person to have a "ban" on events in a particular area of life. All planets related to the house and all their aspects must prohibit the matters of that house. Simultaneously, the context must not provide the default option for the event's realization (see the "The default option" section on page 179). The chance of having such an unfavorable combination is nearly zero. Usually, we observe that things either come together with difficulty or smoothly in one sphere or another. Still, we rarely see a complete prohibition on manifestations of events related to the house, such as a ban on marriage or children, or, on the contrary, a life of constant illness.

Terrestrial Determination

You already know that the house does not change the celestial state of the planets & signs it includes, but it merely conditions (or *determines*) them to manifest in specific areas of life. It forces planets, their copies in places of aspects, signs (i.e., their rulers which are "reflected" in them), and even fixed stars to manifest in particular subjects. We call it *"the house determines the planet/the sign/the fixed star."*

You have already observed that a house determines a planet more effectively than the ruler of an empty sign. Moreover, a house determines a planet or a sign on the cusp much more strongly than when they are at the end of that house.

Therefore, we speak of the *strength of house determination*. Astrological houses condition planets to manifest in a specified area of life with varying degrees of strength—some planets are strongly inclined to play their accidental role, while others are only slightly so. A planet in the horoscope, taking its roles from different houses, may play a central role as a wife, a secondary role in finance, and a very rare role in travel.

You have already seen this in the example of Venus in my horoscope—it plays a central role in overall health protection relative to the 12th house of diseases. Its secondary role is love and marriage. It can only episodically create diseases or conflicts over money or unhappy romances by its unfavorable aspects in corresponding house.

It means, for example, that when the favorable or unfavorable aspect of the 1st house ruler (the current favorable or unfavorable period of life) approaches such a Venus as the significator of the 3rd, 8th, or 12th house, I will first consider the sphere of the 12th house, and only then of the 3rd or the 8th.

Types of the House Rulership

Rulership by position: The position of a planet in a house determines its central role. We'll refer to this as *house rulership by position*. It is the most powerful type of terrestrial determination of the planet. It means that if I consider the planet (or its aspect), I will primarily examine its meaning based on the planetary position in the house. For example, if the ruler of the 5th house—Mars—is in the 4th house and casts a favorable aspect to the cusp of the 2nd house, I will interpret this aspect as originating primarily from the 4th house, not the 5th.

I would say that the native will benefit from the parents (4th house) rather than the children or sex (5th house)—for instance, by receiving an inheritance. As for the 5th house, the influence of that area of life on the native's finances is much less noticeable. First, because Mars is less determined to manifest in 5th-house affairs; second, because logically, inheritance from parents is more likely than from children & sex.

The same logic applies to the dispositor of the planet. Suppose the native's siblings are deposited by Mars, and Mars rules the 9th house and is located in the 10th house. I will say that the accidental signification of Mars relative to the siblings comes primarily from the 10th house.

The 10th house for the siblings is their 8th house, which means a mortal threat, aligning with Mars' universal meaning. Therefore, I will say that the siblings are more likely to be involved in extreme sports or otherwise expose themselves to the threat of mortal injury rather than being related to the native's long journeys.

Accidental rulership: Remember that the opposition is the strongest aspect that creates a significant "copy" of the planet in the opposite house. Hence, through the opposition, a planet also assumes the role of the opposite house. Thus, a planet in the second house will primarily represent finances and, secondarily, the death of the native. We will call this *accidental house rulership*.

Rulership by sign on a cusp: The house determines the empty sign on the cusp to influence specific objects. The sign is an active part of the horoscope, which "emanates" the rays of its ruler toward the Earth. So, by conditioning these rays, the house, in fact, determines the sign's ruler to manifest in a specific area of life, although less effectively than if that ruler were within a house. We will denote this with the familiar term—*house rulership*—and call such a ruler *the ruler of the cusp*.

N.B.

Terrestrial determination *by position* and *by rulership* are the strongest of all. This is why we consider the planet in the house, the ruler of the house, and the zodiac degree of the cusp the most apparent significators of the house's affairs in primary directions—giving priority to the planet in the house.

Rulership by aspect: The planet's close aspect to the house cusp creates the "planetary copy" on that cusp. Thus, the house determines that "copy" to specific affairs, and the aspecting planet becomes connected to that house through its aspect to the cusp.

For instance, if Mars (the ruler of the 10th in the 11th) closely aspects the cusp of the 8th house, it is conditioned by the 8th house, but not as strongly as by the 10th house, which it rules, and not as strongly as by the 11th house, which it occupies.

So, relative to the native, such a Mars will primarily signify friends and activities, and to a much lesser extent, death. Since this Mars combines the significations of both the 10th and 11th houses, these two roles may occasionally manifest simultaneously—for instance, when friends originate from the native's profession or when business is primarily influenced by friends.

However, since Mars is connected to the 8th house, we can interpret it relative to the native's death. Given that an aspecting planet primarily derives its meaning from the house it occupies, such a Mars will signify the 11th house relative to the 8th. Therefore, friends or income from business can be one of the causes of the native's death.

We cannot interpret this the other way round. The native's death cannot cause the appearance of friends or influence them in any way. This would defy logical reasoning. We always seek intersections of meanings that both make sense and provide the simplest possible explanation within the given life context.

Wrapping it up, Mars has the most apparent roles: first, friends; second, the native's actions and activities; and lastly, the native's death. When such a Mars comes to the ASC, it may create (in descending order of probability):

1. New friends or friends originating from the profession.
2. New social activities or starting a new project influenced by or together with friends.
3. A violent death, a deadly wound, or accidental death at the hands of a friend (which undoubtedly needs to be understood in context).

As you can see, relative to ASC (the native's life), Mars promises different events with different likelihoods.

However, as a promissor of friends, when it comes to the cusp of the 11th house, it may only confer new friends (who may have connections with the native's profession), but nothing else.

As a promissor of death, when it comes to the ruler of the 8th, it may only confer death (which may occasionally have a connection with the 11th house), but nothing else.

Remember that aspects have varying degrees of strength—they act like the planet's "copies" of different sizes on the zodiacal circle. For instance, for a planet with a small orb (like Mars) to take on significant rulership of the 8th house through a weak sextile, it must cast an extremely close aspect (within a few degrees) to the cusp. When a planet casts an almost exact aspect to the house cusp, its rulership of that house becomes no less effective than rulership by sign. We call this type of rulership *rulership by aspect*.

Rulership by exaltation: If a planet rules the sign of the cusp by exaltation, its best qualities are reflected by that sign. Since the house cusp strongly focuses these rays on a specific subject, the planet influences that subject—that is, it takes on the role of the house. We call this *rulership by exaltation*. However, this is less effective than regular rulership by cusp. For instance, if the 9th-house cusp is in Aries, the Sun will be the ruler of the house by exaltation. While the Sun will signify long journeys, it will do so less effectively than Mars—the regular ruler of that house.

Co-rulership of the house: The rulers of the signs following the one on the cusp are less conditioned to manifest in house affairs than the ruler of the house. However, remember that if the house cusp is at 29° Leo, and Virgo occupies the remaining part of the house, then Mercury becomes as effective a ruler of the house as the Sun. We will call the rulers of the following signs *co-rulers* of the house.

Secondary rulership: We know that each planet manifests itself through its dispositor. It applies to the ruler of the cusp. If the house cusp is in Leo, then the Sun is the ruler of the house. But if the Sun is in Taurus, it primarily manifests through Venus and operates in the environment signified by Venus. Thus, Venus becomes the *secondary ruler* of the house. However, Venus will govern the house much less than the Sun.

However, if the Sun is the ruler of the 7th house of love, and is disposited by Venus, then this connection to Venusian nature, which has common meaning with the 7th house, enforces Venus's determination towards love and relations.

We cannot apply this logic further down the chain of dispositors. We cannot say that Mars becomes the tertiary ruler of the house if the secondary ruler is in Aries. The influence of planets in this chain diminishes exponentially. The influence of the secondary ruler is significantly weaker than that of the primary ruler. And the impact of the tertiary ruler is negligible, and we never consider it.

Rulership by disposition: A planet may take the accidental role of the house not only through its cusp (via close aspect or rulership of that cusp) but also through a planet in that house.

The dispositor of a planet in a house will have a relationship with the house through that planet. For example, if Mercury is in the third house, it signifies the native's siblings. Its dispositor, Saturn, is in the tenth house.[15] Since siblings manifest themselves through Saturn, Saturn also relates to the 3rd house matters. The tenth house relative to siblings is their 8th, indicating life-threatening situations. It is the environment in which the sibling regularly manifests in the native's life. In other words, in the primary direction, Saturn will have several roles:

- It will show the native's work relative to the 10th house (it may occasionally be connected with siblings, but not necessarily).
- It will also show a life-threatening situation for the sibling relative to the 3rd house.

So, when it is directed to the ASC, we first consider its primary role and verify whether the solar return chart confirms it. If not, we then examine the secondary role (life-threatening situations for siblings). It might occur that neither of these roles is confirmed by the solar return. In that case, no significant event will manifest.

But if we direct Saturn to the significator of the 3rd house, it will only manifest its particular role relative to siblings.

We'll call this type of connection *a rulership by disposition*. Similarly, Saturn may cast a close aspect to the planet in the third house and link itself to that house through that aspect.

N.B.

Please note that sometimes, a house simultaneously determines a planet in several ways, making the planets more conditioned by this house. For example, if the ruler of the house occupies that house, it will manifest itself more prominently in the house's affairs than other planets in the same house. Or the house may have a whole stellium of planets—the further the planet is from the cusp, the less it is associated with it. But it may turn out that the farthest planet in the stellium is the ruler of the stellium itself or has a direct analogy with the house. In that case, it will be the leading planet, the primary significator of that house's affairs.

---

[15] Please note, when assessing the terrestrial state of the dispositor, we only take into account the most powerful determination *by position*, ignoring all the other types of connection of the planet's dispositor with other houses.

Coincidence of the Planet's and the House's Natures

When assessing the strength of a house's determination, it is essential to remember that a planet may have a common nature with the house. For example, the Sun, the universal significator of fame and recognition, has much in common with the 10th house of fame and recognition. Mars, the ruler of wars and conflicts, has much in common with the 7th house of war and conflicts, and so on.

A planet determined by the house and sharing a common nature gains an additional connection to that house.

Morinus explained it this way: "An astrological house does not modify a planet's rays; it merely redistributes their effect among different subjects."

Naturally, the Sun influences various subjects such as the native's fame, father, and vitality. However, the Sun in the 4th house will primarily affect the father, since the 4th house determines the Sun to concentrate its influence on a particular subject. The celestial state of the Sun, which the house does not modify, will determine the final effect of the Sun on the father's state.

However, the Sun's primary signification relates to fame and success due to its central role among planets. So, the Sun acts more effectively in the 10th house than in the 12th, showing hidden enemies of Solar nature. This is precisely why the analogy between a planet and a house prevails over the celestial state of a planet.

For instance, the 7th house directs the action of any planet towards conflicts, wars, and lawsuits. If Mars, whose nature is conflict, is placed in the 7th house, it will always manifest its nature and create conflicts. When in Libra, Mars causes severe conflicts associated with physical violence. When in Aries, Mars still causes conflicts, although they will be milder, shorter, or end in a quick victory. In any case, it cannot avoid conflicts due to its direct analogy with the 7th house.

Apart from direct analogy, a planet may be consonant with the favorable or unfavorable determination of the house by being a malefic or benefic planet *per se*. For example, Mars does not have a direct analogy with death, but Mars will manifest itself more naturally in the unfavorable 8th and 12th houses than in any other favorable ones.

Consider Mars in Aries in the 8th house: Mars is malefic and in an unfavorable house, so it creates threats of violent death and does not protect against them. Even in an excellent celestial state (in Aries), it will create deadly threats, though it will protect against death due to its state. Such a Mars can create a severe car accident with survival.

The same Mars in Aries in the 2nd house acts differently. It does not cause the same harm as in the 8th or 12th house (since these are favorable houses, which dissonates with the malefic nature of Mars). Mars in Aries in the 2nd can bring money, but still according to the Martian nature. Since Mars naturally denotes conflicts or abrupt separations, applied to money, this can mean money obtained through violent means or sudden expenditures, such as extravagance. However, in any case, Mars in Aries will ultimately grant money, not prevent it.

Thus, Jupiter, the natural ruler of riches, in the second house, denotes money more effectively than Venus in the second. Since both planets are beneficial, they will not deny money even in a bad celestial state. But Jupiter in Gemini still grants money due to its direct analogy with the second house, although quite modestly because of its celestial state, whereas Venus in Scorpio does not. Venus lacks a sufficient analogy with the second house to produce money when debilitated. However, Venus is not a natural malefic, so it does not create serious financial issues even when in detriment. Such a Venus will only mildly harm the financial state or bring nothing.

A similar situation occurs when a planet, acting against the house (according to its celestial state), also happens to have a nature opposite to it. For example, a debilitated Mercury in the 7th house creates relationship obstacles. But a debilitated Saturn, the natural ruler of loneliness, will do so much more effectively.

Example №29: Strength of Terrestrial Determination

Take a look at my horoscope (Fig. 3.1 on page 317). Saturn creates problems relative to the 7th house, especially since its intrinsic nature (solitude) is opposite to the nature of the 7th house (union). The harm would be less if a debilitated Jupiter or Mercury were in the 7th house. Mercury is less determined towards matters of love than Saturn in its directly opposite action (solitude).

Chapter 3. Natal Astrology

On the other hand, if Saturn were more strongly determined by the 7th house (by a close aspect to the Sun or the cusp of the 7th house), this would enhance Saturn's significance (solitude). But this is not the case, so the situation is not as dramatic as it might seem.

Now, let's consider this same Saturn relative to the 1st house. It indicates an unhappy life to a much lesser extent than the Moon—a planet in the 1st house—indicates a happy one with a good outcome, as it ultimately applies to Jupiter with mutual reception.

On the other hand, this same Saturn inclines me toward seeking publicity (as it manifests against the background of the Sun and simultaneously resides in the 7th house, which, in terms of publicity, indicates a broad audience rather than lovers).

Saturn, on the one hand, inclines me to public performance, while on the other hand, it creates problems by bringing hidden enemies as the accidental ruler of the 12th or the natural ruler of isolation.

Indeed, publicity has a downside for me—I quickly grow tired of attention or become weary of the persistent attacks from envious people (according to Saturn as the ruler of the 12th), which makes me seek solitude away from the public (according to Saturn's nature in the 7th house), without diminishing my desire to be in the spotlight (according to the ruler of the 1st in Leo in the 7th).

However, this conflicting action of Saturn is not as terrifying as it might seem at first glance:

- Besides being the ruler of the 1st, Saturn is connected with the 1st accidentally by being in the 7th. It means it casts an opposition in the 1st house that falls into Aquarius (Saturn's domicile), which somewhat mitigates its malefic influence on my life.
- Saturn serves more as a background, while the leitmotif of life is given to the Moon, which is in the 1st house. It has a mutual reception with Jupiter (co-ruler of life) and an applying aspect with it.

At first glance, it may seem that the ruler of the 1st house—a malefic planet in exile in the 7th house—foretells a life full of unhappiness and isolation. However, if you prioritize and focus on what is essential relative to the 1st, the Moon stands out as the primary ruler of life. At the same time, Saturn's negative influence is not as severe as it initially appears.

As Morinus wrote, if you concentrate only on the main significators of the 1st and 10th houses, you can immediately see life's overall happiness or unhappiness.

Multiple Aspects of Planets

Now that you are familiar with celestial and terrestrial states, we can delve deeper into the topic of multiple aspects received by the same significator, which we briefly discussed in the section "Multiple Aspects Received by the Same Significator" on page 15.

Consider the ASC, the significator of life, receiving both a favorable aspect from Jupiter and a harmful aspect from Saturn simultaneously. In this case, the ASC is subject to opposing influences: a beneficial effect from Jupiter and a destructive one from Saturn.

In this case, the question arises: Will the overall impact on the ASC be more destructive or constructive?

To answer this question, we need to consider several factors:

- **The form of the aspect:** You already know that the closer the aspect is to 180 degrees, the more effective it is. For this reason, a favorable sextile from Jupiter will be weaker for ASC than a harmful square from Saturn. And a trine from Jupiter will be more powerful *per se* than a square from Saturn.
- **The celestial condition of the planets:** It is clear that if Jupiter is debilitated, then even its favorable aspect is unlikely to protect against the evil influence of Saturn. This is especially true if Jupiter is under the dominion of Saturn, say, in Capricorn. On the contrary, if Jupiter and Saturn are in an excellent celestial state, their mixed effect will not harm the ASC but benefit, though with some difficulties of Saturn's nature.
- **The terrestrial condition of the planets:** Suppose Saturn harms life by co-ruling the 8th house, e.g., ruling the sign in the latter part of the house. Conversely, Jupiter confers benefits by ruling the 2nd house, residing in the 2nd house, and having a direct analogy with it. In this case, Jupiter's favorable financial influence on the ASC outweighs the mortal threat posed by Saturn, since Saturn's connection to the 8th house is weaker than Jupiter's ties to the 2nd.

- **The signs where the aspects fall:** If Saturn's aspect to the ASC falls in a sign of its detriment (such as Leo), it will cause significantly greater destruction. At the same time, Leo neither amplifies nor diminishes the beneficence of Jupiter's aspect. Consequently, the cumulative destructive effect will increase.
- **Distance in the aspect:** Suppose Jupiter casts an aspect to the ASC with a distance of 1 degree, and Saturn casts an aspect to ASC within 5 degrees distance. In that case, Jupiter's influence on the ASC will be greater than Saturn's, as the closer the aspect to exact, the stronger its impact.
- **The dynamics of the aspects:** If Saturn's aspect separates from the ASC, a harmful influence on life decreases over time. This effect is particularly pronounced when Jupiter forms an applying aspect with the ASC, as Jupiter's influence strengthens progressively. Conversely, if Saturn (as ruler of the 8th house) approaches the ASC while Jupiter's aspect separates from it, the risk of mortal threats escalates over time, while Jupiter's protective function against mortal threats weakens, indicating a higher probability of early death.

Examples of Delineation

Example №30: Delineating the 10th House

Let's see how all these techniques, including aspects, work in practice. Let's return to my horoscope (Fig. 3.1 on page 317) and examine the 10th house.

We first start with identifying the planets, determined by the 10th house:

- Two planets—the Sun and Mars—are right on the cusp, and Jupiter rules the 10th house.
- Venus, the *secondary ruler*, is associated with the 10th house to a lesser extent. No planet casts a significantly close aspect to the 10th cusp.
- Saturn expresses itself through the Sun, the planet in the 10th, so Saturn is also determined by the 10th house. We can call this *a rulership by disposition*. However, its influence is negligibly small in comparison with Mars and the Sun since determination by position is much stronger than by disposition, so we can safely ignore its influence.

The 10th house determines the three main planets: the Sun, Mars, and Jupiter. Each of the three planets brings a particular shape to the native's social activity. Let's examine those shapes, assessing each planet's celestial state.

The Sun

The Sun is a natural benefic in its triplicity. Its dispositor, Jupiter, is also a natural benefic without any debilitation, making the Sun even more dignified. The Sun receives an aspect from the Moon, but this aspect is neutral and weak due to the considerable distance. It does not affect the Sun's state. We can say that the Sun is a moderate benefic, creating good things of the 10th house.

According to the first determination, the Sun signifies fame and publicity, which correlates well with the nature of the 10th house. Additionally, the Sun rules the 7th house, which means the audience, partners, spouses, or enemies.

Which of the 7th house's meanings is more suitable for the native's public activities? We follow Occam's razor principle to choose the most relevant and straightforward option for realization.

Every public activity necessarily includes the audience. In contrast, partners, enemies, or spouses are not always involved in the native's publicity. We prefer the most straightforward role of the 7th house ruler relative to public activity—the audience. It perfectly correlates with the Sun's signification.

So, the Sun promises publicity.

Mars

Now, let's move on to Mars. It's a natural malefic in a peregrine state. According to its nature, Mars hinders the good things of the 10th house by bringing conflicts. According to its terrestrial state, it connects the native's activities with the 9th house. Various interpretations are possible here.

– It could involve working abroad or frequent relocations associated with conflicts.

– It could entail scientific/religious activities involving ideological disputes.

Both options are equally plausible. We lack evidence suggesting one option over the other. Here, the dispositor comes to our aid.

As mentioned earlier, planets manifest themselves through their dispositor. Jupiter is the dispositor of Mars. Naturally, it shows higher knowledge (including science), jurisprudence, religion, riches, and nobility.

At the intersection of Jupiter's and Mars' significations, we see common meanings—scientific/religious disputes or legal activities. If the planets have something in common, we always prefer the significance from the area of overlapping meanings.

Thus, we expect judicial or scientific/religious activities with ideological disputes from Mars.

Dynamics of aspects: Please note that Mars and the Sun form a separating conjunction, meaning that Mars's conflicting influence on public activities will diminish over the years, or my public reputation will not suffer from ideological disputes.

In addition, the Sun prevails over Mars relative to the 10th house since the Sun has a much stronger connection to actions by analogy than Mars, even though the Sun is separating from MC, while Mars applies to it. It means the Sun will benefit my activity and its results more than Mars will harm them.

Jupiter

Finally, the third planet, Jupiter, is a natural benefic without debilitations. Although its dispositor, Venus, is a benefic, she has no particular dignity and occupies an unfavorable house. Summary, such a dispositor does not change Jupiter's celestial state.

Although Jupiter receives a favorable aspect from Venus (a trine which falls in place of Venus's rulership), Venus's hostile reception nullifies the aspect's effect. However, the favorable aspect of the Moon (sextile in place of her exaltation) and the Moon's positive attitude toward Jupiter significantly improve Jupiter's celestial state—it will effectively produce the good things of the 10th house according to its nature, despite its retrograde motion. It will grant noble positions or connect the native's activities with science, religion, jurisprudence, or a combination thereof.

It *accidentally rules* the opposite 9th house, responsible for science and religion. Since accidental rulership is stronger than rulership of the cusp, science and religion are much more probable than noble positions or jurisprudence.

Most importantly, Jupiter rules the third house by position. The third house could signify the native's siblings or pupils. We need to combine these meanings with what we said earlier about Jupiter.

We follow simple logic and ask ourselves, what is more likely to manifest—scientific/religious activity associated with siblings or that with students? The obvious answer is that the intersection of science and students is a more likely option, since scientific activity almost always involves teaching.

So, Jupiter promises educational activities.

Main Significators of the 10th House

Let's summarize what we have found:

- The Sun promises publicity or recognition.
- Mars promises legal practice or scientific/religious disputes.
- Jupiter promises educational activities.

The Strength of Determination

If we consider the Sun, Mars, and Jupiter individually, we would say the following about the native:

- It's a well-known figure in the realm of religion or science.
- It's a lawyer or an ideological fighter.
- It's an educator.

All of this should manifest, but what prevails? The Sun and Mars prevail over Jupiter because they both are in the 10th house and are more determined by this house by position than Jupiter by rulership.

The Sun has a much stronger connection with the 10th house than Mars since its nature coincides with that of the house. So, the Sun prevails over Mars.

Thus, we see a clear social activity pattern—the native is well-known in science or religion. To a lesser degree, his activities are associated with ideological disputes that bring moderate misfortune (shown by Mars) and include constant educational work (shown by Jupiter). I use the term "constant" because Jupiter is stationary in my chart. Stationary planets indicate prolonged processes that unfold in the background.

Note that at each step, I took the logical intersections of planetary significations and followed the principle of Occam's razor.

Contextual Confirmation

Reality proves the promises of the planets. Indeed, from an early age, I was captivated by science, and I dedicated the first half of my life to it. Already in my youth, I felt a pull toward teaching—at 23, I received permission to lecture on Riemannian geometry at Moscow State University.

There was a brief period in my life when I dedicated myself to career advancement and quickly rose through the managerial ranks. However, I continued teaching. Nevertheless, the office period ended quickly. I found myself back in science, this time in astrology, which I have been practicing and teaching for the last 15 years.

From time to time, I entered ideological conflicts with my opponents. My first battle began in elementary school when I tried to refute some of Newton's laws of mechanics publicly. In my postgraduate studies, I had significant confrontations regarding the postulates of Einstein's theory. Even now, in astrology, I stand in opposition to the existing mainstream at the peak of its flourishing, according to which there are no exact forecasts, and astrology is either divination or a tool for spiritual growth.

The fixed star Antares, of Martian nature and conjoined with Mars, greatly supports this. Much like a scorpion fighting a hero at the peak of glory, I engage in ideological battles with systems of belief at the height of their flourishing.

However, the tension and number of conflicts in my professional activities have decreased over the years, thanks to the separation between Mars and the Sun.

My PhD dissertation and later my scientific career were interrupted by a period of office work, but they were resumed in the field of astrology.

This occurred due to Jupiter's retrograde motion, as retrogradation often signifies unfinished processes.

Thanks to the Sun, I have always tended towards publicity and recognition. As a scientist, I received prestigious scholarships. While working in office environments, I served as the spokesperson for large companies. As an astrologer, I appeared on television, founded a school, and gained recognition in Russia.

You can see that the Moon supports Jupiter—my scientific or astrological activities—through mutual reception and an applying aspect. This support is strengthening over the years.

The Moon, in a close aspect to the ruler of the 4th house, represents my mother among my parents. And being in the 1st house, the same Moon signifies my wife by *accidental rulership* of the opposite house.

Indeed, in the earlier part of my life, my mother helped me get an education—she assisted in finding tutors and provided financial support. My father (indicated by Saturn in this chart, closely aspecting the ruler of the 4th house) could not provide adequate help due to his stationary and debilitated state. In fact, my father did not participate in my upbringing at all.

Currently, my most faithful helper and support in my research is my wife—and this support has only grown over the years, in accordance with the applying aspect between the Moon and Jupiter.

As you can see, the overall pattern of my activity fully confirmed the promises of the 10th house rulers, which created an incredible passion for science, teaching, ideological disputes, and public engagement.

Verification Through Events

We can verify whether we were correct in understanding the meaning of these planets by observing the specific events they produce. For example, the Sun is the most favorable and prominently manifesting planet in relation to the 10th house. It creates success and recognition. Therefore, when a favorable aspect of the Sun approaches the significators of work or the native, I expect success in my activities.

Chapter 3. Natal Astrology

When a destructive aspect of the Sun approaches the significators of work or the native, I expect destructive events in my activities, often associated with conflicts. Why conflicts?

- The Sun rules the 7th house, so its secondary role is conflicts.
- The Sun closely conjuncts Mars—a natural ruler of conflicts.

The Sun itself cannot take on that destructive role due to its nobility. However, its unfavorable aspects can easily do so, especially if they fall into the 7th house conflicts.

Let's test this hypothesis. Below, I will provide a list of primary directions with the Sun's aspect and my expectations. I'll provide the facts that confirm or refute my expectations. I will look at the period from my 20s to the present moment.

Direction 1: △☉ in 7° ♈ approaches ♃ (March 2002)

- **Expectation:** I expect success from this aspect. Success will come not as a coincidence but as a result of my own efforts, as the aspect falls into the 1st house. We should interpret this aspect in relation to Jupiter (a significator of some area of my life in this direction). According to the nature of Jupiter, success will manifest in science, education, or social status.
- **Reality:** After a long period of scientific activity, I began working in an office for the first time in October 2002. Later, I quickly rose through the ranks in my career. It was a prominent date in my biography.

Direction 2. △☉ in 7° ♈ approaches ASC (September 2004).

- **Expectation:** Again, I expect success in 10th-house matters related to my life path (ASC). This could manifest as a job promotion, a scientific award for a discovery, or another achievement. The specific details will be clarified by the context of my current life circumstances and solar returns.
- **Reality:** This aspect occurred during my office work period. In September 2004, I got a leadership position in a well-known IT company.

Direction 3. ✶☉ in 7° ♎ approaches ♂ (July 2007).

- **Expectation:** I expect misfortunes in my activities due to conflicts. Since the conflicting aspect approaches Mars—the natural ruler of

enemies—and falls into the 7th house of disputes, this further reinforces my expectations. Additionally, the sextile falls into the dignity of Venus, which, as we know, signifies the 12th house matters. Prisons, illnesses, or captivity cannot cause conflict, but secret enemies (plots, intrigues) can.
- **Reality:** This aspect occurred at the peak of my office work career. In the summer of 2007, a group of colleagues testified falsely against me, leading to a public conflict and subsequent dismissal.

Direction 4. ✶☉ in 7° ♎ approaches MC, and right after that it approaches the Sun (October 2008, then February 2009).

- **Expectation:** I expect a similar conflict situation, but slightly milder, as the Sun's conflicting aspect approaches not Mars but the Midheaven.
- **Reality:** At that time, I worked in a branch of a major international company. At the end of 2008, a new director who began to violate corporate standards arrived at our branch. I stood up for the company's rules, and this conflict escalated to headquarters. As a result, in early 2009, I and the branch director were fired. It was also a public and resonant conflict.

Direction 5. ✶☉ in 7° ♒ approaches ♃ (January 2023).

- **Expectation:** Due to the Sun's opposition aspect falling into the 1st house, I expect misfortunes in my activities caused by myself. However, the conflict should be slightly softer, as the sextile falls not into the 7th house of disputes but into the first.
- **Reality:** Nothing happened.

As you can see, some primary directions are not realized. It happens because they are either not confirmed by corresponding solar and lunar returns, which also specify the month and day of the event, or because there is not enough context for realization.

However, as you can see in practice, noteworthy directions are more likely to manifest than not. Also, note that observed events confirmed expectations regarding the Sun's action with accuracy up to several months.

Also, pay attention to the fact that significant events the natal chart portends do not occur daily. This confirms what I wrote above—the natal chart indicates significant life events; it cannot predict everyday occurrences, such as a successful presentation at the end of the week or a transfer to a new department with a salary increase. Such predictions are the domain of horary astrology.

Example №31: Non-Determining Chart

The above horoscope determines the native's specific activity. You noticed that the planets repeatedly reproduced three central motives—a passion for teaching, research, and ideological struggle—at the intersection of their significations. In addition to the planets, the star Antares also supported the last promise.

When we see many indications for the same specific activity represented differently, we call such a chart *strongly determining* the native for particular occupations.

In reality, most natal charts do not make such explicit determinations. They are more general and leave a person free to choose what to do in life. Let's consider a typical natal chart, in which we can say little specific about the native's activity except for the most general aspects.

Planets Conditioned by the 10th House

This chart (Fig. 3.2) shows no planets in the 10th house or planets in the opposite 4th house. Jupiter, the ruler of the 10th house, represents the matter of that house most of all.

Saturn is another planet significantly conditioned by the 10th house. Not only is it the *secondary ruler* of the 10th house, but it is also in an antiscia conjunction with its primary ruler. The 10th house determines Saturn twice.

Two more planets—Mercury and Mars—cast a close aspect to the cusp of the 10th house. They rule the 10th house *by their aspects*. They primarily indicate the matters of the 6th and 12th houses by their position and *accidental rulership*.

Hence, more than anything else, Mars and Mercury denote illnesses, secret enemies, and menial work, which manifests in the 10th house. It's unlikely that these planets can create anything good in the 10th house.

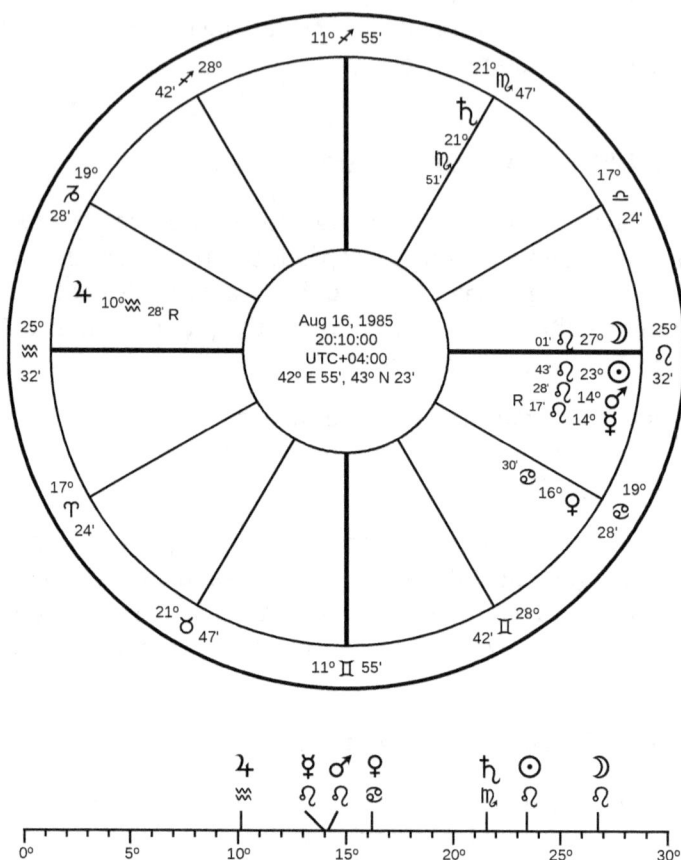

Figure 3.2: *A Non-Determining Chart*

Recurring pattern

Let's see if there's anything similar among these planets. The ruler of the 10th, Jupiter, is in the 12th house. At the same time, Mars and Mercury accidentally rule the 12th house. Both concord indications strongly connect the native's activity with the 12th house. It could be:

- Activity involving secret enemies and rivals.
- Activity in exile or leading to imprisonment or illnesses.

It was an ordinary girl with no criminal past leading a healthy lifestyle. The *determination by context* excludes the last two options. Moreover,

Mars and Mercury are natural rulers of aggression and false rumors, which indicate precisely secret enemies at the intersection of significations.

So, for now, all we can definitively say is that the activity will take place amid envy and secret enemies.

Each planet manifests itself through its dispositor, meaning the native's activity (Jupiter) will manifest through Saturn. Saturn primarily indicates matters of the 9th house by being placed in it. It implies the native's activity will occur in foreign companies, abroad, or connected with science/religion or something similar. According to Saturn's nature, it will be difficult and involve overcoming obstacles.

N.B. on logical synthesis

If, for instance, the Moon were Jupiter's dispositor in the 9th, we would say that the native socially operates in the backdrop of the 9th house matters of the Moon's nature, i.e., travel or distant journeys. The Moon's nature would specify the 9th house in the intersection of its accidental and universal meanings. However, we have Saturn, whose nature only suggests overcoming obstacles in certain (unknown) matters of the 9th house. We lack determination.

Let's assess the celestial conditions of the planets to evaluate their ability to bestow success in the 10th house.

I've already mentioned that Mars and Mercury are not inclined to produce any good deeds in the 10th house; instead, they tend to harm it. Therefore, we will skip these planets.

Although Jupiter is a natural benefic, it lacks dignity, receives an unfavorable aspect from Mars, and its dispositor is also malefic. Such a Jupiter is not inclined to effectively produce good things in the 10th house, at least by its bodily position.

However, since Jupiter carries no negative connotations and doesn't act against the 10th house, its favorable aspects can result in career advancements. Given that these aspects are minor reflections of Jupiter, all we said about Jupiter also applies to its replicas. These aspects will show success due to the native's diligent efforts. The native can expect success in certain realms of the 9th house, accompanied by envy.

Now, let's move on to Saturn. It is malefic without dignity, and its dispositor is also malefic in an unfavorable house. However, Saturn is still unharmful. It is in the favorable 9th house and receives supporting aspects. By its bodily position, it neither harms nor helps; it simply associates the native's activity with the 9th house, as described earlier.

Since it doesn't act against the favorable house, being in a "neutral" celestial state, its favorable aspects can also bring success abroad in education, foreign companies, or other matters of the 9th house.

Space for the Native's Decisions

The context excludes activities leading to imprisonment or illnesses, making the picture more certain—we know that success will be in the aid of envy. But this is the only sure thing that we know. Unlike my horoscope, the girl is not inclined to a specific activity. She will operate in *some* areas of the 9th house, but we do not know which one is more probable. The chance to be captivated by exploring new lands is no more likely than by teaching, researching, or something else.

Contextual Confirmation

From a very young age, the girl had an inexplicable inclination to work in foreign companies. Predictably, all her professional activity took place amidst colleagues' envy.

The native's preference for working in a foreign company rather than engaging in scientific activity is primarily the result of random factors such as upbringing conditions, informational environment, and so on. Even in this case, the native is not determined for a specific work profile. She could be a programmer, translator, or manager in a foreign company. And indeed, the girl worked in various fields. On the contrary, I have spent most of my life in research and education, according to a more specific indication of my horoscope.

As you can see, some people are more inclined towards certain types of work than others, which relates to what can now be called "destiny." We will discuss this in detail in the next section.

Chapter 3. Natal Astrology

Verification Through Events

Now, let's see how the favorable aspects of Jupiter and Saturn will contribute to success and at which dates.

- The most favorable aspect of Jupiter is ✶♃ at 10°♐ in the 10th house of success.
- The next in terms of benevolence is the ✶♃ at 10°♈ in the 1st house and the △♃ at 10°♎ in the favorable 7th house of helping partners. Both aspects are in the places where Jupiter is peregrine, making them less effective.
- Saturn has only one favorable aspect—the ✶♄ at 21°♑, though it falls into an unfavorable 12th house of secret enemies, making it less effective.

As you can see, only the first aspect has constructive potential regarding the 10th house. What does this mean? It means that the girl will have fewer directions for success—that is, fewer moments in life when she can succeed.

But this doesn't necessarily mean that the native will be unsuccessful. To determine the level of success, we need to find a strong connection between the 10th house (career, recognition) or the 1st house (native's life) with the Sun, the natural significator of fame, recognition, and success.

In this horoscope, such a connection exists. Look,

- The Moon (the planet taking *accidental rulership* of the 1st house) is conjunct with the Sun and in its domicile. Quite literally, the native's life will revolve around recognition.
- The Sun squares Saturn—the ruler of the 1st house, again linking the native's life with achievements.

The Sun is in an excellent celestial state; it will bring success to the native's life. But we already know that this success will take work. The ruler of the 1st in the dignities of Mars (the natural significator of intense efforts) supports this idea. Indeed, the girl was remarkably hardworking compared to her colleagues. It largely determined her success.

The girl told me the five dates on which she achieved outstanding career successes:

- December 2005

- Early 2007
- October 2009
- May 2011
- Late 2013

Let's compile a list of primary directions and compare the chart's promises with these dates. I will use the mentioned above aspects as promissors. As significators—the second participant in the aspects—I will use the native herself, her work, and the financial success indicator, the Part of Fortune.

It often happens that an event occurs not only when the significator of the object approaches the native in an aspect but also when one significator of the object approaches another significator of the same object. It signifies the manifestation of the object in the native's life. For example, the conception of a child can be shown by

- The aspect of the ruler of the 5th house to the cusp of the 5th house or
- The aspect of the planets in the 5th house to the natural significator of the child, the Moon, if it has a strong connection to the 5th house
- And so on

Therefore, I will consider the significator of the 10th house in aspect.

In that case, I will take the degree of the ASC and Saturn as significators of the native, Jupiter and MC as the significators of work, and the Part of Fortune as a signifier of financial success. I will look at the period from the native's 20th year to the present and see the following list of aspects in chronological order:

Table 3.4: *Blind Chart: Directions for Career*

Aspect	Expected Date	Real Date
△ ♃ in ♎ to ☽ (native) ⁎ ♄ in ♑ to the ASC (native)	Dec 2005 Mar 2011	Dec 2005 May 2011
⁎ ♃ in ♈ to the ASC ⁎ ♄ in ♑ to ⊗ (fin. state) △ ♃ in ♎ to ♄ (native)	April 2013 May 2013 Nov 2013	Late 2013
⁎ ♃ in ♈ to ♃ (professional or social activity)	July 2022	Nothing happened

Chapter 3. Natal Astrology

As you can see, three directions in 2013 were related to the same central event. It often happens that several directions go one after another in the same year, enforcing the realization potential. The final direction will wrap up these promises and point to the final date.

Six out of seven possible favorable aspects precisely confirmed the dates. I have already written that some directions do not produce an effect since no suitable conditions—confirming solar and lunar returns, or suitable context—happen in a particular year. By 2022, for example, she was already happily married. She had left her professional office job, fully dedicating herself to her family. Knowing that context, and considering that these aspects weakly contribute to success without the native's proper involvement, we would confidently disregard the last direction.

Cumulative Effect of Sequential Directions

Notice that three consecutive directions promised the same outcome—success in 2013. The final direction in this sequence, occurring in November, manifested the cumulative potential of all preceding directions. It should be a year of maximum career advancement. I consulted the girl for clarification, and it was confirmed. That year, she achieved a significant promotion at work and soon led a department of 50 people at a young age.

Even if the girl had not provided us with the dates of her successes, we would still have found them through this table and then confirmed the first three dates using solar charts and current circumstances.

Directions That Promise vs. Directions That Allow

I want to draw your attention to the following. In October 2009 and early 2007, the native achieved success without any apparent confirmation from the stars. That is, we, as astrologers, would hardly have seen these dates.

A critical reader may retrospectively identify the appropriate directions in which two career advancements occurred.

- It is the approach of a moderately favorable sextile of Mercury in Libra to the Moon (native) in February 2007.

- It is the approach of a favorable square of Mars in Scorpio to the MC in December 2009.

Here we recall that Mars and Mercury cast a close trine to the 10th house cusp, so they *rule the 10th house by aspect*.

But I argue. Analyzing the chart post-factum doesn't work like that. As previously noted, both Mercury and Mars reside in the 6th house, which conditions them to menial labor. They harm the 10th house by their trigonal aspects, and they can hardly generate significant career benefits even by their best facets.

For example, Mars's barely favorable square in Scorpio cannot create outstanding success relative to the 10th house if we interpret Mars as menial labor due to its position in the 6th house. However, the girl moved to another city to get the desired position in a vast international company with a 4-times salary increase.[16]

Mercury's sextile in Libra—the sign where it gets no additional dignities—while Mercury's primary role relates to the menial labor, is not enough to produce such a notable effect, such as the high-level managerial position held by a 21-year-old girl overseeing employees older than herself.

Furthermore, I counted a minimum of eight directions from favorable aspects of Mars and Mercury, all of which did not produce deeds in the 10th house worth attention, except these two. Looking at these eight aspects, an astrologer can hardly predict in advance (unless they look further into the specific solar and lunar returns and the current context) whether only two, all, or none of them will materialize, because these aspects neither forbid nor promise success.

What does this indicate? Thanks to her incredible efforts, the native took two out of eight opportunities where success was possible but not promised by the primary directions.

From this example, a straightforward conclusion follows. Events that happen in "neutral" directions, which neither promise nor disrupt events

---

[16] Retrospectively, we know that this particular year, Mars acted as the ruler of the 9th house. In that case, Mars's square in Scorpio can be interpreted as a favorable aspect of a long journey, logically capable of bringing success. But by default, just looking at directions for success, we could not have known whether the girl would move to another city, which is why we did not take this interpretation into account without proper contextual knowledge.

in various spheres of life (and most directions are such), occur by chance or by the action of the native unless solar and lunar returns do not forbid them.

Such "neutral" directions occur one after another and happen most often in our lives. They provide excellent opportunities for the natives or for mere coincidence to shape the flow of events in one way or another.

That is why we can see post-factum that "weak" directions easily explain events in a particular year. However, we cannot confidently forecast events by looking in that "neutral" direction. Occasionally, they produce notable events, but most of the time, they bring nothing worth attention. I suggest sticking to the prominent aspects that are strongly favorable or unfavorable regarding a specific house. That way, we will see slightly fewer events but with more accuracy.

Example №32: Fatal Chart

It is another example of a highly determining chart (Fig. 3.3). To understand what the chart inclines the native towards, let's consider the 10th house (the native's activity) and the 1st house (the native's life in general).

Planets Conditioned by the 10th House

In the 10th house, there is the debilitated malefic Saturn. It acts against the matters of the 10th house to the fullest extent, creating obstacles, hindering fame, or even nullifying it. However, it operates against the backdrop of the Sun, the natural significator of fame and recognition and the ruler of MC. Therefore, it is more likely to create obstacles to fame or dishonorable deeds rather than nullify them. If Saturn were in Cancer, it could restrict publicity and recognition. Still, being in the dignity of the Sun (that has a direct analogy with the 10th house and rules both Saturn and MC and hence prevails in its determination over Saturn), it cannot.

The Sun, against which it operates, is placed in the 7th house.

- Either these are other people of high social rank (wives, enemies, partners) involved in his activity.
- Or it is publicity (Sun) among other people, such as the masses (7th house). It is a fairly common pattern for people who perform on stage.

Predictive Astrology Textbook

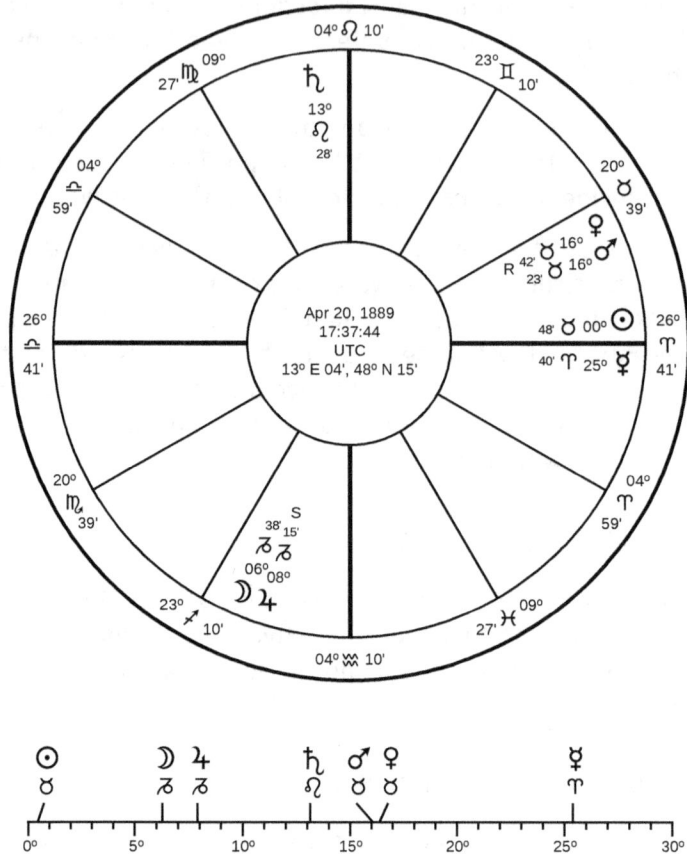

Figure 3.3: *A Highly Determining Chart*

Now, let's consider the second planet, related to the 10th house. It is the Sun, the ruler of the MC. Being the ruler of the 10th house (house of fame and recognition) accidentally and the ruler of fame and recognition naturally, it strongly links the native to public activities, fame, and recognition.

In this case, the Sun in the 7th house indicates either performing for the masses or victory over enemies (if the 7th house has a clearly negative connotation in the chart).

The Sun (public activity) operates against the backdrop of Venus, the natural signifier of love, attractiveness, and art. It again reinforces the idea that it most likely refers to performances in front of a large audience, great personal attractiveness, or activities in the arts, according to the nature of Venus.

But accidentally, Venus suddenly shows an entirely different picture. It rules the 8th house of deadly threats and is connected to Mars, which confirms this picture. Naturally, Mars rules wounds (which represent deadly threats) and battles, and accidentally, it rules the 7th house of wars and conflicts.

Since Venus's natural and accidental celestial state is beneficial, it acts against the 8th house matters, meaning it denotes miraculous salvation from the deadly threats that Mars generates. Such a contradiction puts us in a deadlock.

Logical Synthesis

We must find something that could unite these two contradictory indications: performance before the public/victory over enemies (Sun in the 7th) and fame gained through deadly threats and bloodshed (with miraculous salvation).

The only conclusion we can draw is that fame is acquired through battles, avoiding deadly threats, victory over enemies, and personal charisma, clearly visible to the masses. We have excluded interpretations of artistic activities that do not fit the general picture.

This commonality of the two meanings also clarifies Saturn's role now— it's not just "*some* heavy obstacles on the path to fame," it's deadly threats and even poisoning, as Saturn receives an adverse aspect from the pair of Mars/Venus (deadly threats), and is on the poisonous star Alphard (Alpha Hydrae).

The Modern Readings of Venus

Modern astrologers may disagree with such statements, as they consider Venus the natural ruler of money and therefore well-suited to the 8th house's meaning as "other people's resources." This thought would conclude that we are dealing with a stockbroker, a bank founder, etc.

But I object. **Firstly**, Venus is in no way associated with money. The fact that *Venus rules the 2nd sign of the zodiac*, and the *second house from* *the horizon denotes money*, connects Venus with finances no more than the second train carriage with the second course of my lunch, as they are united by the number two. There is no connection between the train and the food, just as there is none between the ecliptic plane and the sectors of the sky relative to the local horizon.

Secondly, as I said earlier, we avoid ultra-specific meanings of houses in the natal chart. We do not consider the 8th house as other people's money or my son's real estate, as all the houses in the natal chart denote the circumstances of the native, not of other people around them (until we specifically look at wives, brothers, etc.). We often use these ultra-specific meanings in charts closely connected to current events, like transits or lunar return charts. Therefore, relative to the native's life and actions, the 8th house is counted from the 1st house (native's life), representing deadly threats to the native.

Thirdly, the malevolent Mars, both by nature and by accidental signification, indicates wars and bloodshed. It applies to retrograde, i.e., weakened Venus, prevailing over her relative to the 8th house and influencing Saturn in the 10th (which receives the aspect of mixed natures from Mars & Venus). That excludes the idea of peaceful activities.

Additionally, pay attention to the dynamics of the aspect—right after meeting the deadly Mars, Venus (the ruler of life), in its retrograde motion, performs a square to Saturn. This means that the evil caused by mortal threats will inevitably be followed by destructive activity against the backdrop of publicity, as Saturn operates in Leo.

Fourthly, the evil star Algol, responsible for losing the head on Mars, the ruler of the 7th house, in combination with bloodshed, again speaks of military activities. And this once again confirms the overall picture.

Moreover, relative to the 8th house, the conjunction of this same star with Venus—the ruler of the native's death (in combination with Mars)—speaks of violent death from a head wound, which fits into the overall picture of constant deadly threats and salvation from death, against the backdrop of which fame comes. At the same time, the interpretation suggesting that the native "knocks heads (according to Algol) with money bills" lacks common sense.

Fifthly, we can easily verify the signification of Venus through a couple of events that Venus initiates. Suppose we are wrong, and Venus signifies money rather than deadly threats and salvation from death in connection with activity. In that case, Venus's unfavorable aspects should bring financial losses rather than create, together with Mars, deadly threats connected with the native's actions.

Verification Through Events

But, when Venus on Algol approached the ruler of the 10th, the native suffered severe gas poisoning while performing his official duties. Algol is the star of "Losing the Head." The gas poisoning damaged the native's head, more precisely, his eyes.

Later, when Venus's aspect at 16° Virgo (place of its fall) approached Saturn—the significator of his misfortune deeds—then in the same year, the native was the target of the first assassination attempt during a public appearance. As you can see, Venus is not associated with other people's money, and our signification is correct.

In addition to everything we've said, the Sun—the significator of the native's fame, which they will gain in battles associated with deadly threats—is closely connected with Mercury, which, by its position on the 7th house cusp, is also most closely related to fighting and bloodshed (being in the dignity of Mars) and accidentally signifies deadly threats, as it *co-rules the 8th house*. It again repeats the same pattern that we discovered earlier.

Predestination

As you can see, the stars compel the person in various ways to engage in a highly specific and unfortunate activity. They urge them at every opportunity to engage in the bloodiest battles or to provoke them. And this will intensify over the years since Venus, in its retro-motion, approaches a deadly Mars. And it's not about ideological disputes but real war. At the same time, the stars incline the native toward publicity, toward charismatic performances before the masses.

If there is war, this person will inevitably be involved in it. If there is no war, they will arrange it on a scale allowed by the circumstances—from organizing criminal gangs in the district to militarizing the entire country if, by chance, they come to power.

In any case, this is a highly determining horoscope, the holder of which is not entitled to choose their occupation.

This was the horoscope of Adolf Hitler, who initiated World War II and survived more than 20 assassination attempts. He safely survived them not only because of the favorable nature and state of Venus—the ruler of the 8th—but also because the most protective star of the sky, Spica, was right at the top of his first house when he was born in a small town in Austria.

The Myth of Destiny

As you can see from the examples above, some charts incline a person toward particular activities, while others allow them to engage in whatever they desire.

Most charts are not deterministic—they merely outline a general pattern of actions. In contrast, deterministic horoscopes leave individuals no choice. The natives are not free to decide what to engage in—their inner voice guides them in a strictly defined direction.

As you can see, this is only sometimes beneficial, as in my case. Other deterministic horoscopes, such as Hitler's, are less fortunate, where the "evil demon" leads the natives to suffer. In any case, being predetermined is less advantageous than having the freedom to choose what to do.

However, the idea that a person must necessarily have a unique passion for a particular pursuit has been actively promoted in recent years. This idea is now commonly referred to as *destiny*. This idea also suggests that not having a strong passion for something special means one is living the wrong way.

I am deeply convinced that this idea is false. And here's why:

Firstly, experience shows that only some people have highly deterministic horoscopes. Passionate individuals always stand out among others—they attract attention with their devotion and achieve considerable success because they dedicate their lives to one thing and acquire excellent skills in a particular field.

They do not seek their destiny, having no time for it—their pursuit consumes them. Those who have greater freedom of choice in their horoscope are the ones who seek their destiny. Fighting against one's horoscope and considering this innate nature unhealthy is clearly an artificially created trend.

Secondly, people consumed by their passion for a specific activity have no choice. This activity often contradicts socially accepted norms, as in the case of Giuseppe Garibaldi, Joan of Arc, Hitler, and others who found "their path." Even Steve Jobs, who followed a fairly peaceful "destiny," encountered trouble by going against the market in his passion.

To assume that one's "destiny" must necessarily be socially acceptable, not contradict the norms, and simultaneously evoke enthusiasm from the individual and their surroundings is an infantile position. In this case, we disregard examples of individuals clearly following their own path, which we hardly call pleasant, such as Joan of Arc, Garibaldi, etc.

Thirdly, the idea that the absence of a compelling inner voice is a bad thing makes most people unhappy. They seek their path only to rid themselves of the feeling that something is wrong with them. It creates very favorable marketing conditions for an entire industry of destiny-seeking. Simultaneously, the development of this industry further solidifies the false idea of destiny.

Unfortunately, modern astrology has removed its prognostic roots and become an appendage of this marketing trend. Astrologers readily help choose the sphere of realization, not even admitting that by that service, they reinforce the idea that something is currently wrong with their clients, that a regular life without a particular inclination to a specific occupation is subject to correction and a visit to an astrologer.

This further amplifies the background of low self-esteem in most people, which is already fueled by social media with exaggerated examples of artificial success.

Therefore, my message to all readers of this book is the following. Living simply, without a compelling inner voice, is not just the norm; it is a gift of freedom that you can use as you please. At the same time, having an inner voice that inclines you towards a particular pursuit is deep bondage. Being a hostage to your inner voice and achieving great results is like being an all-powerful genie (or genius) trapped in a bottle.

Predictive Astrology Textbook

Homework Assignment №21

So, it's time for your assignment. Here is a woman's horoscope. It is a "blind" chart, meaning you know nothing about the person (Fig. 3.4). Your task with this chart is to determine which planets (and what aspects of these planets) are most likely to bring children.

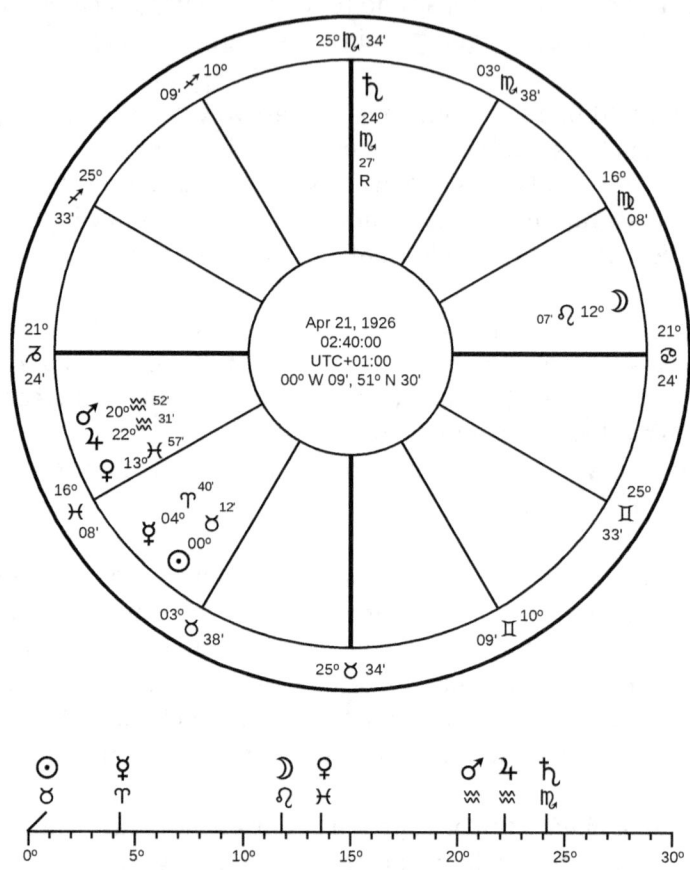

Figure 3.4: A Blind Chart №1

Hint: According to its natural signification, the Moon represents everything that appears for the first time, particularly newborn infants. Use this in your analysis.

After you complete this task, I will show you the correct answer, and then you can compare it with actual events.

Chapter 3. Natal Astrology

Solution

In this chart, there are no planets in the 5th or opposite 11th house, but there is Mercury, ruler of the 5th house. It is maximally determined to manifest in matters of this house. Mercury is a benefic planet, peregrine, placed in a favorable house. There is nothing bad about it. However, its dispositor—Mars—is a natural malefic. It slightly diminishes Mercury's beneficial nature. Overall, Mercury modestly promises children.

Two other planets cast close aspects to the cusp of the 5th house. These are the Moon and Venus—the *rulers of the 5th by aspect*. The Moon, like Mercury, is a natural benefic without dignities. But unlike Mercury, it is in the power of the benefic Sun, located at an angle, meaning it has great power to manifest, and most importantly, it is a *natural ruler of infants*. Thus, regarding children's birth and pregnancy, the Moon has apparent advantages over Mercury—it promises children more vividly.

Venus is accidentally benefic—it is in the sign of its exaltation, and its dispositor is a noble planet. Venus promises more good deeds in the 5th house than Mercury. Moreover, its dispositor—Jupiter—is a natural significator of fertility, making Venus a bright promissor of children.

As you can see, the two planets, the Moon and Venus, clearly stand out. Mercury remains in the shadow. The *secondary ruler* of the 5th house, Mars, will not bring anything for two reasons. First, Mercury is unexpressive compared to the Moon and Venus, making its dispositor (i.e, the secondary ruler) ineffective. Second, Mercury's dispositor (Mars) is a natural malefic whose nature acts against the matters of the house.

So, the Moon and Venus are the only planets that promise children more brightly than anyone else. They can realize this promise by their bodies or by their favorable aspects. Let's list all of these aspects:

- The Moon's trine accumulates all the good that the Moon promises into the signs of Aries and Sagittarius in favorable houses, which do not modify the Moon's action for better or worse. The same applies to the Moon's two sextiles, which accumulate the promise of children in the signs of Gemini and Libra. However, the last aspect is slightly less effective as it falls in the unfavorable 8th house.
- The Moon also has a notable dexter square in Taurus in a favorable house. The square minifies all the good in the Moon, making the copy almost neutral. Still, on the other hand, this aspect falls in the sign

of the Moon's exaltation, enhancing its good qualities. It is not as effective as if the Moon were in that sign, but still, such a replica of the Moon produces good things relative to the 5th house.
- All these aspects have roughly the same chances of bringing a child as the bodily position of the Moon.
- The trine of Venus in Cancer accumulates Venus's best qualities in the sign, which does not change the celestial state of that trine, though it falls in an unfavorable house, making it less effective. The same applies to the sextile of Venus in Capricorn. Finally, the sextile of Venus in Taurus—in the sign of its rulership that occupies a favorable house—is the most promising.

The two planets' bodily positions and favorable aspects are the places of the horoscope that promise children. We call them *promissors*. Let's list them all again in Table 3.5.

Table 3.5: *Homework: Promissors and Their Action*

Promissor			Action
	Degree	House	
☌ ☽	12° ♌	7	Moderately favorable
△ ☽	12° ♈	2	Moderately favorable
△ ☽	12° ♐	11	Moderately favorable
✶ ☽	12° ♎	8	Less favorable due to the terrestrial state
✶ ☽	12° ♊	5	More favorable due to the position in the 5th; it is more determined to the birth of children
□ ☽	12° ♉	3	More favorable due to the celestial state
☌ ♀	13° ♓	1–2	The most favorable of all due to the celestial state
△ ♀	13° ♋	6	Moderately favorable due to the terrestrial state
✶ ♀	13° ♑	12	Moderately favorable due to the terrestrial state
✶ ♀	13° ♉	3	Very favorable due to celestial state of Venus and her aspect

If you found these *promissors*, you were right.

Chapter 3. Natal Astrology

Verification Through Events

Now let's check in practice which birth dates these *promissors* indicate. We will let these points apply to the significators of the 5th house in their primary motion, thereby actualizing a child in the native's life.

As significators, we usually take the planets most determined by the house—that is, the planets inside the house and the ruler of the house by sign. We also take the cusp of the house, since the degree of the empty sign is also well-determined by the house. In our case, these are the cusp of the 5th house and Mercury. Additionally, if the natural ruler of babies (the Moon) has *at least some* connection with the 5th house, we can take it as a natural significator of children. In our case, the Moon *rules the 5th house by aspect*, so we can use it as a natural significator of children.

We have already said that although Mercury is maximally determined to manifest itself in the affairs of childbirth, it produces moderate results. It's like having a clear road without traffic jams, but your car is slow. With all the opportunities given to you to drive without traffic jams, you will still be late for work. Likewise, Mercury is not the most effective significator for children compared to the cusp or the Moon.

On the contrary, the favorable aspect of the Moon, promising children, strongly fortifies the cusp of the 5th house. So, the cusp is much more effective in receiving promissors and directing their actions to the matters of the 5th house than Mercury.

We will consider the period from 20 to 40 years when the likelihood of having children is highest. Since many promissors of children approach the two significators of the 5th house, we will get many possible dates. However, primary directions indicate all possible dates over 180 years. And we are interested in the small fraction of that period from 20 to 40 years of life. Hence, only some of these promissors will approach the significators during this period, and we will get fewer dates than you think.

If we consider all possible combinations of promissors and significators for the specified period, we will get the following dates (Table 3.6):

In my observations, the approach of promissors of children to the cusp of the 5th house (at least in female charts) more often indicates the moments of conception rather than birth, as if the 5th house distributes the

Table 3.6: *Blind Chart: Expected Dates of Child's Birth*

Promissor	Significator	Expected Date
✶ ♀ in ♉	The 5th house cusp	December 1947
☐ ☽ in ♉	The 5th house cusp	October 1949
☐ ☽ in ♉	Mercury	May 1952
✶ ♀ in ♉	Mercury	July 1956
✶ ☽ in ♎	The Moon	December 1959
△ ☽ in ♈	The 5th house cusp	April 1963

power of the promissor within itself, creating a pregnancy. At the same time, the planet-significator of the 5th house is an active participant in external events. It indicates the appearance of a child in the native's life. Therefore, we will add nine months to the dates of appropriate directions to the cusp.

We will also consider that the cusp of the 5th house and the Moon are more inclined to accept promissors than Mercury. Therefore, we will make two tables with a list of the more expected (Table 3.7) and less expected (Table 3.8) birth dates of a child:

Table 3.7: *Blind Chart: Most Expected Dates of Child's Birth*

Promissor	Significator	Expected Date
✶ ♀ in ♉	The 5th house cusp	September 1948
☐ ☽ in ♉	The 5th house cusp	July 1950
✶ ☽ in ♎	The Moon	December 1959
△ ☽ in ♈	The 5th house cusp	January 1964

Table 3.8: *Blind Chart: Less Expected Dates of Child's Birth*

Promissor	Significator	Expected Date
☐ ☽ in ♉	Mercury	May 1952
✶ ♀ in ♉	Mercury	July 1956

Please remember that these are approximate dates, accurate up to several months. We will later learn how to adjust these dates and pinpoint the exact month and date of the event.

Now, it is your turn to compare our expectations with reality. It will either confirm or refute the correctness of our significations.

It was a chart of Queen Elizabeth II of Great Britain. Her life is well documented (as is her time of birth). Find some time, use Google, and discover in which years and months she welcomed new royal family members into the world, and compare it with our table.

Primary Directions

Now that you know how to distribute the signification of the house among the planets, let's move on to the most crucial technique of astrological forecasting—*primary directions*. In essence, they resemble exact aspects of horary astrology. However, there are fundamental differences.

Firstly, the planets perform these aspects in the first hours after birth. As I mentioned in the section "How The Stars Affect Us," as the celestial sphere rotates during the first hours of life, the moving planets form new "chemical patterns," which I believe shape the primary imprint at birth. From a celestial geometry perspective, this appears as the rotating celestial sphere overlaying its initial position at birth. In their daily (or *primary*) motion, the moving planets and their aspects approach the planets and house cusps from the natal chart.

Secondly, there is a fundamental difference in the interpretation:

- In horary astrology, an aspect is the collision of two specific objects. In natal astrology, the applying promissors (planets and their aspects) signify the affairs of a particular house relative to a specific area of life, shown by the significator. The aspect means the manifestation of these affairs (objects and circumstances) in some area of life. I'll give you supportive examples below.
- In horary astrology, we evaluate the potential of the aspect based on the context of the situation, the motives of the two participants in the events (receptions), and their ability to act (accidental strengthening). In natal astrology, we look at the promissor's ability to create, destroy, or negate the house's affairs—how much it is beneficial or malefic relative to a given life area.

Promissors and Significators

As you already know, the same planet can take on different roles. In my horoscope, for example, Venus signifies romances and marriages, money, illnesses, and death. Consequently, considered relative to the 7th house, favorable aspects of Venus will bring new love into my life. The same aspects relative to the 2nd house will bring wealth.

In primary directions, we move the promissors (planet and its aspects), promising something good or bad regarding a specific house, to the significator of that same house.

For example, to find out the date of a severe illness in my horoscope, we would direct an unfavorable aspect of Venus to the significator of the 12th house of the disease, since unfavorable aspects of Venus create diseases relative to the 12th house.

To find the date of a significant romance, we would move a favorable aspect of Venus to the significator of the 7th house, since favorable Venus's aspects relative to the 7th house produce romance.

In Hitler's chart, Venus signifies deadly threats and salvation from death relative to the 10th house. Thus, "threats to life while on duty" or "threats during public activity" are among Venus's specific roles. Therefore, to determine when this particular role will come into play, we would direct a malefic aspect of Venus (ruler of the 8th house) to the significator of the 10th house—this would show us the date of the assassination attempt during a public appearance.

Thus, directing the same planets' aspects (promissors) to the different houses' significators resembles answering the horary question, "When will a particular event manifest in a native's life?" The degrees in the aspect denote the years from birth to that event in question.

Who Can Be a Promissor?

- Promissors can be planets or their aspects that produce or destroy the affairs of a specific house, as shown in the examples above.
- Promissors can also be planets' antiscia. Antiscia is the copy of planets similar to the aspect. The difference is that an aspect suppresses planets' bad or good qualities depending on its form (square, trine, etc.), while antiscia does not.
- Promissors can also be fixed stars if they occupy the house in question.

Who Can Be a Significator?

- Significators are planets most determined by the house, i.e., planets occupying or ruling the house by sign.

- The cusp of the house is also a significator, as the zodiac degree on the cusp is maximally determined by the house to a specific area of life.
- Regarding financial success, the Part of Fortune is a general significator of wealth.

Finally, if there is a planet that has a direct analogy with the house's affairs, and this planet is determined by that house (by rulership, position, aspect, etc.), then this planet can also act as a natural significator of the affairs of the house.

- For example, in a question about a child's birth, the Moon will indicate children, but only if it is associated with the 5th house, for instance, by aspect, rulership, dispositors, and so on (see the section "Terrestrial Determination").
- Regarding career advancement, the Sun will indicate fame and recognition, but only if it is associated with the 10th house.
- Jupiter will indicate wealth in a question about profit, but only if it is associated with the second house.
- And so on.

Special Role of the 1st House

The 1st house, representing the native and their life path, can act as a significator in almost any question. For example, the direction of the promissors of the child towards the significator of the 5th house brings the birth of a child. Similarly, the direction of the promissors of the child to the significator of the native can produce the same effect. Both aspects are equally capable of bringing children.

But when it comes to the 1st house, you must exercise caution. For example, in my horoscope, a very favorable sextile of Venus in Pisces approaches the ASC, indicating a positive event in October 2000. But what could it be? Venus co-rules the 2nd and 7th houses. This aspect can equally bring a new love or an influx of money. I will have to look at other directions this year to choose the correct option.

In 2000, I had no prominent directions indicating enrichment. However, right after the successful direction of Venus to the ASC in October 2000, a "neutral" aspect of Mercury (co-ruler of the 7th house) approached the 7th house cusp in November 2000. The second aspect followed the first and pertained to the 7th house. It rules out the option of enrichment. Thus, the aspect of Venus to the ASC promises big love at the end of the year. And so it was—in December 2000, I embarked on a passionate romance that left a mark for years.

It is safe to direct the promissor of the 1st house to the significators of the corresponding house. For example, in my horoscope, a favorable aspect of the ruler of the 1st house (literally, a favorable period of life) approached the cusp the 10th house in January 2003. A fortunate circumstance entered the 10th house between 2002 and 2003. So I expect only one thing from that aspect—success in my undertakings. And so it was. After prolonged scientific activity, I started my first work in an office for the first time in October 2002. Later, I quickly rose through the ranks in my career. It was a prominent date in my biography.

> **N.B. on technical terms**
>
> In matters of death, the most harmful planet (or its unfavorable aspect) related to the 8th house is the promissor of death relative to the 1st house of life. It is called *anaereta* or *abscissor*. We direct the *anaereta* to the most unfavorable significator of life—it will most effectively receive the deadly aspect and complete the native's earthly journey. You may hear terms like *hyleg* or *apheta*, which all denote the significator of the native's life in life-duration questions.

Celestial State of the Promissor

As you have seen, **prominent promissors**—whether explicitly beneficial or harmful—almost always bring about events. Exceptions occur when there is no suitable solar/lunar configuration in the corresponding year or simply no context for the event.

> **N.B.**
>
> Please note that if the promissor is an aspect or an antiscion rather than the planet itself, we consider both the condition of

the aspecting planet and the condition of its copy in the degree of the aspect when assessing the promissor's ability to act. It includes the celestial and terrestrial condition of the planet's copy.

Insignificant promissors, which neither create nor prohibit the house's affairs, usually produce nothing. If events do occur during their directions, it is more likely due to chance or the free will of the native, who is not compelled to do anything during these "neutral" periods.

This is why I divide directions into those that **vividly promise events** and those that merely **allow an event to happen**, opening up possibilities but nothing more, as I mentioned earlier in the section "Directions That Promise vs. Directions That Allow" on page 349.

In the promissor-significator pair, the last word always belongs to the promissor. It is the active side in the aspect; it produces the event relative to the specific area of life. At the same time, the significator merely indicates that area. It is the passive side in the aspect. You can imagine it as receiving the impulse from the promissor and then forwarding it to the corresponding area of life it represents.

For example, suppose the significator of the favorable 2nd house is in a favorable celestial state. In that case, it effectively redirects promises of wealth from beneficial promissors into the financial sphere. However, if the promissor is "neutral," not creating or destroying the affairs of the 2nd house, approaching such a promissor will not produce anything. No matter how good the significator is, if the promissor does not produce anything, the significator has nothing to pass into the area of the 2nd house.

The significator can only channel the promises of events into the area of life they are responsible for with varying degrees of effectiveness, but it cannot cancel them. Therefore, if a destructive promissor, portending financial losses, approaches a favorable significator of the 2nd house, the significator will still allow this misfortune to happen, albeit in a softer form than if it were itself debilitated. In the latter case, the effect of financial disruption would be maximal.

So remember, the last word in directions is with the promissor; it promises to create good or bad events in a particular area of life once it reaches a significator of that area.

Initiating Directions

Often, directions indicate not so much a significant event as a turning point that opens a lengthy process. It could be the onset of a prolonged illness that will eventually lead to death. It could be the completion of a project that leads to long-term career growth.

At the same time, these prolonged periods can also end through directions. For example, a favorable direction from the promissor, releasing from imprisonment, could end a long period of incarceration. A favorable direction from the promissor of wealth could end a prolonged period of financial hardship.

It does not mean that the absence of a finalizing direction implies eternal financial hardship or eternal illness. For instance, regular self-care will eventually lead to recovery without any direction—it is simply a manifestation of natural laws.

I call directions that initiate lengthy periods *initiating directions*. You will often encounter them in your practice.

Example №33: Initiating Directions in Action

Here is the "blind" chart (Fig. 3.5). I will examine the 1st and 10th houses to understand the overall "profile" of the native's life and activities.

Planets Conditioned by the 10th House

Inside the 10th house is a whole stellium of planets, but one stands out sharply against the others. It is the Sun, which simultaneously shares a similar nature with the 10th house and is closer to the cusp of the house than any other planet. So, it is more determined to manifest in the 10th house matters than other planets.

Moreover, it is conjunct with this cusp and simultaneously rules over a whole stellium of planets in the 10th house by exaltation. Additionally, it hides these planets within its rays, further dominating them.

Chapter 3. Natal Astrology

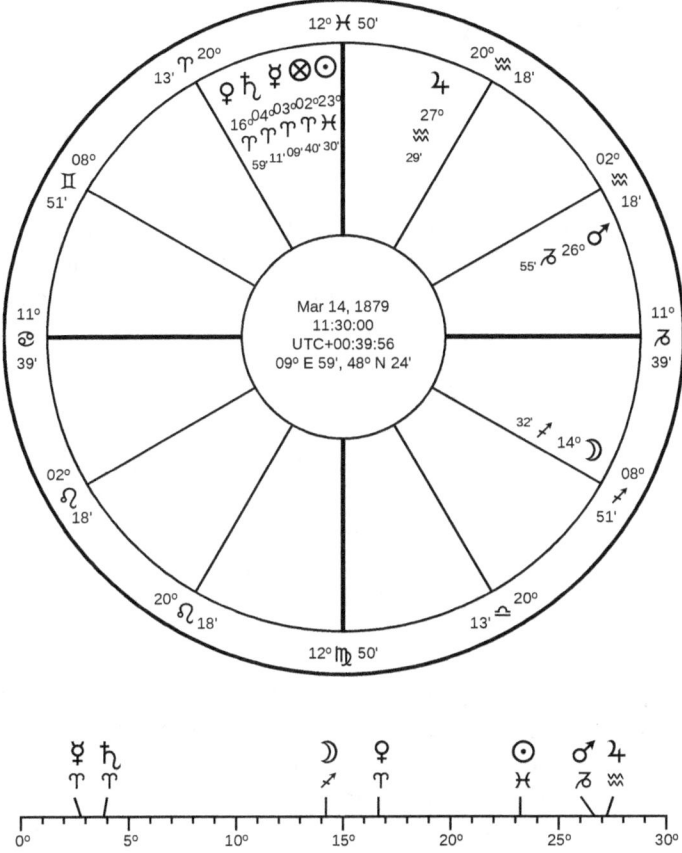

Figure 3.5: *A Blind Chart No. 2*

Undoubtedly, the Sun is the primary planet regarding the affairs of the 10th house. According to its nature and celestial state, it promises to bring significant fame and recognition. But what will this fame be associated with?

The Sun expresses itself through its dispositor and simultaneously the ruler of the 10th house, Jupiter, who by nature signifies science, jurisprudence, and religion among professions and is located in the 9th house of science and religion. At the intersection of these significations, Jupiter immediately outlines the area of manifestation of fame. We see the portrait of a prominent scientist, lawyer, or priest.

On the other hand, the next most significant planet, determined by the 10th house, is Mercury. By its nature, Mercury indicates any scientific activity but has no relation to religion or jurisprudence. At the intersection of significations, only science remains the most likely activity, supported by a multitude of different indications. Thus, an outstanding scientist is more likely than a famous priest or judge.

Saturn in the 10th house is a significant troublemaker—a malefic in exile. It promises to bring misfortune to the 10th house—hardships according to its nature, along with open enemies and mortal threats as indicated by the unfavorable houses it rules.

Saturn is closely connected with Mercury, meaning Mercury is inclined to take on roles with negative connotations because of Saturn. In Mercury's nature, nothing is negative, but accidentally, Mercury rules the 12th house. Therefore, on the one hand, Mercury contributes to scientific activity; on the other—it brings misfortune to the 10th house due to its connection with Saturn. Mercury indicates severe illnesses, secret enemies, exile, or imprisonment associated with the native's activities or publicity.

At the cusp of the 10th house lies the star Fomalhaut (it conjuncts MC in the ecliptical plane). The legend of this star is associated with escaping from pursuing enemies—it portends persecution but promises eventual success. What else in the chart supports this pattern? Exalted Mars on the cusp of the 8th house speaks the same—it creates mortal threats and immediately protects from them, according to its favorable celestial state.

Let us intersect these testimonies with what we know about Mercury: threats of persecution with a happy outcome (according to Fomalhaut), direct enemies or mortal threats (according to Saturn's terrestrial state), and illnesses (according to Saturn's nature) are much more aligned with the significations of exile and severe diseases of the 12th house than with prisons and intrigues. Therefore, we expect primarily diseases, exiles, and persecution from Mercury.

Planets Conditioned by the 1st House

Let's delve into the 1st house, which represents the native's life.

Chapter 3. Natal Astrology

Its ruler, the Moon, is located in the 6th house, symbolizing material deprivation and hard work for scarce earnings. Additionally, it takes on the role of the opposite 12th house, implying a life in exile (remember that naturally, the Moon shows relocations and movements).

Jupiter is the second planet strongly associated with the 1st house. It serves as the secondary ruler of the 1st house and its lord by exaltation. While the Moon's placement suggests a life in constrained conditions or exile, Jupiter's position and natural disposition indicate a life in science, further confirming the profile of a scientist in exile.

Jupiter also rules the 6th house, linking the native to restricted circumstances. However, since Jupiter is a mild benefic planet, and its nature of abundance acts against the 6th house matters, we expect such a Jupiter to, if not rid, at least mitigate the harsh conditions of life. More specifically, scientific pursuits will provide support during times of financial hardship.

Note the numerous recurring indications of identical life and activity patterns. It is highly deterministic horoscope of a very famous scientist with a very complicated fate, destined to experience many illnesses, to be exiled or pursued by enemies, to face mortal threats, but to escape from them.

Who is It?

It is the horoscope of Albert Einstein, whom the Germans persecuted during World War II, who was expelled from the country and experienced periods of dire existence, leading to lifelong illnesses. Despite these hardships, he was passionately devoted to one thing—science. His genius compelled him to pursue this field, even when his teachers closed doors to it during his youth.

With such a strong inclination towards science, we should anticipate that during intervals between significant directions, which influence the native toward realizing particular events, Albert Einstein would not be left to his own, unlike an average person. He had no time to search for his calling. All his time was dedicated to the subject of his passion, emanating from the 1st and 10th houses.

Testing Directions

Let's move on to primary directions. We will study examples of how the same promissor, promising multiple events in different areas of life, creates specific events when it reaches the significator of the corresponding life area.

For instance, Jupiter's position relative to the 10th house cusp signifies scientific endeavors in general, and relative to the Sun in the 10th house, it indicates notable scientific achievements leading to recognition and fame. Let's direct Jupiter to the Sun. This direction should bring recognition or start a process that will lead to recognition in science at the end of 1907.

You have probably heard that Einstein is the founder of the general theory of relativity, which is named after him. The year 1907 is considered the beginning of the development of this theory. This year, Einstein formulated his equivalence principle, which was later proved by experiment and brought him world fame. It is a classic example of an *initiating direction*. It did not bring an outstanding event, but it gave a turning point in his scientific path.

Regarding the 9th house, the same Jupiter signifies long-distance travel. If we direct Jupiter to the ruler of the 9th house, we will get the date of his long-distance trip. The first direction is performed by Jupiter's antiscion—it approaches Saturn in 1922. In that year, Einstein and his wife embarked on a grand tour of East Asia.

As you can see, Jupiter and its aspects hold different promises regarding different areas of life. But when we direct them to the significators of these areas, the corresponding promises materialize.

Thus, planets align their different roles into a chronological sequence of events. It is the essence of primary directions. It's appropriate here to recall the legend from the section "Primary Directions & Spindle of Ananke."

Now you understand the absurdity of modern astrology's questions, such as "What does my Venus in the horoscope represent?" It's like asking, "What does Jupiter represent in Einstein's horoscope?" The correct question is, "What does Jupiter indicate during a certain period of life (that is, during a specific direction relative to a specific significator)?"

Chapter 3. Natal Astrology

Example №34: False Prediction

As I mentioned earlier in the example on page 247, *cherry-picking* is a method of data manipulation where astrologers only showcase successful predictions while concealing all their failures. This creates a false illusion that their predictive techniques work when in fact they do not. To avoid such manipulation, I believe it is necessary to include cases of my obvious predictive failures in this book.

Not long ago, I made a prediction about whether Trump had a chance to win the 2024 election. I found no primary directions indicating elevation that year, so I concluded that Trump would not win the election. And this prediction did not come true (Fig. 3.6).

Let us examine how I reasoned then and how I reason now.

Planets Conditioned by the 10th House

First, we shall identify the planets conditioned by the 10th house and select from them the most prominent promissors of fame and success.

The Sun is located within the 10th house. Its nature of fame and success perfectly corresponds to the meaning of the 10th house of fame and success in the context of gaining power. The best aspects of the Sun can bring electoral victory.

These include:

- ✱☉ at 22°♈ in the 9th house. It promises maximum elevation through support from foreign services (9th house), though this elevation will involve elements of scandal (due to Mars—the dispositor of this aspect)
- ✱☉ at 22°♌ in the 1st house. It promises maximum elevation through one's own efforts (1st house)

These two degrees—22° Aries and 22° Leo—are bright promissors of success in the political context.

Next, in the opposite 4th house, we find the Moon. It is both the *accidental ruler* of the 10th house and the *ruler of the 10th house by exaltation*. The Moon is doubly conditioned to influence the native's actions. However, the Moon has no aspects that would fall in Taurus or Cancer—the signs of its exaltation and rulership. Thus, the Moon cannot provide the

Predictive Astrology Textbook

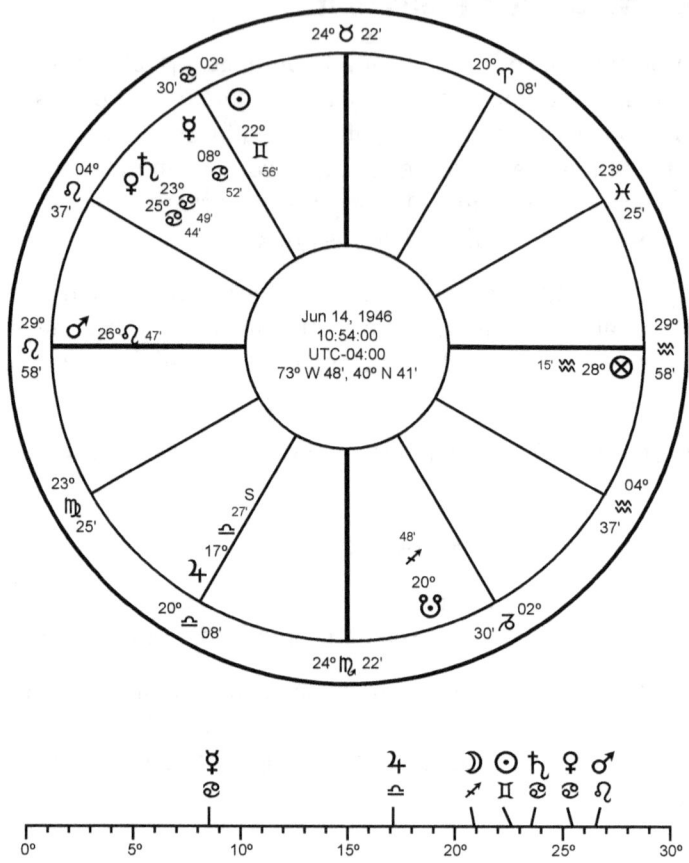

Figure 3.6: *Donald Trump*

same level of elevation through its best aspects as the Sun does through its bright promissors.

The 10th house itself is ruled by Venus. This natural benefic is not in fall or detriment.

Unlike the Moon, Venus has at least two aspects that promise great success in 10th house matters:

- ✶♀ at 25°♉ in the 10th house. It promises great success with little effort from the native.

Chapter 3. Natal Astrology

- □♀ at 25°♎ in the 3rd house. Logically, the 3rd house (siblings) is unlikely to be a source of success, so the celestial condition of this aspect can be disregarded. It simply indicates elevation.

However, Venus has a clearly negative trait regarding the 10th house: it is conjunct with debilitated Saturn, thus carrying its heavy imprint. Saturn represents direct enemies as the ruler of the 7th house. The second promissor at 25° Libra exactly hits Saturn's exaltation point, promising not just elevation but also difficult struggle associated with it.

Two planets cast close aspects to the MC—Saturn and Mars—but their aspects are harsh: they hinder the native's actions rather than bring fame and success, so we will not consider them.

Promissors and Significators of Victory

Thus, we have four promissors capable of bringing a significant breakthrough in Trump's career:

- ✶☉ at 22°♈
- ✶☉ at 22°♌
- ✶♀ at 25°♉
- □♀ at 25°♎

To fulfill their promises regarding the 10th house, these promissors must approach either the significators of life or the significators of the native's actions and undertakings.

The significators of life are:

- Ruler of the 1st house, the Sun
- Planet in the 1st house, Mars (though technically in the 12th house, its orb is in the 1st)
- The ASC degree itself

The significators of actions and undertakings are:

- Ruler of the 10th house, Venus
- Planet in the 10th house and natural ruler of power and success, the Sun
- The MC degree itself

None of the bright promissors of success approach any significators of life or activity in 2024. This is precisely why I predicted that Trump would not become president.

Where Was the Mistake?

As you already know, primary directions indicate the timing of an event. When searching for directions indicating elevation in 2024, we follow the logic: "If a presidential candidate has indications of success in 2024, then the election will occur in that year and not another, because the year of elevation is already determined by the horoscope."

But this logic is inherently flawed. It is not Trump's horoscope or his opponent Kamala Harris's that determines the election date. That is determined by the U.S. Constitution.

Therefore, victory in the prolonged election race should be sought not at its conclusion in 2024 but at its beginning, when candidates, inclined by their horoscopes, first initiate the process whose outcome interests us.

Here we return to the topic of *initiating directions*. We must find the moment when the initiating event—entry into the election race—occurred.

Trump began his election campaign in November 2022, several years before the election. What was happening in the sky shortly before this? In August 2022, two months before the campaign began, □ ♀ at 25° ♎ approached the significator of life—♂.

This is exactly what I was looking for. This is a classic *initiating direction*. At this direction begins the lengthy process of the election campaign, whose outcome (elevation) is already predetermined by the favorable state of the promissor. Meanwhile, the date of the campaign's conclusion is set not by the participants' horoscopes but by the White House.

As you can see, the mistake was not so much technical as it was logical. Yet the primary directions themselves work flawlessly, like Swiss clockwork.

Geometry of Primary Directions

You have probably already tried calculating primary directions in the astrological software you know, and you may have noticed that their results do not match the calculations given in the books. Unfortunately, most astrological programs do not support the methods of calculating directions proposed by Morinus. Therefore, I had to create the software that calculates them accurately.[17]

First, we must understand the *mundane conjunction*, i.e., the conjunction of two planets in the celestial sphere (Fig. 3.7).[18] A line from south to north through the significator is called the *significator's horizon under its pole* or its *circle of position*. If the significator is a house cusp, this line coincides with the dividing line between the houses.

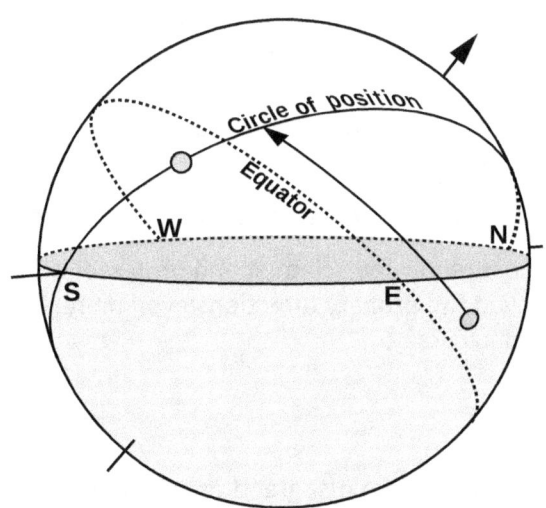

Figure 3.7: *Mundane Conjunction*

Next, we keep the significator's horizon stationary and allow the promissor (star, planet, its aspect, or antiscion) to reach that line. Once it reaches it, we call this a *mundane conjunction*. The promissor's path to the significator's stationary circle of position, in degrees, indicates the number of years from birth to the event.

---
[17] https://morinus-astrology.com/natal-app/
[18] The promissor is approaching the significator's circle of position

Converse Directions

Sometimes, the path from the promissor to the significator's circle of position takes more than 180 degrees. In this case, astrologers sought ways to calculate the shortest route. Some astrologers mistakenly rotate the sphere in the opposite direction, allowing the promissor to reach the significator's horizon by the shortest path.

However, as Morinus pointed out, this calculation method contradicts common sense. The celestial sphere does not rotate in the opposite direction in the first hours after birth. We need to find a way to direct the rotating horoscope to the stationary radix figure to calculate the shortest distance between one planet and the circle of positions of the other.

For this purpose, ancient astrologers proposed a more straightforward method: leave the promissor and its circle of position stationary and move the significator along with the sphere until it reaches the promissor's horizon. If the significator is the house cusp, we direct its zodiac degree to the promissor's circle of position.

This approach changes the length of arcs in directions and, in practice, confirms incredible accuracy. We call such directions *converse*.

Morinus, the most renowned scientist and professor of mathematics of his time, improved the primary directions even more, bringing them to the next level of accuracy.

Circle of Aspects

For a long time, astrologers disagreed on which plane to plot planets' aspects for primary directions. Figure 3.8[19] shows the surface of aspects parallel to the ecliptic. Directions utilizing aspects in this plane are called *zodiacal directions with the planet's latitude*.

Morinus brilliantly resolved this problem. He proposed constructing the plane of aspects called *a circle of aspects*, considering the apparent motion of planets (including their loops). He built a surface that passes through two points—the planet's current position and the point of maximum elevation above the ecliptic on the planetary path from the past

---

[19] Fig. 3.8: The planet is in the center, and its aspects are on a surface parallel to the ecliptic. The planet is slightly above the ecliptic at the moment.

Chapter 3. Natal Astrology

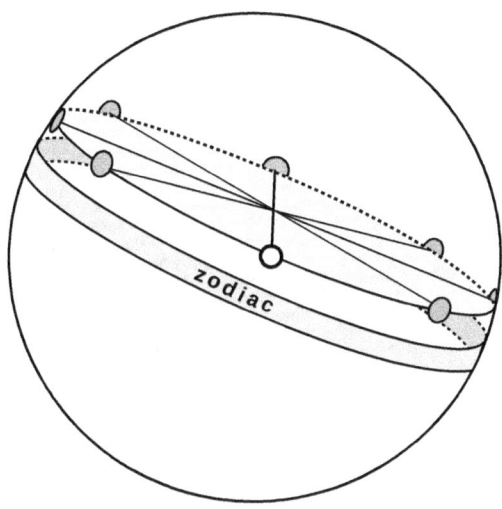

Figure 3.8: *Zodiacal Directions With Latitude*

to the next node (Fig. 3.9).[20] Thus, the plane of aspects depends on the planet and the current moment.

The promissors (planetary aspects) plotted in this plane, approaching the significators, indicate the most accurate timing of events. You have already seen that the deviation between the direction indication and the event amounts to only a few months. At the same time, aspects of planets plotted in other planes give a difference of several years.

Antiscia on 3D Sphere

But Morinus's genius did not stop there. He also considered that planets' *antiscia* are not just a mirror reflection of the planet on the zodiacal circle but the intersection of the arc of its diurnal motion with the ecliptic surface. Therefore, on the three-dimensional sphere, planets have not one but two antiscia (Fig. 3.10).[21] These two positions of the antiscia also provide a more accurate result in primary directions.

---

[20] Fig. 3.9: Planet (white dot) and its aspects on a surface, constructed by Morinus. Black dots represent the places where the planet deviates most from the zodiac circle along its apparent motion path (bold dashed line).

[21] Fig. 3.10: Planet (white dot) is slightly above the ecliptic; hence, it has two antiscia.

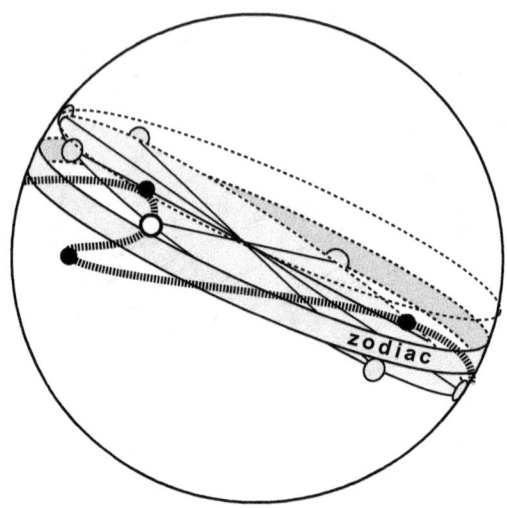

Figure 3.9: *A Circle of Aspects*

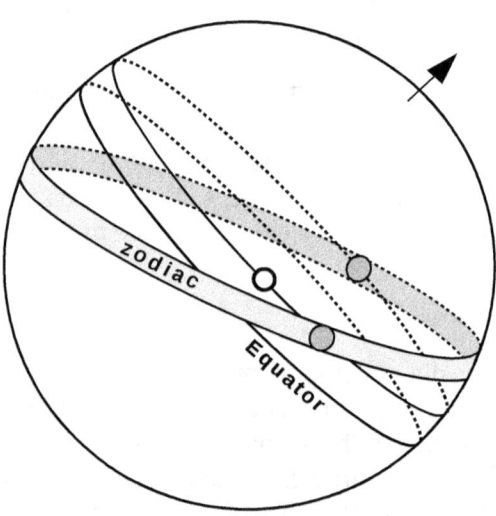

Figure 3.10: *Antiscia*

Chapter 3. Natal Astrology

For example, as you remember, in Hitler's chart (Fig. 3.3 on page 352), Venus rules the 8th house; it conjuncts Mars and Algol. Relative to Saturn in the 10th house, it indicates deadly threats or violent death from a head wound (according to Mars and Algol) due to the native's own actions.

The far antiscion of this Venus (a Venus copy, at 11°♊, which fell in the middle of the 8th house of death) approached Saturn, indicating September 1945. Several months before that, in April 1945, Hitler shot himself in the head. So, you can see the accuracy of our results when we apply Morinus' calculations.

Naibod Key

But that's not all Morinus left us. Astrologers have long noticed that the number of degrees the celestial sphere rotates corresponds to approximately, but not precisely, the number of years. Over the years, astrologers have tried to find a key that could accurately translate the degrees of directional arc into years of life so that they would closely match reality. One such key was suggested by the German scientist, professor of mathematics Valentin Naibod. He proposed taking one year of life not as 1° of the planet's diurnal path but the Sun's mean daily motion along the equator, which is 0°59'08" (or 0.9855°).

Morinus examined many keys, applying them to the plane of aspects he constructed. He found that Naibod's key gave the most accurate timing.

Since one year of life corresponds to 0.9855°, then 1° of the arc of direction corresponds to approximately 1.0147 years of life. The slightest error in the key would lead to a significant deviation in terms by age 50–60. But Naibod's key and Morinus's plane are devoid of this drawback—they accurately indicate the timing of events throughout the native's life.

You will shortly see the fatal direction in Einstein's horoscope ("Example №39: Solar Return Confirming Initiating Direction" on page 412), which triggered deadly illness in his 75th year with a difference of only a couple of months between the direction's indication and reality.

Rectification of Birth Time

The birth time reflected in the birth certificate or the one you recall from memory is not inherently accurate. Even a minute's deviation in the birth time can change the timing of events according to primary directions by months.

Therefore, astrologers use a procedure known as *birth time rectification* to refine the exact minute of birth. Its essence lies in making predictions based on your natal chart and comparing how accurately these predictions align with known events. If the discrepancy is significant, the astrologer adjusts the birth time forward by a minute, then backward, attempting to determine the direction of adjustment in which the deviation between predictions and known events decreases.

The astrologer further adjusts the time until finding a minute where the deviation between predictions and reality is minimal. The logic here is this: if the rectified chart accurately reflects the timing of already known events, it will similarly predict future events with the same accuracy. Usually, the rectified time can differ by a few minutes from the time on the birth certificate.

Primary directions are well-suited for rectification. Shifting the birth time by 1 minute moves the expected time of an event by several months, especially in the case of directions to house cusps. Converse directions extend the time until the event, while direct ones, conversely, shorten it (if we move the birth time forward). Let me demonstrate how to conduct rectification using my horoscope as an example.

Example №35: Rectification

According to official records, my birth time is 12:15 (Fig. 3.11).

To rectify the chart, I will select areas of life to compare against. For example, I will consider the 10th house (my professional activity) and the 7th house (love and relationships). I will only consider these houses' most prominent directions (constructive or destructive).

Chapter 3. Natal Astrology

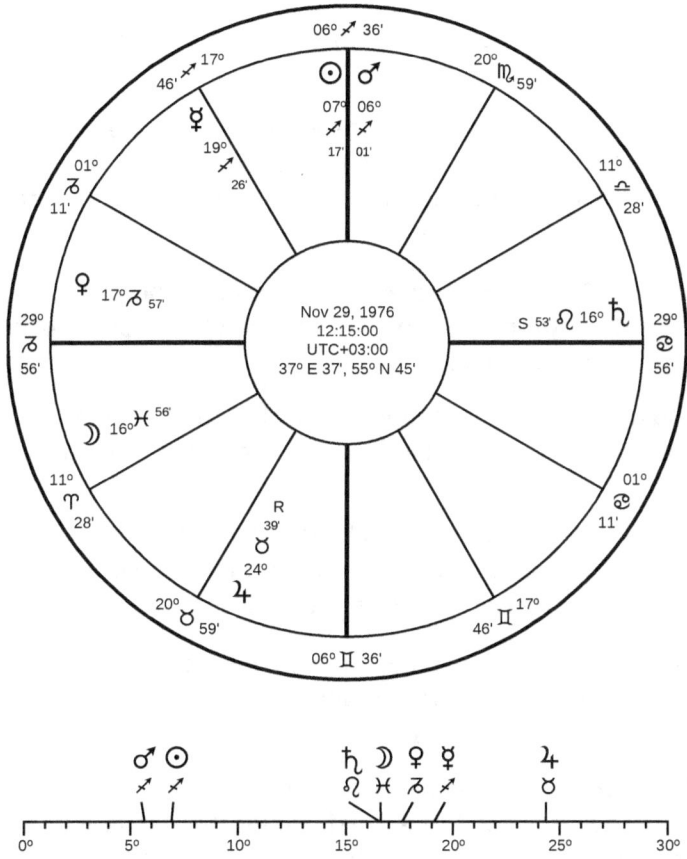

Figure 3.11: *Alexey Borealis. The Birth Chart According to Records.*

Career Events

The Sun is the most prominent indicator of success in the 10th house. Therefore, if I take favorable aspects of the Sun and direct them to favorable significators of the 10th house—MC, the Sun, or Jupiter—I will see success dates in my professional activity to compare with known events.

By now, only one such aspect has occurred:

Direction: △☉ in ♈ approaches Jupiter: **April 2002**.
Reality: In **October 2002**, after leaving the academic environment, I began my career advancement in business.

Success is also possible with the direction of a favorable aspect of the Sun (professional success) to favorable significators of the 1st house (my life path)—ASC or the Moon.

Direction: △☉ in ♈ approaches the Moon: **October 1990**.
Reality: I was only 13 years old then and not yet working. According to the fourth determination, the Sun cannot indicate success in endeavors during this period.

Direction: △☉ in ♈ approaches ASC: **December 2004**.
Reality: In **September 2004**, I obtained a leadership position in a major IT company.

I can also direct favorable aspects of my life to favorable significators of the 10th house. It will also indicate the dates of my professional successes.

Direction: ✶♄ in ♎ approaches MC: **December 2002**.
Reality: In **October 2002**, I began my career advancement in business, leaving the scientific environment.

Direction: ✶♄ in ♎ approaches the Sun: **July 2003**.
Reality: In **May 2003**, I started working at a major IT company, where I later obtained a leadership position.

I can direct unfavorable aspects of Mars—the worst promissor of the 10th house—to Mars itself (the worst significator of the 10th house). In that case, I will obtain dates of the worst episodes of my activity. By now, there have been two such directions:

Direction: ✶♂ in ♎ (in place of exile and the 7th house of conflicts) approaches Mars: **January 2007**.
Reality: In the **summer of 2007**, I left the highest position I ever held amid scandal.

Direction: □♂ in ♍ (located in the house of conflicts) approaches Mars: **December 2014**.[22]
Reality: In **early 2015**, I attempted to start a hotel business in Asia, which quickly failed, resulting in financial loss and conflict with partners.

---

[22] I note that this direction also pertains to the money issue since Mars is also the significator of the 2nd house—this direction promises financial losses as the destructive promissor of finance approaches the unfavorable significator of wealth.

Chapter 3. Natal Astrology

Since I do not remember the exact dates of the last two events, I will not use them for rectification.

Relationship Events

Venus, while not the most prominent indicator of the 7th house (as it only partially rules it), is nonetheless the planet of love. It shares the nature of the 7th house, thus becoming an effective promissor of relationships.

I can direct favorable aspects of Venus to favorable significators of the 7th house—its cusp or Venus as the natural significator of love (which I can do as it is associated with the 7th house) or to favorable significators of the 1st house—ASC and Moon. In that case, I will obtain dates of significant romantic relationships.

Direction: ✶ ♀ in ♓ approaches ASC: **January 2001**.
Reality: In **December 2000**, I embarked on a passionate romance that left a mark for years.

Direction: △ ♀ in ♉ approaches ASC: **July 2019**.
Reality: In **May 2019**, I entered into my third marriage. I filed for marriage registration in April and received the marriage certificate in May.

Direction: △ ♀ in ♉ approaches the Moon: **February 2006**.
Reality: There was nothing remarkable in that year, just a regular romance.

I can also direct favorable aspects of life (Moon or Saturn) to Venus or DSC to achieve a similar effect. But by now, only one such aspect has occurred:

Direction: ✶ ♄ in ♎ approaches DSC: **February 2013**.
Reality: I was already married then, so this aspect did not manifest. However, an unfavorable △ ♄ in ♈, which approached Venus in **March 2016**, resulted in my second marriage in **January 2016**, which lasted only several months due to the detrimental condition of the promissor.

Note that my descendant is on the cusp of signs, meaning the first degrees of Leo are relatively close to the horizon. Therefore, the 7th house strongly determines the sign of Leo and the Sun's influence on relationship matters. Thus, the Sun becomes as significant in the 7th house as the Moon, associated with the 7th house by just one (although powerful) degree on the cusp.

Therefore, the Sun can also be a promissor of good deeds in the 7th house. We can direct favorable aspects of the Sun to beneficial significators of the 1st and 7th house. In that case, we will also obtain dates of notable relationships.

Direction: △☉ in ♈ approaches Venus: **February 2008**.
Reality: In **April 2008**, I entered into my first marriage.

Direction: △☉ in ♈ approaches ASC: **December 2004**.
Reality: There was nothing remarkable in that year.

Rectification

We've gathered enough events for verification. Let's record them all in Table 3.9 and assess how the directions deviate from reality (in months). If the directions precede the event, I will indicate the difference with a minus sign; otherwise, I will use a plus sign.

Table 3.9: *Events for Rectification*

Prm.	Sgn.	Frcst	Reality	Event	Δ
✶♀♓	ASC	Jan 2001	Dec 2000	A passionate romance that left a mark for years	+1
△☉♈	♃	Apr 2002	Oct 2002	The start of career advancement in business	−6
✶♄♎	MC	Dec 2002	Oct 2002	The start of career advancement in business	+2
✶♄♎	☉	Jul 2003	May 2003	The start of work at a major IT company, followed by obtaining a leadership position.	+2
△☉♈	ASC	Dec 2004	Sep 2004	Obtaining the first leadership position	+3

Continued on next page

Table 3.9 – Continued from previous page

Prm.	Sgn.	Frcst/Reality		Event	Δ
△☉♈	♀	Feb 2008	Apr 2008	First marriage	−2
△♄♈	♀	Mar 2016	Jan 2016	Second Marriage	+2
△♀♉	ASC	Jul 2019	May 2019	Third Marriage	+2

Now, I will arrange the deviations in ascending order [−6, −2, 1, 2, 2, 2, 2, 3] and then select the central element from this sorted list. It will allow me to find the *mean average* deviation value of 2.

This means that, on average, events occur approximately two months before the onset of directions, which is quite suitable accuracy for predictions. After all, directions are only needed to indicate the year of the event to cast the appropriate solar return chart for further details. Our task is to avoid making a mistake with the year.

However, suppose we want to be detailed and increase the degree of correlation between predicted and actual events. In that case, we can adjust the birth time forward and backward by a few minutes to assess how the mean average deviation changes (see the Table 3.10).

Table 3.10: *Rectification: Shifting the birth time*

Birth Time	The list of Deviations	The ordered list	Mean Average	σ
12:13	7, −5, −1, 4, 10, −2, 2, 8	−5, −2, −1, 2, 4, 7, 8, 10	3	4.96
12:14	4, −6, 1, 3, 7, −2, 2, 5	−6, −2, 1, 2, 3, 4, 5, 7	2.5	3.86
12:15	1, −6, 2, 2, 3, −2, 2, 2	−6, −2, 1, 2, 2, 2, 2, 3	2	2.83
12:16	−2, −7, 3, 1, 0, −2, 3, −1	−7, −2, −2, −1, 0, 3, 3	−0.5	3.04
12:17	−5, −8, 4, 0, −3, −2, 3, −4	−8, −5, −4, −3, −2, 0, 3, 4	−2.5	3.78

Notice that as we shift from the official birth time, which I initially consider reliable, the mean average of deviations between actual and predicted dates grows, and deviations become highly uneven. It happens because the converse directions shorten the time until the event, while the direct ones extend it.

For example, at 12:15, almost all events lead the forecasted time by two months, while at 12:13, some directions lead events by five months, while others lag by nine months. This spread is minimal when we are close to the correct birth time.

I mathematically expressed this spread in the last column using the formula for the so-called *standard deviation*, sigma.[23] You don't necessarily need to evaluate the spread mathematically as I did. It's enough to visually confirm that as we shift from the correct birth time:

- The spread between the indications of directions and actual dates increases.
- On average, forecasts will either lead or lag behind the confirmed dates.

Based on what we observe in our table, the official recorded birth time is very accurate. However, I still lean towards thinking of a slightly later moment—between 12:15 and 12:16. Somewhere in that interval:

- The spread of deviations is still low.
- On the other hand, on average, the directions indicate the timing of events very close to reality, as the *mean average* equals zero somewhere in this interval (Fig. 3.12).

Without bothering with the futile pursuit of the exact second of birth, I safely shift the birth time by 1 minute forward, and this will be slightly more accurate based on the forecast results than the time according to official records.

Final Verification

Now, let's verify our rectified time against random events from different areas of life. To do this, we'll take a different approach. First, we'll

---

[23] The formula is $\sigma = \sqrt{\frac{1}{n} \sum_{i=1}^{n}(x_i - \mu)^2}$, where $\mu = \sum_{i=1}^{n} x_i/n$, n denotes the number of rows in the Table 3.10, and x_i—an element in the list of deviations. If you familiar with Excel, please use the STDEV.P() function for automatic calculation of σ-value.

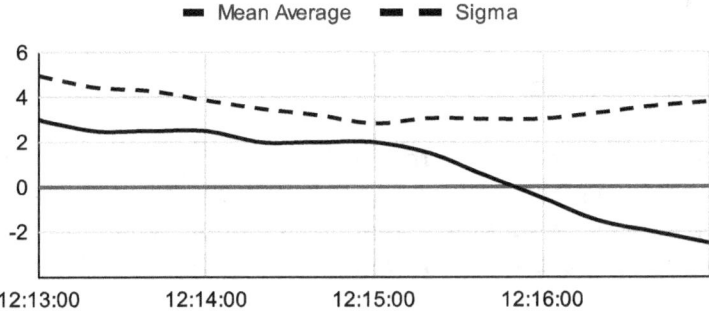

Figure 3.12: *Mean Average and Standard Deviation*

arbitrarily select significant life events and then see if any corresponding directions point to these dates.

For instance, in **May 2001**, I traveled to Australia to write my doctoral dissertation. It was a key event for me, and I had diligently prepared for it. I completed the PhD candidacy requirements two years before the scheduled date, received a Vice-Chancellor's of Australia scholarship, and finally embarked on my journey in May 2001. Brian Schmidt, the current Nobel Laureate in Physics, was my guide on this journey. I am still immensely grateful to him for his assistance.

However, this event wasn't arbitrary. In **July 2001**, a highly favorable trigon of Mars (ruler of the 9th house) in its domicile, Aries, approached Jupiter—the accidental ruler of the 9th house, the ruler of my scientific endeavors, and the natural ruler of science.

Another event happened in **April 2019**. I was managing my business when the landlord of my business premises breached the contract, leading to a conflict that escalated into a legal dispute.

In **April 2019**, Mars, representing conflicts related to my activities, by its opposition on the cusp of the 4th house of property, approached the significator of the native, the Moon.

As evidenced by these control examples, the directions in the rectified birth chart accurately indicate the timing of events. As you can see, rectification is a helpful but time-consuming technique.

Revolutions

General Principle

As I previously mentioned in the section "How The Stars Affect Us," the degree where a planet was located at birth is perceived by the native's body in a special way. If the planet, in its motion, returns to the same degree, the human body sensitively reacts to this moment.

Although the returning planet is in the same zodiacal degree, it may fall into a different house or receive aspects from other planets. Suppose that in the natal chart, this planet is conditioned by the 3rd, 5th, and 9th houses, having different roles simultaneously. At the moment of its return, it becomes connected to one of these houses (by position, rulership, aspects, etc.). In that case, we say that the planet repeats its specific natal role.

The moment when the chart returns to its original natal position is called a *revolution*, and the chart cast for this moment—the *revolution chart*.

It is a special kind of transit that actualizes the planet's particular role, which it plays until it completes its current revolution around the zodiacal circle and returns to its original position. The following transit will refresh the planet's role again—and so on—cycle after cycle.

We always consider return charts relative to the radical figure, i.e., the birth chart. If the planet plays the same roles that it has in radix, these roles are reinforced for the period of revolution. If it starts to show something that it doesn't signify in radix, it will hardly manifest.

It may happen that a returning planet repeats several natal roles in the revolution chart, and we do not know which are more likely to manifest. Therefore, we consider return charts relative to the main promises of primary directions, which occurred shortly before or right after the revolution.

Suppose in the preceding direction, the planet actualized the role of illness—it either acted as a promissor of disease, which approached the significator of the 12th house, or as the significator of the 12th house, which received the promissor of illness.

Chapter 3. Natal Astrology

Then, we will consider the revolution chart solely as a transit, triggering (or not triggering) trends toward forming illnesses in the nearest revolution cycle.

For example, we may observe that in the revolution chart, the returning planet becomes a prominent ruler of the 12th house—it rules it by sign or occupies it. Simultaneously, it receives numerous malevolent aspects, debilitating its celestial state.

Additionally, we may see that the natal ruler of the 12th house casts an exact aspect to the revolution's 12th house cusp—it also reinforces its relations to the disease. We can technically overlay the revolution chart onto the radix figure since revolution is always considered relative to the radix.

Such a revolution confirms the promise of the direction—it establishes favorable conditions for the manifestation of ill health, which will intensify over the course of the revolution cycle. Therefore, the direction has a high chance of realization during this revolution.

If the returning planet in question is not connected to the 12th house, then the revolution chart does not confirm the direction. In that case, the direction has very little chance of realization on that revolution.

But suppose the revolution chart acts contrary to the promises of primary directions. It promises the native good health, strengthening the 1st house. For instance, the planet that signifies disease in the primary direction became the dignified ruler of the first house and received a favorable aspect from other planets in the chart of revolution.

In that case, such a revolution will initiate trends of health strengthening throughout its entire cycle of influence. The revolution chart *actively suppresses* the direction's promises, and illness will certainly not manifest while the revolution chart is active.

Thus, the revolution chart either confirms, does not confirm, or suppresses the promises of the primary directions.

Let's consider this with an example.

Example №36: Venusian Return

You've already seen in my horoscope that the direction of Venus's most favorable aspect—17° Taurus—to my ASC points to April 2019, marking my third marriage. Let's cast the chart of Venus' return (Fig. 3.13), which happened shortly before this direction occurred.

Figure 3.13: *Alexey Borealis. Venusian Return Chart*

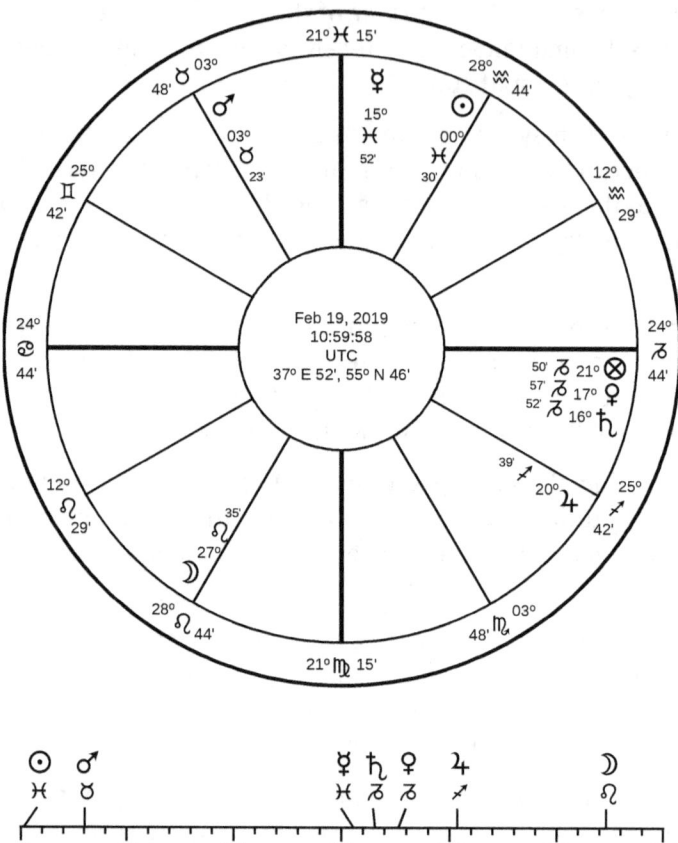

We're interested in Venus's role relative to the 7th house in this chart. Venus conjuncts the ruler of the 7th house (Saturn), and she is under his influence. Furthermore, Venus, within her orb, conjoins with the cusp of the 7th house. Additionally, Mars—the ruler of the 7th house by exaltation—manifests itself through Venus. Undoubtedly, Venus has repeated her natal role as a planet related to the 7th house this year.

Let's examine Venus's celestial state. Her sign hasn't changed since she returned to the same point she was at birth. But what about her

Chapter 3. Natal Astrology

dispositor? Saturn has become the accidental benefactor in this chart and conjoins Venus. It significantly improves Venus's condition compared to her natal state for the next 294 days (until the next Venusian return).

So, we have two confirmations of what direction promises:

- Venus has a strong connection with the 7th house.
- Venus's celestial condition has improved compared to the natal one.

This year, she repeated her role—the *promissor* of love and marriage. Marriage could be the only option since I was already in a favorable relationship at the beginning of the revolution.

We do not examine other houses and spheres of life—we only focus on Venus and its connection with the 7th house as we consider this chart relative to the nearest direction, promising good deeds in the 7th house.

So, we have several confirmations that Venus will produce good deeds in the 7th house for the next 294 days. As a sequence, the corresponding direction will take effect in that period.

In the first part of this book, I wrote about how unique transit charts, particularly revolution charts, can be radical figures for subsequent transits—they lay down tendencies for realizing the main events they promise. Since this chart sets trends for marriage during the Venus revolution period, we can consider that chart as radix for the main event it promises.

It means we can apply the same predictive technique to this chart as to the birth one—the primary directions. We can take the most outstanding aspect of Venus—at 17° Taurus in favorable 11th house—and direct it to the favorable significators of marriage—Venus/Saturn—or to the significators of the native's life and activities for the next 294 days—ASC/Midheaven.

Then we get the following directional arcs (see Table 3.11):

Table 3.11: *Borealis: Directions from Venus' return chart*

Promissor	Significator	Arc	Days	Date
△ ♀ in ♉	ASC	303.21°	248	Oct 2019
△ ♀ in ♉	MC	54.48°	44	Apr 2019
△ ♀ in ♉	Venus	172°	140	Aug 2019
△ ♀ in ♉	Saturn	174.90°	142	Aug 2019

Since the complete revolution of the sphere (360°) corresponds to the duration of the revolution chart's influence (294 days), translating these directions into days indicates the dates as shown in Table 3.11.

Look. One of the dates coincides with the promise of the primary direction, derived from radix, and points to April 2019. It is not a mere coincidence. Later, you'll see that we will use primary directions derived from revolution charts to refine the approximate event date with an accuracy of several days.

This direction occurred on April 5. Ten days later, on April 15, I filed for marriage, and I received the marriage certificate in May.

P.S. To ensure that such a remarkable connection between Venus and the 7th house doesn't occur frequently, we can cast a Venusian return chart for the date following the direction, promising marriage (Fig. 3.14).

You can see that Venus is primarily connected with Saturn through conjunction and disposition and with Mars through disposition. Still, neither Saturn nor Mars has any essential relation to the 7th house, Venus's aspect does not fall on the cusp of the 7th, and Venus is not the ruler of the 7th house. In the subsequent cycle, Venus assumes entirely different roles unrelated to love and marriage.

Solar and Lunar Returns

Unlike the revolutions of other planets, when two luminaries—the Moon or the Sun—return to their original positions at the moment of birth, they refresh not only their roles but also the roles of all other planets in the horoscope.

We can examine any planet in solar and lunar returns and compare its natal roles or ones in primary directions with those it receives in the solar or lunar chart. The planets significantly refresh not only their terrestrial but also celestial states.

Therefore, solar and lunar returns are more adaptable charts—we can apply them to verify the potential of any direction with the participation of any planet.

In solar and lunar return charts, there are more indicators to confirm the planets' roles.

Chapter 3. Natal Astrology

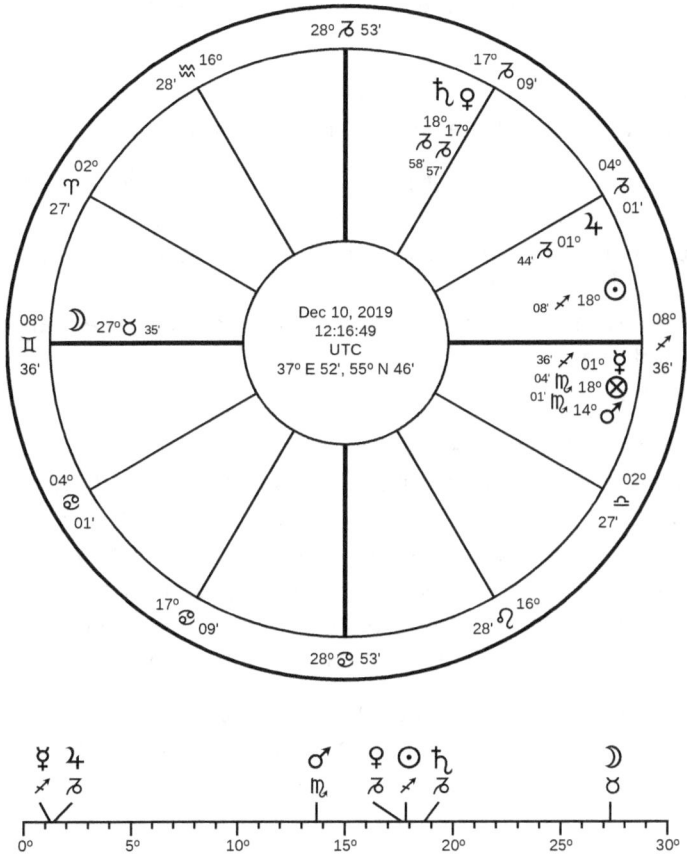

Figure 3.14: *The Following Venusian Return Chart*

- When the cusps of identical houses in the natal and solar return charts fall in the same sign, the house rulers (by sign or exaltation) repeat their roles. It is especially true if the house cusps fall in the same degree, meaning the natal planets that rule that house by close aspects reinforce their roles—their natal aspects again coincide with the solar cusp. Most house rulers repeat their roles, making the affairs of that house manifest easily this year.
- If a planet returns to its natal sign, it repeats its natal dignities/debilities, and gets the same dispositors—it also strengthens its natal role.
- Suppose a planet in the solar chart receives a close aspect from the same planet as in the natal chart. In that case, this also strengthens

its natal role regarding the circumstances signified by the aspecting planet.

Similarly, any contradiction between the solar chart and the radical figure suppresses the promises of the primary directions.

- For example, the solar return chart replaces an unfavorable aspect received by a planet in the radix with a favorable one.
- The cusp of a house in question in the solar return chart opposes the same cusp of the natal chart.
- A solar return chart replaces a debilitated state of the planet with a dignified one.
- And so on.

Since the 1st house in the solar/lunar chart indicates the native's life for the next year/month, the opposition of the 1st and 7th houses establishes an opposing flow of events in all spheres of life during this period. Morinus called this a "reversed sky." You can compare it to the action of the South Node in horary astrology. Bright promises of directions for this year will encounter resistance and are unlikely to materialize. Such a solar return usually leaves room only for minor events.

The reverse is also true. Suppose the signs and especially the degrees of the 1st house cusps of both charts coincide. In that case, the directions' promises will meet a "concurrent flow of circumstances."

Event Details in Solar/Lunar Return Charts

Similar to how a third planet may intervene in a horary question, certain houses—through their rulers and cusp degrees—can also influence the main significators in a revolution chart.

For example, in matters of childbirth, you might observe that the 5th house is negatively affected by the 4th house. The 4th house operates through its rulers and the cusp:

- The ruler of the 4th house (a debilitated planet) falls into the 5th house,
- At the same time, the 4th house cusp of revolution chart falls into the natal 5th house (or vice versa),
- Simultaneously, planets in the 4th house cast malefic aspects to the 5th house cusp, etc.

Chapter 3. Natal Astrology

The radical 4th house (your parents) cannot influence the child's birth and health. However, the 4th house as the child's 12th (illness) can. The solar return confirms the birth while adding crucial details—the newborn's fragile health. Such nuances might not appear in primary directions that simply promise a child's arrival. Thus, solar/lunar returns do not merely confirm events but can reveal surrounding circumstances. We will see this in the section "Example №40: Relocated Solar Return."

The same applies to the two most important houses of a solar/lunar return chart—the 1st and 10th. They indicate the native's life and activities during the following year or month. If they are influenced by an unknown house (i.e., one not relevant to the question) through its rulers or cusp, this can specify the accompanying circumstances of the main event.

However, it is essential to remember that without detailed knowledge of the specific context of the current year and month, it will be challenging (if not impossible) to determine the particular significance of other houses interposing the event.

Let us continue predicting marriage using my natal chart as an example, casting both solar and lunar return charts to confirm or reject the main event.

Example №37: Solar Return Chart

We will cast a solar return chart (Fig. 3.15) during which the marriage direction[24] occurred. In this chart, we will not limit ourselves to Venus as we did in Venusian return, but consider all natal planets conditioned by the 7th house in the radical figure (see the section "Alexey Borealis. Rectified Figure" on page 317).

Planets, Conditioned by the 7th House in Radix

As you may recall, the 7th house matters are represented by multiple planets in the natal chart. If most of these planets simultaneously repeat their natal roles as rulers of the 7th house in the solar return chart, the solar return will confirm the promise of the preceding direction. Let us recall which planets rule the 7th house in the natal chart.

---
[24] △ ♀ in ♉ approaches ASC, pointing to April 2019

Predictive Astrology Textbook

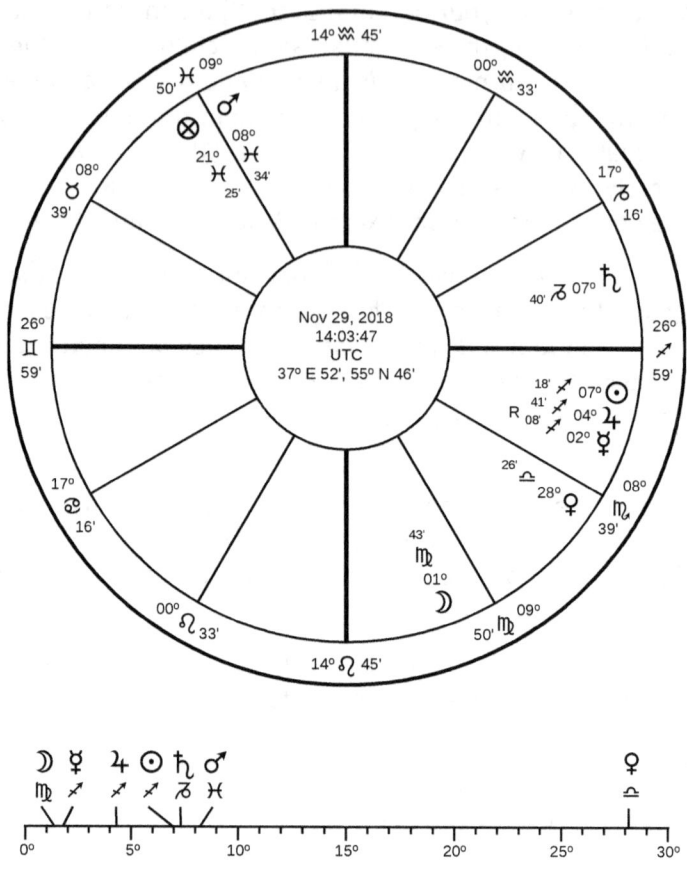

Figure 3.15: Alexey Borealis. A 43rd Solar Return Chart

- Saturn is the primary significator of the 7th house in the radix since *it occupies* it.
- Additionally, the Moon is the *accidental ruler* of the 7th house as it opposes it.
- The Sun *rules the 7th house by sign*.
- Venus is the *universal significator* of love and marriage in my chart. It can play that role since it relates to the 7th house, being its *co-ruler*, and shares the same nature.
- Mercury is less associated with the 7th house, being its *co-ruler*.
- The *secondary ruler* of the 7th house is Jupiter.

Two of these planets, Saturn and Mercury, are troublemakers. However, Mercury's disruptive influence is considerably small:

- Firstly, it is inherently beneficial, having no connection to malefic houses.
- It is under the Sun's beams, thus weakened.
- Its co-rulership of the 7th house is weaker compared to Saturn.

Such Mercury is unlikely to cause significant problems and will not produce anything good in the matters of the 7th house. Therefore, it is the least considerable planet on our list in terms of contributing to the 7th house for better or worse.

Let us examine whether these planets repeated their 7th-house-related roles in the solar return chart (Fig. 3.15).

Saturn—A Planet in the 7th House in the Radical Figure

Saturn is in the same house as in the natal chart, repeating its association with that house. However, this time, it has completely changed its celestial state. In the radix, it was debilitated, whereas in the solar return, it is dignified. The solar return suppresses the negative role of loneliness associated with Saturn in the radix. One could say that this year, the solar return gives a "green light" to the good deeds of the 7th house.

Moon—The Accidental Ruler of the 7th House in the Natal Chart

The Moon throws a close trine to the cusp of the 7th house (the boundary of the signs is not a problem) and a close aspect to the ruler of the 7th house. Additionally, the Moon throws a close aspect to the Sun—the ruler of the 7th house in the natal chart. It ties itself to the 7th house threefold.

Furthermore, the Moon becomes a co-ruler of the 1st house, repeating its natal connection with the 1st house. If, in the natal chart, the Moon ruled both the 1st and 7th houses, linking the native's life to positive episodes in the matters of the 7th house, then the Moon does the same here. It effectively creates such a positive episode.

Sun—The Ruler of the 7th House in the Natal Chart

In the solar return chart, the Sun is closely conjunct with the ruler of the 7th house. Within its 18-degree orb, the Sun also touches the cusp of the 7th house. And finally, the Sun manifests itself through its dispositor—Jupiter—who becomes the ruler of the 7th house. The Sun ties itself to the 7th house threefold.

At the same time, the Sun improved its celestial condition. The dispositor turns out to be a noble planet, and it is conjunct with the Sun. The Sun repeats and reinforces its role as the giver of good deeds in the 7th house.

Venus—Universal Significator of Love and Marriage, Co-Ruler of the 7th House in the Natal Chart

Finally, the main planet on the stage is Venus. In the natal chart, it is more capable than others of bringing love and marriage, as it is associated with the 7th house and has the similar nature. Moreover, Venus' aspect serves as the primary *promissor* of marriage this year.

Venus throws a close sextile to the cusp of the 7th house, thereby reinforcing its connection with it. Additionally, Venus has attained the most noble celestial condition. Its dispositor by exaltation is the noble Saturn, who also links Venus to the 7th house. Through an aspect, Venus receives support from the Moon, which also has a strong connection with the 7th house in this chart, as we discussed above.

Without a doubt, Venus repeats the promise of the directions.

Jupiter—Secondary Ruler of the 7th House in the Natal Chart

Let's look at the last significant planet related to the 7th house: Jupiter. It has become the ruler of the 7th house in the solar return and is conjunct with the ruler of the natal 7th house. Additionally, Jupiter is in an excellent celestial state.

Look at how many different ways the solar return reproduces the promise of the directions. We anticipate marriage this year.

Chapter 3. Natal Astrology

The 1st and the 10th Houses of the Solar Return Chart

It is also helpful to consider the 1st and 10th houses of the solar chart (life and activity for the next year) regarding the matters of the 7th house.

The ruler of the 1st house, Mercury, entered the strong dignities of Jupiter, whom we discussed earlier. Additionally, it closely approached the Sun, the ruler of the natal 7th house. This year, the native's life will be intricately woven with the events of the 7th house, emphasizing its profound significance.

The ruler of the 10th house is dignified Saturn in the 7th. Moreover, the square of natal Saturn at 16° Aquarius—Saturn's domicile—falls right on the solar MC. This promising alignment links the native's activities to successful matters of the 7th house, promising favorable results.

We have found two more confirmations of the upcoming marriage in question.

Directions from the Solar Return Chart

Let us apply primary directions to the solar return chart. First, we need to find promissors of love and marriage in that chart, similar to what we did in the radical figure.

Venus in Libra is the brightest promissor of love and marriage affairs, together with its nearest antiscion at 4° Pisces. They are more likely to produce the event the solar return chart promises. Venus's other aspects are not as favorable. Also, we will consider the promissor of marriage for this year—the natal trine of Venus at 17° Taurus. It can also produce the event and participate in directions derived from the solar return chart.

Venus and Jupiter are the brightest significators of the 7th house in the solar chart. This year, we have several directions involving these promissors and significators (see Table 3.12).

But look. One of the possible marriage dates aligns perfectly with the indications from primary directions and Venus' return.

- Primary directions point to a time around April 2019.
- Venus' return specifies the date as April 5.
- The solar return specifies it to be April 9.

Table 3.12: *Alexey Borealis: Directions From 43rd Solar Return Chart*

№	Promissor	Sgn.	Arc	Days	Date
1	Antiscion of ♀ at 2°♓	♀	129.59°	131	09 Apr
2	Antiscion of ♀ at 2°♓	♃	111.13°	113	22 Mar
3	☌ ♀ at 28°♎ (in the 5th house)	♃	341.54°	346	10 Nov
4	Natal △ ♀ at 17°♉ (less effective, since falls into the solar 12th house)	♀	234.40°	238	25 Jul
5	Natal △ ♀ at 17°♉ (less effective, since falls into the solar 12th house)	♃	221.36°	225	12 Jul

It is not a mere coincidence. As I've previously explained, primary directions provide a broad time frame, revolution charts narrow it down to a few days, and the final transit pinpoints the exact day and hour. What you're witnessing is the accurate behavior of the stars.

Some may wonder if we can find enough connections between the planets and the corresponding house each year. The answer is no. Let's cast a solar return that follows the direction of marriage and see if it can confirm marriage as effectively as the preceding return chart (Fig. 3.16).

We will consider the same planets as before.

- Saturn—the planet primarily determined by the 7th house in the natal chart—has no connection with the 7th house of this solar return. It does not repeat its role.
- Venus and Jupiter jointly rule the 7th house. Jupiter is twice connected to the 7th house—through rulership by sign and a close aspect to the cusp. Venus is associated with the 7th house only once—through rulership by exaltation. Moreover, Venus's celestial state is not as outstanding as in the previous solar return.
- The Moon—the accidental ruler of the 7th natal house—does not replicate its natal role in the solar return and does not link the 1st and 7th houses—life and love/marriage this year. Moreover, it is in exile.

Chapter 3. Natal Astrology

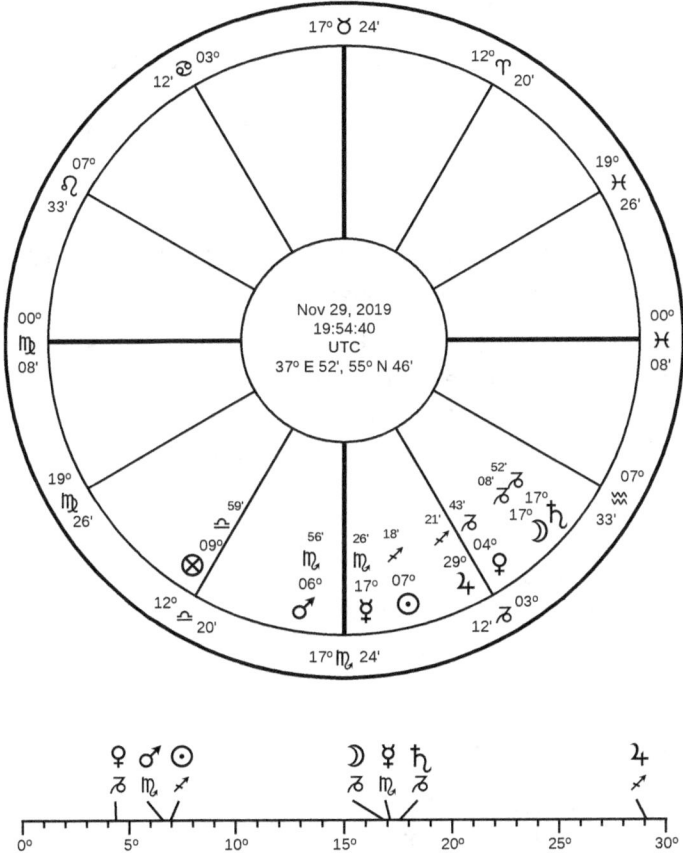

Figure 3.16: *Alexey Borealis. A 44th Solar Return Chart*

- Finally, the Sun—the ruler of the 7th house in the natal chart—is not connected to the 7th house this year except for a weak aspect to its cusp. However, such a weak aspect is insufficient to produce notable results in that house's affairs.

As you can see, compared to the first solar return, this chart is much less capable of producing good deeds related to the 7th house, so we do not expect the realization of the marriage direction while this solar return is active.

Example №38: Lunar Return

We will continue with predicting a marriage date based on my horoscope. Now, we will cast the lunar revolution chart. Lunar returns function similarly to solar return charts, except they confirm or refute the occurrence of events in a specific month of the year.

Since we have three confirmations of the timeframe (April 2019) for marriage, we can immediately cast the April lunar return to ensure that the event will indeed happen in that month.

Alternatively, for a more thorough approach, we can cast all the lunar returns throughout the year. It ensures that the lunar return for the corresponding month stands out distinctly among the others, thereby confirming the indications of the previous solar return and primary directions in that month.

I won't cast all 13 lunar return charts happening this year to show you the difference between a regular and an outstanding lunar return chart. Instead, I will examine the sixth lunar return for May and the fifth for April so you can feel the difference.

A 6th Lunar Return in 2019

This lunar return occurs at the end of April and extends throughout May (Fig. 3.17). The first thing to note is the "reversed sky" effect. The cusps of the 1st and 7th houses are in opposition (by signs) to the natal cusps, immediately weakening any promises of this lunar return chart.

Natal Saturn once again governs the 7th house here. By its celestial state, it rewrites the role of "loneliness" from the natal chart, giving the green light to the 7th house's good deeds. It does not promise love and marriage for the next 27 days; it simply removes the limitations imposed by the natal Saturn.

However, in this chart, no planets can produce good deeds in the 7th house. If we look at the planets associated with the 7th house of the natal chart, we will see that they do not repeat their roles this month.

- Jupiter, which governs the last 3 degrees of the lunar 7th house, is insignificantly conditioned to the affairs of love and marriage, so it cannot repeat its role.

Chapter 3. Natal Astrology

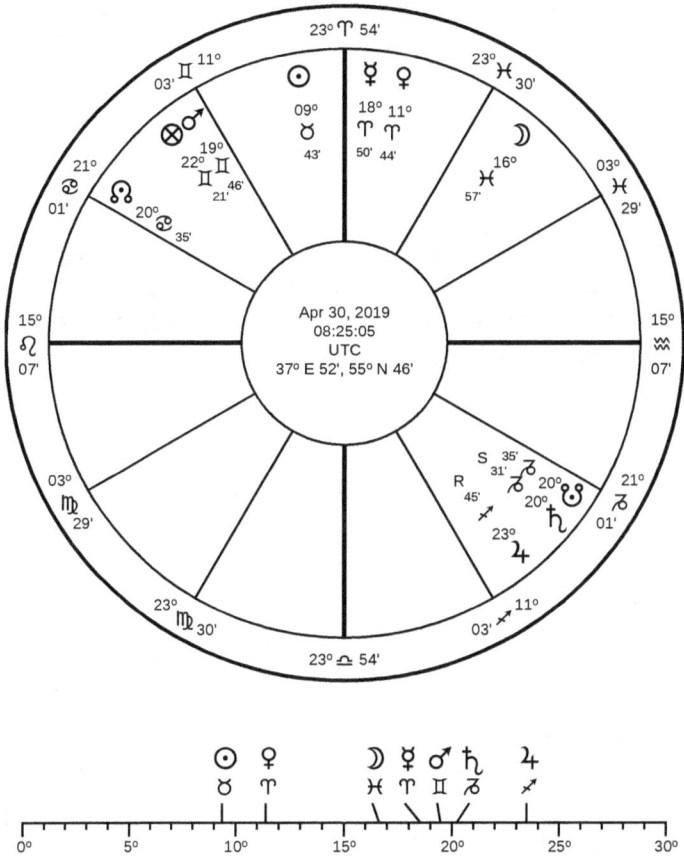

Figure 3.17: *Alexey Borealis. A 6th Lunar Return.*

- Venus, casting a close aspect to the 7th house cusp, is detrimental and suppresses its role in love and marriage for the next 27 days.
- The Sun has no significant connection with the 7th house (except for a distant aspect to the cusp, which is weak to confirm its role).
- Only the Moon remains, casting an aspect to the ruler of the 7th, Saturn. But this aspect is unfavorable—it falls into the Moon's fall. Therefore, with this aspect, the Moon does not create anything good regarding the affairs of the 7th house, i.e., it does not repeat its role of a wife-giver.

Predictive Astrology Textbook

As you can see, this chart barely confirms the indications of the previous solar return and directions. But a lunar return cast at the beginning of April shows an entirely different picture.

A 5th Lunar Return

This lunar return shows an entirely different picture (Fig. 3.18). First, note that the degrees of the cusps of all houses in the natal and lunar charts almost coincide. This rare phenomenon powerfully reinforces any promise this lunar return has.

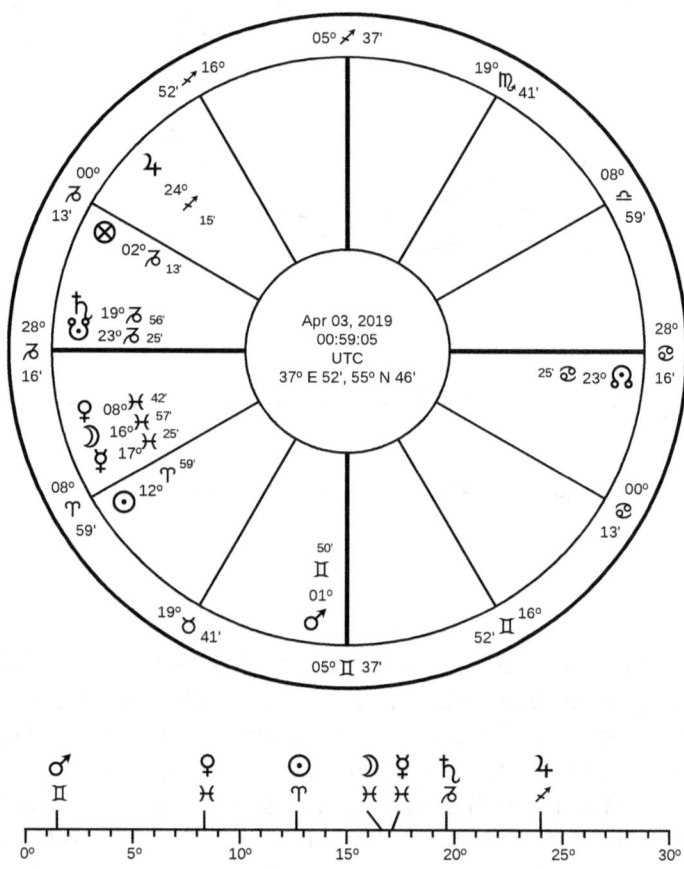

Figure 3.18: *Alexey Borealis. A 5th Lunar Return*

Chapter 3. Natal Astrology

Planets Conditioned by the 7th House in Radix Now, let's see if the same natal planets determined to bring good in love affairs—Venus, Moon, Saturn, Sun, and Jupiter—repeat their roles in the lunar return. For this, we consider their terrestrial and celestial states in the lunar return chart. We will be interested in their connection with the 7th house.

Two planets, Venus and the Moon, which create good deeds in the natal 7th house, accidentally rule the 7th house in this lunar return, placed in the opposite 1st house.

The Moon repeats its natal role as the planet in the 1st house, which connects life and good episodes of the 7th house. Now, along with Venus, it does the same even more effectively. Additionally, the Moon rules the 7th house in the solar return chart.

Besides accidentally ruling the 7th house, Venus co-rules it as in the natal chart. Moreover, it has acquired maximum dignity this month, promising wonderful deeds of love and marriage. Like the Moon, by its position in the 1st house, it favorably connects the 1st and 7th houses for the next 27 days.

Both planets are under the rulership of dignified Jupiter and manifest through it. Jupiter, in the natal chart, is the secondary ruler of the 7th house. In the lunar return, it is the ruler of the 7th house by exaltation.

Saturn casts a close aspect to the Moon—the ruler of the 7th house in the lunar return chart—thus again connecting itself with the 7th house. Saturn also conjoins with the natal Venus, once again linking itself with what she signifies in the natal chart in general and in this lunar return in particular, namely, love and marriage.

This time, Saturn cancels its role of "loneliness" from the natal chart, giving the green light for benefic Venus, Jupiter, and the Moon to fulfill their promise of marriage this month.

The Sun in the lunar return chart is close to the 7° Aries. Please recall that this degree is one of the prominent promissors of love and marriage, the place of favorable △☉ at 7°♈ in the radix. It even produced the first marriage earlier (see the table "Events for Rectification"). Thus, in this lunar return, the Sun reestablishes its connection with its natal role as the 7th house ruler. The Sun's exalted state confirms that it will bring much good to the affairs of the 7th house.

The 1st and 10th Houses of Lunar Return The connection between the 1st and 10th houses (life and actions this month) and the 7th house of love & marriage is also clearly visible in this chart. Regarding the 1st house, we have already mentioned:

- Both planets promising marriage are located in the 1st house.
- The ruler of the 1st house is dignified Saturn, closely linked by aspect to the ruler of the 7th house and conjoined with the natal Venus.

The connection between the 10th and 7th houses is also notable.

- Jupiter, the ruler of the 10th house, is the dispositor of the Moon and Venus. Both planets portend love and marriage and manifest through Jupiter.
- Jupiter itself is the ruler of the 7th house by exaltation.
- In addition, Jupiter is dignified.

You can see how this lunar return stands out compared to others. We have found a dozen confirmations that prove the promise of the preceding direction and solar return chart for this month.

Directions From the Lunar Return Chart

Now, we can calculate the primary directions from the lunar return chart to find the date of the event within the current month.

Venus and the Moon are the most prominent planets determined by the 7th house and simultaneously promise love and marriage. However, I would prefer the Moon in this chart, as besides being the promissor of marriage, the Moon is the primary planet in the lunar return chart. It's her return to the initial position (in a position that connects the native's life with a good episode of the 7th house) that refreshed the states of all planets, including those we have just discussed.

I also chose the most favorable aspect through which the Moon is most likely to produce the event. It's her trine in Cancer. This aspect has more dignity than the Moon's bodily position, thus having more chances of realization. Additionally, the events can be triggered by the main promissor of the preceding direction—the trine of the natal Venus at 17° Taurus.

Let's direct these promissors to the significators of the 7th house of the lunar return chart, the Moon, Venus, and DSC.[25] Here's what we get (see Table 3.13).

Table 3.13: *Alexey Borealis: Directions From Lunar Return Chart*

Promissor	Significator	Date
Lunar △ ☽ in ♋	DSC	29 Apr
Lunar △ ☽ in ♋	Venus	09 Apr
Lunar △ ☽ in ♋	The Moon	08 Apr
Natal △ ♀ in ♉	DSC	23 Apr
Natal △ ♀ in ♉	Venus	05 Apr
Natal △ ♀ in ♉	The Moon	04 Apr

The dates indicated earlier in the Venus return chart (April 5) and the solar return chart (April 9) are repeated here. This means we have a narrow window from April 5 to 9 when a transit can trigger the event.

Our next task in the forecast will be to find a suitable transit on a specific day and hour within that short time range. We will discuss the transit technique further in this book. For now, let's stick to the fact that the direction's central promise must be realized sometime around these dates.

The attentive reader may have noticed that I described how I filed an application for marriage registration on April 14 and received the marriage certificate on May 15. So why does the chart insist on either April 5 or 9?

The answer is simple. Indeed, after deciding to start a family, my future spouse and I went to the registry office on April 9 to file for marriage. However, my passport lacked space for the marriage stamp, so we had to spend a few more days renewing the passport and resubmitting the application later.

As you can see, the minor circumstances of life make their adjustments. Interestingly, from the perspective of the celestial schedule, the wedding date turned out not to be the date of celebration, not the date

---

[25] Morinus wrote that in solar and lunar return charts, one must include directions to the ASC and Midheaven as significators of life and activity for the upcoming year/month, as well as directions to the Sun and Moon as the primary planets making the solar/lunar returns. However, for simplicity of demonstration, I skip this step at this stage. You will see a full example of how to construct directions from the return chart in the section "Example №41: Predicting the Exact Day of the Event."

of receiving the marriage certificate, but the very day when I took the initiative to get married. It indeed happened on April 9, 2019.

Such behavior of natal charts makes me quite skeptical of modern astrologers' attempts to make mundane forecasts based on horoscopes of states constructed at the moment of signing constitutions or declarations of independence. Such moments are determined mainly by the schedule of official ceremonies on a particular day, not by the stars.

Traditionally, mundane forecasts assume different logic, but this goes beyond the scope of this book.

Narrowing Down Planetary Meanings

Observe how planets refine their roles and timing of manifestation through predictive techniques. For example, Venus in my natal chart has multiple significations—it represents money, love, illnesses, and mortal threats.

Primary directions: Venus's benefic aspect approached the ASC, eliminating the roles of illness and mortal threats. We expected a positive event regarding finances or love in **April 2019**.

Preceding Venusian return: It confirmed that Venus's primary role in the coming 294 days would concern love—Venus conjoined the ruler of the 7th house and entered its domicile. Directions from the Venusian return chart point to the same **April 2019**.

2019 Solar return chart: It confirmed that Venus would signify love and marriage that year, not wealth. First, Venus achieved maximum dignity through a double connection with the solar return's 7th house. Second, the solar return's 7th house compelled (determined) all other natal marriage significators to manifest specifically in matters of love and marriage that year. Directions from the solar return also pointed to **April 2019**.

April 2019 Lunar return: It confirmed Venus would indeed act as marriage significator that month. First, Venus attained excellent celestial state with a double 7th house connection. Second, the lunar return

Chapter 3. Natal Astrology

similarly inclined all natal marriage significators toward 7th house matters specifically in April 2019. Directions from the solar return further narrowed the timing to a specific period within April when the marriage would occur.

This is precisely how predictive astrology functions. By systematically applying forecasting techniques, you determine:

- Which specific role a planet will assume during a particular period of your life
- In which year this role will manifest
- During which month of that year the manifestation will fully mature
- On which exact day the promised event will occur

Revolutions Confirming Initiating Directions

As I wrote earlier in the section "Initiating Directions," some directions initiate a long-term process rather than create a short-lived event, for example:

- They may initiate a severe illness that will lead to death; or
- They may bring an unsuccessful marriage that will result in a quick divorce; or
- Create a lawsuit, followed by bankruptcy over time.

The logical outcomes resulting from such processes are often no longer reflected in the directions. You saw this in the chart of Donald Trump, who won the election race in 2024. He had a clear direction for success when he started the race in 2022, but no directions for success in 2024.

You can observe this in the chart of Cardinal Richelieu or King George VI, who died from a severe illness. They have clear directions for deadly diseases but no directions for death.

At the same time, the solar return chart cast for the year of illness only confirms the disease. The solar return chart for the following year may occasionally show the outcome of the disease—either death or recovery—even though no explicitly fatal or recovery directions occurred that year. But often, it shows nothing. It means that the timing of specific events is not the subject of the horoscope. These events are simply a consequence of the processes initiated by preceding directions.

For example, in Trump's case, the year of a presidential election—the outcome of the initiated race—is no longer a consequence of the directions derived from the natal chart or the solar return chart. The election year is determined by the mechanics of terrestrial processes.

Therefore, you must exercise great caution in long-term forecasts—primary directions may not always reflect sudden career successes, death, bankruptcy, divorce, and so on if they are the logical consequences of the preceding processes, that started on suitable *initiating directions*. But the revolution charts may occasionally indicate such events.

Example №39: Solar Return Confirming Initiating Direction

Let's go back to Albert Einstein's horoscope (Fig. 3.19).

In March 1953, a notable direction occurred—an unfavorable Jupiter's trine in Gemini approaching debilitated Saturn.

It may have several meanings, and we do not know in advance which of them will manifest. Therefore, we must first consider all possible meanings and choose the most obvious one in the context of the current year. Below, I will show how to do this.

Saturn signifies several areas of life:

- Matters of the 10th house,
- Matters of the 8th house, and
- Matters of the 9th and 7th houses.

The unfavorable event promised by Jupiter relates to one of these four areas of life. Jupiter has many promises regarding these areas, for example:

- It may signify an unfavorable period in scientific activities (as it rules the 9th house relative to the 10th).
- It may be a mortal threat (as it rules by exaltation the 1st house relative to the 8th house of death).
- It may show dramatic relocation (as it rules the 9th relative to the 9th house of other countries).
- It may signify conflicts (as it rules the 1st house relative to the 7th).

Chapter 3. Natal Astrology

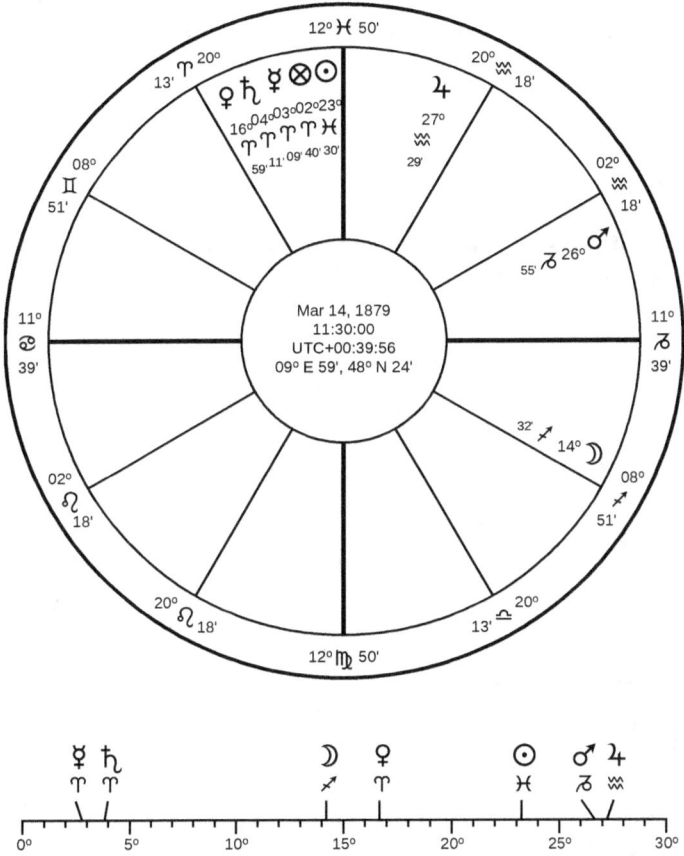

Figure 3.19: *Albert Einstein*

Jupiter's trine falls into the 12th house of the chart, ruling out the significance of all houses except the 12th. It narrows the list of options but still needs clarification.

So, we also need to consider the context. This year, Einstein was 75 years old, had recently had an operation, lived in Princeton, and didn't have open enemies at the time.

The context completely rules out Saturn's meanings, such as dramatic relocation or open enemies. According to the third and fourth determinations, Saturn can only signify mortal threats connected to diseases (as it is connected with the ruler of the 12th house).

Predictive Astrology Textbook

So, we see a classic direction initiating fatal illness. The next direction, which happens a month after that, is Algol approaching ASC—the significator of health and bodily state. It supports the testimony of deadly disease.

Solar Return

Let's check if the solar return, happening after this direction, confirms this promise (Fig. 3.20).

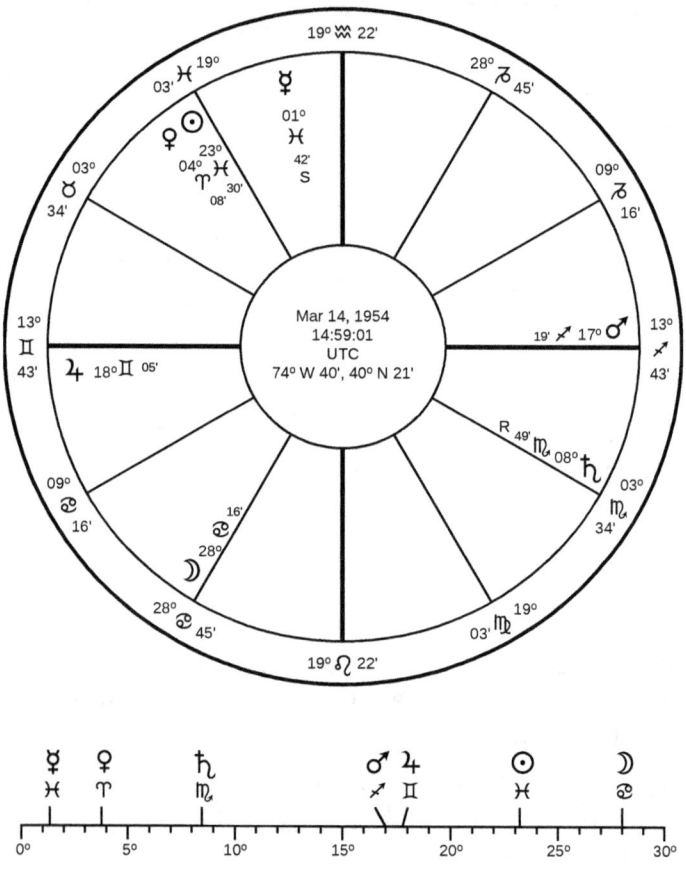

Figure 3.20: *Albert Einstein's Solar Return*

The first thing we see in the chart below is malefic Jupiter, indicating fragile health—the role inheriting from the primary directions as discussed above, afflicting the 1st house. Poor health will affect the native's life in the coming year.

Next, natal Mercury, which signifies illness and conjoined with Saturn, the significator of mortal threat in the direction, became the ruler of the native's life this year. Moreover, it fell into a bad celestial state, being in Jupiter's domicile, and became stationary. Mercury connects illness with the native's poor and immobile state this year. It is another strong confirmation of the onset of disease.

Jupiter (fragile health) has become almost exactly opposite Mars—the secondary ruler of the 8th house that partially conjunct its cusp in the natal 8th house and the ruler of the 8th house of solar return charts by exaltation. Fragile life is under mortal threat.

In the natal chart, Mars creates mortal threats but also protects from them due to its exaltation. This year, this exaltation is absent. Mars repeats its role of mortal threat but loses any significance of protection from death. In other words, Mars becomes the significator of possible death—a possible *anaereta* in the solar return chart.

Saturn, which signifies death in the natal chart and the significator of mortal threat in the preceding direction, repeats its role this year. Still, this time, it takes on an additional (clarifying) significance of illness, as its significant "copy" in place of its opposition falls on the cusp of the 12th house of diseases. It again connects illness with death.

For the coming year, Venus has become the ruler of illness. Judging by her celestial state, it should be a severe disease. Moreover, Venus casts an aspect to the Moon—the significator of the native's life—the ruler of the natal 1st house and co-ruler of the solar return 1st house. By itself, such an indication is unlikely to cause illness. Venus is not associated with the 12th house of the natal chart and cannot assume a role it does not inherently possess.

However, as a momentary accidental significator of illness in the solar return chart, it can contribute to clarifying the overall picture. In this case, this clarification fits perfectly with the central promise of the solar return.

Look at how many indications of a fatal illness we have discovered. I want to emphasize that this is not a deadly solar return, as it predicts a severe disease associated with death, not death itself. The end of this illness may occur later, upon the completion of the solar return cycle.

If we did not know the context of life and were unaware of the previous direction of illness, we could have randomly chosen entirely different interpretations of this solar return. For example, we could say that the malefic Jupiter in the 1st house signifies a harsh life and failures due to the native's actions.

Based on this initial postulate, Mars, opposing Jupiter from the 7th house of open enemies, indicates conflicts with scientific opponents. In this context, we would consider Venus, a planet, determined by the 11th house in both charts, as conflicting friends, who cast an aspect to the Moon—the significator of the native's life in both charts. Therefore, we would forecast significant conflicts with opponents in which close friends will participate.

Alternatively, we could start with Mercury, the ruler of the 1st house, being in a terrible state in the 10th house, foreshadowing business problems. From this randomly selected perspective, the ruler of the natal 10th house, afflicting the 1st house, also indicates life in the following year, affected by professional failure. In this case, we would arrive at a completely different interpretation.

It once again confirms the idea: *Considering the solar return chart outside the context of the previous direction turns the forecast into a guessing game of "whose astrological intuition is better." But astrology is not divination.*

N.B.

The next direction, involving Saturn, occurs in January 1955, when the antiscion of Saturn (the *promissor* of death) approaches the cusp of the 8th house (the significator of death). Albert Einstein passed away two months after this killing direction.

Clarification of Event Details

Now, let's explore how to specify the event. Since the chart indicates illness rather than anything else, we can consider it from a medical perspective.

Mercury, the significator of illness in the natal chart and the significator of the ill body for the next year, becomes debilitated in Jupiter's dignity. It manifests through Jupiter, indicating that Jupiter is the cause of the severe disease. In medical astrology, Jupiter signifies blood vessels, the liver, and the state of blood. Therefore, the cause of the disease could be vascular wear, liver dysfunction, or internal bleeding.

Jupiter (liver, worn vessels, state of blood or internal bleeding) opposes Mars, indicating ruptures and resulting bleeding. In such a close aspect, these two planets act together and jointly indicate the exact cause of the illness.

At the intersection of their significations, we see the shared meaning—internal bleeding (the cause of impending death).

Once again, I emphasize that this solar return proves the onset of a fatal disease, not death itself. His death, however, occurred in April 1955, under the influence of the subsequent solar return. The cause of death was the rupture of an aortic—the body's main artery—with a significant loss of blood.

The subsequent direction (Algol approaching the ASC in January 1955), as well as the subsequent solar return, do not promise death but merely leave open the possibility. If the native is bedridden due to old age, triggered by the initiating direction toward a fatal illness, he may well pass away in the following year, 1955.

However, if the native is young and full of vitality, the directions and the solar return in 1955 alone are insufficient to cause death—the direction of a single star is weak evidence for such an event, and the subsequent solar return also does not clearly foreshadow the passing.

It is a classic example of events occurring not in connection with directions but as a logical consequence of preceding processes. In *Astrologia Gallica*, Morinus particularly emphasized the significance of this behavior of natal charts[26]. He explained the confusion of many medieval

---

[26] J.-B. Morinus. *Astrologia Gallica, Book 24. Progressions and Transits.* Hagae, 1661d

astrologers who often could not find the date of monarchs' coronations. The answer is simple—coronations occur not as a result of directions but as a consequence of inevitable earthly processes to which the stars exert no influence.

Relocation

General Principle

Perhaps you noticed I used the native's current location rather than the birthplace for solar return charts. The solar return confirms or rejects the indications of the previous direction relative to a specific geographic area.

You can consider the revolution chart as a multitude of transit charts simultaneously constructed in different locations worldwide. These charts confirm and refine the year's main event differently, depending on where corresponding trends unfold.

In other words, if a direction promises something good or bad, it will be realized or not, depending on where you live in that particular year. This makes long-term predictions challenging for individuals who frequently travel. You never know which city they will live in a specific year or which place on Earth their lives and fates are connected to.

Many astrologers believe that selecting a place where the solar return is most favorable and experiencing the moment of solar return in that place allows one to encounter the most promising events—career advancements, the birth of a child, wealth, success, and so on. But that's not the case.

Firstly, if there is no corresponding direction for success, children, or finances, even the most prominent solar return will yield no significant changes.

Secondly, the solar return influences not only the moment of occurrence but also continues throughout the entire planetary cycle, laying down and sustaining the daily flow of events leading to the realization of the event in that place.

By briefly visiting a new city and returning, individuals find themselves back in the stream of events they sought to escape. This stream, as before, will either contribute to or hinder the realization of the event promised in the primary directions relative to the current location.

If you see an unfavorable event confirmed by a solar return chart constructed in a specific place, the only way to avoid the event is to relocate to another place for the entire duration of the solar return, where there is a directly opposite trend: the solar, lunar, and other planets' return charts in the new location should suppress the promises of the vivid direction.

Even if you find such a place and organize relocation for a year, it still implies a radical change in context. It means that, according to the fourth determination, the promise of the *promissor* in the direction may not materialize due to an incompatible context.

Also, keep in mind that if the event is a consequence of an inevitable process, like death due to a fatal illness, the relocation won't help at all.

Example №40: Relocated Solar Return

Here is the horoscope of a young woman (Fig. 3.21). In 2012, a significant event was expected in her life (according to her natal chart). She and her husband were on a short tour of several countries, and she celebrated her solar return while traveling. Let us use this example to test whether meeting the solar return in a new location—followed by a return home—can indeed alter the key event of the year.

Our verification plan will be as follows:

— We will determine the key event of 2012 based on primary directions.
— Then, we will verify whether the solar return for her place of residence confirms this event.
— Next, we will confirm that the solar return celebrated during travel does *not* confirm the event.
— Finally, we will compare the promise of the relocated solar return with reality and draw conclusions.

In 2012, there was only one significant direction in her life: a noble promissor, △♀ at 8°♎ approached Jupiter (the significator of a particular area of life where this positive event will occur).

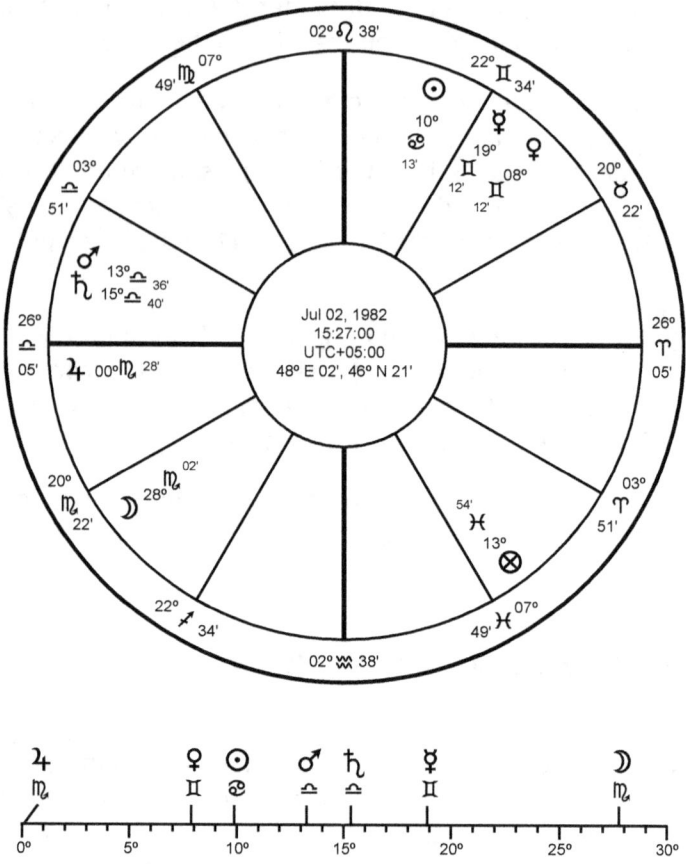

Figure 3.21: *Radical Chart for Relocation*

Promissor and Significator

Let's start with Jupiter:

- It is located in the 1st house, representing life as a whole. This doesn't specify a particular area of life.
- It rules the 3rd and 5th houses, indicating siblings or children.

In the context of the woman's life, no events related to siblings are anticipated, but the birth of a child is a pretty plausible option. If our hypothesis is correct, Venus must directly connect to the 5th house to signify a child. Let's verify this:

- Venus rules the 5th house by exaltation.
- It casts an almost exact aspect to the cusp of the 5th house in its place of exaltation. This specific aspect of Venus relative to the 5th house promises a child.

Indeed, we see that the *promissor* of a child approaches Jupiter, the *significator* of children and life as a whole, which indicates the birth of a child in 2012.

Additionally, it's worth noting that in the natal chart, Venus is under the influence of Mercury, the ruler of the 9th house. Literally, conception occurs in the context of Mercury and what it represents—namely, a long journey or being abroad.

Now, let's check our hypothesis and see if any promissor is approaching another significator of a child—the cusp of the 5th house.

And there is such a direction: △ ♀ at 8°♒ approaches the cusp of the 5th house, pointing to July 2012. We already know that, relative to 5th-house matters, Venus promises a child. This serves as a second confirmation of the year's key event.[27]

Solar Return for the Place of Residence

Now, we cast the solar return for the place of residence (which coincides with the birthplace) to check whether conception will occur if the woman does not relocate this year (Fig. 3.22).

I selected the solar return starting in July 2012 for the following reason: the timing of conception indicated by directions (March–July 2012) closely aligns with the beginning of that solar return, where its potential is at its peak.

Thus, we expect conception to occur in the spring or summer of 2012.

Planets conditioned by the 5th house: In this solar return, I focus on just two planets—Jupiter and Venus.[28] Do they repeat their roles as planets of children? Let's see:

---

[27] Although this promissor lacks essential dignity—i.e., it is "neutral" and merely opens the possibility of an event—it reinforces and complements the primary direction for children, actively realizing this window of opportunity.

[28] No other planets are determined by the natal 5th house to manifest in the 5th house affairs.

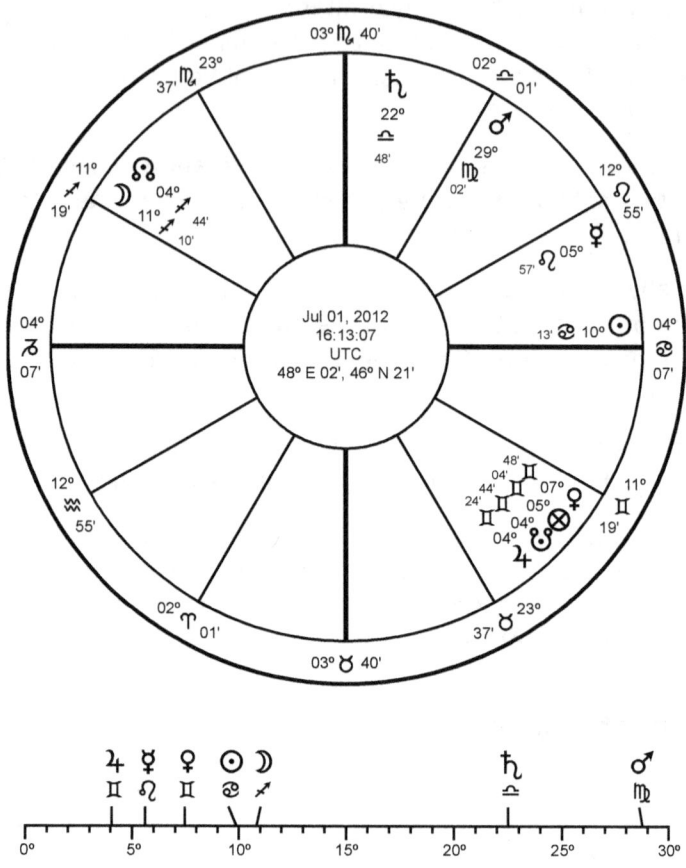

Figure 3.22: *Solar Return for Place of Residence*

- Venus in the solar return conjuncts its natal position, strengthening its natal role. As we recall, it predicts a child. This is the first confirmation.
- Venus is placed in the 5th house of children, not elsewhere in the chart. This is the second confirmation.
- Jupiter is also in the house of children, reaffirming its natal role as the ruler of the 5th house.
- Jupiter (the significator of children) conjuncts Venus (the promissor of children) in this solar return, repeating the configuration of the primary directions.
- Finally, Venus, in the solar return, becomes the ruler of the 5th house of children.

Chapter 3. Natal Astrology

We also consider the 1st and the 10th houses—life and activity this year. The ruler of the upcoming year, Saturn, who rules the 1st house, will manifest under the influence of its dispositor, Venus. This indicates that the year will be centered around conception and pregnancy. This is the fifth confirmation of conception around July of this year.

We have six confirmations.

Thus, the solar return confirms six times that conception will occur around July 2012 (as promised by primary directions).

Clarification of event details: Moreover, the solar return provides additional details about the circumstances of conception:

- This year, Venus is again under Mercury's influence, reiterating its meaning of "conception abroad," as noted earlier.
- Venus becomes the ruler of the 9th house of long journeys, linking conception to foreign countries.
- The ruler of active endeavors, i.e., the 10th house this year, Mars, also comes under the influence of Mercury, the significator of foreign lands in the natal chart. This suggests that part of the year will involve travel.
- Saturn, the ruler of the year's life direction, is located in the 9th house of the solar return. Its trine at 22° Gemini precisely aligns with the cusp of the 9th house in the natal chart—another indication that part of the year will involve travel.
- Venus in the solar return casts a close aspect to the cusp of the solar return's 9th house, once again connecting conception to a distant journey.
- Jupiter in the solar return is in Gemini. This indicates that either conception will not occur, as Jupiter is in detriment, or that conception will happen during travel, since Jupiter operates under Mercury's influence, the ruler of the 9th house in the natal chart. Considering all the above, the second interpretation is chosen, further confirming the conception away from home.

Therefore, the solar return for the birthplace clarifies that the year's key event is conception around July 2012, which will occur abroad.

Solar Return for the Relocation

The woman celebrated her solar return in Munich. This gives us a perfect opportunity to test whether a short-term relocation works. Let's analyze the solar return for Munich (Fig. 3.23).

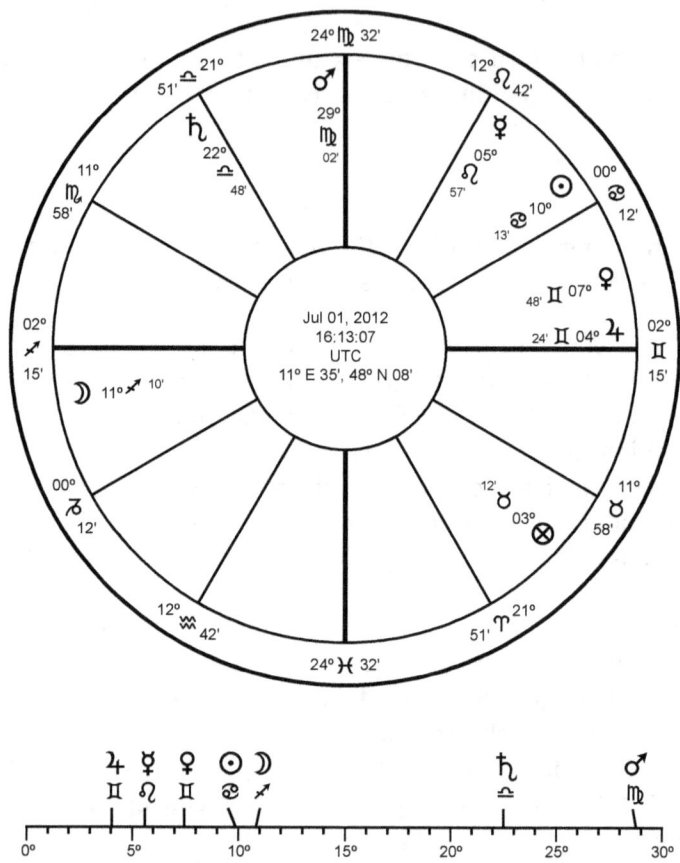

Figure 3.23: *Relocated Solar Return*

Planets Conditioned by the 5th House: Again, we start by analyzing the natal planets—Venus and Jupiter—to see if they repeated their natal roles:

- Here, Venus also returned to its natal position and conjoined Jupiter, reaffirming its natal role related to children. However, that is where the confirmations end.
- Venus lost its connection to the 5th house in the solar return—it no longer rules or resides in it.
- In the solar return, Jupiter also lost its connection to the 5th house—it is no longer positioned there.

The 1st and the 10th houses: Jupiter, the ruler of the natal 5th house, became the ruler of the year's life (i.e., the ruler of the solar ASC). This is the second confirmation of conception.

Mars, the planet in the MC, becomes the ruler of the 5th house—it connects the main activities of the year with the child's arrival. However, Mars is not determined by the 5th house, so it cannot repeat the role that it inherently does not possess.[29]

> **N.B.**
>
> Please note that Venus's return to its natal position and its conjunction with Jupiter do not depend on the city—this celestial phenomenon is equally visible from everywhere at the moment of solar return.
>
> For the sake of the rigor of the experiment, we should not give preference to one or another solarium based on these indicators. The terrestrial place where this happens matters. In the first solar return chart, this happened right in the 5th house.

The few confirmations in the relocated solar return are clearly insufficient to realize the year's main event. In other words:

The solar return calculated for the relocation place does not confirm the conception this year, while the solar return for the city of residence does.

---

[29] Strictly speaking, Mars rules the last 3 degrees of the 5th house, where the power of terrestrial determination tends to zero. Hence, it is not enough to consider Mars as an evident co-ruler of the 5th house.

Verification through event: So, we have two astrological hypotheses:

1. **Predictive astrology:** A brief stay in a new location for the solar return does not work; the solar return for the place of residence continues to operate. In this case, we expect that the woman will conceive somewhere away from home around July 2012.
2. **Modern astrology beliefs:** Relocation works; in this case, the brief trip to Munich does not create suitable conditions for the realization of conception.

Here is what happened in reality. The woman described the events of that year as follows:

> "My husband and I were in Munich from June 27 to July 7, then we went to the Czech Republic and stayed there until July 20. That's when conception occurred—around July 20. I also gave birth to my first daughter while traveling. My friends even joked that I needed to go abroad to get pregnant."

And there's a grain of truth in this joke—the birth chart clearly reveals a pattern: Venus, which connects the native's life path and their children (as the ruler of the 1st house by sign and the 5th house by exaltation and aspect), operates against the backdrop of Mercury—the ruler of the 9th house of foreign countries.

As you can see, in this specific example, Hypothesis 1 was confirmed: with a short stay in a new place and subsequent return to the place of residence, the solar return for the place of residence continues to operate.

Why do we see a short-term relocated solar return not working? As I see it, the answer is that a solar return is tied both to the person's location and natal chart. The essence of a solar return is to form a flow of events or circumstances that facilitate the realization of the year's main event within the conditions where the person spends most of their time.

In our case, the woman spent most of her time living in her hometown, where she already had a family: her husband and first daughter. A brief trip to Munich and subsequent return did not change this context—her husband, family, and living conditions remained constant. If, under these conditions, the stars predetermined a journey, conception, and pregnancy, then this scenario would unfold based on the circumstances of her permanent residence.

Chapter 3. Natal Astrology

For the Munich scenario to manifest, she would have needed to move to Germany beforehand and live there for some time, creating a new life context to let the local solar return chart operate within this new framework. In that case, according to the Munich solar return, conception would not have occurred in 2012.

The takeaway from this case is to focus on the solar return for the place of permanent residence, where the person is tied to their current circumstances and spends most of their time.

Planetary Transits

General Principle

This technique allows us to specify the exact day of an event's realization. As you have already seen, the primary directions derived from revolution charts indicate short periods of time (usually several days) during which we expect the event to manifest.

Planetary transits denote specific moments within this short interval when planets replicate their natal roles in their movement—entering corresponding houses in the current moment, ruling them, aspecting their cusps or rulers, and acquiring the corresponding celestial state.

For example, if Mars promises financial disruptions, to repeat this role, it should afflict the 2nd house of the transit chart in its daily motion. First, it should lack any dignity or even be debilitated to act as an accidentally malefic planet. Second, it should either be inside the 2nd house, become its ruler, or cast an adverse aspect on its cusp or its ruler. Additionally, it could afflict the ASC of the current moment as the debilitated ruler of the 2nd—that would also be a suitable configuration, echoing the promise of financial collapse.

Suppose in the natal chart Jupiter also relates to the 2nd house but acts contrary to Mars—it casts a favorable aspect to the cusp of the 2nd house, protecting against financial losses. In this case, it is essential that transiting Jupiter nullify its protective function. For instance, at the current moment, Jupiter might become afflicted, receive adverse aspects from malefic planets, combust under the Sun's rays, or in any other way diminish its natal significations as the guardian of wealth.

We always superimpose the transit chart on the natal one. The transiting planets must not only repeat their roles in transit but also pass through the degrees of the natal chart responsible for the event in question to reinforce their meaning again.

For instance, if we are searching for transits regarding illness, we want to select a time when the ruler of the momentary 12th house not only repeats its role but also afflicts the radical 1st house or strengthens the radical 12th. For example, it could pass over the natal ASC, approach the natal ruler of the 12th or its adverse aspect, or conjoin with the 12th house cusp of the natal chart.

The same applies to house cusps. Suppose the natal ASC falls on the cusp of the momentary 12th house or vice versa. In that case, this is also an auspicious moment for the onset of illness.

In a well-selected transit, several planets simultaneously replicate their natal roles and pass through corresponding degrees of the natal chart. Such transit configurations typically persist for several minutes and then dissipate.

It is the most thorough forecasting technique, as you must cast transit charts with an interval of several minutes over the desired period of a few days when you expect an event.

- If it turns out that a significant transit does not occur within the specified period, then with high probability, the event will only happen if the context highly suggests the event realization. So, you should be aware of the context.
- Suppose there are several suitable transit moments within a short time interval. In that case, we choose the one where the number of planets repeating the promised event and the number of their transits through the corresponding points of the natal chart is maximal. We also give priority to transits that occur right after the beginning of the lunar return cycle, as the start of a planetary revolution holds the greatest potential for realization.

How Not to Use Transits

Some astrologers attempt to use transits as a standalone prognostic technique. They cast transit charts to forecast tiny events of the day.

Chapter 3. Natal Astrology

But this is different from how natal astrology works. Transits serve to refine the timing of significant events when we know:

- Which planets and which cusps are in question, and
- A short interval of several days when the expected event should occur.

Transit planets pass through various points of the horoscope each day. But this does not mean that all major life events occur daily. There is no decisive way to distinguish a transit that produces nothing substantial from a transit that brings an essential event of the year on a particular day.

Therefore, use transits only as a final refinement of the event, which is already well known and expected to occur within a defined period of several days.

Note that events do not occur minute by minute at the moment of transit. Sometimes, the natural flow of events may delay an event by several hours or days. For example, you receive a significant promotion at work on a specific transit, but the transit occurs over the weekend, so the order for your new assignment will be signed two days later, on Monday.

While it is possible to predict an exact date, I recommend avoiding the extensive use of transits for the following reasons. Although you may often be right—and this will certainly impress your clients—an error of even a day will be perceived as if you could not make a correct forecast at all. The client often does not care whether you were off by just one day or a whole year—in their eyes, you still made a mistake.

From a practical standpoint, transits are not particularly necessary for natal forecasting—if you manage to pinpoint the month and year of an event and see that the life context has already begun to favor the realization of the promised outcome, then almost certainly, the event will occur in the specified month and year. So, indicating the correct month and year of the event is already an excellent forecast. Few people demand an exact date from you. However, there is a rare situation where transits can indeed be helpful.

Imagine that directions derived from revolution charts indicate an event in early January or mid-August. Meanwhile, lunar returns confirm both months equally. In this case, selecting the appropriate transit can help determine the correct date.

Let us see how transits work in practice.

Example №41: Predicting the Exact Day of the Event

We have the natal chart of a young woman, and our goal is to determine the exact date of her wedding.

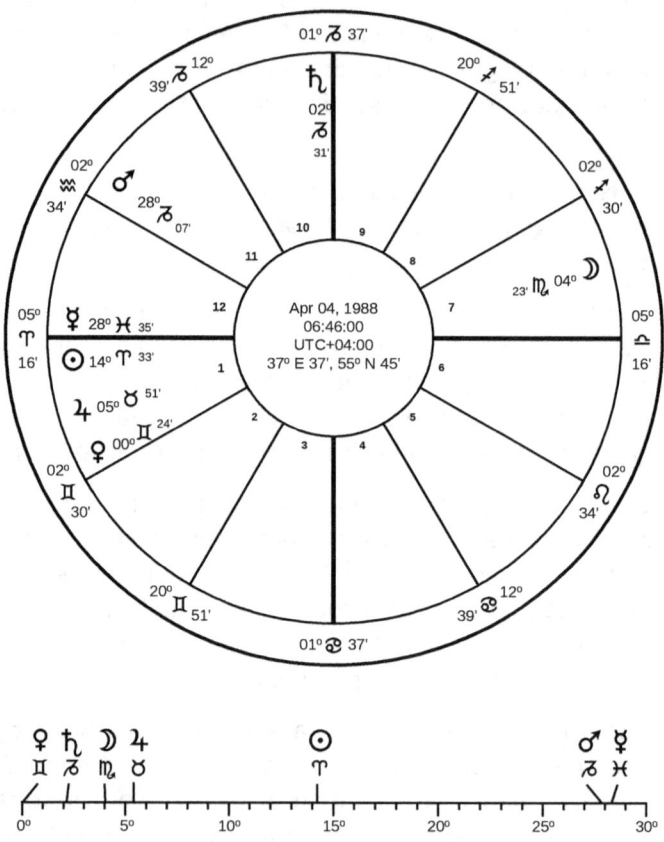

Figure 3.24: A Woman's Chart

Planets Conditioned by the 7th House

The 7th house governs love and marriage. There are several planets associated with it:

— First, the Moon, which is located in the 7th house.

- Second, the planets that accidentally govern the 7th house by being positioned in the opposite 1st house—Mercury, the Sun, Jupiter, and Venus.
- Additionally, the ruler of the 7th house—Venus. It is already included in our list.

Although Venus appears to be on the cusp of the 2nd house, this is not the case. We only see the projection of Venus onto the zodiacal circle, whereas, in reality, it is situated in the middle of the 1st house.

Look at Figure 3.25. The segments on the sphere represent the houses. Astrological programs show houses as sections of the zodiacal circle, but in reality, they are segments of space. Venus is positioned in the middle of the first sector, not at its lower edge.

Figure 3.25: *Venus in a 3D Sphere*

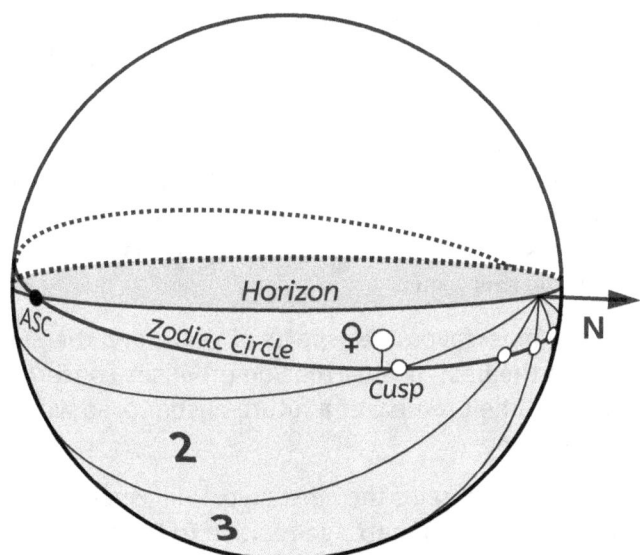

The projection of Venus onto the zodiacal circle creates the illusion that it is close to the boundary of the 2nd house, but this impression is deceptive. This is because Venus was slightly above the ecliptic at birth. Similarly, Mercury is physically in the 1st house below the horizon, even though its projection falls into the 12th house.

Determining the Planet Most Likely to Bring Marriage

Thus, the five planets are related to the 7th house. But which one is most likely to lead to marriage? We use the following approach:

Since marriage is a favorable event, the planet that brings it should not be malefic. We exclude planets that are in poor celestial state. Thus, we immediately exclude the Moon.

We select those that naturally govern marriage or a spouse among the remaining planets. Venus symbolizes marriage, so it remains on our list. The husband is represented by the Sun and Jupiter, but we prefer the Sun because:

- It is in a place of exaltation, meaning it is maximally productive concerning favorable houses.
- It is closer to the cusp of the 1st house, which strengthens its connection to the opposite 7th house.
- The Sun, rather than Jupiter, symbolizes the masculine principle, i.e., the leader of the hierarchy, which indicates a man in the context of the patriarchal family model.

Thus, we are left with two planets most capable of bringing marriage—Venus and the Sun. This does not mean that Jupiter cannot bring marriage. However, if we focus our search on the most obvious planets and their best aspects, we will arrive at the most probable wedding dates. Therefore, I follow this logic.

Now, we find the most favorable aspects of Venus and the Sun. The △☉ at 14° ♌ contains the best of what the Sun promises concerning the 7th house. It contains the promise of a future husband, so we will call it a *promissor of husband*.

Similarly, △♀ at 0° ♎ contains the most favorable aspect of Venus, i.e., a particular role of love and marriage relative to the 7th house. We will call 0° Libra a *promissor of marriage*.

Primary Directions From the Radix

We expect that when in primary directions, 0° Libra or 14° Leo approach the significators of the 1st or 7th houses (that is, life as a whole or its specific sphere—romantic relationships), the promises of a husband and marriage will be realized.

Chapter 3. Natal Astrology

Significators of the 7th house are:

- The planet in the 7th house—the Moon.
- The cusp of the 7th house.
- The ruler of the 7th house and the natural ruler of marriage—Venus.

Significators of the 1st house are:

- Planets in the 1st house—Mercury, the Sun, Jupiter, and Venus.
- The ASC.
- The ruler of the 1st house—Mars.

Now it remains to determine when the promissors of marriage reach these significators.

Table 3.14: *A Woman: Directions for Marriage*

№	Promissor	Significator	Date
1	△☉ at 14°♌	☾	Dec 2014
2	△☉ at 14°♌	♀	Jul 2009

We excluded from this table cases of extreme old age, childhood, and times beyond the span of human life (over 120 years), so only two directions remain.

Selecting the Most Effective Direction

As you can see, the woman has two most evident windows of opportunity for marriage throughout her lifetime. These are the summer of 2009 and the fall–winter of 2014. A solar return for either 2009 or 2014 will confirm one of these dates. However, before verifying both dates with solar returns, let us examine which of the two directions has a greater potential to bring about marriage.

What interests me are the directions that occur immediately after and just before these directions for marriage.

I will start with the year 2009. In that year, the marriage direction is surrounded by the following neighboring directions:

I pay attention to neighboring directions to see if they also point to marriage.

Table 3.15: A Woman: Directions in 2009

№	Promissor	Significator	Date
1	△ ☽ at 4° ♓	♃	May 2009
2	△ ☉ at 14° ♌	DSC	Jul 2009
3	□ ☽ at 4° ♒	♃	Aug 2009

If I consider Jupiter to be a significator of the 1st house in the preceding direction (direction No. 1 in Table 3.15), then the trine of the Moon cannot contain the promise of marriage for two reasons:

- First, the Moon is in detriment, so her role is to be a troublemaker.
- Second, this trine does not fall into any dignities of the Moon; this is a particular (neutral) facet of the troublemaker—it cannot bring anything favorable to the native's life path.

Similarly, the promissor in the subsequent direction (direction No. 3 in Table 3.15) also does not contain promises of marriage and will not manifest anything related to wedlock. Thus, the primary direction for marriage in July 2009 (the middle row in Table 3.15) remains without the necessary support.

Now, let us examine the direction for 2014 and analyze what surrounds it (Table 3.16).

Table 3.16: A Woman: Directions for 2014

№	Promissor	Significator	Date
1	✶ ♂ at 28° ♏	♄	Nov 2014
2	△ ☉ at 14° ♌	☽	Dec 2014
3	Ant. of ♂ at 4° ♐	♄	Jan 2015

Look: right before it is a favorable sextile of exalted Mars, which has fallen into Scorpio, the domicile of Mars, approaches Saturn—the significator of the native's actions (Saturn rules the 10th house).

Mars governs the native's life as a whole. Its favorable aspect indicates a particularly favorable facet—or rather, episode—of the life path. But what exactly is this favorable aspect related to?

The aspect of Mars is at 28° Scorpio, right in the 7th house of the chart. This means that this favorable aspect of life is related to matters of the 7th house, particularly marriage. When it approaches Saturn, the ruler of

Chapter 3. Natal Astrology

the native's activities, it stimulates the native's actions toward marriage that year. We say that the native takes action to realize the best aspect of her life related to the 7th house. This occurs in November, and the main direction for marriage comes into play the following month.

Thus, the autumn direction for marriage received support from the preceding direction. The marriage will most likely occur in the fall of 2014, not in the summer of 2009. However, it is essential to ensure that the solar return confirms this.

N.B. on Strategy

Please note that I am following a strategy of identifying the most prominent indicators of marriage—the most capable planets, their best aspects, and the brightest directions. This does not imply that marriage cannot occur under less prominent directions. A woman's life may present multiple windows of opportunity—and consequently, multiple marriages. However, my present objective is to determine the precise date of one specific marriage. I am seeking the most definitive window of opportunity where marriage becomes virtually inevitable.

Solar Return Chart

Now, we cast the solar return for the year 2014 (Fig. 3.26) based on the native's place of residence.

Planets conditioned by the 7th house: I will examine the planets, conditioned by the natal 7th house—the Sun, Venus, Jupiter (accidental ruler), and Saturn (ruler by exaltation and by aspect)—to see if they repeat their natal roles this year.

The Sun: The first thing I see is that the Sun, which indicated the husband in the natal chart and acted as his significator in the direction, has become the ruler of life this year. The year's main event is related to the husband—this is the first confirmation of the directions by the solar return.

Predictive Astrology Textbook

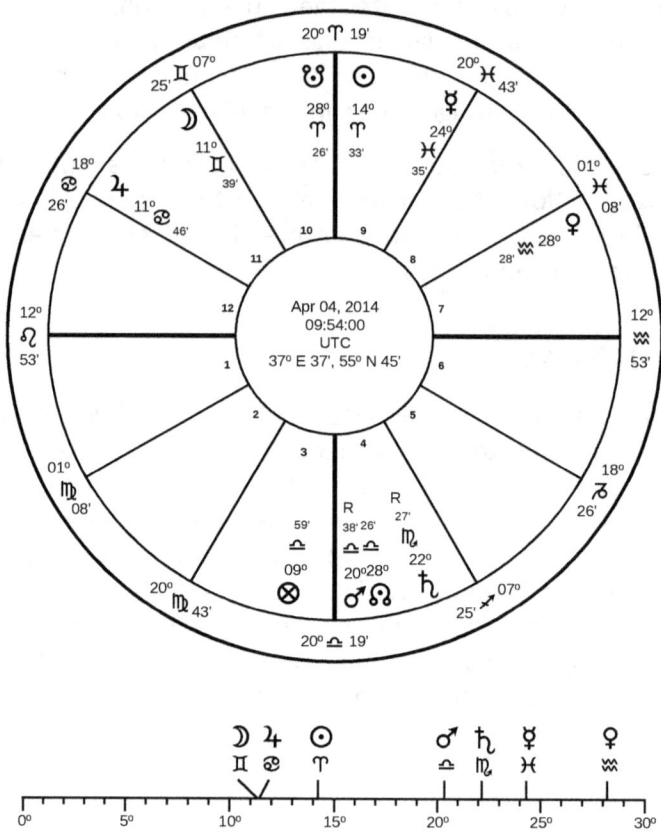

Figure 3.26: *A Woman's Solar Return Chart*

Now pay attention: the trine of the Sun at 14° Leo—the significator of the husband from the previous direction (see Table 3.14)—rises on the ASC of this year. It literally means that the husband will appear on the horizon this year. This is the second confirmation of the preceding direction.

Venus: This year, it is located in the 7th house. Among all its natal meanings, it explicitly repeats the role of love and marriage this year, once again confirming the promise of the directions.

Saturn: We saw in the previous direction that a favorable aspect of life related to marriage (△♂ at 28°♏, see Table 3.14) was approaching

Chapter 3. Natal Astrology

Saturn—the native's own actions. This direction promised to encourage the native to take steps toward marriage this year.

Saturn, as the ruler of the native's actions, repeated this promise: it has become the ruler of marriage this year, combining two roles—the native's actions and her marriage, once again repeating the promise of the previous direction: urging the native to take decisive action—getting married. This is the fourth confirmation.

In addition, it twice repeated the natal role as the ruler of the natal 7th house—in addition to being the ruler of the 7th house this year, it also falls into the natal 7th house.

The 1st and the 10th Houses The Sun—the significator of the husband from the natal chart—by its wide orb, covers the cusp of the 10th house in the solar return. It links the native's actions this year to the husband's appearance, repeating the promise of the preceding direction (Direction No. 1 from Table 3.14), which is the sixth confirmation.

However, the solar ruler of activities this year and the natal ruler of life—Mars—has moved into Libra, which might mean:

- Either Mars annuls its favorable promise contained in 28°♏ —the favorable aspect of life related to marriage may not manifest due to external challenges, since Mars in Libra is in detriment this year.
- Or the year will be full of love, as Mars is in the sign of Venus—the natural significator of love and marriage.

We cannot read both simultaneously. It is either Mars operating in the Venusian environment or debilitated Mars. Here, knowing the context of the native's life helps. If the year began under difficult circumstances, then Mars in detriment would bring impending challenges, particularly in the 4th house, where it is located. If, however, the native's life was calm, this points to the influence of Venus—love and marriage—on Mars.

At the beginning of the year, the native did not experience significant difficulties in the sphere of property or family. This means the solar return indeed shows Mars (that is, the period of life for the coming year) influenced by love and marriage.

In addition to that, solar Mars falls into the natal 7th house.

We remember that in the previous direction (Table 3.14), Mars's "copy" at 28° Scorpio in the 7th house pointed to a specific aspect of life—a period related to marriage. In the solar return chart, Mars repeats this same role twice (by operating against Venus and by falling into the natal 7th house), indicating a year of love and marriage. This is yet another confirmation of the promise of the directions.

Note that I am not analyzing every sphere of life in the solar return. I am focusing on confirming the two directions that promise marriage, and I have already found seven such confirmations.

Seven confirmations satisfy me. The marriage will take place this year. Now that I am confident that the marriage will occur in 2014, closer to autumn (according to the directions), I can determine the specific month.

Directions From the Solar Chart

To determine the specific month of the marriage, I will calculate the primary directions from the solar return chart.

I will leave the two main promissors of marriage from the natal chart untouched—they represent general lifetime promises of marriage. These are:

- 14° Leo, the degree promising the future husband,
- 28° Scorpio, the favorable aspect of life related to marriage.

Now, I will add the promissors of marriage specifically for 2014, derived from the solar return chart.

Saturn: We have already established that this year, Saturn represents both the native's actions toward marriage and the marriage itself (as the ruler of the 7th house in the solar return chart). Thus, its favorable aspects will indicate promises of marriage specifically for 2014.

Saturn has two favorable aspects, located at 22° Capricorn and 22° Aquarius. However, I will prioritize the latter, as it falls directly into the 7th house of the solar return chart.

Venus: The second ruler of the 7th house by position in the solar return chart is Venus. Its favorable aspects, located in its signs of rulership—28° Libra and 28° Taurus—also indicate marriage promises for 2014. However,

Chapter 3. Natal Astrology

I will prioritize the latter, as it falls directly into the 10th house of the solar return chart for the following reason:

We have already seen that marriage is promised through the native's actions, and Venus in the solar return expresses itself through its dispositor, Saturn (which rules the 10th house in the natal chart and represents the native's own actions). Thus, the second aspect (28° Taurus in the 10th house) aligns much more closely with the overall picture.

Promissors & significatos: Therefore, these four points are the main promissors of marriage for 2014, relative to the solar return chart:

1. 14° ♌ (future husband)
2. 28° ♏ (favorable aspect of love tied to marriage)
3. 22° ♒ in the 7th (native's actions toward marriage)
4. 28° ♉ in the 10th (native's actions toward marriage)

N.B. on Promissors

The highest art in constructing directions from revolution charts is selecting the correct *promissors* capable of triggering an event. They could be rulers of a house from the natal chart, prominently aligned with the revolution chart, or even the ruler of the house intervening in the question in a given context. In this example, the selection was fairly obvious because we initially chose a strategy of looking for the most prominent marriage indicators, which led us to the most significant and clear solar return for marriage.

I will direct these four points to the significators of life and activity for this year: the ASC and MC of the solar return. Additionally, I will direct them to the Sun—the main planet of the solar return and simultaneously the significator of the husband in the previous direction—as well as to Saturn and Venus, the significators of the 7th house this year.

Next, I will record the dates when the promissors approach the significators, resulting in a fairly long list—20 dates for this year (Table 3.17).

Predictive Astrology Textbook

Table 3.17: *Directions for Marriage from the Solar Return*

	\multicolumn{5}{c}{Significator}				
	ASC	MC	☉	♀	♄
14° ♌	06 Apr	01 Aug	08 Aug	28 Oct	18 Jan'15
28° ♏	12 Sep	10 Nov	12 Nov	16 Dec	07 Apr
22° ♒	01 Dec	08 Feb'15	11 Feb'15	25 Mar'15	03 Jun
28° ♉	08 Jan'15	11 May	19 May	13 Aug	30 Oct

Then, I sort these dates and look for clusters that occur within a few days of each other.

As a result, I identify the following short periods: April 6–7, May 11, October 28–30, November 10–12, and February 8–11. The marriage will take place within one of these periods.

On the one hand, the directions from the radix point to fall 2014; on the other, the directions from the solar return specify four date ranges (Table 3.18).

Table 3.18: *Intersection of Dates*

\multicolumn{2}{c}{Directions}	
From Radix	From Solar Return
Sep-Nov 2014	8–11 Feb 2014 6–7 Apr 2014 28–30 Oct 2014 10–12 Nov 2014

At the intersection of indications from both charts, I identify two periods in the fall: October 26–29 and November 10–12.

This means the marriage will most likely occur during one of the lunar returns containing the specified dates and confirming the marriage.

Lunar Return

Fortunately, we have one lunar return that includes both dates. It is the eighth lunar return of the year, which begins on October 28 and ends on November 20. Let's examine it (Fig. 3.27):

The 1st and the 10th houses: Let's recall that Mars,

Chapter 3. Natal Astrology

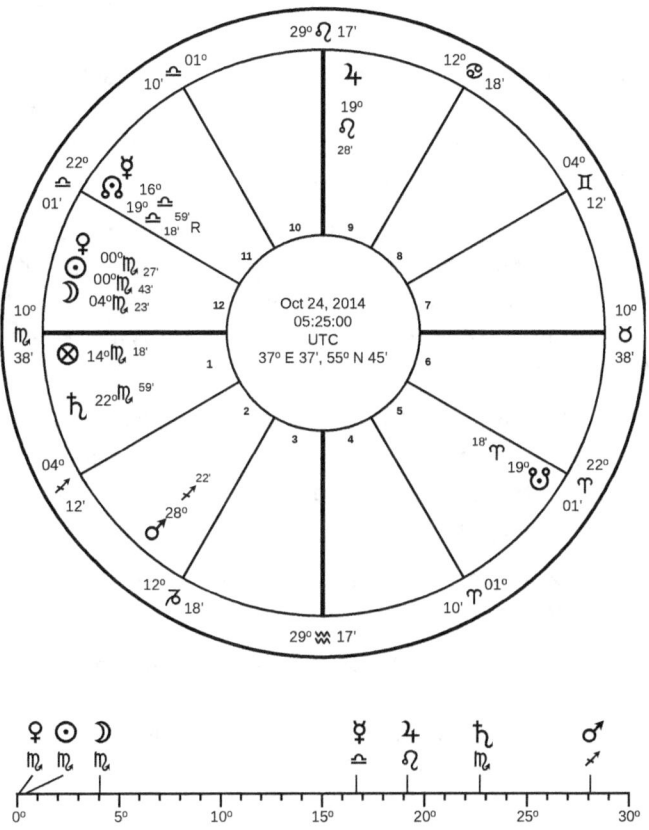

Figure 3.27: *Eighth Lunar Return for 2014*

- In the natal chart, governs life in general;
- In the preceding direction, it indicated a wonderful aspect of life related to marriage;
- In the preceding solar return chart, it represents a life period marked by Venus.

This month, Mars becomes the primary ruler of a 27-day short period as the lord of ASC. In addition, Venus forms a nearly exact sextile with Mars, once again signifying a "period" or "aspect of life" connected to marriage, which occurs this month.

Let's recall that the Sun,

- In the natal chart, signifies the spouse, who will appear due to the native's actions;
- In the preceding direction, it promised a future husband (14°♌);
- In the preceding solar return, it shows the husband's appearance (14°♌ were ascending) and the native's activities toward the marriage (it conjoined the 10th house cusp).

This month, it begins to show decisive action toward marriage—it again becomes the ruler of the 10th house. The connection between the decisive action toward marriage is especially evident in the following aspect: Mars (ruler of life for the next 27 days) forms a nearly exact trine to the MC.

Moreover, the Sun conjoins Venus—the marriage significator in the natal chart. This suggests a literal connection between the Sun (husband) and marriage (Venus) this month. It also confirms the promises of previous directions and the solar return.

Additionally, we see that the house cusps also repeat the promises of preceding directions:

- The 1st house cusp falls into the 7th house of the natal chart, linking life in the next 27 days with marriage;
- The 10th house cusp falls into the solar 1st, again linking life for this year with actions toward marriage this month.

Planets conditioned by the 7th house: I will again examine the planets, conditioned by the natal 7th house—the Sun, Venus, Jupiter (accidental ruler), and Saturn (ruler by exaltation and by aspect)—to see if they repeat their natal roles this year. We have already discussed the Sun, so let's continue with Venus.

Venus: Let's recall that Venus,

- In the natal chart rules the 7th house by sign;
- In the preceding solar return, it ruled the 7th house by position.

In this lunar return chart, it becomes the ruler of the 7th house, once again emphasizing its role as the marriage planet. You see how the lunar return confirms the promises given by previous directions and the solar return in multiple ways.

Venus is placed in Scorpio, which can be interpreted in two ways:

Chapter 3. Natal Astrology

- Either Venus neutralizes its promise of marriage, being in its detriment in Scorpio.
- Or it manifests itself through its dispositor, Mars—the ruler of the current month. This means that the marriage will manifest within this short 27-day period.

Considering all previous indicators (i.e., the absence of contrary factors), I choose the second option—a marriage within the next 27 days.

Saturn: Let's recall that Saturn,

- In the natal chart, rules both the 10th and 7th houses, linking the native and her actions with marriage;
- In the preceding direction, it received an impulse from Mars's aspect (28°♏)—that again inclined the native toward marriage;
- In the preceding solar return, it became the ruler of the 7th and fell into the radical 7th house.

This month, Mars—the ruler of the following 27 days—again comes into contact with Saturn—it conjoins its natal degree within its orb (as seen in the chart overlay). This suggests that the native will take a step toward marriage during this specific month in 2014.

Jupiter: Finally, let's examine Jupiter. Recall that:

- In the natal chart, it accidentally rules the 7th house;
- It did not participate significantly in either directions or the solar return.

But here it again repeats its natal role. Take note of 14° Leo—a promissor of husband in natal chart. In the solar return chart, it was rising on the ASC, and now, in that lunar return chart, it conjoined Jupiter—the significator of the husband in the natal chart. This is yet another confirmation that the husband will appear on the horizon this month.

Thus, there are sufficient confirmations that this lunar return will fulfill the promises made by the previous solar return and directions.

Primary Directions From the Lunar Return

The event should occur during the lunar period, around October 27–30, though the exact date is not yet defined. There may be deviations of a few days. To specify the date more precisely, we may calculate primary directions from the lunar return chart.

Promissors and Significators: I retain the previously chosen marriage promissors from natal and solar return charts:

1. 14° ♌ (future husband)
2. 28° ♍ (favorable aspect of love tied to marriage)
3. 22° ♒ in the solar 7th (native's actions toward marriage)
4. 28° ♉ in the solar 10th (native's actions toward marriage)

Two planets that rule the solar 7th house are Saturn (by position) and Venus (by sign). They can facilitate marriage this month through their strongest aspects: △ ♀ at 0° ♉, □ ♄ at 22° ♒, and ✶ ♄ at 22° ♑, so I add these aspects to my list of promissors.

Now, I sequentially direct the marriage promissors to the following significators:

- ASC, MC and planets in these houses—the significators of the native's life and activity for this month.
- The Moon—significator of the main event of the month in the lunar return chart.
- The significator of the 7th house for this month—Venus.

Here are the dates (Table 3.19):

Table 3.19: *Directions for Marriage from the Lunar Return*

	Significator				
	ASC	MC	☾	♀	♄
14° ♌	10 Nov	19 Nov	11 Nov	12 Nov	09 Nov
28° ♍	26 Oct	30 Oct	26 Oct	27 Oct	24 Oct
22° ♒	01 Nov	06 Nov	01 Nov	02 Nov	30 Oct
28° ♉	04 Nov	13 Nov	04 Nov	05 Nov	02 Nov
00° ♉	02 Nov	11 Nov	03 Nov	04 Nov	01 Nov
22° ♑	30 Oct	03 Nov	31 Oct	01 Nov	29 Oct

I again sort these dates and look for clusters that occur within a few days of each other.

As a result, I identify the following short periods:

- October 24–31

Chapter 3. Natal Astrology

- November 1–6
- November 9–13

The marriage will take place within one of these periods. Now, I expand the Table 3.18 with these new dates (see Table 3.20).

Table 3.20: *Intersection of Dates from All Charts*

	Directions	
From Radix	From Solar Return	From Lunar Return
Sep–Nov 2014	8–11 Feb 2014 6–7 Apr 2014 28–30 Oct 2014 10–12 Nov 2014	24–31 Oct 2014 1–6 Nov 2014 9–13 Nov 2014

As you can see, two of these periods coincide with testimonies of preceding directions: 9-13 Nov and 24-31 Oct. This is not a random coincidence. Morinus wrote that if you accurately construct directions for the same event from both the solar and lunar return charts, you will end up with the same dates.

Somewhere between October 24–31 or November 10–13, a transit in the sky will occur that fulfills the promises of the directions, confirmed by both the solar and lunar returns.

Our task now is to cast transits charts for these days with a very short interval—about 5–10 minutes—to find the moment when several promises from the previous directions, the solar return chart, and the lunar return chart coincide simultaneously.

We may identify multiple such moments. In such cases, we prioritize:

- The transit showing the greatest number of concurrent repeating indications;
- The transit that occurs closer to the beginning of the lunar return cycle, when the lunar return's promise has maximal potential for fulfillment.

Transit Chart

After thorough research, the necessary transit was found. It not only provides striking simultaneous confirmations of the primary directions, but also occurs practically at the very beginning of the lunar cycle, where the potential for the fulfillment of promises is at its peak.

Indeed, on October 24, 2014, an hour before the lunar cycle begins, at 04:27:36, several significant coincidences occur (Fig. 3.28):

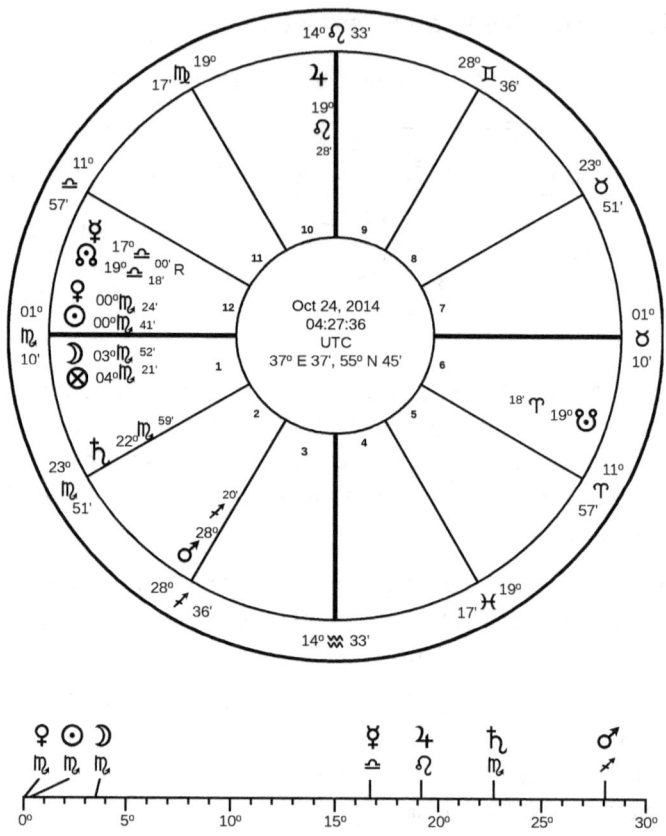

Figure 3.28: *Transit Chart: 10 Oct 2014*

Testimony 1. You remember that 14° ♌ is an extraordinary point:

- It is a promissor of the husband in the preceding direction for marriage;
- It was rising on the ASC in the solar return chart;
- It conjoined the second significator of the husband—Jupiter—in the lunar return chart;
- It participated in directions from the solar and lunar return, indicating the time of the event.

Chapter 3. Natal Astrology

In the transit, I found it culminates right on the MC, dominating over the whole chart.

Testimony 2. The Moon, embodying the central promise of the lunar return and serving as the 7th house significator in the preceding direction for marriage (see Table 3.14), simultaneously:

- Became the ruler of the 7th house by exaltation and conjoined with the ruler of the 7th;
- Rose on the ASC.

This can be interpreted literally—the marriage will appear on the native's horizon that day.

Testimonies 3-6. At the same time:

- The husband's significator (Sun) conjoined Venus, which you can understand literally.
- The Sun also rose on the ASC, again indicating the husband's arrival in the native's life on this day.
- Venus became the ruler of the 7th house, thrice repeating its role of marriage—originating from the natal chart, solar return, and lunar at this very moment.
- Venus ascended on the ASC, signifying the realization of the thrice-promised marriage on this day.

All these independent confirmations converge in a single moment and begin to dissipate within a few minutes.

Please note that I use the transit chart not to predict various events but to confirm the main one that is meant to happen on this day. I know this main event before casting the transit chart rather than searching for it within the chart. That is, I analyze only those degrees that indicate marriage, including 14° Leo, where there are no planets at all.

So, the forecast is as follows: the native will get married on October 24, 2014. Indeed, the woman married on this day, when the entire potential of the natal chart—focused on a single event (marriage)—was triggered by the suitable transit on the morning of that day.

Focusing Natal Chart Promises on a Specific Day

Notice how the planets in the natal chart enhance their specific roles closer to the day of the event's realization.

Example of Mars:

- **Mars' role in natal chart:** It is a broad significator of life path, including all possible events.
- **Mars' role in 2014:** It manifested its particular beneficial aspect in 2014—a favorable life episode associated with marriage (28° Scorpio, falling into the 7th house ruled by Venus).
- **Mars' role in October 2014:** The lunar confirmed marriage in a specific month of 2014, once again making Mars the ruler of life for the next 27 days and tightly linking it with Venus.
- **Mars' role on a specific day:** The transit fulfilled the promise by making Mars the ruler of the moment and placing Venus (marriage) directly on the ASC.

Example of the Sun:

- **The Sun's Role in the Natal Chart:** In the natal chart, the Sun represents many things—husband, liberation from hard labor, personal fame, and so on.
- **The Sun's role in 2014:** But in the directions, the Sun specifically reflects the meaning of its particular aspect (at 14° Leo) in relation to the 7th house—it shows the husband and only the husband. In the solar return chart, the Sun again signifies the husband, appearing on the horizon in 2014: 14° Leo (the promissor of the husband) rises above the horizon, and the husband himself (the Sun) becomes the ruler of the 1st house—the main theme of the year.
- **The Sun's Role in October 2014:** In the lunar return chart, the Sun becomes the main significator of the month: it conjoins the Moon, as well as Venus (the significator of marriage), and 14° Leo (the promissor of the husband) conjoins Jupiter—another significator of the husband in the natal chart.
- **The Sun on a Specific Day:** Finally, in the transit chart, the Sun once again becomes the main significator of the husband at a certain moment: these same 14° Leo reach culmination, and the Sun, conjoined with two indicators of marriage, rises above the ASC.

Thus, the overall potential of the natal chart gradually focuses on ultra-specific meanings on a specific day.

A Final Note on Transits

Although this example shows that the transit technique can be used to predict with an accuracy of up to a day, we were rather lucky in this case.

Imagine a suitable transit happening on a weekend when the registry office is closed. We would not be able to say for sure whether the wedding would take place on Friday or Monday.

As always, life makes its adjustments. In practice, if you correctly name the event, year, and month but miss the date by 1–2 days, then, in the eyes of the client, your forecast will be 100% a failure.

Therefore, my advice is not to strive for excessive precision. If the event occurs within the specified period, a forecast accurate to the month is already a good one.

Astrological Compatibility of Couples

When examining the horoscopes of couples, I have consistently observed the same pattern—major life events for both individuals are clearly reflected in their respective charts. Very often, they share the same dates for significant events such as the birth of children, relocations, and so on. In one case from my practice, I even found the exact same moving date in both horoscopes of a married couple.

This leads me to conclude that people unite not just (or even primarily) due to personality compatibility, but rather because of shared destinies. If two people's horoscopes "prescribe" major joint events, there is a high probability that they will form a couple—at least for the duration of those shared events.

Of course, this does not mean that all events in their lives will be identical. For example, my students have encountered cases where the birth of a child (usually not the first) is visible in only one spouse's chart. I also observed this phenomenon during my Professional Assessment Process to become a member of APAI.[30] While making a public prediction based on a "blind chart," I identified a few major events of the year—except one related to the couple: the birth of a child. This event was not reflected in the chart.

The same signs of both ASC and MC also play a significant role. If two people share similar inclinations or are drawn to the same pursuits, this strengthens their bond. For instance, my spouse and I have the same ASC and MC signs—we have much in common and understand each other intuitively. As expected, our horoscopes contain indications of shared family events.

Example №42: Shared Events

Let us return to the homework assignment on page 358. We examined the horoscope of Queen Elizabeth II and identified four dates with a high probability of the birth of a child. Let us recall these dates (Table 3.21):

Table 3.21: *Key Dates in Queen Elizabeth II's Horoscope*

Expected Date	Real Date	
Sep 1948	Nov 1948	Charles
Jul 1950	Aug 1950	Anne
Dec 1959	Feb 1960	Andrew
Jan 1964	Mar 1964	Edward

Now, let us analyze the horoscope of her spouse—Prince Philip, Duke of Edinburgh (Fig. 3.29). We will examine which dates of the child's birth are indicated by his horoscope.

Planets Conditioned by the 5th House

As usual, we will begin by identifying the rulers of the 5th house. The 5th house is ruled by Jupiter, with Mars and Mercury acting as accidental rulers. Additionally, three planets cast close aspects to the cusp of the 5th house:

- △ ☽ —a favorable aspect of life
- ☍ ☉ —a favorable aspect of life

---
[30] Association of Professional Astrologers International, https://professionalastrologers.co.uk/

Chapter 3. Natal Astrology

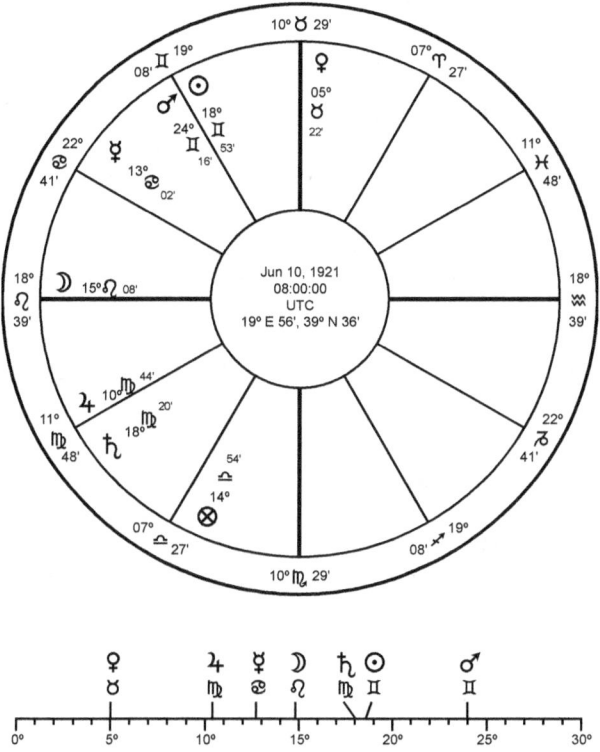

Figure 3.29: *Prince Philip*

- □♄ —a neutral aspect of marriage

We will focus on the planets most capable of bringing children.

- **Jupiter:** Although Jupiter is a natural benefic, in this chart, it has become an accidental malefic due to being in its sign of exile. This means such a Jupiter is unlikely to produce good deeds relative to a favorable house. But since it is a natural ruler of fertility, relative to the 5th house, it can produce offspring by its most favorable aspects.
- **Saturn and Mars:** These are natural malefics lacking dignity. They are unlikely to grant children.
- **The Sun:** This is a natural benefic, not in exile or fall, and receives no significant afflictions through aspects or its dispositor. Such a planet can produce moderate benefits relative to favorable houses. However,

considering that the Sun is the natural ruler of life and birth, it is quite capable of granting offspring in relation to the 5th house.
- **The Moon:** The same applies to the Moon. Although it is a benefic without significant dignity, concerning the 5th house, it will bring children for two reasons. First, it is the natural ruler of infants; second, the Moon operates in the context of the Sun, which signifies new life in relation to the 5th house.
- **Mercury:** Mercury is also a benefic without dignity, but it lacks the strong connection to the 5th house that the Sun and Moon have. Therefore, we will not focus on it.

Thus, the three planets most capable of bringing children are the Moon, the Sun, and Jupiter.

Promissors and Significators

As usual, the promise of offspring is concentrated in the degrees where favorable aspects of these planets fall. Let us list them (Table 3.22).

Table 3.22: *Prince Phillip. Promissors of Children*

Aspect	House		Potential
✶☉ in ♌	ASC	Favorable	High
✶☉ in ♈	9	Favorable	High
✶♃ in ♋	11	Favorable	High
☐☉ in ♍	2	Favorable	Neutral
☐☉ in ♓	8	Unfavorable	Neutral
☍☉ in ♐	5	Of children	High
☌☽ in ♌	ASC	Favorable	Moderate
✶☽ in ♊	11	Favorable	Neutral
✶☽ in ♎	3	Favorable	Moderate
☐☽ in ♉	10	Favorable	Moderate
△☽ in ♐	5	Of children	High
△☽ in ♈	9	Favorable	Neutral
✶♃ in ♏	IC	Favorable	Neutral
☐♃ in ♐	4	Favorable	Moderate
△♃ in ♉	MC	Favorable	Moderate

When assessing the potential of an aspect, I also considered its dispositor. For example, aspects falling in the sign of dignified Venus or Jupiter (the natural ruler of fertility and accidental ruler of the 5th house) have a higher likelihood of manifestation than aspects in other signs.

Chapter 3. Natal Astrology

Typically, the strongest promissor brings the first child, while subsequent children may arrive in moderate directions. Since we are looking for the birth of more than one child, in Table 3.22, I have listed not only the most favorable but also moderately strong aspects capable of producing children.

As significators of the 5th house of children, I will consider:

- Jupiter, the ruler of the 5th house,
- The cusp of the 5th house,
- The Moon, as the natural ruler of newborn children.

Now, I will direct aspects with high and medium potential to these significators. During Philip's lifetime, only three promissors reached these significators (see Table 3.23).

Table 3.23: *Prince Phillip. Directions for Children*

Promissor	Significator	Date
✶ ☉ in ♌	Jupiter	Dec 1948
☌ ☽ in ♌	Jupiter	Jan 1951
✶ ☽ in ♍	Jupiter	Apr 1964

Now let's compare the horoscopes of the royal couple.

Table 3.24: *Prince Phillip & Queen Elizabeth II. Shared Dates*

Queen Elizabeth II	Reality	Prince Phillip
Sep 1948	Nov 1948	Dec 1948
Jul 1940	Aug 1950	Jan 1951
Dec 1959	Feb 1960	—
Jan 1964	Mar 1964	Apr 1964

Take a look. In both horoscopes, not only do the dates of most children's births coincide, but the exact months of their births also fall roughly midway between the peak potentials of the directions in the two charts.

Note also that Prince Philip's horoscope contains no explicit indication of a child being born in 1960. However, there is a direction that opens the possibility for a birth but does not guarantee it.

This is the direction of a neutral aspect, □☉ in ♍, approaching the ASC, pointing to April 1960. This direction creates opportunities for various 1st-house (life path) events—from financial support from allies to the birth of a child. But whether any event occurs under this direction at all depends entirely on external factors.

In our example, that factor turned out to be the spouse's horoscope. It was hers that brought Prince Philip a child in the year when his chart opened the possibility for a son's arrival.

Forecasting as a Part of Life

Using Natal and Horary Charts

When I first started forecasting, I was so captivated by horary astrology's ability to provide answers that I would make predictions for absolutely everything—when a café table would free up, whether it would rain that day, and so on. But over the years, I realized that this approach only satisfied curiosity or simply fascinated me, without actually improving my quality of life.

As time passed, I began using horary astrology only when it came to matters of safety or serious decisions. And it turned out that this application aligns quite well with using directions in the natal chart.

For example, if the question of moving to another country or selling a house arises, I first note the time of the question. Then, I refer to the natal chart: directions and solar returns will indicate whether a major event is likely to occur. If it is, I consult the horary chart to refine future details within the unfolding context. This way, I gain the ability to influence future events—for instance, by preparing measures in advance.

Another way I use natal forecasting is for strategic planning.

Strategic Planning

When I conceive a long-term plan spanning several years, I first examine directions for the next 3–5 years to identify the optimal year for my plans to come to fruition. It might turn out that the favorable time for realization is three years away—so I prepare the groundwork in advance to "seize the opportunity" when it arrives.

As part of my regular practice, I also look into the near future (the next year or two) for myself and my loved ones to anticipate upcoming threats.

This allows me to take preventive measures—crafting a life context that prevents the foreseen events from occurring.

This is what Morinus called "rational will"—applying effort at a known time and in a known direction to improve one's life.

Chapter 4

Conclusion

Refutation of Modern Astrologers' Arguments against Accurate Forecasting

In 2024, I surveyed modern astrologers to determine their arguments against the existence of accurate astrological predictions. Modern astrologers mostly repeat the same three arguments against accurate forecasts, which I want to respond to.

Argument 1: *Astrology is divination. An accurate forecast based on logical analysis is impossible.*

This statement is a classic axiom in which a particular assertion (in this case, that astrology is divination) is accepted a priori.

In reality, such an assertion contradicts the mathematical core of astrological techniques. Directions, revolutions, mathematical timing techniques, spherical geometry formulas, and angular distance calculations prove a logical, not intuitive, approach to astrology.

Moreover, numerous examples from this book and a vast collection of books preserved over the centuries demonstrate examples of predictions made based on purely logical conclusions. Therefore, the reader cannot consider the first argument to be valid—it contradicts historical evidence.

Argument 2: *Modern Uranian individuals have become free, and the stars no longer influence them.*

The emergence of modern genetics and neurophysiology has proved otherwise—we are not entirely free in our decisions. Furthermore, the idea that physical laws governing the movement of planets (gravity), altering the composition of the atmosphere (chemistry), and stimulating neural networks (neurobiology)—and other material regularities underlying astrology—have always worked but suddenly ceased to work for Uranian individuals in modern society contradicts the fundamentals of science.

If the laws of astrology, according to which stars influence visible social collisions and events in life, existed somewhere in the past, then the same laws should manifest themselves now. They will also manifest in the future as long as our Universe exists. Exceptionally material principles of astrological influence are as immutable in this Universe as gravity, electricity, and other known laws of physics. They cannot be "turned off" for individual generations. So, this argument also cannot be considered justified.

Argument 3: *Forecasts are nothing more than a form of manipulation where the astrologer programs the client for a predetermined outcome.*

A large number of preserved forecasts from renowned astrologers contradict this thesis. William Lilly predicted the Great Fire of London, but he couldn't program an entire city to self-immolate. You have seen examples where an astrologer accurately named the date of the lockdown in Baku or the place and time of a businessman's murder. However, an astrologer couldn't program the government of an entire country or an individual killer to take a specific step on a particular day. Morinus predicted the day of Cardinal Richelieu's death from a severe illness, but he couldn't "program" him to die on a specific day.

At the same time, from a purely mathematical standpoint, the probability of randomly guessing exact dates and event details correctly multiple times in a row approaches zero.

This last argument also contradicts observed experience.

Chapter 4. Conclusion

Memo for Reading Ancient Texts

If you want to refer to ancient texts, read them with caution. Most rules and aphorisms are given without proper logical argumentation or practical confirmation.

Many of these contradict common sense, the theories of other authors, and the practical examples provided. Astrologers adopted techniques from predecessors without subjecting them to criticism, doubt, or proper verification. Accumulated historical errors in transmitting information in this way are almost inevitable.

You may find many internal contradictions even within the same book. For example, in some charts, Lilly considers close aspects across sign boundaries, while in others, he does not. In some examples, he uses symbolic time in aspects, but in others, he suddenly uses transit time without explaining the reason for doing so.

How to Correctly Read Ancient Texts

Most books from previous centuries contain such contradictions. Therefore, please do not follow the rules stated in them literally, or you will inevitably fall into errors. Ignore the rules if they do not make astrological sense. For instance, you may find that the 10th house represents the price of the property you sell or buy. But it does not make sense:

- The 10th house of "actions and recognition of the querent" has no logical connection to the house's price.
- It also cannot show the price of real estate as the 7th from the 4th, since the 7th house is not related to price, and the 7th house as a transaction must be considered from the querent—it is the querent who participates in selling the house, not the house selling itself.
- The 7th house of enemies and other people, derived from the 4th, also has no logical connection to the price.
- Finally, the price is initially given as part of the context—there is no need to search for it in the chart. Suppose the billionaire asks, "Will the price I'll pay for this castle in auction be high?" Look at how much the lord of the 4th house affects the querent's finances and assess the state of their pocket as if you were looking at a photo of the future moment.

When thinking critically about each ancient rule, you will ignore most of them. But do not read the text only to reject the contradictions. On the contrary, knowing the most general principles of astrology, pick up ideas from ancient texts that:

– Align with general principles and common sense;
– Underlie the seemingly baseless but still repeating rules.

For example, Lilly repeatedly sought correspondence between the querent's planet and the special marks of the client who came to their office before judging the chart. This rule looks bizarre; there are no logical arguments for that. But this is what may attract your attention. In this recurring pattern of astrologers' work, you may find an underlying idea—they sought a reflection of current reality in the chart to consider it radical.

Understanding this main idea will bring you to a simple conclusion—a reflection of reality is not limited to the external features of the querent in the chart; on the contrary, these features are least important in the context. From this, you may conclude that you need to look for a reflection of essential elements of the context in the chart to consider it radical. By testing and proving this hypothesis in practice, you'll further refine ancient astrological knowledge. It is the most effective way to read ancient astrological texts.

Some traditional astrologers who unthinkingly follow the rules from the old books may argue that it is not permissible to criticize ancient astrologers and that their authority is unquestionable. I respond: There is no right or wrong *opinion* here; the only criterion will be the *accuracy of regularly made forecasts*.

So, if some ancient rules do not prove themselves in forecasts, bravely reject them. But if you found a tool that allowed ten different astrologers to provide ten identical answers without using intuition, and these answers were later confirmed by reality, pick it up.

Some rules must be rejected immediately, as they defy common sense. For example, in the books of Al-Qabisi and Guido Bonatti, you can find frequent mentions of the triplicity rulership technique attributed to Al-Andarzaghar.

Chapter 4. Conclusion

According to these astrologers, if a house cusp falls in a certain sign, each triplicity lord indicates strictly defined meanings for that house and control over a specific part of life.

For instance, the first ruler of the element where the 8th house falls, per Bonatti, signifies death—but only in the first third of life. The second triplicity ruler denotes old things, yet only those encountered in middle age. The third ruler represents inheritance, but solely what the native receives in old age.

All these claims lack any argumentation or logical basis and entirely contradict statistically observable patterns:

- Death typically occurs at the end of life, not the beginning.
- People usually inherit in youth or middle age when wealthy elderly relatives pass away, rarely in advanced old age.

Such techniques must be discarded without hesitation.

Avoid Cherry Picking

I frequently observe how astrologers, particularly traditionalists, enthusiastically collect predictive techniques, inevitably developing "favorites." When I inquire about their selection criteria, the response typically amounts to: "This technique works better—my personal experience suggests so."

The most dangerous professional trap for an astrologer is relying on subjective impressions or conclusions drawn from isolated successful predictions. In reality, individual coincidences may be random. An objective evaluation of many colleagues' work reveals: they readily showcase accurate predictions while systematically ignoring cases where the same methods produce errors with comparable frequency.

This reflects a cognitive bias: the human brain naturally registers confirming examples that reinforce existing beliefs while subconsciously filtering contradictory data. Consequently, astrologers overestimate their chosen methods' effectiveness, failing to recognize that their accuracy doesn't exceed probability thresholds.

Such selectivity is known as "Cherry Picking"—a manipulative data-handling tactic. Professional growth requires abandoning this approach and implementing rigorous statistical tracking of prediction outcomes.

Statistical Verification

To properly test astrological techniques, you'll need fundamental knowledge of mathematical statistics—particularly t-tests, p-value calculation, effect size measurement, and an understanding of statistical error types.

I recommend completing an introductory course on platforms like Udemy or Coursera, or studying a textbook on statistical hypothesis testing fundamentals. Here are a few tips for you:

When selecting events for verification, ensure they meet these criteria:

- The subject cannot influence the predicted outcome (e.g., predicting SMS arrival time, death dates, or bank transaction timings)
- Events must be objectively verifiable (e.g., "car accident," "relocation," "job termination"). Avoid vague predictions like "large bonus" or "intense emotions"—these lack measurable parameters for statistical validation.

The primary challenge you'll encounter is obtaining sufficient client feedback. My practice shows that when predictions come true but don't meet clients' subjective expectations (which occurs frequently), they typically seek alternative practitioners offering comfort rather than accuracy and withhold their feedback.

What's Next?

You've seen the structure. You've seen the results. Now it's time to bring this predictive method into your consultations.

My full course is now open to practicing astrologers ready to deepen their craft and gain clarity in prediction.

As a reader of this book, you're also invited to download The Case Study Pack — three full predictive examples (natal, horary, and medical) that illustrate how the method works in real consultations.

https://morinus-astrology.com/bookbonus/

Let's make predictive astrology speak with clarity, precision, and confidence.

Appendix A

The Geometry of Celestial Sphere

The Zodiac Circle

The Ecliptic, Solstice, and Equinox

Let's explore how the Earth moves in space and why the seasons change. Take a look at Fig. A.1.

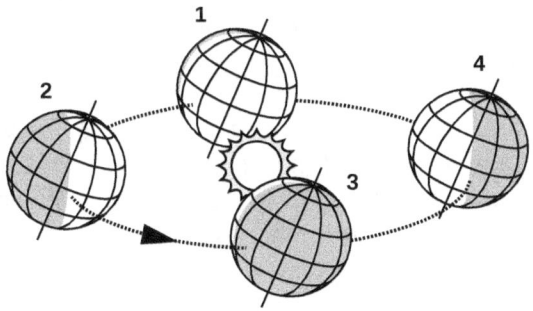

Figure A.1: *Rotation of the Earth*

The Earth moves around the Sun in the direction indicated by the arrow in a particular plane called the *plane of the ecliptic*. In a year, the Earth completes one orbit in this plane. At the same time, the Earth rotates around its own axis, which is tilted 23.5 degrees from the perpendicular to the plane of the ecliptic. This small tilt is called *inclination of Earth's axis*. During the year, the Earth rotates around its axis 365.24 times while orbiting the Sun.

The rotation of the Earth around its axis appears to us as the change between day and night: we find ourselves on the sunny side or the shadowed side of the Earth's surface.

The Earth's orbit around the Sun appears to us as the changing of the seasons. It is precisely because the axis of the Earth's rotation is not strictly perpendicular to the plane of the ecliptic but slightly tilted that we feel the cold in winter and the heat in summer. Look again at the diagram above.

- When the Earth is at point 2, in the northern hemisphere, the day is significantly longer than the night. The Earth's surface warms up well during the day and does not have time to cool down at night. We feel the warmth of summer with its long days.
- When the Earth is at point 4, the picture is opposite: in the northern hemisphere, the day is short, and the Earth does not have time to warm up and quickly cool down—we feel the cold of winter with its long nights.
- When the Earth is in positions 1 and 3, the day equals the night both in the north and the south. The Earth does not have time to either warm up or cool down—we feel the transitional seasons of spring and autumn, respectively.

Points 1 and 3 are called the *vernal and autumnal equinoxes*—day equals night. Points 2 and 4 are called the *summer and winter solstices*—day or night, respectively, are maximally prolonged. You will learn why these points are called solstice points later in the section "Cardinal Signs and Mystical Cults."

We know that the Earth rotates around the Sun. But if you observe the Sun from the center of the Earth, it will seem that not the Earth, but the Sun, is moving around you. Look at the Sun's apparent movement around the Earth's stationary center, represented by Fig. A.2: the Sun moves in the direction indicated by the arrow in the ecliptic plane.

Appendix A. The Geometry of Celestial Sphere

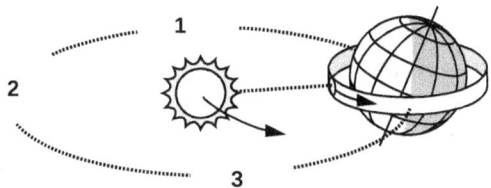

Figure A.2: *Rotation of the Sun*

Make sure to distinguish this movement from the visible movement of the Sun during the day. We are currently ignoring the Earth's own rotation around its axis and following the slow annual movement of the Sun around the center of the Earth. The circle that the Sun traces during the year is called the *ecliptic circle*. It is illustrated in the diagram as a belt surrounding the Earth: the Sun moves along this belt during the year. This belt is the *zodiac circle* itself.

Like any circle, it consists of 360 degrees. What should be considered the beginning of the circle at 0 degrees? In Western astrology, it is customary to consider the degrees of the zodiac circle from the position of the spring Sun, when day equals night, that is, from the point of the vernal equinox. Look at Fig. A.3.

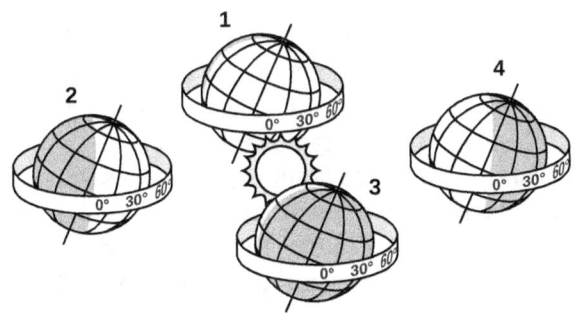

Figure A.3: *Zero Degree of Zodiac Circle*

- When the Earth is at point 1 (vernal equinox), the Sun, from the perspective of the center of the Earth, is at the beginning of the zodiac circle.
- When the Earth reaches point 2 (summer solstice), the Sun will be at 90 degrees of the zodiac circle.
- When the Earth reaches point 3 (autumnal equinox), the Sun will be at 180 degrees of the zodiac circle.
- Finally, in winter, when the Earth reaches point 4 and the day is the shortest (winter solstice), the Sun will be at 270 degrees of the zodiac circle.

As you know, the zodiac circle consists of 12 equal parts of 30 degrees each. These equal parts are called the *signs of the zodiac*. Look at how the zodiac signs are arranged (Fig. A.4):

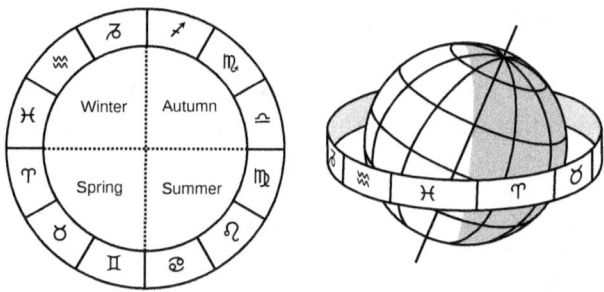

Figure A.4: *Zodiac Signs*

- On the day of the vernal equinox, the Sun is at 0 degrees of the 1st sign, called Aries and denoted by the symbol ♈;
- On the day of the summer solstice, the Sun is at 0 degrees of the 4th sign, called Cancer and denoted by the symbol ♋;
- On the day of the autumnal equinox, the Sun is at 0 degrees of the 7th sign, called Libra and denoted by the symbol ♎;
- Finally, on the winter solstice day, the Sun is at 0 degrees of the 10th sign, called Capricorn, and denoted by the symbol ♑.

So, the zodiac circle is a "belt" surrounding the Earth and divided into 12 equal segments of 30 degrees each. Each of these segments has its unique properties. Why precisely 12 segments? One of the explanations, provided by the Italian medieval astrologer Guido Bonatti[31], involves the idea that each of the four primary states or elements of matter (Earth, air, fire, and water) exists in any phenomenon of the sublunar world in one of three stages: formation, development, and completion. Each zodiac sign is responsible for a particular stage of one of the elements of the sublunar world.

There are 12 possible combinations: three stages for each of the four primary states. Twelve zodiac signs are necessary and sufficient to form changes in the ever-changing sublunar world.

The beginning of the zodiac circle is taken at the vernal equinox. The Sun slowly moves along this "belt" throughout the year, and its passage through these equal segments (zodiac signs) causes the seasons to change. In Western astrology, zodiac signs are conventionally drawn counterclockwise, as shown in the diagram above.

Remember the sequence, names, and symbols of the zodiac signs.

- Aries (♈), Taurus (♉), and Gemini (♊)—spring signs.
- Cancer (♋), Leo (♌), and Virgo (♍)—summer signs.
- Libra (♎), Scorpio (♏), and Sagittarius (♐)—autumn signs.
- Capricorn (♑), Aquarius (♒), and Pisces (♓)—winter signs.

Zodiac Signs and Constellations

As the Sun moves along the zodiac circle, it also passes through certain constellations in the celestial sphere, as shown in Fig. A.5.

There is a common mistake—confusing zodiac signs and constellations due to their identical names. Constellations are groups of fixed stars. Constellations have unequal lengths, and their boundaries have been redefined in different historical epochs. A zodiac sign is a 30-degree arc of the ecliptic circle, not related to constellations except for their names. Moreover, zodiac signs slowly shift against the backdrop of fixed stars and constellations. We will explain why constellations and zodiac signs have the same names later.

---

[31] G. Bonatti. *Book on Astronomy. Volume 1.* Cazimi Press, 2007

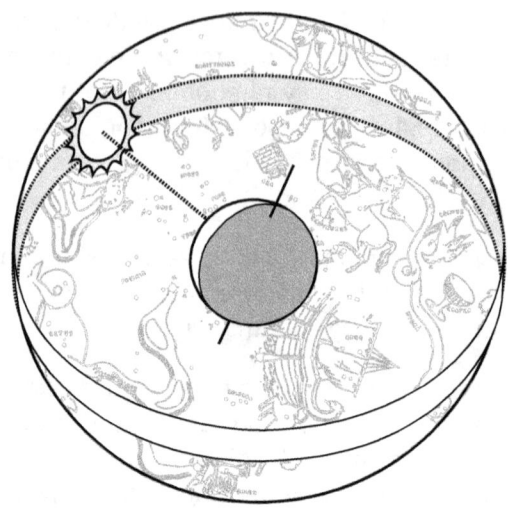

Figure A.5: *Signs vs Constellations*

Precession

If you have yet to hear of *precession*, the best way to understand it is to imagine a spinning top. When you spin a top, you rarely manage to make its axis of rotation perfectly perpendicular to the ground. It will still be slightly tilted, and as a result, you will notice that while the top spins rapidly around its axis, the axis itself makes smooth circular motions around the axis perpendicular to the ground. This effect is called precession. The same effect happens with the Earth. It is called the precession of the Earth's axis (Fig. A.6).

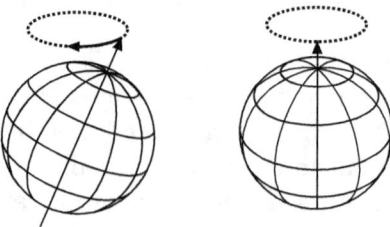

Figure A.6: *Precession*

The Earth's axis makes one big precession cycle, called *Cosmic Epoch*, in about 26,000 years or about 9 million rotations of the Earth around its axis. Ancient Greeks made the first calculation of the precession period with very high accuracy. Look at Fig. A.7.

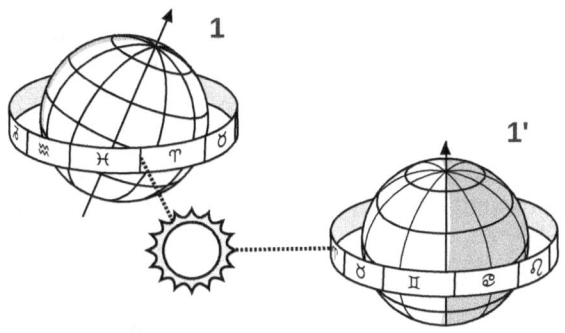

Figure A.7: *Cosmic Epochs*

Due to precession, the Earth's axis changes its orientation. If the Earth's axis is currently pointing to the right and position 1 is the point of the vernal equinox, then after a quarter of a great cycle (in 26,000 years), the Earth's axis will be pointing towards you—the Earth will be facing you with its North Pole. At the same time, to be evenly illuminated both in the south and in the north (so that day equals night), the Earth needs to be in position 1'. In other words, due to the precession of the Earth's axis, the point of the vernal equinox has shifted from position 1 to position 1'.

If every year on the day of the vernal equinox, we observe the position of the Sun, decades later, we will notice the prolonged shift of this position against the background of fixed stars. Hence, the point of the vernal equinox shifts against the backdrop of fixed stars. And since the entire zodiac circle is tied to the point of the vernal equinox, it turns out that all 12 signs slowly shift against the backdrop of constellations, completing one full rotation in 26,000 years. You can look at it differently: constellations change against the backdrop of the zodiac circle.

Tropical and Sidereal Zodiac Circles

The 12 zodiac signs we've discussed, tied to the vernal equinox point, represent the *tropical*, or *movable*, zodiac circle. As we've just understood, this zodiac circle is not stationary—it slowly shifts against the backdrop of the fixed stars.

If, at a particular moment, we fix the position of the tropical zodiac circle against the backdrop of the fixed stars, such a "fixed" zodiac circle would be called the *sidereal*, or starry, zodiac. It will no longer be associated with the "walking" point of the vernal equinox but with the fixed stars. It will be firmly "attached" to the stars and constellations. However, even in this case, the signs of the sidereal zodiac circle will not coincide with the constellations—constellations have different extents and represent groups of stars called "constellations" by convention. A sign of the sidereal zodiac is a 30-degree arc of the ecliptic circle, firmly "anchored" against the background of the stars.

It is clear that when the tropical zodiac circle shifts against the backdrop of the fixed stars, it also shifts against the background of the sidereal zodiac circle. In other words, the sidereal zodiac shifts relative to the tropical zodiac. The sidereal and tropical zodiac circles coincided about two millennia ago.

Great Cycles and Ages

The sidereal zodiac circle slowly shifts against the tropical one. Once every two thousand years or so, a new sign of the sidereal circle crosses the zero degrees of Aries of the tropical circle—this marks the beginning of a new *astrological age*, which lasts slightly over two millennia until the point of the vernal equinox enters a new sign of the sidereal zodiac circle. The sidereal and tropical zodiac circles coincided about two thousand years ago (during the Hellenistic astrology era). Nowadays, the Age of Pisces is ending, giving way to the Age of Aquarius.

The ancients were well aware of the changing epochs. The sign of Pisces symbolized the Christian era. Now, it is fading, giving way to the era of Aquarius, associated with the power of logic.

Planetary Loops

The Sun moves smoothly along the zodiacal circle relative to the Earth, and the planets revolve around it. Suppose you mentally draw a line showing the planet's trajectory on the ecliptical plane from the perspective of the Earth's center. In that case, you will see that this trajectory has *loops*.

When the planet is at its maximum distance from Earth, it overtakes the Sun and moves quickly along the zodiac signs. But when the planet is closest to Earth, it moves against the signs (Fig. A.8).

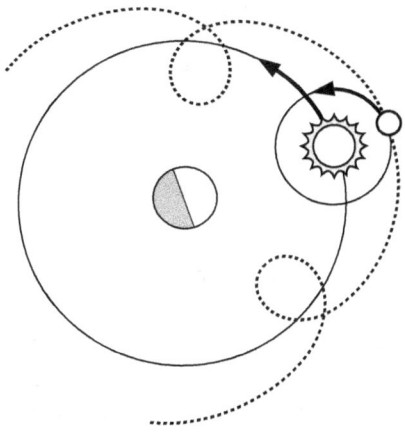

Figure A.8: *Planetary Cycles*

In this case, we say that the planet's apparent movement is *retrograde*. In brief moments, when the planet changes its direction, it appears to stay relative to the zodiacal circle. During these moments, the planet moves directly toward or away from the Earth's center—its projection on the zodiac is immovable. We say that the planet is *stationary*.

The Moon and the Sun are the only two planets that do not make loops and always move uniformly along the signs of the zodiac. It distinguishes these two luminaries from all other planets. The planetary movement along the zodiacal circle, as seen from the center of the Earth, is called *apparent* or *Secondary motion* motion.

The Local Horizon

Until now, we have not considered the rotation of the Earth around its axis. Let's imagine an astrologer is in the Earth's northern hemisphere.

He sees a small portion of the Earth's surface around him, bounded by the local horizon.

Due to humans' small size compared to the Earth, the astrologer perceives the local ground surface as flat. The observer and his local horizon rotate with the Earth around the axis of the Earth's rotation (Fig. A.9).

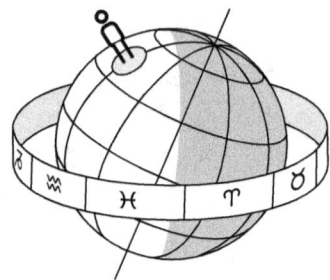

Figure A.9: *Local Horizon*

Now, let's place the astrologer along with the rotating local surface at the center of the world. The observer will perceive the world as if the heavens are revolving around him while he remains stationary. The astrologer will observe a celestial sphere rotating around an axis coinciding with the axis of the Earth's rotation. All the stars, the planets, and the degrees of the zodiac circle rise on the eastern horizon and then set in the west. Such a daily motion, connected with the rotation of the celestial sphere, is called a *primary motion* in contrast to the secondary motion of the planets along the zodiac circle. In the Fig. A.10, you see the moment when 0° Aries ascends right to the East. A few hours before it, 0° Capricorn ascends much closer to the South.

The power of gravity, which rotates the Earth (and consequently the heavens from the observer's perspective), is called the *Primum Mobile*.

In the Northern Hemisphere, the axis of rotation of the celestial sphere points to the pole star.

The further north a person is, the higher the pole star appears. The closer he is to the equator, the closer the pole star is to the horizon. Strictly speaking, the angle of deviation of the axis of rotation of the celestial sphere coincides with the astrologer's geographic latitude. When the astrologer is at the Earth's equator, this angle is 0°; when he is at the North Pole, this angle is 90°, and the pole star is directly overhead.

Appendix A. The Geometry of Celestial Sphere

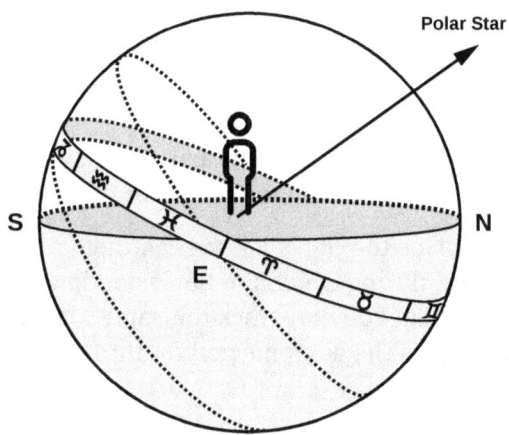

Figure A.10: *Primary Motion*

The zodiacal circle rotates along with the celestial sphere. Its northernmost point is 0° Cancer, and its southernmost is 0° Capricorn.

- When the Sun is at 0° Cancer, the Sun's daily path from sunrise to sunset is much longer than the short path from sunset to sunrise, making the day significantly longer compared to the short night. It is called the *summer solstice*.
- When the Sun is at 0° Capricorn, the opposite effect occurs — the night is significantly longer, and the day is very short. It is called the *winter solstice*.
- When the Sun is at the points 0° Libra or 0° Aries, the Sun's daily path above the horizon and below the horizon coincide. It is called the *equinox*.

Cardinal Signs and Mystical Cults

The signs Aries, Cancer, Libra, and Capricorn are called *cardinal*. Notably, many religious and mystical cults are associated with moments when the Sun ingress into these signs.

If you observe the Sun's daily motion every autumn day, the path from sunrise to sunset progressively further southward while the Sun approaches 0° Capricorn. The day will become shorter and shorter.

The closer the Sun gets to 0° Capricorn, the slower the movement of its daily path southward will be. Near the point of the winter solstice, the Sun's daily path will seem to "freeze" in its northernmost position for 3 days. That is why we call that point winter solstice.

When the Sun passes through 0° Capricorn, its daytime trajectory will shift back southward, increasing the length of the day.

The observer perceives the Sun's passage through 0° Capricorn as the three shortest days, during which the Sun's daytime arc remains in its southernmost position. You may track the same idea in many religious cults—darkness engulfs the supreme god for three days, after which the god resurrects again.

Another example. You may notice that some ancient temple structures had a narrow entrance that was strictly oriented towards the east. It was not accidental.

As you can see from the illustration above, when the Sun is at the point of equinox, it rises directly in the east. The rays of the rising Sun penetrate the narrow entrance of the temple structure, fully illuminating the sacred altar located opposite. It was a signal from the heavens of the onset of the new astronomical year.

Different Coordinate Systems

Planets' orbits are not strictly in the ecliptic plane but are slightly inclined to it. Consequently, planets can be slightly above or below the plane of the zodiac circle (Fig. A.11).

To describe a planet's coordinates on the zodiac circle, we can use its zodiacal degree, counted from 0° Aries, and the deviation from the ecliptic plane (in degrees).

The first coordinate is *celestial latitude*, and the second is *celestial longitude*. Together, these two coordinates are called *ecliptic coordinates*.

For practical purposes (especially in calculating the primary directions), we must describe the coordinates of planets relative to the celestial equator. The *celestial equator* is the line dividing the celestial sphere into northern and southern parts. It is perpendicular to the axis of rotation of the celestial sphere and passes through 0° Aries and 0° Libra.

Appendix A. The Geometry of Celestial Sphere

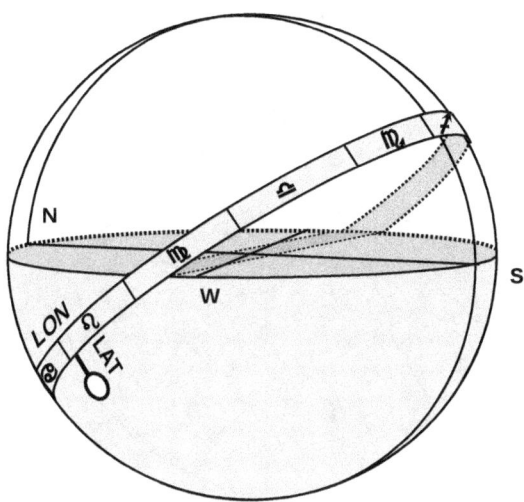

Figure A.11: *Ecliptical Coordinates*

In astrology, it is customary to count degrees of the equator from the point of intersection with 0° Aries. In this case, the direction of the degrees of the equator coincides with the direction of the degrees of the ecliptic (Fig. A.12).

Then, the planet's position can be described by its equatorial degree and the magnitude of deviation from the equator. The first coordinate is *right ascension*, and the second one is *declination*. Together, they form *equatorial coordinates*.

Finally, you can measure the position of a celestial body relative to the horizon. The projection of the planet onto the horizon is called *azimuth*. Usually, azimuth is a degree of the horizon relative to the true north. The elevation of the planet above the horizon (in degrees) is called *altitude*. The pair of azimuth and altitude form the *horizontal coordinates* (Fig. A.13).

We will actively use these coordinates to calculate so called primary directions—the royal forecasting technique in natal astrology.

Predictive Astrology Textbook

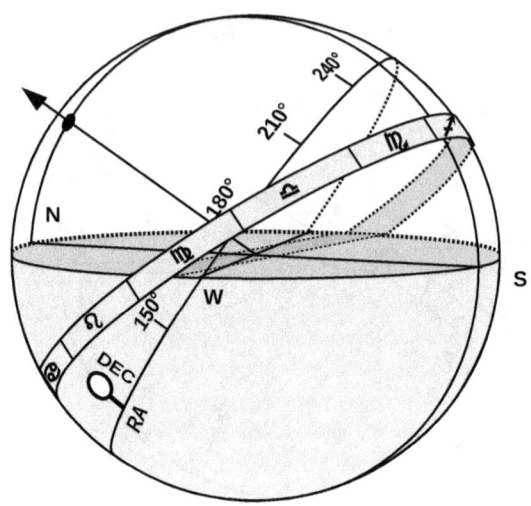

Figure A.12: *Equatorial Coordinates*

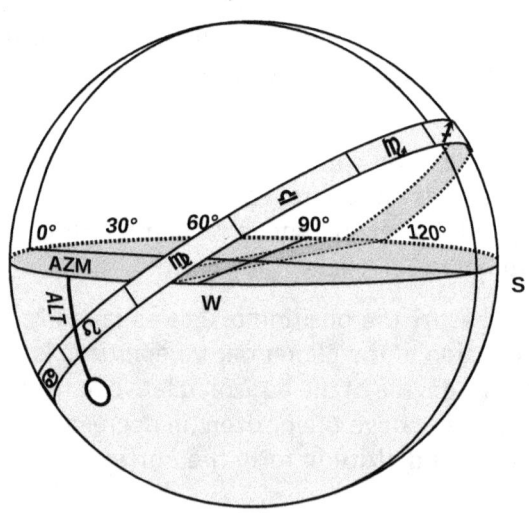

Figure A.13: *Horizontal coordinates*

Appendix B

List of the Brightest Stars

Here are the most influential fixed stars. The section "Descriptive Techniques: the Fixed Stars" discusses working with the stars.

Remember that fixed stars can be conjunct with cusps and planets in three planes—on the equator (proximity by equatorial latitude), on the ecliptic (proximity by right ascension), and on the circle of positions (proximity of mundane positions). The orb of these stars is 6 degrees, and the coordinates of the stars are for 01.01.1980.

The last column in the table represents the influence of the star.

- "+" stands for favorable influence,
- "–" stands for unfavorable one.

Experience confirms that in directions, stars by themselves rarely produce significant events. However, the directions of stars can refine the actions of prominent directions. For example, if a promissor of injury, the square of malevolent Mars from the 7th house approaches the ASC, and following this, Algol approaches a planet in the 1st house. The direction of Algol will specify the type of injury—it will be a head injury, according to the nature of Algol.

Table B.1: *List of royal stars*

The Star	Location	Longitude	Latitude	Infl.
Alcyone	η Tauri	59° 43'	4° 3'	−
Algol	β Persei	55° 53'	22° 26'	−
Alhena	γ Geminorum	98° 50'	-6° 45'	+
Alnilam	ε Orionis	83° 11'	-24° 31'	+
Alnitak	ζ Orionis	84° 24'	-25° 18'	+
Alphard	α Hydrae	147° 0'	-22° 23'	−
Alphecca	α Coronae Borealis	222° 0'	44° 19'	+
Altair	α Aquilae	301° 29'	29° 18'	+
Arcturus	α Boötis	203° 57'	30° 45'	+
Antares	α Scorpii	249° 29'	-4° 34'	−
Castor	α Geminorum	109° 58'	10° 6'	+
Deneb	α Cygni	335° 3'	59° 55'	+
Fomalhaut	α Piscis Austrini	333° 34'	-21° 8'	+
Mintaka	δ Orionis	82° 5'	-23° 33'	+
Pollux	β Geminorum	112° 57'	6° 41'	+
Regulus	α Leo	149° 33'	0° 28'	+
Spica	α Virginis	203° 34'	-2° 3'	+
Sirius	α Canis Majoris	103° 49'	-39° 36'	+
Vega	α Lyrae	285° 1'	61° 44'	+

Appendix C

Determination by Ecliptic

This Appendix is provided as a historical reference.

Morinus described the scheme of creating "copies" of a planet at the locations of aspects based on a three-dimensional sphere. He used the word *virtue*, meaning the energy that emanates. For simplicity, I will use the modern term "energy."

You can find a detailed explanation of Morinus's approach in Section 1, Chapter 4 of Book 14.[32]

Morinus wrote that the pole[33] of any great circle on the celestial sphere is the focus of energy distributes along the circle (he referred to this as the "center of virtue").

Therefore, the ecliptic pole P_1 is where all the energy of all zodiac signs is concentrated (Fig. C.1).

Since the planet is on the ecliptic and determines the radiation of the primary heaven to manifest according to the planet's intrinsic nature, a unique "energetic circuit" arises between the ecliptic pole P_1 and the planet P, dividing the ecliptic circle into two equal parts (Fig. C.2).

On the other hand, like any circle, it has its own pole P_2, which is the focus of the "energetic circuit" passing through P and P_1 (Fig. C.4).

---

[32] J.-B. Morinus. *Astrologia Gallica, Book 14. The Primim Caelum and its Division into Twelve Parts.* Hagae, 1661b

[33] The pole of a circle is where the celestial sphere intersects with the perpendicular line to the circle, originating from its center.

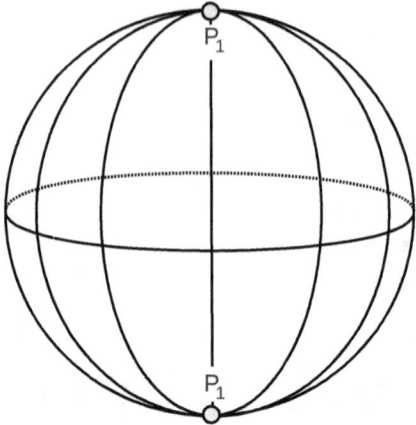

Figure C.1: *The north and south poles of the ecliptic*

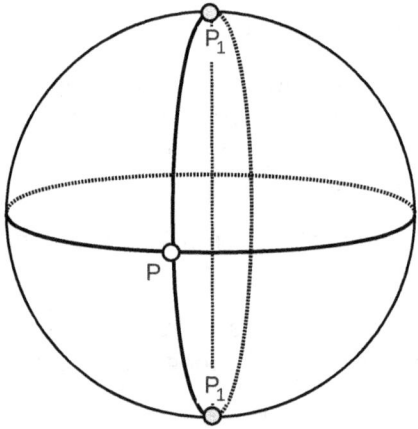

Figure C.2: *The circle from the planet to the pole*

Since poles P_1 and P_2 are places of concentration of the planet's "reflected" energies and simultaneously belong to the same plane, they initiate a new "energy circuit" passing through P_1 and P_2 with the pole P (Fig. C.4).

Morinus further assumed that each pole always has two "copies" at distances of ±120 degrees in the plane of the "circuit" it belongs to. He considered this to be a profound property of the very nature of space, which he called the Trinity.

Appendix C. Determination by Ecliptic

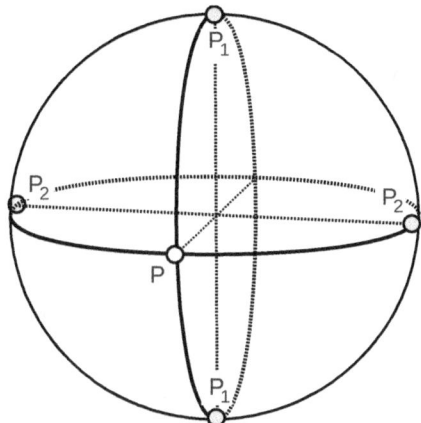

Figure C.3: *Four poles*

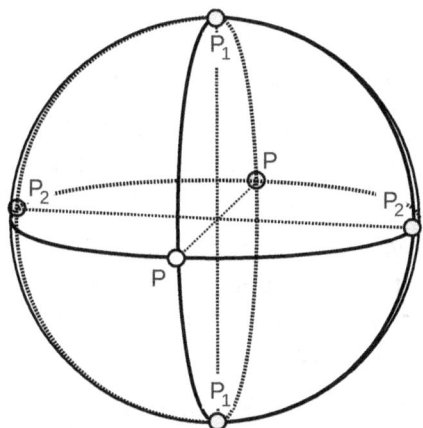

Figure C.4: *Three main circuits*

Thus, 12 energy focuses are formed in each plane[34] (Fig. C.5).

For this reason, Morinus did not exclude the existence of *semi-sextile* (30° aspect) and *quincunx* (150° aspect). However, in his practical examples, Morinus mainly adhered to Ptolemaic aspects in primary directions.

According to Morinus, a semi-sextile has only 1/6 the strength of an opposition, which is insufficient to realize significant events in primary

---

[34] It should be understood that everything said here about the ecliptic applies to the circle of aspects that we discussed earlier

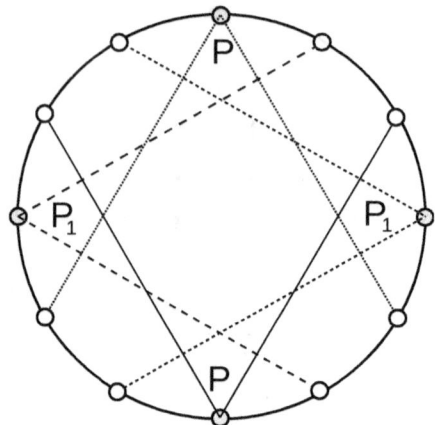

Figure C.5: *Twelve aspects*

directions. Morinus also pointed out the weakness of the quincunx, so this aspect also doesn't have a significant effect.

Now note that this Morinus's statement completely contradicts his idea (see Chapter 12 of Book 18[35]) that the strength of an aspect is proportional to the distance in the aspect, relative to 180 degrees.

According to this logic, a semi-sextile has 30/180 = 1/6 of the strength of a conjunction, a trine is 120/180 = 4/6, while a quincunx should be 150/180 = 5/6, which clearly contradicts experience and Morinus' last statement about weakness of the quincunx.

For this reason, I believe that Morinus was mistaken in introducing minor aspects into consideration. However, we can quickly resolve this contradiction within the framework of Morinus's own theory if we agree that poles perpendicular to the planet do not create the "copies" at 120-degree points, or they at least create negligibly small "copies" (Fig. C.6).

Thus, the final distribution of aspects according to Morinus would look as shown in Figure C.7.

For this reason, I did not consider semi-sextile and quincunx aspects in this book.

---

[35] J.-B. Morinus. *Astrologia Gallica, Book 18. The Strength of the Planets.* Hagae, 1661c

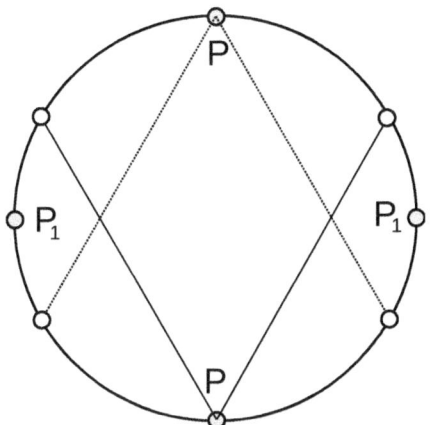

Figure C.6: *Ptolemaic aspects*

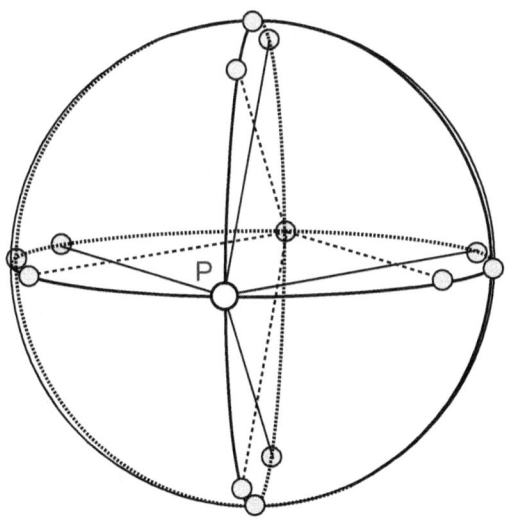

Figure C.7: *Ptolemaic aspects in space*

Bibliography

G. Bonatti. *Book on Astronomy. Volume 1.* Cazimi Press, 2007.

A. Borealis. Pilot study of predicting the timing of events using horary astrology methods. *Correlations*, 36(1):63–68, 2024.

H. Coley. *Clavis Astrologia Elimata: Or the Key to the Whole Art of Astrology New Filed and Polished.* Kessinger Publishing, 1676.

J. Frawley. *The Horary Textbook.* Apprentice Books, 2005.

M. Gansten. *Primary Directions. Astrology's Old Master Technique.* Wessex Astrologer Ltd, 2009.

W. Lilly. *Christian Astrology.* Printed by John Macock, 1669.

J.-B. Morinus. *Astrologia Gallica.* Hagae (ex Typograhia Adriani Vlacq), 1661a.

J.-B. Morinus. *Astrologia Gallica, Book 14. The Primim Caelum and its Division into Twelve Parts.* Hagae, 1661b.

J.-B. Morinus. *Astrologia Gallica, Book 18. The Strength of the Planets.* Hagae, 1661c.

J.-B. Morinus. *Astrologia Gallica, Book 24. Progressions and Transits.* Hagae, 1661d.

A. Parkhomov. Dark Matter as a Cosmic Interaction Agent. (Russian). *Institute for Time Nature Explorations*, 2007. URL http://chronos.msu.ru/old/RREPORTS/parhomov_temnaya.pdf.

C. Ptolemy. *Tetrabiblos: Translated from the Greek paraphrase of Proclus by J. M. Ashmand.* Davis and Dickson, London, 1882.

Index of Terms

Abscissor, 305, 366
Accidental strength, 20, 22, 217, 233, 254
Altitude, 475
Anaereta, 305, 366, 415
Angles, 36, 143
    ASC, Ascendant, 36
    DSC, Descendant, 36
    IC, Imum Caeli, 36
    MC, Medium Caeli, 36
Antiscion, 166, 379
Apheta, 366
Apparent motion, 471
Arabian Parts (lots), 85, 137, 203
Aspect
    applying, 118
    close, 51, 96
    dexter, 95
    exact, 22, 81
    full platic, 100
    mutual, 100
    one-sided, 100
    opposition, 80, 94
    partial platic, 100
    Ptolemaic, 94
    separating, 118
    sextile, 94
    sinister, 95
    square, 94
    trigon, trine, 94
Astrological Age, 470
Azimuth, 475

Cazimi, 228
Celestial equator, 474
Celestial latitude, 474
Celestial longitude, 474
Celestial state, 44, 54, 72
Circle of aspects, 378
Circle of positions, 377
Co-ruler of the house, 329
Combustion, 173, 227
Conjunction, 95, 96
    full platic, 98
    mutual, 98
    one-sided, 98
    partial platic, 98
Coordinates
    ecliptic, 474
    equatorial, 475
    horizontal, 475
Cosmic Epoch, 468

Debilitated state, 49
Declination, 475

Determination, 6, 309
    by context, 311, 344
    by ecliptic, 101, 313, 479
    by house, 29, 325
    by kind of things, 310, 323
    by planet, 5, 6, 31, 45, 312
    by sign, 312
    celestial, 310
    of Primum Caelum, 312, 313
    terrestrial, 310, 325
Direct motion, 125
Dispositor, 59
    by exaltation, 60
Domicile, 46

Ecliptic circle, 465
Ecliptic plane, 463
Elemental qualities, 25
Equinox, 464, 473
Exaltation, 46, 60
Exile (Detriment), 49

Fall, 50

Horary astrology, 11
House, 18, 30
    derived, 73
    primary, 29
    radical, 73
    secondary, 29
House cusp, 30
    in sign, 31
House rulership, 28, 44, 54, 72, 327
    accidental, 17, 30, 245, 326, 338, 340, 343, 347, 373
    by aspect, 327, 343, 350, 359
    by disposition, 330, 335
    by exaltation, 328, 373
    by position, 326, 330
    co-ruler, 77, 355
    secondary, 335, 343, 359
House system, 30
Hyleg, 366

Inclination of Earth's axis, 464
Ingress, 126
Initiating directions, 368, 372

Loops of the planets, 471
Lunar Node, 222
Lunar return, 5, 43, 301, 307
    example, 405, 406

Mean average, 387, 388
Moiety, semi-orb, 109, 110
Mundane astrology, 10
Mundane conjunction, 377

Natal astrology, 8
Node of a planet, 84
North node, 223

Orb, a sphere of virtue, 108

Part of Fortune, 85, 139, 141, 153, 155–157, 159
Peregrine, 50
Precession, 468
Primary directions, 4, 43, 301, 304, 363
    converse, 378
    zodiacal with latitude, 378
Primary motion, 304, 363, 472
Primum Caelum, 5, 29, 312
Primum Mobile, 305, 472
Prohibition, 119
Prohibitor, 119
Promissor, Promittor, 167, 320

Querent, 16

Index of Terms

Quesited, 16
Quincunx, 481

Radical chart, radix, 141, 146, 304
Reception, 21, 22, 59, 72
    in domicile, 59
    in exile, 61
    in place of exaltation, 60
    in place of fall, 62
    in triplicity, 60
    mutual, 65
Rectification, 382
Refranation, 126
Retrograde motion, 125, 471
Revolution (return), 306
    of Venus, 392, 395
Right ascension, 475

Secondary motion, 471
Secondary ruler, 329
Semi-sextile, 481
Significator, 16
Solar return, 5, 11, 307
    example, 398, 403, 414
Solstice, 464, 473
South node, 223
Standard deviation, 388
Station, 125, 471
    first, 125
    second, 125
Strength of determination, 325

To dispose, 59
To exalt, 60
To form a close aspect, 101
To interpose, 119
To intervene, 119

To prohibit, 119
To receive an aspect, 100
Transit chart, 5, 122, 141
Transits, 141
Triplicity, 47

Under the Sun's beams, 227
Universal benefics, 299
Universal malefics, 299
Universal rulership, 17, 29, 30, 66, 87, 91, 245

Virtue, 5, 479
Void of course, 85

Zodiac circle, 31, 465
Zodiac sidereal, fixed, 470
Zodiac sign, 31, 466
    airy, 55
    barren, 56
    bestial, 56
    cardinal (fast), 55, 473
    double-bodied, 56
    earth, 55
    fertile, 56
    fiery, 55
    fixed (slow), 55
    human, 56
    loud, 56, 69
    masculine & feminine, 54
    mutable, 55
    mute, 56
    of short and long ascension, 57
    water, 55
    wild, 56
Zodiac tropical, movable, 469

www.ingramcontent.com/pod-product-compliance
Lightning Source LLC
Chambersburg PA
CBHW071134300426
44113CB00009B/971